P9-CFC-161

Holding Fast the Inner Lines

Supplementary Volumes to *The Papers of Woodrow Wilson*
Arthur S. Link, Editor

THE EDITORIAL ADVISORY COMMITTEE
Katharine E. Brand
Henry Steele Commager, *Emeritus*
John Milton Cooper, Jr.
William H. Harbaugh
August Heckscher
Richard W. Leopold
David C. Mearns, *Emeritus*
Arthur M. Schlesinger, Jr.

A list of volumes in this series will be found at the back of the book.

Holding Fast the Inner Lines

Democracy, Nationalism, and the Committee on Public Information

by Stephen Vaughn

The University of North Carolina Press
Chapel Hill

Wingate College Library

D
632
V38

© *1980 The University of North Carolina Press*
All rights reserved
Manufactured in the United States of America
Library of Congress Catalog Card Number 79-9941
ISBN 0-8078-1373-7

Library of Congress Cataloging in Publication Data

Vaughn, Stephen, 1947–
  Holding fast the inner lines.

  (Supplementary volume to the Papers of Woodrow
Wilson)
  Bibliography: p.
  Includes index.
  1. United States. Committee on Public Information—
History. 2. Propaganda, American. 3. European War,
1914–1918—United States. 4. European War, 1914–1918
—Propaganda. I. Title. II. Series: Wilson, Woodrow,
Pres. U. S., 1856–1924. Papers: Supplementary volume.
D632.V38   940.4'886'73   79-9941
ISBN 0-8078-1373-7

To Mrs. W. J. Vaughn, Jr., and
Alice Vaughn, and to the memory of
William Jackson Vaughn, Jr., Ella C.
Riddle, and Mrs. E. O. Hirsch

078544

Contents

Illustrations

Preface

DEMOCRATIC GOVERNMENT is worth having, and it is also very difficult to maintain, and herein lies an essential awkwardness in judging the activities of the United States government's first large-scale propaganda agency, the celebrated Creel committee, officially known as the Committee on Public Information. The CPI proved spectacularly successful in mobilizing public opinion behind the country's participation in the World War of 1917–18, popularizing the notion that the struggle was a great crusade to save democracy. In retrospect there must be little doubt that its appeal promoted national unity, but there has been considerable skepticism as to whether the CPI strengthened democracy, which, in the United States, has been associated with individual liberty and human equality under law.

The committee was above all a nationalizing agent, encouraging American nationalism. It set up an apparatus that allowed the federal government to communicate with virtually every citizen, no matter how isolated; it promoted a national ideology, namely, American democracy; it reinforced persons who were convinced that the nation was the best and perhaps only vehicle for the progress of democracy, and even civilization. It is quite true that some varieties of nationalism are antithetical to democracy, and at times the committee's work unfortunately encouraged an attachment to the nation that surely weakened democratic government.

Still, the development of democracy in the United States

has often been closely associated with nationalism and vice versa, and the story of the CPI's connection with democratic government is more complex than most writers have suggested. Much of the work of the Committee on Public Information has been remembered for having encouraged hysteria, hatred, an atmosphere of intolerance. Too often it has been assumed that members of the CPI had little understanding of or appreciation for the meaning of democracy and that they used "democracy" merely as a catchword to galvanize opinion behind the war effort. To evaluate the CPI's work fairly, however, one should consider the committee against a broader background than just the war.[1] The committee attracted many intelligent, sincere people—journalists, scholars, educational leaders, orators, artists, even advertising men—who were committed to democracy and whose concern about the fate of democratic government often went deeper than the war. Many of these people before 1917 had been involved in the effort to improve American society. Much of the CPI's work derived from the progressive tradition—the attempt to come to terms with the modern urban-industrial age. The Committee on Public Information not only condemned German militarism, it also publicized reform. The CPI did promote nationalism but in ways that at the time were often calculated to strengthen democratic government.

The study of a government agency such as the Creel committee presents special difficulties. The historian's task should be to detach himself from the present. He must try to avoid reading contemporary values into the events of the past. Anyone who is familiar with the history of the 1930s and 1940s, or who has lived through the 1960s and 1970s, may be tempted to view all forms of government propaganda with a healthy skepticism. "Propaganda" did not have quite the same negative connotation in 1917 that it acquired in the decades after the Great War.[2] Nor did George Creel and his associates have the advantage during these years of witnessing the abuses of later propagandists. The CPI reflected their naive faith in the integrity of the American government and its leaders and in the power of ideas to transform men and society. If some of the

committee's work did foreshadow the sinister propaganda engines of the future, the great power of government propaganda
and its disturbing implication for democratic government were
only dimly perceived in 1917–18.

Although the Committee on Public Information's labors
were worldwide, the present work deals only with the CPI's Domestic Section. The committee's Foreign Section is not treated
in the pages that follow, as it was sufficiently large to warrant a
separate study. Nor has this work attempted to measure in any
precise way the CPI's effect on public opinion. Considering the
enormous volume of propaganda coming from both governmental and nongovernmental sources during the First World
War, and realizing how hard it is to gauge public opinion in a
time before sophisticated polling techniques, such a task would
be extremely difficult, if not impossible. The following pages
do try to provide an accurate accounting of the committee's
work, so that one can compare the CPI with other propaganda
agencies, American and foreign.

MANY debts have been incurred in preparing
this study. A Rotary International Fellowship to the University
of Toronto allowed me to do the initial research on this project
in the excellent facilities of the Robarts Library. I received
assistance from the staffs of other libraries. Ferris Stovel of the
National Archives; Maynard Brichford of the University of
Illinois Archives; Judith A. Schiff, Chief Research Archivist of
Yale University Archives; Kathleen Jacklin, Archivist at the
Cornell University Libraries; and Mrs. James H. Chadbourn of
the Harvard Law School Library were especially helpful. I wish
also to acknowledge the courtesies shown to me at the Library
of Congress, the Lilly Library in Bloomington, Indiana, the
New York Public Library, the State Historical Society of Wisconsin in Madison, and the libraries of Columbia University,
Indiana University, Princeton University, the University of Chicago, the University of Illinois, the University of Minnesota,
and Yale University.

Several people were helpful either by sharing their knowledge on subjects related to this study or by criticizing specific

aspects of this work. In the early stages I profited greatly from discussions with Harold I. Nelson and Kenneth McNaught of the University of Toronto. At Indiana University, George Juergens made suggestions concerning the relation between Woodrow Wilson and the press. I found discussions with Leonard Lundin both enjoyable and helpful. Maurice Baxter was kind enough to read and comment on Chapters 1, 6, and 10. Edward H. Buehrig made important criticisms of the conclusion. John E. Wiltz read each chapter with extreme care and made many suggestions that improved the style and organization. Arthur S. Link, Robert H. Wiebe, and Paul L. Murphy read the entire manuscript and made valuable recommendations. James Diehl, Robert D. Ward, George Blakey, Terry Anderson, and Kenneth Moss offered criticisms on portions of this work. Charles Weeks and David Culbert made worthwhile remarks on parts of chapters 4 and 9, respectively. I wish to thank the staffs of the *Historian, American Journal of Legal History, Indiana Military History Journal,* and *New Jersey History,* where portions of this study were published in somewhat altered form. I must also mention Mrs. W. J. Vaughn, Jr., who read this manuscript from beginning to end, and Beverly Vaughn, who took time from her own work to read and comment on large sections of this study, pointing out many needed improvements.

Finally, I owe a special thank-you to two individuals. It was Martin Ridge who first stimulated my interest in American history and who, by his example, set high standards of scholarship that I have tried to emulate. Robert H. Ferrell was a source of encouragement from the beginning of this work, indeed from the beginning of my training as a historian. No other individual did more in attempting to improve this book, and I am reminded of a remark he once made about his own mentor: "Rarely can one find this sort of assistance from an accomplished scholar."

Holding Fast the Inner Lines

1. Painting of George Creel by J. W. de Rehling Quistgaard
(Courtesy of the Library of Congress)

Democracy is a religion with me, and throughout my
whole adult life I have preached America as the hope of
the world.

—George Creel, May 29, 1918

1

The Origin of the CPI

> Truth and Falsehood are arbitrary terms, ... there is
> nothing in experience to tell us that one is always pref-
> erable to the other. ... There are lifeless truths and vital
> lies. ... The force of an idea lies in its inspirational
> value. It matters very little whether it is true or false.
> —Arthur Bullard[1]

WHEN PRESIDENT WOODROW WILSON an-
nounced to Congress and the world on April 6, 1917, that a
state of war existed between the United States and Germany, he
could not have been sure that he was leading a united country
into battle. For nearly three years his administration had attempted to make a virtue of neutrality. Americans in 1917 were
a heterogeneous people, including German-Americans, Irish-
Americans—all those persons of European origin who had
opposed the declaration of war because of attachment to Germany, or dislike for England. More than 14.5 million people
out of a total population of about 100 million had been born in
foreign countries. There were probably more than 8 million
persons in the United States who considered Germany their
land of origin. Better than 2.5 million of these individuals had
been born in Germany, and another almost 6 million were
second-generation immigrants.[2] Before the declaration of war
a sizable German-language press in the United States had been
largely sympathetic to the German cause.[3] There were also
other worries. Pacifism was strong in parts of the country. Many
Americans possessed deeply held beliefs opposing war.[4] Others
were apathetic to the issues surrounding the war because, living
in the hinterlands, they were out of touch with international
issues. The head of the American propaganda effort during
the war, George Creel, would later describe this state of af-

fairs when he wrote that during the time of neutrality "the United States had been torn by a thousand divisive prejudices, with public opinion stunned and muddled by the pull and haul of Allied and German propaganda. The sentiment in the West was still isolationist; the Northwest buzzed with talk of a 'rich man's war,' waged to salvage Wall Street loans; men and women of Irish stock were 'neutral,' not caring who whipped England, and in every state demagogues raved against 'war-mongers,' although the Du Ponts and other so-called 'merchants of death' did not have enough powder on hand to arm squirrel hunters."[5]

Admittedly, there were many supporters of the war, people who felt that a declaration should have come earlier. In 1917–18 the problem with such persons, as President Wilson well knew, was not convincing them of the justice of entering the conflict but controlling their enthusiasm. These self-styled patriots, aglow with conviction, were ready to stand at Armageddon.

In April 1917, the task of mobilizing America seemed so immense, so formidable. The conflict in Europe had become like no war of the past. Thirty-two months of fighting had shown that war could engulf entire populations. Every man, woman, and child in the principal belligerent nations was becoming a combatant. President Wilson rightly sensed the magnitude of mobilization when he remarked, "It is not an army we must shape and train for war, it is a nation."[6] To create national unity the president in mid-April 1917 therefore issued an executive order establishing a Committee on Public Information —at once an information agency and an instrument for rallying Americans behind the country's war effort.

The activities of the Committee on Public Information in subsequent months proved an unsettling experience. The CPI succeeded all too well. It organized patriotic enthusiasm where it existed and created it where it did not. It publicized the government to the citizenry, and in so doing became an extraordinarily effective nationalizing agent.

It was not necessary in April 1917 for the administration's new committee to begin its work without the slightest idea of what it would be about, for during the preceding weeks and months, as war was coming ever closer, the government in Washington had begun to receive much advice on how to mobilize opinion. The newspaperman Walter Lippmann corresponded with Wilson and apparently had some influence with the president.[7] Lippmann's correspondence in the months before entry into the war revealed a concern with such matters as recruiting an army, censorship, and a rationale for abandoning neutrality and entering the war that would win support of the many dissident groups within the United States. In February 1917 and in early April, Lippmann wrote of the danger to democratic government of recruiting an army. He feared that such an effort would require a newspaper campaign of manufactured hatred that would poison American society, as he believed it had done in Britain, negating Wilson's appeal for a war to save democracy.[8]

Lippmann's ideas were certainly interesting. On the question of censorship he feared that usual military procedures would be dangerous and recommended that such matters be under control of civilians who had "real insight and democratic sympathy." Secretary of the Interior Franklin K. Lane, he thought, would be an ideal censor. Problems with the press would not come from unpatriotic Americans but from "those who persecute and harass and cause divisions." It was important to control untruth but not to suppress truth, as had been done in Europe. A healthy public opinion was of paramount importance.[9]

The specific ideas Lippman had in mind for mobilizing public opinion—a rationale for abandoning neutrality and entering the war—appeared in a letter and memorandum he submitted to Wilson on March 11, 1917. This statement, probably drawn up with the aid of his colleague on the *New Republic*, Herbert Croly, sought to counter the argument that the United States had selectively enforced its neutral rights against Germany, ignoring infractions by Britain. Lippmann sought to show how support could be won from France, Canada, and Britain, as well as to demonstrate to pacifist groups within the United States that a program of war could support the general objective of peace; Lippmann believed the administration had failed to explain such matters. The memorandum said nothing about ways to galvanize opinion and indeed argued that Germany, by violating neutral rights, by "fighting for a victory subversive of the world system in which America lives," had given the United States the right to retaliate. It called on Germany to abandon aggressive purposes and enter a league of nations. In the letter attached to the memorandum, Lippmann elaborated how Wilson might gain support of public opinion. He urged the president to emphasize that the issue with Germany was a concern not simply for commerce but for lasting peace. He called for the capture of liberal opinion in the Allied countries and encouragement of German radicals by a statement of peace terms. Wilson should warn jingoistic groups in the United States that bellicosity would have to be subordinated to liberal policy. These goals could be obtained, he thought, by tying them to a proposal of a league for peace.[10]

There is no evidence that Wilson replied to these suggestions of March 11, but Lippmann likely discussed his ideas with the president in mid-March. His thoughts surely, somehow, must have made an impression. There is evidence that the president's confidant, Colonel Edward M. House, asked Lippmann to help set up a "publicity bureau," and the response was an outline of such an agency on April 12, 1917, just one day before creation of the Committee on Public Information. Lippmann proposed a clearinghouse for information on government activities, a monitoring of the foreign press, a taking into account of the motion-picture industry, and the tracking down of "rumors and lies."[11]

Meanwhile, another young newspaperman, a reporter for the New York *Evening Post*, was presenting proposals on censorship and mobilization of opinion. One of the president's former students at Princeton, David Lawrence, wrote Wilson on March 31, 1917, urging him to make war on the German government but emphasizing that the United States had no quarrel with the German people. Lawrence believed that this procedure would improve the chances for better international relations after the war.[12] Less than a week before establishment of the CPI, Lawrence again wrote Wilson and Secretary of State Robert Lansing about the importance of publicizing war aims abroad, and suggested a confidential publicity bureau or press organization.[13] To Lansing he stressed countering German propaganda in Central and South America. He urged supervision of cables from foreign correspondents, lest they give an anti-American twist to news. He argued for an increased flow of American news in Central and South America, to impress people in those areas with their great northern neighbor's aims and ideals. He recommended that the United States pay the tolls for such news services, as most Latin American countries were too poor to do so. A staff of newspapermen would secretly direct this propaganda. The United States should profit from the mistakes of Britain and France, countries that had withheld information from correspondents, failing to realize the publicity value of the work of such reporters until almost too late. Every effort should be made to present foreign correspondents in the United States with material that would give a favorable impression of America. Lawrence believed that observing foreign correspondents, some of whom might be spies, would assist the work of the Department of Justice. He urged an effort by Wilson to tell the German people of America's preparation for war, as this tactic would weaken the enemy country's morale. Censorship, he believed, should go beyond suppressing military information; it should publicize the American cause.[14]

Still another journalist was attempting to persuade the government of the importance of publicity and the danger of unnecessary censorship: Arthur Bullard, the muckraking reporter and novelist who sometimes wrote under the name Albert Edwards, was offering detailed suggestions to the administration well before 1917. In retrospect, it would appear that Bullard should receive much of the credit for the administration's decision to establish the Committee on Public Information.[15]

Bullard came from an interesting background. In the mid-nineteenth century his grandfather, Artemus Bullard, had apparently been a supporter of early efforts at international cooperation for peace. His father, Henry Bullard, had been a Presbyterian minister and in 1863 a member of the United States Christian Commission to Europe.[16]

After spending two years at Hamilton College, Arthur Bullard had become a settlement worker on New York's Lower East Side, where he was fascinated with the problems of crime and social justice, of the conditions in tenements and the radical views of many young immigrants who lived there. For a while he wrote for the *Masses*, and eventually he became editor of a weekly, the *Call*; in the decade before World War I he was an advocate of socialism of the "aggressively revolutionary" variety and in 1913 could write that plutocracy was "everywhere in a life-and-death struggle with Democracy—and as often as not seems to be winning the fight."[17] He urged a great awakening of the "Social Conscience," or so he put the case; he believed that to inspire the whole nation to "an effective enthusiasm" would require nothing less than a call for social revolution.[18] His interest in reform gradually extended to other countries. The struggle for reform in Russia especially interested him, notably the unsuccessful revolution of 1905–6. He was critical of the czarist regime and later, from a vantage point in wartime Russia, would write about the revolution of 1917.[19]

During the initial stages of the World War, Bullard was a foreign correspondent for *Harper's Weekly*, *Outlook*, and *Century*, and his attention turned to America's position vis-á-vis Europe —and then to what he considered to be the forthcoming problem of censorship, the need for a more open and democratic diplomacy, and the importance of educating public opinion.[20] In long letters detailing the European military and political situation as he saw it he corresponded with Colonel House, who in turn quoted from the letters in conversation with President Wilson.[21]

The occasion for Bullard's initial foray into the problems of censorship came in 1916 when a young army major, Douglas MacArthur, was appointed to the somewhat uncertain duties of "censor" of the War Department. Presumably, MacArthur would oversee newspapers and newspapermen during any future military conflict involving the United States. Major Mac-

Arthur took his appointment seriously and drew up a statement about a proper wartime relationship between the army and the press, citing past military successes that had resulted from information provided by enemy newspapers. General William T. Sherman's famous march to the sea during the Civil War, he wrote, had been made possible by information found in southern publications. He cited similar dangerous examples from the Crimean, Franco-Prussian, Spanish-American, and Russo-Japanese wars. In the formal statement that MacArthur prepared for his superiors he outlined the recent press measures of Britain, France, Japan, Germany, and Bulgaria. He approved Britain's strict censorship, especially the so-called press bureau in London, which gave out only such news as the government desired. As for U.S. problems in a future war, he noted that the plethora of American newspapers and other means of communication made control difficult, but he was optimistic that in the event of the country's entrance into the war the American newspaper press would meet the War Department midway in the matter. In war, he wrote, the army and navy "become paramount, and every utility and influence within the country should be brought to their aid."[22]

Outraged by MacArthur's proposed plan of censorship, Bullard submitted a memorandum to House claiming that "a Prussian staff officer could not have gone farther in asserting the supremacy of the uniform."[23] War was an abnormal activity demanding unusual precautions, he admitted, but an enlightened public opinion required free discussion.[24] MacArthur, Bullard believed, had presented the classic, deplorable case for censorship, urging that a democracy renounce its ideals when it declared war. Censorship of this sort would be a shield to protect the military from civilian criticism. Contrary to MacArthur's assertion that public confidence in the army would disappear because of open criticism of tactics and strategy, he contended that in the long run such criticism would strengthen morale. From MacArthur's proposed censorship, moreover, it was a short step to politics. Any military advantage would be offset by "systematic falsification of Public Opinion."[25] Censorship would protect grafters and incompetents, civil and military.

The way to bolster popular morale was through announcing the truth, for democracy was a "crazy ideal unless we can trust the people to sort the true from the false."[26] Bullard urged faith in the people. The best way to stop enemy propaganda was to meet it with unvarnished facts.[27]

Bullard's hostility to a harsh military censorship derived from his liberal sympathies and also from awareness of the restrictions on newspapermen imposed by Britain and France, which to his mind had subverted democracy in those countries.[28] Censorship in Britain, he held, had done precisely what MacArthur feared from a free press; namely, it had caused the public to lose faith in the military. He complained to House that the British press bureau, backed by the Defence of the Realm Act, had misled the British people.[29]

There was also, Bullard wrote, a problem of the presentation of American ideals abroad. Censors in Britain and France controlled opinion, preventing publication of anything likely to endanger their diplomats or the social classes they represented.[30] The British public misunderstood the American position regarding the war. The traditional good feeling between England and the United States was being threatened because the State Department had not devised any way to counteract the interpretation of American neutrality spread by the press bureau in London. In France, too, what little American news was published was usually reprinted from the Northcliffe press in England, which was hostile to the United States.[31]

Democratic diplomacy was a notable theme in Bullard's published writings at this time. Such a diplomacy, he liked to maintain, would bring international relations into agreement with the purposes of American domestic politics.[32] Diplomacy was the area "least touched by modern ideas," in some ways "an empty survival of medievalism." This situation had resulted in strained Anglo-American relations, because the only official contact of the United States was with a British government composed of an aristocracy "outspokenly hostile to all our ideals."[33] House apparently considered Bullard's ideas on democratic diplomacy interesting, but as late as July 1916 the influential colonel doubted that any government could "go just now as far" as Bullard suggested.[34]

The *Atlantic Monthly* offered to publish Bullard's theories on censorship and democratic diplomacy in the issue of November 1916, but he felt that he had submitted them to House in confidence and could not publish them without House's consent. He seems to have hoped that Wilson would make democratic versus secret diplomacy an issue in the presidential campaign that year. Such an article as the *Atlantic* desired would be valuable just before the election, unless Wilson decided not to speak out on the issue, in which case an article might harm the president's electoral chances.[35] House told Bullard that he did not know what Wilson planned and that he, House, would not see Wilson before mid-September. He encouraged Bullard to use his own judgment without reference to Wilson's purposes.[36]

When Bullard's article on diplomacy appeared in the *Atlantic* in April 1917, it argued that all the nations of Europe had been victims of secret diplomacy and that the United States conducted its foreign policy in a scarcely better fashion; American diplomacy, Bullard contended, was hardly more democratic than that of Russia.[37] The culprits of this depressing situation were the professional diplomats who hated publicity and defended secrecy.[38] Bullard proposed to make it impossible "for a few men in secret and uncontrolled conclave to decide the fate of nations."[39] He would do so by going over the heads of any foreign office that stood in the way, appealing directly to the people.[40] He proposed that American diplomats take messages of good will to the parliaments of countries where they were accredited. Foreign diplomats in the United States should be introduced in Congress and given the right to speak on the floor. Nothing would "be more gloriously American and more heartily welcomed by the Liberals of all the world than the devising and demonstrating of means by which diplomacy could be democratic."[41] Publicity was also a way of influencing the peoples of foreign nations.[42] Britain and Germany were using publicity as a weapon of war—subsidizing newspapers in neutral countries, sending propagandists to the United States. They could not object if someone "returned the compliment," and he criticized the Wilson administration for not having done so.[43] The State Department should cable press bulletins to embassies to counteract local accounts of American news. Newspapers should be a major instrument of disseminating the American story.[44]

An enlightened public opinion at home was necessary, and this required education of the American people in international affairs. Bullard urged the government to "go in wholeheartedly for education."[45]

The problem of a press bureau took on importance as the United States approached war. Bullard wrote House on February 23, 1917, that if war came the State Department would have to set up a bureau, and he called on the department to study the practices of belligerent countries, to be ready to imitate successes and avoid mistakes.[46] A few weeks later he saw House on the subject of mobilizing newspapermen and suggested that he and other writers in New York had experience and were willing to put it at the service of the government.[47] The two men conferred, and shortly thereafter Bullard sent House a memorandum on organization of a press bureau.[48]

It is interesting that in late March 1917, a crucial time when the United States government was about ready to enter the World War, Bullard published a book entitled *Mobilising America*. House, of course, received a copy.[49] The volume nicely complemented the author's ideas on censorship and democratic diplomacy, for it presented a plan for preparing the country for war. In one sense the book must be seen in the context of Bullard's previous writings on censorship and democratic diplomacy. In another sense the work contained a disturbing element not readily apparent earlier, for it called not just for an educated public opinion but for one filled with missionary zeal.[50]

Bullard believed that the experience of the European democracies revealed two requirements for mobilization of public opinion: a clear call to arms, and a plan that would tell every citizen what to do. The call to arms should stress fervent democratic idealism; it should "electrify public opinion," because "first, last and all the time, the effectiveness of our warfare will depend on the amount of ardour we throw into it."[51] *Mobilising America* stressed the theme of absolute war, "national in the widest sense." If forced into the conflict, we should "go in hard!"[52] The war had shown that democracies in time of crisis would give their governments what was needed for defense, that they could be made into efficient "fighting machines."[53] Behind the buildup of men and arms must be "an inward, spiritual mobilisation." People must be made to desire mobilization.[54] Public welfare must be placed above individual gain, as every citizen who was indifferent to the war was "dead weight."[55] The European powers, he said, had demonstrated that a democracy could galvanize its citizenry.[56]

Bullard's ideas for propaganda organization were nothing if not detailed. He clearly had been thinking a great deal about the subject. A healthy public opinion required free discussion. Censoring debate, spoken or written, was self-defeating.[57] The best method of combating dangerous opinion was publicity, "by constantly giving the man in the street something wholesome to think about."[58] A publicity department would keep the public informed of work and needs of men at the front. It would requisition space on every newspaper front page and draft writers to "feed 'Army stories' to the public." It would set up a corps of press agents to make the war understandable and thereby popular.[59]

Bullard was enthusiastic about some of the methods of mobilization employed by France. Nationalization of the telegraph allowed the French to issue daily news bulletins that were "hypnotic in monotonous regularity." He was excited over the tension created by the three o'clock bulletin. "It was stupendous," he wrote, "the whole nation thinking together once every day."[60] The French also had made efficient use of the schoolteacher and schoolhouse, which were especially important as intellectual centers in locales where metropolitan newspapers did not circulate. In France addresses by the premier were usually summarized by the minister of public instruction, who passed information to subordinates, and in a few days

Wingate College Library

every schoolmistress was reading the message to her pupils. This arrangement had "the peasants . . . thinking of the same problem from the same point of view."[61] Such centralization appealed to Bullard.

A friendly critic described Arthur Bullard as "a sensitive and quiet man, scholarly and well informed, detesting the limelight," with a "passion for obscurity and aversion to official position," a person whose influence exercised through Colonel House "should not be underrated." Bullard surely was a leading personality in the organization of the Committee on Public Information. His plan, set out in the article in the *Atlantic Monthly*, in *Mobilising America*, and (months before that) in long, confidential letters to the friend of the president of the United States, brought an enthusiastic response from House, who wrote on April 13, 1917—the very day the Committee on Public Information was established—that *Mobilising America* was one of the most interesting booklets he had read and that he agreed "almost wholly" with all Bullard had written.[62] Perhaps in so responding House was merely being polite, while privately entertaining reservations about Bullard's ideas. But every indication suggests that he was not. The steady correspondence, the stream of recommendations, the clarity of expression, the fact that House usually passed on ideas from any quarter if he felt they would help the president—all this says that Bullard was a major influence in the weeks before the creation of the CPI.

After the committee was established, Bullard in response thanked House for the assistance and said that, though he knew only slightly the man appointed to the chairmanship of the CPI, George Creel, he thought that his fellow newspaperman was a good choice.[63] At the suggestion of Wilson and House, Creel asked Bullard to help organize the committee, and Bullard did considerable work in this regard.[64] Together with Ernest Poole, he helped write one of the first CPI pamphlets, *How the War Came to America*.[65] Shortly thereafter, he went to Russia and there became an important figure in CPI offices.[66]

Executive Order 2594 established the Committee on Public

2. Arthur Bullard (Reprinted by permission of Princeton
University Library)

Information. It was contemplated at the time that a bill would be sent to Congress giving the CPI statutory authority, but this plan was never carried through. The executive order stipulated that the committee be composed of the secretaries of state, war, and the navy, with a civilian chairman to give direction. The executive order designated Creel for this latter post. Secretaries Robert Lansing, Newton D. Baker, and Josephus Daniels were authorized to appoint officials to work with the CPI.[67]

Members of the president's cabinet were much interested in issues surrounding the CPI. Secretary of the Navy Daniels and Secretary of War Baker were particularly concerned with censorship—Daniels as a former newspaperman, Baker because censorship would affect his department—and on March 17, 1917, both men had met representatives of the press, who hoped the mistakes of British censorship would not be repeated if America went to war. Baker, although having earlier expressed irritation with certain "irresponsible and reckless" newspapers, agreed that the mistakes of European censors should be avoided. Daniels's office on March 24 issued guidelines to the press, asking that certain information regarding troop movements not be published. The notice explained that, aside from such limitations, "maximum publicity" was desired. On April 2, Daniels, Baker, and the counselor of the Department of State, Frank L. Polk, spoke to editors in an effort to calm the fear of impending censorship legislation. The following day, Daniels opposed a suggestion for a board of censors offered by the Advisory Council of the Council of National Defense.[68]

It is of interest that Baker and Daniels came from progressive backgrounds, Baker having been a reform mayor of Cleveland, Daniels the editor of the Raleigh (N.C.) *News and Observer*.[69] Baker had confidence in Daniels and turned over many CPI responsibilities to him. Although Creel got along well with the secretary of war, it was probably Daniels more than any other cabinet member to whom the CPI chairman would turn for advice. A week seldom passed after April 1917 when Daniels and Creel did not confer.[70]

As for the appointment of Creel as executive head of the

CPI, President Wilson trusted him and never considered any other person for the chairmanship.[71] Creel's fierce loyalty to Wilson dated to a time early in his career when he had lived in Kansas City. Wilson, then at Princeton, had come to speak to local high school students on the meaning of democracy and had captured Creel's imagination. The young newspaperman read Wilson's books. When Wilson became governor of New Jersey, Creel began to argue for his nomination for president. He campaigned for Wilson's reelection in 1916, producing a book entitled *Wilson and the Issues*. He organized a committee of authors and publicists to write pamphlets and statements in Wilson's behalf. Many of these writers were to work for the CPI, including Harvey O'Higgins, Ernest Poole, and Samuel Hopkins Adams.[72] After Wilson's victory at the polls, Creel rejected an offer to work for the administration, apparently for financial reasons, but by mid-March 1917 he had become concerned over reports that Wilson was moving toward some form of strict censorship, a course he later described as "criminally stupid."[73] Taking advantage of his friendship with Secretary Daniels, he wrote on March 19 that if a censor was to be appointed he wanted "to be *it*."[74] A little over a week later, on March 28, he again wrote to Daniels, saying that a "censorship policy must be based on publicity, *not* suppression." He worried that government policy was not sufficiently positive and that policy makers—hindered by the "evil nagging" of some newspapers—were "being nibbled to death by ducks." He urged creation of a "Bureau of Publicity" that would work with the army and navy, "suppressing all information of a properly secret nature, but minimizing this repressive power by the vigor of its publicity policy." Such a bureau, Creel hoped, would issue "big, ringing statements" that would arouse the nation's patriotism.[75]

Creel again promoted himself as head of government publicity in two more letters to Daniels on April 4, and these communications were followed up by a telephone call. Attached to one of the April 4 letters was a memorandum outlining how he believed a publicity bureau should be organized. "Censorship," he felt, was a word to be avoided if possible, because though there was much that was "properly secret," the total was small when compared "to the vast amount of information that it is right and necessary for the people to have." Creel recommended that "the *suppressive* features" of this agency be "so overlaid by the publicity policy that they will go unregarded and unresented." Government activities, he argued, "must be dramatized and staged, and every energy exerted to arouse ardor and enthusiasm." He suggested that the organization should have a civilian head, because "a military management suggests the censorship we are trying to avoid"; the army, the navy, and the State Department would be represented, but no one department would control the bureau. Carefully selected newspapermen would visit government departments to collect news and "to develop 'stories,'" so that each department could present its work in the best possible manner. Creel urged the use of famous writers but stressed that only small salaries were to be paid to bureau personnel, for such a policy, he thought, would attract the best and most dedicated workers. There was no need to pass judgment on every item appearing in newspapers and magazines, he believed. Material could be sent to the proposed bureau for approval, or it could take its chances with the law if it violated existing statutes. Partisan attacks on the government could be "handled easily without exercise of despotic power," as such stories would be ordered sent to the bureau, where criticisms would be checked for accuracy. If criticisms were honest, delay would be asked, "pending efforts at rectification"; if attacks were dishonest, the mistake would be pointed out. By this procedure, he maintained, "the whole ugly business of lying, malicious nagging" could be avoided. Creel emphasised that the work of the publicity bureau would have to be done in a spirit of cooperation and on the "assumption that the press is eager and willing to do the handsome thing, and its attitude must be one of frankness, friendship and entire openness."[76]

On the ninth of April, Daniels spoke to Wilson about censorship. By this date the president had decided to appoint Creel. Two days later, Daniels forwarded Creel's memorandum, along with two drafts of proposed censorship legislation, to the president. Wilson liked Creel's proposals.[77] Creel met with Daniels and Baker on the eleventh to make plans for a department of information, and on the following day, Baker and Daniels drafted a letter to Wilson suggesting a committee on publicity, with Creel as director. This letter, dated April 13, also signed by Secretary of State Lansing, was to be cited in the press as the basis of President Wilson's executive order setting up the Committee on Public Information.[78]

Creel's background was rather similar to that of Bullard. He had grown up in Independence and Odessa, Missouri, and was largely self-educated. After beginning his journalistic career in Kansas City, he lived for a time in New York, but he returned to Missouri and together with Arthur Grissom founded the *Independent* in 1899. When Grissom returned to New York, Creel was left with responsibility for the weekly. Perhaps the most distinguished feature of his editorship was the publication's attack on the political organization of the boss of Kansas City, Tom Pendergast.[79]

In his journalistic work during the years before the World War, Creel went to Denver to write for the *Post* and *Rocky Mountain News*. Ever the activist and possessor of ardent opinions, he then left the *Post* for its competitor, the *News*; during a trip to Africa with the *Post*'s editor, Frederick G. Bonfils (to deliver a personal invitation to Theodore Roosevelt to come to Denver), he became disillusioned with the paper's attitude toward reform. In 1911 he helped organize a group of public-spirited citizens in Denver to bring reform to the city. This group was headed by Judge Benjamin B. Lindsey and included two other persons who would later work for the CPI, Josephine Roche and William MacLeod Raine. Defeating the local Speer machine in 1912, the group helped elect Henry J. Arnold as mayor, whereupon Creel became police commissioner. One of his first acts at the police department was to deprive policemen of guns and nightsticks, an unpopular course, to be sure. Assailed as a "tramp anarchist" and "crackpot," he cited statistics to prove that attacks on policemen declined after his order. He also shut down the city's red-light district on Market Street and rounded up the unemployed prostitutes, hoping to reform them by placing them in a more wholesome atmosphere. He also believed that his action would check the spread of venereal disease. After a few months he was forced out as commissioner because of a conflict with Mayor Arnold.[80]

Creel obviously believed in "the demonstrated supremacy of American institutions and ideals."[81] Before the World War, he championed many reforms, including child labor legislation (with Judge Lindsey and Edwin Markham, he was author of a book attacking child labor); women's suffrage; municipal ownership; laws to protect labor; and those favorite panaceas of reformers during the early twentieth century, the initiative, referendum, direct primary, and recall.[82] He read Karl Marx's *Das Kapital* but was repelled by its materialism and hate, by what he thought was its rejection of honor and honesty. He nonetheless flirted with socialism, rejecting its doctrinaire form, yet standing for "the highest degree of socialization" short of doing "away with the incentive motive and [denying] proper rewards for initiative, industry, and ability." He was attracted to Henry George and the single tax.[83] Arguing that government must take a larger part in the world's quest for justice, he favored government regulation or public ownership of utilities involving air, water, food, light, heat, and transportation.[84] By early 1917 he was urging universal military training, pointing to its alleged social value in making men better citizens.[85]

In writings and public utterances—before, during, after the war—Creel showed his confidence in the omnicompetent citizen. He saw the average citizen as rational and capable of wise decisions if properly informed. "I do not believe that public opinion has its rise in the emotions, or that it is tipped from one extreme to the other by every passing rumor, by every gust of passion, or by every storm of anger. I feel that public opinion has its source in the minds of people, that it has its base in reason, and that it expresses slow-formed convictions rather than any temporary excitement or any passing passion of the moment."[86] Because Creel was convinced of "the absolute justice of America's cause, the absolute selflessness of America's aims,"[87] he believed "that no other argument was needed than the simple, straightforward presentation of facts."[88]

Ironically, Creel's work with the CPI during the war may have undermined his ideas about public opinion. He had with the CPI desired to weld the American people into "one white-hot mass . . . with fraternity, devotion, courage, and deathless determination." Democracy, he said, depended on the extent to which people were willing to "concentrate and consecrate body and soul and spirit in the supreme effort of service and sacrifice." Americans had to be shown that "all business was the nation's business."[89] So convinced was he of the correctness of America's position that he probably did not appreciate the dilemma of attempting to educate the public while rousing it to such intensity. Others in the CPI, as we shall see, had little interest in educating and made calculated appeals to the emotions.[90]

To say that Creel's appointment to head the CPI in April 1917 met with unanimous public approval is an overstatement. A New York *Times* editorial questioned whether he had the ability to gain the cooperation of the press.[91] He was known to be flamboyant, temperamental, and thin-skinned. The *Times*'s inquiry was prescient, for he proved unable to take criticism calmly and was frequently stung by critics (he once referred to himself as "morbidly sensitive").[92] Asked what he thought about the minds of Congress, he replied carelessly that he did not know because he had not been slumming lately. After that remark only his friendship with the president saved his job as chairman. He referred to one member of the House as a "petty malignant" and likened Senator Henry Cabot Lodge's mind, perhaps aptly if undiplomatically, to the New England soil— "highly cultivated, but naturally sterile." Too clever with words, he later characterized Lansing as a "dull, small man" who carried "conservatism to the point of medievalism."[93] More than anyone else on the CPI, he was gifted with an ability to turn a phrase—Wilson described him as a man with a "passion for adjectives."[94]

Creel's critics were able to turn an occasional phrase also, and he was described as "a little shrimp of a man with burning dark eyes set in an ugly face under a shock of curly black hair." With a nose "large enough to suggest force," with hair fringing his temples and "brushed as straight back as if his hatless head had been shot out of a big gun, face foremost," he was a "fascinating talker who looked like a gargoyle."[95] More energetic than reflective, a passionate man whose heart (in Wilson's judgment) was in the right place, he brought to the war a crusader's zeal for preservation of "the American way of life." He undeniably was a prodigious worker.

Individuals who worked with Creel noticed more important characteristics than his appearance or outspokenness. One of his assistants, Guy Stanton Ford, was impressed with his administrative ability, his "flare for hitting the high spots."[96] Another, James T. Shotwell, who headed the National Board for Historical Service, apparently got along well with him even though he thought him "a roughneck through and through."[97] To Mark Sullivan he was "an enjoyable person," whereas to Heber Blankenhorn, who directed American propaganda sent into Germany, Creel was "that thunderous steam engine."[98] But he surely possessed what is probably a requirement for any good propagandist—absolute faith in the cause he was supporting. He was one of the era's great apostles of Americanism.

THE Committee on Public Information was established out of a desire to avoid repression, out of hope that American democracy would survive, out of belief that the story of American ideals was sufficient to win the support of people both inside and outside the United States. A crusader for liberalism—Bullard—had helped inspire its creation. The chairman, Creel, and many of his associates were similarly crusaders. For Bullard and Creel it was a noble hope, the Committee on Public Information, but it was to fall short in its fulfillment.

2

Foundation of American Propaganda: Reformers and the CPI

> It is not because we have grown any weaker in our
> advocacy of social reform, social justice and industrial
> democracy, but because, more than ever, we are com-
> mitted to those reforms. It is because we see that the
> very foundation of the cause we represent is in deadly
> peril.
>
> —Charles Edward Russell[1]

IT HAS BEEN SAID that the United States could
not have fought in the Great War without the aid of reformers,
that 1917–18 "marked the apotheosis as well as the liquidation
of the Progressive spirit," that President Woodrow Wilson by so
closely associating America's participation in the war with progressive language and values unintentionally assured an intense
reaction against progressivism after the Armistice.[2] Whether
or not this view is correct, much of the responsibility for the
war's being phrased in progressive terms lay with the Committee on Public Information. The CPI acted as a veritable magnet,
attracting intellectuals, muckrakers, socialists, and other reformers.[3] Though not every person listed on the CPI payroll
was of this sort, many of those individuals who held positions of
responsibility on the committee did come from such backgrounds. This aspect of the committee was important in determining the CPI's operations. Perhaps sensing that the threats
to democracy at this time—militarism, industrialism, the un-
fettered growth of cities, the new immigration—were not confined by national boundaries, many of these people believed

the war had evoked a new spirit of self-sacrifice and cooperation.[4] They were drawn to the committee in hope that they
might fight society's evils and make a better world.[5] The presence of such reform-minded people helps explain that, in addition to its major emphasis on the evils of Prussianism, the CPI
sought to impress Americans with the importance of public
health, conservation, thrift, the civic virtues, and the folly of
national isolation in the modern world. A part of the CPI's
work amounted to urging a spiritual awakening. American
democracy, or sometimes simply Americanism, a vague set of
ideas which at that time was capable of inspiring the national
populace, was to be the great secular religion preached by
the committee. Through a renewed, invigorated Americanism,
society was to unite and improve. Not only would the war
be won but reform would be made international, the world
Americanized and made safe for democracy.

THE Committee on Public Information con-
sisted of two parts: the Domestic Section, which attempted to
mobilize the home front and which is the subject of this study;
and the Foreign Section, which dealt in propaganda abroad
and maintained offices in more than thirty countries.[6] Within
these two parts were more than twenty subdivisions, each spe-
cializing in some aspect of propaganda.[7] Subdivisions were
created as the need arose and usually existed so long as money
was available.[8]

The Executive Division, composed of Creel as chairman,
with three associate chairmen, the committee's secretary, and
staff, was central to the CPI's operations. A muckraking journalist, Creel had championed many reforms before 1917, including universal military training and governmental regulation of
industry. He brought to the CPI a crusading mentality (the
Billy Sunday of politics, Mark Sullivan called him). Progressivism he saw as a moral crusade, indeed, "a spiritual revolt."[9]
Shortly after the United States entered the war he told the editor of *Pearson's Magazine*, A. W. Ricker, "We must keep up our
fight for reform, but we must place the emphasis on construction."[10] He hoped the CPI would reform as well as revitalize

American democracy, and he described the war as a struggle for "the principles held by our fathers of old and reaffirmed today as the meaning of America."[11] Shortly after the Armistice he wrote of the war years as a transition and said, "When I think of the many voices that were heard before the war and are still heard, interpreting America from a class or sectional or selfish standpoint, I am not sure that, if the war had to come, it did not come at the right time for the preservation and reinterpretation of American ideals."[12]

Three associate chairmen—Harvey O'Higgins, Edgar Sisson, Carl Byoir—together with a secretary, Maurice F. Lyons, assisted Creel.[13] O'Higgins had attended the University of Toronto and had become an author and playwright.[14] He also had assisted the reform judge Ben Lindsey in the Children's Court of Denver. His sympathies for reform appeared in a series of articles written in collaboration with Lindsey that were published in 1919, in which he praised Lindsey as an "advance agent of the New Freedom" and hailed the judge's writings as reflective of "our great future after the war."[15] He and Lindsey criticized the YMCA's wartime record and praised the work of the Salvation Army. Representatives of the former, he said, both in the cantonments and in France, had denounced drinking, gambling, and immorality, urging soldiers to repent and save their souls. The latter had preached service and justice. The doughboy, O'Higgins thought, symbolized the spiritual revival brought by the war: he evinced self-sacrifice, courage, and humility, never thinking of anything so selfish as saving his soul. Soldiers were not inclined to denounce immorality so much as to put down "cowardice, selfishness, and egotism." The churches' work in the postwar world, he and Lindsey argued, was to take up this ethic, "the religion of Christ in action."[16] In other articles he and Lindsey compared the vested interests of the United States (the invisible government, they called them) with the Junkers of Germany and urged Americans to welcome reform as had Britain, or face revolution, as had Russia and Germany.[17] O'Higgins participated in several phases of the CPI's work and wrote one of the best-known wartime pamphlets, *The German Whisper*, which sounded a warning about

German propaganda and ended by urging citizens to report to the Justice Department the names and addresses of persons suspected of spreading such propaganda.

Edgar Sisson had attended Northwestern University before becoming a reporter on the Chicago *Chronicle* in 1897. He later joined the Chicago *Tribune* and after several years left to become managing editor of *Collier's Weekly*. By 1914 he was editor of another reform periodical, *Cosmopolitan Magazine*; he remained there until called to Washington to serve with the CPI. Sisson's employer, William Randolph Hearst, reluctantly agreed to part with his services.[18] A "sharp, keen man, small and wiry in stature, bursting with energy and patriotic enthusiasm," to some colleagues he seemed distant and impersonal, with "a flair for conspiracy and intrigue."[19] Sisson spent part of the war in Russia and was for a time director of the Foreign Section. An erstwhile Roosevelt Progressive, he found bolshevism distasteful and remarked to Creel that he was turning increasingly against socialism.[20]

Like Sisson, Carl Byoir had been on the Hearst payroll, as circulation manager for *Cosmopolitan*. Interested in nearly all aspects of the CPI, he was known as the committee's "multiple director." He had been president of the House of Childhood in New York City and had become fascinated by the Montessori system of preschool education. He helped set up *John Martin's Book*, a children's publication.[21] Creel considerd Byoir "absolutely indispensable" and secured his exemption from the military service.[22] After the war, Byoir became one of the country's leading public relations men, founding the firm of Carl Byoir and Associates.[23]

In addition to the Executive Division, three other offices were important to the functioning of the CPI: the Division of Stenography and Mimeographing, the Division of Production and Distribution, and the Division of Business Management. The work of the first is obvious. Henry Atwater directed the second, the Division of Production and Distribution, established in June 1917. Its initial purpose was to provide nationwide distribution of the early CPI pamphlet *The War Message and the Facts behind It.* The Government Printing Office handled production during the early months of the war, but as the demand for CPI materials increased it became necessary to use commercial publishing houses and the division expanded its offices to New York. The section handling business affairs was set up in October 1917, taking over from N. P. Webster, disbursing clerk at the White House. Clayton D. Lee headed this division and supervised the committee's finances.

Other divisions were established within the Domestic Section as the war progressed.[24] The CPI did not grow according to a precise plan; its organization was improvised, and its structure and personnel were constantly changing.[25] Some divisions were set up early—such as the Division of News—whereas others, like the Division of Advertising, were not established until 1918. Several divisions were out of existence before the Armistice, after Congress in June 1918 cut the committee's appropriation.

Some of the best-remembered work of the committee came from publicists writing for the Division of Civic and Educational Cooperation, later known as the Division of Civic and Educational Publications. Pamphlets in the Red, White and Blue and War Information Series sold millions of copies and were translated and sent across the world. The list of writers for this division ranged from the dean of the muckrakers, S. S. McClure, to the youthful historian Carl Becker. The division's director and one of the CPI's most influential members, Guy Stanton Ford, estimated that he had from two to three hundred scholars working for him, including such well-known figures as Evarts B. Greene, Andrew C. McLaughlin, and Edward S. Corwin. Ford thought of his division as a "new educational agency," and it is clear that many of his assistants viewed the committee as a forum from which to present the vital issues confronting the country. They attempted to tell of American ideals, the threat of German militarism, and the danger of American isolation. Becker, McLaughlin, and Ford each sought to justify America's intervention in the war and to bring the Monroe Doctrine in accord with modern conditions.[26] Ford told his scholars to produce pamphlets "as accurate as scholarship could make them . . . the kind of work which they would not be ashamed to own twenty years after the war."[27]

The division was responsible for a school bulletin, the *National School Service*, sent to public schools across the country. J. W. Searson, who had been a teacher of English at Kansas Agricultural State College, and William C. Bagley, of Columbia, edited the bulletin. Bagley thought of it as an opportunity to use the federal government to raise the quality of education at the local level.

The Committee on Public Information made several efforts to reach American laboring men. Ford's busy division published pamphlets for workingmen under the Loyalty Leaflet Series. Written by well-known Americans, the tracts were simple appeals to support the war. The CPI established a Division of Industrial Relations, but after a month the work of this division, headed by Roger W. Babson, was transferred from the CPI to the Department of Labor. Babson always had voted a straight Republican ticket until 1916, when he backed Wilson. He was apparently one of those people who helped formulate and advertise the president's campaign slogan of that year, "He kept us out of war."[28] Earlier, in 1907, he had established what he described as Babson's Statistical Organization, in Wellesley, Massachusetts, which studied industrial relations and other problems facing large employers. Before 1917 he had traveled to South America and written of investment opportunities there.[29] He became concerned about eliminating the economic causes of war and helped organize a society to that end.[30] As a statistician, employer's counsel, and business analyst concerned with efficiency, he hoped during the war to "bridge the chasm" between industrial leaders and laborers. Though he had reservations about entry in the war he joined the CPI in February 1918, perhaps hoping that through the committee he could improve industrial relations.[31]

When Babson withdrew from the CPI after his short tenure, and his division went to the Department of Labor, the appeal to labor was primarily through the Labor Publications Division and through the American Alliance for Labor and

Democracy, the latter an organization under the presidency of Samuel Gompers, technically independent of the CPI, but in reality strongly influenced by Creel.[32] Robert Maisel was director of both the publications division and the alliance. A prowar socialist, he had been a staff member of the New York *Call* but resigned after the Socialist party's antiwar stand in April 1917. He supplied information to Gompers about the activities of the antiwar People's Council of America for Democracy and Terms of Peace. During the war some critics suspected Maisel's patriotism, but Creel defended him, pointing out that Gompers had selected him and that he was in charge of the committee's work against German socialists on New York's East Side.[33] J. G. Phelps Stokes, another prowar socialist, was treasurer of the alliance. A millionaire from New York, Stokes had resigned from the Socialist party in July 1917. Along with John Spargo and other prowar socialists, like Charles Edward Russell and William English Walling, he hoped to create a separate socialist movement that would support the war, and, in fact, he helped establish the Social Democratic League of America.[34] Within six months the American Alliance for Labor and Democracy had established 150 branches in 40 states, given out nearly 2 million pamphlets, conducted 200 mass meetings, and obtained newspaper space totaling about 10,000 columns.[35] Some of the pamphlet literature published by the alliance supported reform measures, such as the tracts by John R. Commons, which favored the universal eight-hour day and greater worker participation in industrial management.[36]

Realizing that many Americans did not read the front pages of newspapers and would not read patriotic pamphlets, the CPI, in August 1917, created the Division of Syndicated Features, under L. Ames Brown, in the hope of capturing the attention of those persons who read only the feature sections of Sunday papers. When Brown left the division for the Shipping Board he was replaced by the newspaperman and western novelist William MacLeod Raine, associated with Creel in the earlier effort to reform Denver.[37]

Brown had worked for the Nashville *Tennessean* (1912–13) and had been White House correspondent for the New York

Sun (1913–16) and the Philadelphia *Record* (1915–17). During the political campaign of 1916, he supported President Wilson, explaining presidential programs and defending policies.[38] He wrote articles in 1915 and 1916 against the saloon. He opposed national prohibition, arguing that it would be uneconomic and un-American and would work against the survival of the fittest. Drinking was a problem best left to the states. He did not oppose moderate drinking and argued that the American way was self-reliance rather than legislation. Americans made great sacrifices, he believed, only for some spiritual reason.[39] After the war he became president of the public relations firm of Lord, Thomas and Logan.[40]

Brown's division attracted the volunteer services of about fifty essayists, novelists, and short-story writers and many professors and college presidents. Arthur McFarlane wrote a half dozen articles for the division, Donald Breed fourteen, Raine ten. Writers included O'Higgins, Spargo, Walling, Wallace Irwin, and Will Irwin.[41] The Indiana writer Booth Tarkington wrote for this division, as did the muckraking novelist Samuel Hopkins Adams. The latter, incidentally, published *Common Cause: A Novel of the War in America* in 1918. The story's central character, a young newspaper owner, Jeremy Robson, had to struggle in his community not only with a powerful German-American group that supported Germany in the war, but also with strong business interests trying to corrupt his paper with advertising.[42]

The Division of Syndicated Features provided stories for Sunday newspapers whose weekly circulation was often as high as seven million. The stories related "the racial, the social, the moral, and the financial aspects of the war."[43] It popularized material from the News Division and from the Division of Civic and Educational Publications, always with the theme of patriotism.[44] Before its work ended, after the budget cut in June 1918, its stories were reaching almost twenty-five million people each month.[45]

For the occasional readers and nonreaders the Committee on Public Information established a national speakers' network, largely through the Division of Four Minute Men, but also through the Speaking Division. By the war's end almost seventy-five thousand Four Minute Men had delivered perhaps one million speeches to perhaps four hundred million people. Donald Ryerson, William McCormick Blair, and William H. Ingersoll in turn directed this division. Ingersoll hoped that the division could continue after the war and serve as an updated version of the old New England town meeting, bringing important issues to public attention. The Speaking Division, less centrally controlled than the Four Minute Men, routed nationally known speakers across the country. Arthur Bestor, president of the Chautauqua Institution, was in charge of the Speaking Division. J. J. Pettijohn, who had been director of the extension division of Indiana University and in charge of the Indiana State Speakers' Bureau, followed Bestor as director. When the Speaking Division combined with the Division of Four Minute Men in September 1918, Pettijohn became associate director of that division.[46]

Among the reform-minded individuals who were routed by the Speaking Division were Ida Tarbell, Jane Addams, and Charles Edward Russell. Tarbell spoke on behalf of the Woman's Committee of the Council of National Defense.[47] Addams undertook a speaking tour in early 1918 for the Food Administration. She spoke in Ohio, Louisiana, Texas, and California, hoping that the effort would further her ideas about international order. Russell had been perhaps the most prolific writer of all the muckrakers.[48] Shortly after the United States declared war, he had been named to the Root mission that was sent to Russia. Later he headed the committee's offices in England. Replaced in that post by his son John Russell, and back in America, he undertook a speaking tour across the country under the direction of Bestor's division, delivering fifty-eight addresses between October 1917 and February 1918.[49]

In the unlikely event that Americans failed to read the CPI's message or to hear it via the spoken word, the committee enlisted the powerful forces of advertising and art. In the Division of Advertising it brought together some of the leading advertising figures in America. With the assistance of the Division of Pictorial Publicity, this division turned out some of the most famous posters of the war. One of the leading spirits of the advertising section was Herbert S. Houston, who before the war had sought to reform his trade by calling for elimination of fraudulent advertising.[50] The Division of Pictorial Publicity was under Charles Dana Gibson, America's best-known illustrator in 1917.

The CPI established a Bureau of War Expositions and a Bureau of State Fair Exhibits. In twenty cities the former bureau set up exhibits of war machinery and trophies taken from the Germans on the western front. These displays, such as the one in Chicago in late August 1918, were popular, and admission receipts brought returns of about four hundred thousand dollars. The Bureau of State Fair Exhibits displayed war equipment, but its primary message was conservation. To exhibits at some sixty state fairs it drew an estimated seven million people.[51]

Thanks in part to the CPI, the federal government exerted an enormous influence on the dissemination of news during the war. One of the earliest creations of the committee was the Division of News, which sought to rectify the chaotic procedure for news releases that had plagued both the army and the navy. It expanded beyond the military and eventually issued about six thousand releases. Though not able to command publication, the division sent releases to the press, which in turn chose material to be printed.[52] Some contemporaries complained that this division was staffed by men of radical social views sympathetic to bolshevism. J. W. McConaughy was the first director, followed by Leigh Reilly. Ranking assistants were Marlen E. Pew and Arthur W. Crawford, and Kenneth Durant and Maurice Strunsky were associated with the division.[53] Closely connected with the office's work was the *Official Bulletin*, an official newspaper published daily by the government and edited by Edward S. Rochester.

The Foreign Language Newspaper Division, directed by William Churchill, also dealt with the news. Created in April 1917, it watched virtually every foreign-language newspaper in the United States, with an eye toward violations in the special permits required by these publications under the Trading-with-the-Enemy Act. It provided translating service to other CPI divisions and translated several committee pamphlets into foreign languages. After eleven months the division combined with the CPI's Division of Work with the Foreign Born.

To mobilize cartoonists for commentaries on current events, the Executive Division set up a Bureau of Cartoons. Directed by Alfred M. Saperston, it published a *Weekly Bulletin* to instruct every cartoonist in the country.

Both the Film Division, established in late 1917, and the Picture Division dealt with the production of news. These two sections, which were combined in early 1918, attempted to capture war activities on film. The Film Division produced newsreels that played in movie houses across the country. In the beginning this division limited its efforts to distributing Signal Corps movies, but later it developed an Educational Department and a Scenario Department.[54] It dealt with commercial producers and sometimes made motion pictures of its own.[55] Charles S. Hart, director of the Film Division, spent more than a million dollars but recovered nearly three-fourths of the amount in film rentals. In the early days of the division, Hart received assistance from William A. Brady and D. W. Griffith. Brady was concerned with the expression of ideals in movies; Griffith, who sought to reform the motion-picture industry, believed that movies could help establish a universal morality.[56] The Picture Division and the later Bureau of War Photographs granted permits for war pictures, and the latter circulated widely. The Department of Slides, connected with the Bureau of War Photographs, took over Signal Corps production work and distributed more than two hundred thousand slides.[57]

A Division of Women's War Work established on November 1, 1917, sought to mobilize the nation's women. The division sent material to nearly twenty thousand newspapers and also to women's publications. It sent out approximately fifty thousand letters to women who raised questions concerning the war, and produced about two thousand feature articles and news stories concerning the work of women. Used by editorial writers and columnists, the stories showed what women had done at home and abroad through national organizations, government departments, state and local organizations, schools, colleges, and churches.[58] An effort also was made to present work by black women. The division was headed by Mrs. Clara Sears Taylor of Denver, a newspaper writer who for more than fifteen years had specialized in Sunday stories for magazine sections of eastern newspapers, and who was a member of the Colorado Suffrage Association.[59] Taylor sought to cover the work of the Women's Division of the Council of National Defense, which included Anna Howard Shaw, Carrie Chapman Catt, and Ida Tarbell. When Congress cut the CPI's budget in June 1918, this latter organization took over the Division of Women's War Work.[60]

The Division of Work with the Foreign Born, with Josephine A. Roche as director, attempted to ensure the loyalty of new immigrants. Roche, after graduating from Vassar in 1908, and after studying on a Russell Sage Foundation Fellowship, had received a master's degree from Columbia; she then went to Denver, where "with a heartful of dedication and a headful of liberal ideas" she joined Creel in an effort to reform that city.[61] In 1912 she supported Roosevelt.[62] Between 1913 and 1915 she was executive secretary of the Colorado Progressive Service. She was appointed special agent for England and the United States in 1915, for the Commission for the Relief of Belgium. Between 1915 and 1918 she served as director of the Girls' Department of the Juvenile Court for Denver and the surrounding area. By 1918 she was connected with the National Consumer's League. When the CPI set up its Division of Work with the Foreign Born in May 1918, she took over as director.[63] In her work with the CPI she helped the committee organize along patriotic lines twenty-three foreign groups within the United States. The division tried to ensure the loyalty of the foreign born by providing them with information and giving them a sense of participation in government. Working through the foreign-language press, foreign-language organizations, field work, and pamphlets, the division set up sections to work with the foreign-language groups and through the sections issued more than twenty-three hundred news releases concerning the work of various government departments.[64]

The Committee on Public Information attracted many other reform-minded individuals. The socialist Algie Martin Simons urged the CPI to do more in the way of supporting social reforms. He viewed the World War as "the supreme opportunity of social service" and broke with the Socialist party over the issue of supporting the war.[65] He attacked his former comrades as un-American. He wrote and distributed CPI literature in his home state of Wisconsin; many of his writings on labor were sent abroad; and he toured England, France, and Italy, with CPI publicity, to ask support of labor and socialist groups.[66] He hoped the war would bring a social revolution that would make possible "the conscious organization of society."[67] An ardent nationalist by early 1917, Simons believed that the war was having a constructive influence on society, that it presented an opportunity for democratization of industry, and that there should be "national control of distribution."[68] The war had swept away more obstacles to progress than a century of legislation and agitation. Observing that militarism could block social legislation, he argued that the struggle was for human rights and called for "radicals, reformers, revolutionists, and progressives to recover from their war shock," to dry their "unnoticed and ineffective tears," and to use "war-created forces" to advance social progress and strengthen labor, women, and the poor. War collectivism must be democratized. If the war were a part of the death of an outgrown society, people favoring revolution should not attempt to block the conflict.[69] Simons took an interest in the American Alliance for Labor and Democracy, and along with Stokes, Russell, and others helped organize the Social Democratic League in July 1917.[70] Simons urged that CPI publications take a "new outlook in the direction of social transformation, reconstruction, rebuilding of men and society."[71] He thought the war had unleashed the "most powerful social forces ever unchained," and he worked to use the opportunity to bring about something resembling "the Cooperative Commonwealth."[72]

John Spargo was another socialist drawn to the CPI. He had resigned from the Socialist party in June 1917 and joined the American Alliance for Labor and Democracy, hoping to support the war without abandoning his socialist principles. In the summer of 1917 he complained to Creel that there had been no statement of American and Allied war objectives and peace terms. Creel hurriedly sent Spargo a list of such aims to incorporate in a speech before a convention of the Alliance.[73] Spargo later, in June 1918, accompanied Simons to Europe.

Upton Sinclair, perhaps anxious to demonstrate his patriotism, was attracted to the CPI. In September 1918 he sent Creel the first few chapters of his novel *Jimmie Higgins*. As he then planned the novel, its hero was a socialist workingman who opposed the war but changed his mind after realizing he had been misled by German propaganda. The hero went to France and gave his life for democracy. Sinclair suggested that this work might be published as a serial, translated, and sent to countries abroad. Creel expressed interest in the idea but decided to turn down the project as too large for the committee's program. Afterward the author became disgusted with American intervention in Russia and concluded the novel by having its hero give his life for the Russian revolution.[74]

It should be mentioned parenthetically that many reformers worked for the CPI abroad. The journalist Will Irwin had a realistic, indeed enlightened, understanding of modern warfare and was not optimistic that the war would bring a social transformation or restrain capitalism or purify society.[75] He saw it, instead, as destroying the finest youth in each country.[76] Creel considered him "the best of all war reporters" and a "brilliant advocate of the Allied cause."[77] In articles for the *Saturday Evening Post*, Irwin sought to expose German tyranny and atrocities; he served as director of the Foreign Section in 1918.[78]

Ernest Poole directed the Foreign Press Bureau, which was established in November 1917. A student of Wilson at Princeton, he had worked with Bullard on New York's Lower East Side. He abandoned pacifism when he saw what the war had done for France and England, "the new social ideals and visions and the drastic methods of cooperation which the demands of this mighty combat were forcing upon the governments there, while infusing hearts and minds of the people with the idea of

comradeship and universal service—service in a cause world
wide." He came to believe that the war he had hated "was in
some ways on a higher plane than was the peace" he had
extolled.[79] Poole tried to educate American soldiers in France
on problems of reconstruction and wrote a series of articles
entitled "The Blind Revolutionist," distributed with Creel's assistance, attempting to describe the unsettling changes brought
by the war.[80]

Charles E. Merriam, the scholar-activist from the University of Chicago who did so much to gain recognition for the
academic discipline of political science, headed the CPI offices
in Italy for a considerable time. Vira B. Whitehouse, an active
participant in the woman suffrage movement before 1917,
directed the CPI effort in Switzerland; Frank Bohn, a specialist
in international relations whom Creel described as occupying
a "commanding position in the world of liberal thought," assisted Whitehouse. James Kerney, publisher of the Trenton
Times and a friend of Wilson, directed propaganda in France.
Ben Lindsey, Creel's close friend from Denver, made a speaking tour of Europe in 1918. Lindsey wanted to establish a moral
alliance among the Allied countries through an exchange of
social workers and urged Creel to promote a plan for "an
International Commission of Social Work."[81]

THE Committee on Public Information was
thus an organization composed of liberal, reform-minded journalists and intellectuals—some of the most forward-looking
members of American society. It is likely that many of them
agreed with Ford that the CPI was a new federal educational
agency that promised to be not only an instrument to mobilize
the nation for war but an instrument of reform.

Most of the progressives who joined the CPI had been publicists for reform before the war.[82] The militant spirit so evident
in 1917 and 1918 had been rehearsed, and these writers expressed their ideas in moralistic terms. The city boss, the large
corporation, graft, corruption—such had been the earlier enemies thwarting democracy. The new enemies were the kaiser,
the German militarists, and Prussianism. They called for a new

campaign for American ideals to make the world safe for democracy. Creel, Bullard, Russell, Ford, and others spoke for reaffirming the fundamental ideals of the Republic. The Creel committee was a part of the bureaucracy during the war, but bureaucratic values and concern for efficiency, though present (especially in the minds of men like Babson, Brown, and Simons), seem to have been secondary to a spiritual awakening.[83] Some of the committee's efforts were misguided, and phases of its work had disturbing implications for democratic society. Still, the reforming impulse, the desire to improve society, helped determine the work of the CPI.

3

The Literature of the CPI: American Democracy

> . . . if this war shall eventually unite the old America to
> the New America in a spirit of understanding, a bond of
> true national fellowship, it will be well worth the heaviest
> price that we may have to pay. . . .
> —Samuel Hopkins Adams[1]

THE PROMOTION OF DEMOCRACY offered large
opportunity for speculation not merely about what American
democracy was but about what it should be, and was a major
theme in the literature of the Committee on Public Information.[2] Secretary of War Newton D. Baker remarked in November 1918 that victory had resulted not only from physical
superiority but from the "persuasive and unending flood of
ideas that aroused a correct apprehension of the true spirit and
idealism of America in the war."[3] The task of selecting pamphlets for this grand purpose fell to Guy Stanton Ford and his
associates of the Division of Civic and Educational Publications.
Ford beheld the CPI as a new educational agency, "a war emergency national university," to inform citizens of the duties and
privileges of and dangers to American democratic institutions.[4]

How Ford came to his task of guardian of
American democracy is an interesting story. In 1917 the CPI
had first turned to Arthur Bullard to prepare documents detailing German-American diplomatic relations. With little prece-
dent save perhaps what other belligerent nations had done,
Bullard began working with the State Department to select
such material. It was soon decided that thick books and long

state papers were not likely to capture public attention, and the project was dropped in favor of a series of popular pamphlets.[5] Bullard was the logical choice to conduct the pamphlet campaign, but he was interested in Russia and spent much of the war in that country with the CPI's Foreign Section. Creel also realized that the ideal person for such a position would be a university man who could attract the scholars a journalist would not be able to reach. At about this time, in spring 1917, Ford— then dean of the University of Minnesota graduate school— wrote an open letter to public school principals suggesting that high school commencements be devoted to patriotic purposes. A copy was given to Creel, most likely by James T. Shotwell of the National Board for Historical Service, and made such an "instant impression" that Creel brought Ford into the CPI.[6]

In his mid-forties in 1917–18, Ford was a professor of European history. As a youth he had attended school in Wisconsin and Iowa and in the early 1890s had enrolled at Upper Iowa University in Fayette. After a year of teaching in the rural schools of Bremer County, he went to the University of Wisconsin, wrote an undergraduate paper under the direction of Frederick Jackson Turner, and graduated in 1895. After three years as superintendent of schools in Grand Rapids, Wisconsin, he reentered the university for graduate work. He studied again with Turner and also with Charles H. Haskins, Richard Ely, Paul Reinsch, and Victor Ely. From Wisconsin he went to Germany to study mainly in Berlin, but he visited the universities of Leipzig and Göttingen. In the autumn of 1900 he entered Columbia University to study for a doctorate. In 1901, Yale engaged him as an instructor. He went later to the University of Illinois, and eventually to Minnesota. His doctoral dissertation, *Hanover and Prussia*, was published in 1903.[7]

Ford's group within the CPI became known as the Division of Civic and Educational Cooperation, a title later changed to Division of Civic and Educational Publications. He was assisted by Samuel B. Harding, professor of European history at Indiana University, who had been "booming the war" to his classes in Bloomington. Harding joined Ford's staff in No-

3. Guy Stanton Ford (Courtesy of the University of Minnesota Archives)

vember 1917 and was a leading contributor to the division's pamphlet output.[8]

On his arrival in Washington, Ford found himself in the midst of a storm of activity. So hectic was the pace that he did not see Creel for nearly two weeks. Yet his efforts were rewarded, for he soon assembled a formidable group of writers.[9]

His division worked with the National Board for Historical Service (NBHS), created early in the war during a conference sponsored by the Carnegie Institution. The first chairman of the NBHS, Shotwell, explained that it sought a connection with state archives and state libraries in the United States to make certain that there would be an accurate record of the war. The board did background work for many of the documents used by the CPI, especially the Red, White and Blue Series and the best-known War Information Series pamphlet, *The War Message and the Facts behind It*.[10] Ford was a member of the NBHS, as were several other people who wrote for the CPI. There is every indication that the NBHS took advantage of Ford's position to use his division to advance its own projects.[11]

It is difficult to know how many publications were put out by Ford's division. The final report of the CPI lists more than ninety.[12] However, this figure does not include articles by people on the CPI payroll that found their way into periodicals, nor articles turned down by the CPI but recommended for publication elsewhere.[13] It does not include articles in *History Teacher's Magazine*, written by the scholars involved with Ford's bureau, nor books inspired by the war and the CPI. The best known of the publications were the thirty-odd pamphlets that made up the Red, White and Blue and the War Information Series, and the seven pamphlets in the Loyalty Leaflet Series. Circulation of the ninety-plus publications was estimated to be more than seventy-five million, and this number does not include the circulation that metropolitan dailies gave these writings (newspapers often reprinted CPI pamphlets). Nor does it account for the thousands of copies printed by state organizations.[14]

Such was the organization and extent of the publications of Ford's division. How, then, did Ford's writers define American democracy, the political system for which the country had gone to war? To many people, the challenge to American values and democratic institutions ran deeper than the war and seemed bound up with the conditions of modern living. The industrial revolution and growth of cities transformed American society; the closing of the frontier raised doubt about the nation's capacity to absorb immigrants.[15] These concerns were intensified by the war, as the specter of German aggression appeared to threaten democracy's survival. It cannot be denied that a part of the committee's literature oversimplified and even distorted the issues of the war. But putting aside this aspect of the CPI's work, there remained a conviction that American democracy must function under modern conditions. A desire for reform, so as to preserve democracy, was inseparable from the purpose of the CPI's literature.[16]

Probably the clearest, most visible expressions of American democratic ideals during the war, certainly the most frequently used by the Creel committee, were the speeches of President Wilson. Seldom have the utterances of a president been more eloquent, and the CPI gave them wide circulation. Two of the committee's pamphlets were annotated printings of Wilson's speeches, whose circulation exceded nine million copies.[17] The president's words appeared in other CPI pamphlets.[18] *How the War Came to America* was published in nearly six million copies and translated into at least seven languages, and an appendix reprinted three of Wilson's speeches.[19] Other publications, such as Carl Becker's *America's War Aims and Peace Program* and the *War Cyclopedia*, were laced with statements from the chief executive.[20] The most famous expression of American ideals during the war, Wilson's Fourteen Points, was widely circulated by the CPI.[21]

Democracy often was described as being identical with American ideals, or Americanism. Secretary of the Interior Franklin K. Lane, in *Why We Are Fighting Germany*, spoke of America in mystical terms. "America," he wrote, was not the name of mere territory but "a living spirit" that had "purpose and pride, and conscience." It was "more precious that this America should live than that we Americans should live."[22] In a speech before an Americanization conference in the spring of 1918, Lane expanded on his idea of the meaning of America: "America is an aspiration. America is a spirit. America is something mystical which lives in the heavens. It is the constant and continuous searching of the human heart for the thing that is better." Each listener, he said, was "a religious leader" in whose soul lay "a mystical quantity which represents ... Americanism." Americanism was the "most advanced spirit" that had come to man "from above."[23] After the war, Lane was to speak of the spirit of Americanism as "a living flame" and to suggest that Americanism was "a spirit that meets challenge; a spirit that wants to help." Though the United States welcomed different cultural heritages, Lane wanted every citizen to love America "because it is holy ground—because it serves the world."[24] He was responsible for an anthology of prose and poetry published by the CPI under the title *The Battle Line of Democracy*. The anthology, which tried to inspire love of country, contained such selections as John Ireland's "The Duty and Value of Patriotism"; Ireland said that patriotism "goes out to what is, among earth's possessions, the most precious, the first and best and dearest—country." Patriotism was essential to human life, even innate to man, Ireland believed, and its absence was a perversion of human nature. After God and religion came patriotism. Another of Lane's selections was by the well-known poet Katharine Lee Bates, who had written "America the Beautiful." Bates's poem, "The New Crusade," began:

> Life is a trifle
> Honor is all
> Shoulder the rifle
> Answer the call.[25]

An interesting wartime effort to explain American democracy was made by a professor of English at the University of Illinois, Stuart P. Sherman, who would be one of the editors of the *Cambridge History of American Literature*, a landmark in American letters. At Harvard, Sherman studied under Irving Babbitt; in early 1917 he considered himself a humanist, offering a critique of modern society similar to that of Babbitt and Paul Elmer More. He was an admirer of Matthew Arnold and a strong critic of naturalism in literature.[26] It was in 1917 that Sherman began to think about the importance of national groups for civilization's survival. He believed that "an inflamed egotistical nationalism" had brought on the war.[27] Yet even if national groups were the most powerful force corrupting civilization, they were the strongest redemptive agent. People who loved humanity would make more progress by attempting to purify the national spirit than by trying to destroy it. Sherman spoke of a "religion of democracy," and even after the war, well into the 1920s, he was concerned with arousing a religious feeling, of defining a national faith, that would unite Americans spiritually.[28] He also apparently believed that Americanism provided a basis for international order.

Sherman was something of a dissenter and in 1917 had written an article about Theodore Roosevelt for the *Nation*, rejecting Roosevelt's chauvinistic attitude toward the war. He accused the former president of being "temperamentally and philosophically an ardent admirer of the German system." TR was not at war to make the world safe for democracy; he was at war to make the world safe for the United States.[29]

Sherman's CPI essay, *American and Allied Ideals*, had originally been prepared as an address before the National Council of Teachers of English.[30] When he went before the teachers in early December 1917 to ask them to become propagandists on behalf of American ideals, he was speaking from a conviction about the national heritage.[31] A peaceful nation, he argued, had the right to protect itself. A country's life included more than the property and lives of the present generation: it included the common ideals and principles, the national culture, which the living generations had received as a sacred inheritance from its forefathers, a priceless possession to be passed on to their posterity. The inheritance constituted "the spiritual mold in which our fluid thoughts and emotions

take the shape of American characters." Such ideals linked
the present generation with Franklin, Washington, Jefferson,
and Lincoln.[32]

The intense interest of the Illinois professor in American
democracy had been stimulated by the war, but his concern also
went deeper; he believed that American democratic values
were being attacked in several ways, one of which involved a
challenge to traditional American literature.[33] An insidious
anti-American campaign, involving magazine editors, novelists,
poets, critics, professors, and even brewers, had been conducted
with the English language, seeking to destroy America's literary
heritage by sneering at democratic government. It attacked the
Puritan tradition, which was at the center of Americanism.
It denigrated efforts at moral reform and the humanitarian
movement connected with Christianity. It laughed at classical
American literature and every other revered American tradition. The campaign celebrated "the biological-political ideals of
Prussian statecraft, the biological immoralism of Nietzsche, and
the literature of Berlin and Vienna, especially that nastiest part
of it which they are certain will offend what they scoffingly
call the Puritanical sensibilities of Americans."[34] Contemporary
German thought was "prehistoric, reversionary, paradoxical,"
and Sherman believed German literature, ethics, and politics,
the works of Schopenhauer, Nietzsche, Treitschke, Bernhardi,
and Hartmann, to be the antithesis of the American ideal.
American principles expressed the great literature of the ages,
such as the writings of Confucius, Cicero, Milton, and Goethe
(who had said that national hatred was strongest in countries
with the lowest culture).[35]

American civilization, according to Sherman, was a very
special proposition. Each national culture developed in response to local needs. Its values related to place, time, and
circumstance. Each culture had a principle of expansion and a
principle of contraction. Herein lay the difference between
German and American culture. The American ideal was external freedom and inner control. In the United States the
government looked after the citizen's liberty while the individual looked after his conduct. "Puritanism" was the American

principle of contraction, an indispensable check on democracy, the American principle of expansion. Puritanism, as defined by Sherman, was "the inner check upon the expansion of natural impulse."[36] The German ideal, by contrast, was "external control and 'inner freedom'"; the government looked after the individual's conduct and he looked after his liberty.

Sherman saw the attack on American democracy as coming not merely from assaults on traditional American literature but also from unassimilated immigrants. He believed that there existed a campaign to destroy the melting pot: immigrants were being organized to resist Americanization.[37] They insisted on speaking their native tongues, usurping the place that belonged to the English language; they were "deliberate colonists for a foreign empire, and enemies of the American republic."[38] Immigrants, when they came to America, left behind the contractive principle of their national culture: the German left behind the strict regulatory force of the German government, the Frenchman the discipline of the French family. New arrivals were unaware of any government check on their freedom, and Sherman feared that unless they were made aware of "the check of individual responsibility which the good American's moral culture imposes upon his liberty," immigrants might conclude that the United States was "a paradise for the lawless." When immigrants accepted the civic liberty guaranteed by the government but refused to accept the restraints and obligations America imposed upon the individual conscience, anarchy resulted.[39] Anarchy, one senses, was as much a threat to democracy as was autocracy, because it provided fertile ground for the growth of authoritarian government. Sherman believed that America was in the midst of anarchy, and any person not indoctrinated with American ideals was a menace to the republic.[40]

In the attempt to redefine American democracy, few individuals spoke out more enthusiastically than did Carl Becker. From the first, Becker was interested in reinterpreting American democratic institutions—the Great Experiment he called them—so that they would meet the realities of the twentieth century. He prepared one of the last CPI pamphlets, *America's*

War Aims and Peace Program, and began working on a book for Ford, which tried to explain the American democratic experiment.[41] The latter work was not published until 1920, but Ford assisted Becker from the beginning and many years later still referred to the book as the best effort he had seen to explain American democracy.[42]

Becker hoped the war would bring a regeneration, not just of German society, but of the social and economic order in the United States and other countries. Although the United States enjoyed political democracy, in industrial and economic organization it had been undemocratic. Such developments made it difficult to attract foreign-born workingmen. Arrivals from Europe had a different idea of America than did Carl Schurz's generation. Rather than being a land of democracy, the United States had come to be a capitalist, bourgeois regime. "The last thing the average foreign workingman, either in Europe or in this country, wants is to establish American institutions as he knows them—the Capitalist and Bourgeois regime is precisely what he wants to destroy." To reach the foreign-born worker, Becker believed it was necessary to persuade him that this was not a capitalist war but "the culmination of a generation of Imperialistic reaction," a reaction not confined to Germany. It was a war "to save our own soul," not only to safeguard democracy from Prussian militarism but also to prevent our own backsliding.[43]

Becker's book continued this theme. America had a place in the world as a symbol of democracy. Changed conditions threatened this legacy. Political democracy remained, but because of the disappearance of free land, economic democracy was becoming a thing of the past. Without such economic freedom, political freedom became a sham. It was the great task of the coming years to remedy this situation.[44] Becker called attention to the fact that the industrial revolution divided citizens into classes, making democratic government more difficult. He expressed concern over extending the power of the state to solve political and economic problems (he advocated a decentralization of the nationalist state) and observed the potential for a tyranny of majority rule. Concentration of economic power, control of the state by an entrepreneurial class —such was the threat before American democracy. He called for more democratic control of industrial enterprises.[45]

Becker also worried about assimilation. Though he condemned slavery and the social philosophy that justified it as a denial of America's meaning, he was concerned about assimilating blacks into American life and observed that where racial, cultural, or economic differences made for deep-seated division in society, the application of democratic principles became difficult, if not impossible. Failure to assimilate blacks and the newly arrived immigrants into the "general type, with common interests and ideals," presented a serious problem for democracy.[46] Americanizing the immigrant was related to the disappearance of free land and the simultaneous industrial transformation. Recent arrivals from southern and eastern Europe came from different cultural backgrounds, with no ability to speak English, and had to take the most undesirable jobs.[47] The problems of assimilating these immigrants, coupled with pressures created by the industrial revolution, posed major difficulties for democratic government.

Becker's remarks about the immigrants pointed up a very important concern of the CPI. For many of its members, the immigrant appeared to be one of the chief obstacles to the establishment of democracy in the United States. For these writers, democracy's survival seemed to depend on the acceptance of common beliefs: thus the concern with explaining American ideals, or Americanism. The desire to establish such a consensus and the apparent challenge posed by these newcomers were important in determining whatever thoughts Wilson, Lane, Sherman, or Becker had in explicating American values. American democracy, or often simply Americanism, was defined somewhat differently by each person. But their writings, taken together, formed a vague set of ideas that served as a secular religion, one that might unify everyone, including hyphenated Americans, around a common idea.[48]

The CPI gave much attention to immigrants, and many pamphlets were written for their benefit, in the hope of Americanizing them and ensuring their loyalty. The committee published at least nine pamphlets in German for the Friends of German Democracy, including *The Meaning of America*; *The Democratic Rising of German People in '48*; *On Loyalty, Liberty, and Democracy*; *Democracy, the Heritage of All*; and *No Qualified Americanism*.[49] Pamphlets like Evarts B. Greene's *Lieber and Schurz* described German-Americans who had renounced Prussian culture and embraced democratic ideals. Another pamphlet, *American Loyalty*, consisted of seven statements by citizens of German descent, including F. W. Lehmann's "National Service Knows No Hyphen" and Franz Sigel's "The Spirit of '48 in 1917."[50] More than 700,000 copies of this pamphlet were published in English and another 560,000 in German.

Some CPI literature was unqualified in condemnation of treason by first-generation immigrants. Joseph Buffington, a senior U.S. circuit judge, wrote a pamphlet entitled *Friendly Words to the Foreign Born*, in which he urged them to make every effort to avoid even the appearance of treason: "The crux is not the fact of the hyphen, but whether the man's heart is at the American end of the hyphen."[51] No American, he said, should be treated badly because he was foreign born, and no one should be interned unless he had demonstrated an intent to harm the government. The highest duty of any government was self-protection, and he advised every first-generation immigrant to "put a flag at your door, another on your coat, and above all keep one in your heart."[52] The man who knew of treason and did nothing was as guilty as one who participated in a treasonous act. The CPI printed 570,000 copies of Buffington's pamphlet, and it was translated into German, Bohemian, Italian, Hungarian, and Russian.[53]

The committee did not undertake harassment of German-Americans or other foreign-born people, but did expect recent arrivals to abandon ideas hostile to American democracy. It usually took pains to point out that the great majority of German-Americans were loyal and law-abiding, and Creel deplored the harassment the hyphenated American often received from various self-appointed patriotic groups.[54] There was no indiscriminate attack on any immigrant group. The CPI was not attempting to prohibit the teaching of German in public schools, although some of its staff favored such a move. Harding believed that the German language was but a means of Germanizing the United States. Both Harding and the pamphlet writer Earl E. Sperry were critical of such organizations as the German-American Alliance and constantly were on guard against efforts to make the teaching of German compulsory in public schools. They were suspicious of efforts to include German propaganda in American school books.[55] But President Wilson believed that the opposition to teaching German in schools was "childish," and the United States commissioner of education, Philander P. Claxton, who worked closely with the CPI, agreed with him.[56] Creel said he was interested not so much in proving the disloyalty of the German press as in making it more loyal.[57] Ford felt that emphasis should be on teaching English rather than erasing German. He believed that the loyal foreign-language groups not only could hasten Americanization but could take a stand that would make impossible the survival of an un-American or anti-American press. He probably expressed the sentiment of most committee members toward German-Americans when he urged Sherman not to alienate this group, because it was a permanent element in American society. Many advocates of the German political system, he felt, were having their confidence shaken, and the best thing the CPI could do was to see that the number of such persons increased rather than decreased.[58] Something of a revolution could be brought about in the thinking of German-Americans, indeed, of all the foreign born, and they would embrace the democratic ideals of the United States.

Defining and preserving American democracy were central to the work of Ford's division, and in relation to that task one must lastly turn to the committee's efforts to publicize ideas aimed at reforming society. Here one speaks of the desire to move the country toward new goals, new hopes. It was not by accident that the Committee on Public Information was so named. Such men as Creel and Ford had carried their sympathy for reform into the war, took the words "public information" seriously, and felt that their work differed from "propaganda" as the Germans used that term.[59] The reforming impulse, the desire to improve society, lay at the center of CPI literature.

In his capacity as chairman of the CPI, Creel attempted to avoid anything that seemed like "advocacy or anticipation of legislation or executive action."[60] He did not hesitate, however, to articulate publicly his theory of democracy, nor did he refrain from pushing for democratic reform behind the scenes. Without "vision, spirit, ideals," Creel maintained, America was "unintelligible." "Democracy has never been, and never can be, other than a theory of spiritual progress. . . . Democracy is not an automatic device but the struggle everlasting."[61] Privately he tried to get President Wilson and Secretary of the Navy Daniels to issue statements in favor of women's suffrage, justifying this effort as an opportunity to increase support for the war by showing that women were part of the democracy for which the country was fighting.[62] He praised Wilson in November 1918 for having described the conflict as a war for democracy, attracting radical, progressive, and other democratic elements of the country.[63] He believed that the war had "quickened the pace of policy that made for better social order" and that every emergency measure strengthening democratic government should be a permanent part of government policy.[64] Slowly but surely "the equal justice dreamed by Jefferson" was coming about. Every day saw "new victories for progress . . . in solving the age old problems of poverty, inequality, oppression and unhappiness."[65]

As mentioned, Ford saw his division not only as a vehicle for mobilizing support for the war but as possessing an educational purpose, that of informing citizens of democracy's advantages and problems. As he explained to W. H. Stout of the International Lyceum and Chautauqua Association, democracy was a political philosophy from the eighteenth century, a heritage that until recently had been easy to live with because the United States had been an isolated, frontier country. This state of affairs had disappeared, and he believed that the problem had become how "to put the meanings of [the] industrial world community age of the twentieth century into the ideals inherited from the age that is gone—or else find new definitions and institutions that do fit."[66] Though he was anxious to avoid coming out too strongly in support of controversial programs, he was willing, where possible, to have material from his division support reform measures. He once remarked that the CPI's first task was to establish itself as an exponent of the national cause. With that accomplished, confidence in the committee secure, he saw no problem with proceeding "cautiously with occasional and constructive suggestions." One means of accomplishing this goal was by "a clear exposition of the social experiments necessitated by war in various other countries."[67]

In pursuing his division's educational purpose, Ford presided over the compilation of a *War Cyclopedia*, which circulated in nearly two hundred thousand copies and was widely used by the committee's public speakers. Algie Simons, who worked for the Creel committee distributing literature in Wisconsin, was a source of recommendations for this publication. As a socialist he wanted the committee to support direct governmental action to increase production and control prices and distribution. Realizing that the CPI could not come out for such a measure, he suggested telling the American public about what Australia, England,and France had done in the way of having government distribute the burdens of the fighting.[68] He was asked to prepare essays on labor, food control, and the news associations for the *War Cyclopedia*, and was probably responsible for the entry on "Price Fixing in Australia" describing the "highly successful scheme of State marketing and distribution" in operation there.[69]

The *War Cyclopedia* contained several entries that explained or tried to justify government regulation of the economy. War profiteering was condemned: George Washington was quoted as saying that no punishment was too great for the profiteer, and Wilson that "Patriotism leaves profits out of the question."[70] The problem of excess war profits was treated with a discussion of how Britain had taxed them and an explanation of the American law of October 3, 1917. War profits should support the war in the interest of social equity, "for the idea of one part of a nation profiting by a war from which the other parts derive nothing, and for which still others make great sacrifices, is abhorrent to the concept of democracy in which each should share burdens and advantages alike."[71] There was an entry explaining the American income tax and comparing it to its British counterpart. The *War Cyclopedia* dealt with reasons for national control of food and fuel.

One of the cyclopedia's editors, Edward S. Corwin, believed that the war had come "at a peculiarly favorable moment for affecting lasting constitutional changes" and sought to have the publication justify in general terms the expanding power of the national government during the war.[72] As one of the country's constitutional authorities, Corwin probably was responsible for entries on "Police Power" and "States Rights versus National Power," and almost certainly he wrote the sections on "War Powers" and on Abraham Lincoln's view of such matters. "Police Power" was defined as ability of the government to provide for the general welfare. Development of this idea was of great importance to American constitutional law, the cyclopedia said, because prior to its appearance the validity of legislation depended upon the legislation's effect on private rights. With the appearance of this doctrine, "the primary test became public utility."[73] Although this power was once thought to belong to the states, the pamphlet argued that the national government should now use it "in a way to promote all the great ends of good government."[74] The cyclopedia discussed the relation between the wartime power of the federal government and states' rights. According to Article VI, paragraph two, of the Constitution ("This Constitution and the laws which shall be made in pursuance thereof . . . shall be the supreme law of the land. . . ."), the national government's war powers were "limited in no respect by the powers or rights of the States. The only relation which the States can occupy legally toward the National Government in war time is that of cooperation."[75] The power of Congress and the president in conduct of war "ought to exist without limitation," because, as Alexander Hamilton said, "it is impossible to foresee or define the extent and variety of national exigencies, or the correspondent extent and variety of the means which may be necessary to satisfy them."[76] In Corwin's opinion, Lincoln during the Civil War understood "perfectly" the nature of the presidential authority in wartime. Lincoln argued that temporary suspension of liberties and increase in presidential prerogatives would not have a lasting effect on the United States government once the war ended. History, Corwin believed, had proven Lincoln correct.[77] Such arguments, as presented in the *War Cyclopedia*, helped justify the expanded power of the national government. Especially when combined with the great publicity given Wilson's utterances, they must have enhanced the prestige of the presidency.

The division's educational effort ran into many areas, in addition to such concerns as those of Corwin. The Committee on Public Information desired to win the support of laboring men. Publications for workingmen were short and written in a style that would capture attention. Seven were published in the Loyalty Leaflet Series and perhaps a half dozen others for the American Alliance for Labor and Democracy.[78]

As mentioned in the preceding chapter, the CPI had a division that sought to mobilize workers, the Division of Industrial Relations, headed by Roger Babson, but it lasted a short time and was absorbed by the Department of Labor. The CPI thereafter operated largely through the American Alliance for Labor and Democracy, whose headquarters were in New York, with branches in 164 cities. Creel supported the alliance financially at least through July 1918 and exerted influence on its publication policies.[79] Material deemed too radical for the CPI was published sometimes by the American Alliance for Labor and Democracy.

Most pamphlets connected with Ford's division and directed toward workingmen were concerned with the loyalty of laborers and with increasing their productivity. The effort included offering a colorful picture of German brutality and frightfulness, assuring workers that conditions in America were far superior, and holding out hope that labor's chance for improvement lay with an American victory.[80]

In addition to vilifying Germany, encouraging production, and stressing loyalty, CPI literature suggested to laboring men that social gains would come with an American victory. In this regard, John R. Commons of the University of Wisconsin wrote three pamphlets (published by the alliance), including *Why Workingmen Support the War* and *Who Is Paying for This War?* Simons was enthusiastic about *Why Workingmen Support the War* and felt it was the most effective appeal yet made to labor.[81] Commons began by asserting that labor had never made so many democratic gains as during the last six months of the war. "If this continues," he said, "American labor will come out of this war with the universal eight-hour day, and with as much power to fix its own wages by its own representatives as employers have."[82] Labor had benefited from the war because it was "on the inside," helping run the government.[83] Commons criticized antiwar socialists and cited Camille Huysmans, international secretary of the Socialist Bureau in the Netherlands, to the effect that President Wilson's war aims were identical to those of the international socialists. A German victory meant that the United States would be subject to attack and would need a large standing army that would drive down wages, lengthen working hours, and negate labor legislation for women and children. Free speech would be suppressed. The wage earner who wished to aid labor would support the American cause.[84]

In *Who Is Paying for This War?* Commons pointed to the measures to finance the fighting and sought to tie the ideas of American victory to combating excess wealth. The tax burden was easier on those with low incomes than during the Civil War, he said, because two-thirds of the population paid little in taxes, whereas the other third was taxed on income and excess war profit. Commons emphasized that a start had been made in taxing excess profits and that the government was seeking to reduce such profits. The government had been fairly successful, he said, in holding down sugar and flour prices. The workingman had as much say in fixing prices as did the farmer and capitalist. "Instead of objecting, why not join together to help the Government both to win the war and to finish the start already made towards taxing excessive wealth and keeping down the cost of living?"[85]

Labor's Red, White and Blue Book published the American

Alliance for Labor and Democracy's "Declaration of Principles," adopted at its national conference in Minneapolis in September 1917. This statement declared labor's interests "wholly compatible with supreme loyalty to the Government" but opposed any lowering of standards with regard to workingmen. It supported taxing incomes, excess profits, and land values "to the fullest needs of the Government."[86] It urged government control of industries where differences between labor and capital threatened to halt work. To lower food prices and increase food the alliance favored having the government commandeer land for public purposes while taxing idle, privately owned land on its full rental value. It supported collective action for wage earners involved with the government in activities connected to the war. Workers were to have a say in determining conditions under which they were to give service. The alliance advocated universal suffrage and, while noting the value of free speech and press to democratic institutions, declared for prosecution of those persons whose expressions were obstructive to the government.[87] Approximately one hundred thousand copies of this pamphlet were printed.

President Wilson's speeches printed by the CPI supported the progress made by labor and assured workers that gains would not be taken away. In a speech in Buffalo on November 12, 1917, Wilson condemned Germany, asked workers to increase production, and warned of the mob spirit. He said, "We shall see to it that the instrumentalities by which the conditions of labor are improved, are not blocked or checked." He commended labor for being more reasonable than capital.[88]

The Creel committee did not publish a large amount of material for farmers. Simons and others in the Midwest noted this omission and urged the CPI to do more. Ford wanted greater use of the post office and the rural free delivery system.[89] In a pamphlet addressed to the farmer the president emphasized that the United States had agencies to help agriculture that no other government in the world possessed. The Department of Agriculture, he asserted, was without question the biggest scientific and practical agricultural organization in existence. The farmer's condition had improved because of

land-grant colleges, the Smith-Lever act, and banking legislation that gave farmers ready capital and credit. By direct purchase of nitrates and creation of nitrate plants, the government
had helped solve fertilizer problems. Wilson pledged support
to farmers in meeting sacrifices required by the war.[90]

The pledges to workers, both wage earners and farmers,
were effective propaganda to keep the groups loyal. CPI literature tried to convince workers that only through an Allied
victory would their long-sought social gains be possible. Had
the writers of the tracts not shared a belief in social improvement, the committee literature would have been less specific in
the hopes it held out.

In addition to appealing to workingmen, committee pamphlets sought to inform citizens of their responsibilities during
the war, providing them with information about how to serve
the country. The *National Service Handbook*, which ran to nearly
250 pages, was one such publication, prepared under Ford's
supervision, with most of the organization and editing done by
John J. Coss and James Gutmann. It discussed everything from
domestic welfare to the army and navy and was packed with
information about where one should go and whom one should
see to assist the many war-related agencies. It began with a
short statement by Creel, who said that if our military effort
was to be successful, every citizen had to give his all, "whether
this be time, or money, or life, or all three." What was needed
was centralization and organization, or as Creel called it, "intelligent efficiency."[91] The booklet suggested ways to "win the war
by giving . . . daily service."[92] It discussed domestic welfare, arguing that social gains of the past generation must not be even
temporarily suspended because of the war. Safeguards of public
health and efficiency, of workers on the job, had to be maintained. Standards for female employees should be retained,
and "any infraction of present labor laws, or any attempt to
evade them under cover of war stress, should be reported
immediately to the State industrial commission."[93] It was important that colleges and universities be kept open.[94] Citizens
should take part in social and settlement endeavors. "Next to
education and labor legislation, the most important means of

securing national vitality and efficiency is social and philan-
thropic work."[95] More than 450,000 copies of this pamphlet
were printed.

Another publication to inform the populace of its duties
was the *Home Reading Course for Citizen-Soldiers*, prepared by
the War Department and published by Ford's division. It offered thirty daily lessons for men selected to serve in the national army, including how to become a good soldier: loyalty,
obedience, physical fitness, and also intelligence, cleanliness,
cheerfulness, spirit, tenacity, and self-reliance were considered
important. Lessons were devoted to preparing for camp,
marching and care of feet, close-order drill, guard duty, "getting ahead in the army," military courtesy, the spirit of the
service, and the soldier in battle. Discipline was emphasized,
but so were fair play and humane treatment of the enemy. The
American soldier always fought for principles and rights. The
individual soldier was important.[96] Service was an obligation of
citizenship. It was a post of danger but also of honor.[97] To give
the citizen some idea of the American forces, the CPI published
a *Regimental History of the United States Regular Army*, prepared
by the adjutant general's office.

Other pamphlets of the Division of Civic and Educational
Publications tried to be purely informative. Charles Merz, who
later became editor of the New York *Times*, listed in *First Session
of the War Congress* all the legislation passed during that session.[98] Another pamphlet, *The Activities of the Committee on Public
Information*, discussed the CPI up to February 1918.[99]

In later years, Guy Stanton Ford would re-
mark that "the Germans spoiled some perfectly good enterprises by ending the war when they did."[100] He was referring to
the work of his pamphlet writers, their attempt to "educate"
the public about the meaning of American democracy in the
modern world. Ideology helps to provide stability for societies
undergoing rapid change. Facing the problems of industrialization, urbanization, immigration, and the closing of the frontier, not to mention the Great War, the United States was such a
society in 1917–18. Democracy, it has been observed, is "the

generating principle of American cohesion," and Ford's writers tried to strengthen this national ideology, so important to unifying the country.[101] But it was the war and the apparent menace of German militarism that gave urgency to their appeal and made their arguments seem compelling.

4

The Literature of the CPI:
The German Menace

> Through the eyes of hate and paranoia, [Germany] saw
> Belgium annexed, France crushed, occupation of the
> channel ports, Serbia reduced to vassalage, and the rest
> of the Balkan States instructed in obedience; Turkey,
> Austria-Hungary, and Italy mere suzerainties; Asia and
> Africa left helpless for the taking; Russia, England, and
> America to be dealt with at leisure. A dream of madmen,
> perhaps, but one that had every chance of success.
>
> —George Creel[1]

GUY STANTON FORD argued that the dominant
theme of CPI literature was antimilitarism.[2] He might also have
said antiauthoritarianism, but, whatever the terminology, the
CPI's indictment of Germany portrayed that country as the
very antithesis of the American tradition. American nationalism has been linked with the idea of democracy, of individual
liberty; America has symbolized a "haven of liberty" for those
people "escaping authoritarianism."[3] The American tradition
of opposing arbitrary power has complemented the emphasis
on the free individual, and the CPI appealed to this sentiment
by presenting the menace of German Kultur.

In their incessant writing about German militarism, the
authors of some committee pamphlets surely encouraged fear,
suspicion, and intolerance. There were, however, real points of
difference between German and American institutions, and
much of the writing about the enemy came from conviction
about these differences. The appeal struck a responsive chord
and promoted unity at home. From its description of Germany
the committee was able to argue that intervention was not a

break with the past but an affirmation of the national heritage. Circulation of CPI pamphlets passed into the millions and helped convince Americans that they were in a life-and-death struggle with an enemy determined on world domination.[4]

CREEL believed that the tracts characterizing the enemy made the "most sober and terrific indictment ever drawn by one government of the political and military system of another government." Although prone to rash statements, he did not make this comment in haste. Both he and Ford ardently maintained that the committee's indictment of Germany was more than a momentary attempt to sway opinion and that it would stand the test of time.[5]

There is no simple explanation for the strength of anti-German sentiment in 1917–18. There were Americans, some of them on the CPI staff, who admired the social progress Germany had made. Popular literature, such as best-selling novels, had made few references to a German menace before 1914. Although American school books by the late nineteenth century had begun to take note of the military cast of German society, they portrayed Germany and Germans favorably. There apparently was little in the American German-language press prior to 1914 to indicate serious differences between Germany and the United States.[6]

Still, there were sources of distrust. Tensions existed between the native born and German-Americans, and these differences were often reflected in such issues as prohibition and women's suffrage; they had been beneath the surface for several years before 1914 and were brought to a head by the war.[7] Then, too, chauvinistic nationalism was strong in the late nineteenth and early twentieth centuries, in both Germany and the United States. Since 1870, relations between the two countries had often been less than cordial. Both nations had undergone rapid industrialization, both countries had grown in military power, and relations had been strained by events in the Samoan Islands, the Philippines, and Venezuela. In the decade or so before the Great War, occasional newspaper editorials and magazine articles warned of a German naval buildup and showed

DOWN at Washington stands the Nation's capitol. It is more than a pile of stone. It is a monument to an idea: "The people *are* the Government." Under no other idea is there so great an opportunity to work out individual prosperity and individual happiness.

Back of the American idea suddenly has arisen the black menace of the opposing Prussian idea. Under it the people are not the Government. Under it the people live and prosper, or sacrifice and die, by grace of "Me und Gott."

Militarism is the mailed fist which supports the divine-right Government. It is typified in Hindenburg.

What a contrast is offered to Hindenburg's *militarism* by Pershing's military! Freedom's military is the *people embattled*. Autocracy's militarism is the *people driven*.

Our boys in France and Italy are the expression in military form of the people's own stern will. When Pershing speaks of them to President Wilson, he says, "Sir, *our* armies." The German soldiers are the servants of militarism. Of them Hindenburg says to the Kaiser, "Majesty, *your* armies."

The billions of dollars we are gathering here at home for military purposes have no taint of militarism on a single coin.

Germany began her war with no plans for elaborate taxation of her people; the Junkers expected to saddle the cost of the war upon quickly conquered nations. Not so does a free people make war! From the start we have gone down into our own pockets for every cent we expend; we have never thought of taking; we have thought only of spending our blood and our treasure to protect our ideal of free national life.

The menace of Hindenburg makes no American tremble. But it makes us grit our teeth and either fight or give! What the Government (which is the people) wants to borrow, we, the people, as individuals will lend.

The menace of Hindenburg shall cease to exist in the world even as a shadow; and we shall return to our individual pursuits under the protection of our national ideal successfully defended; and, please God, other nations, as the result of this struggle, shall join us and our already free Allies in the enjoyment of our blood-bought and blood-held freedom.

BUY U. S. GOV'T BONDS FOURTH LIBERTY LOAN

Contributed through Division of Advertising · United States Govt. Comm. on Public Information

This space contributed for the Winning of the War by

The Publisher of

4. (Courtesy of the National Archives)

Germany as a potential enemy, while at the same time encouraging an increase in United States naval strength. An influential minority of Americans, military and naval officers and others, warned that Germany threatened American security in the western hemisphere.[8] There were people who suspected the German government of secretly using German immigrant organizations in America to accomplish imperialistic aims. For some Americans, Kaiser Wilhelm II symbolized this imperialism before 1914. For persons already suspicious, anti-German sentiment was no doubt increased by the so-called Zabern affair; by the Delbrück Law (1913), which allowed a German emigrant to retain his citizenship while obtaining citizenship in a new country; and by the appearance in 1913 of the English-language edition of General Friedrich von Bernhardi's *Germany and the Next War* (1911). Although all of these things may not have caused popular opinion to be greatly apprehensive, it must be remembered that once the war in Europe began, the American public was subjected to a highly successful British propaganda campaign. It is true that Germany sought to influence American opinion, and the German-language press often tried to present the German case, but Britain controlled the transatlantic cables and was far more successful in setting up a propaganda network in America. What suspicions might have existed about Germany before 1914 were also magnified many times by the invasion of Belgium, the sinking of the *Lusitania*, and the Zimmermann telegram.[9]

Several explanations exist, in addition to British propaganda, for the indictment of Germany. Some people, such as President Wilson, may have had deep attachments to English civilization before the war began.[10] For some journalists the moral indictment of Germany may have been an extension of the prewar muckraking that had condemned city bosses and business corruption; it is worth observing that two of the men who eagerly publicized German atrocities in Belgium—Brand Whitlock and S. S. McClure—came from such a background.[11] Many writers were unquestionably caught up in the emotions of the period. Other people may have been overwhelmed by having been so close to the center of power. It has been suggested also that many academicians, particularly historians, were insecure about their new profession and eager to demonstrate the relevance of their work to major issues of the day.[12]

There may have been yet another reason for belief in the German menace. It is interesting to speculate on the influence of personal experiences with German culture on the committee's pamphlet writers. For scholars concerned with the formal study of history and government, who took their graduate training in the late nineteenth century, it was not uncommon to spend a year or more in Germany. The thoroughness of German scholarship and the convenience of the great libraries attracted American students.[13] Moreover, those universities in the United States that pioneered the study of political science —Columbia, Johns Hopkins, Michigan—were modeled after German schools and often heavily staffed with German-trained scholars. It has been argued that up to the First World War the German idea of the state dominated the American discipline of political science and much of the writing about history.[14]

Guy Stanton Ford's experience as a student in prewar Germany may be illustrative of that of other writers in his division of the CPI. Having arrived in Berlin too late to study with the Prussian historian Heinrich von Treitschke,[15] he had entered the seminar of the military-political historian Hans Delbrück, who stimulated his interest in the Napoleonic era. His dissertation dealt with neutrality between 1795 and 1803, focusing on Prussia and English-controlled Hanover.[16] While in Germany, Ford kept a diary of his travels in the summer and autumn of 1899; in addition to giving a fascinating picture of life in Marburg and Berlin, this diary shows that even then he was concerned by the spirit of militarism that he believed existed in parts of Germany. He noted the "ever present uniformed official," poems and songs calculated to instill loyalty to the fatherland, castles destroyed by the French and often left dismantled to keep alive a hatred of Germany's neighbor. He commented on the crowds following marching soldiers, and the potential danger of standing armies. He observed German soldiers when they gathered to drink: they "looked at war as quite the regular thing. . . . Where they joined in and sang the

Prussian Hymn or the soldiers' songs it had, to me, a grim earnestness about it though all done in a rousing, hearty, unconstrained way. . . . You felt in it all the difference between the German character and spirit and the American."[17] He returned to the United States in September 1900, impressed by the militarism in Germany. He came to believe that Prussians were different from the Bavarians and other groups to the south. "The Hohenzollerns by fraud, cunning and military force had pushed themselves up in Germany until Prussia was two-thirds of the German Empire." Later he would claim that the origins of the war lay not in violation of neutral rights but in the militarism he first witnessed as a student in Berlin. He believed this attitude subordinated everything to the army, demanding that the individual pay allegiance not merely to the state but to a particular ruler.[18] In a scholarly paper in 1914 he discussed militarism in Prussia and the establishment of universal military service a century before.[19] In another work substantially finished before 1914, but put aside during the war and not published until 1922, Ford wrote of Heinrich Friedrich Karl vom Stein, the reformer who had sought a Prussian government based on limited monarchy and self-determination.[20] Thus, Ford had opposed German militarism well before America entered the war.[21]

Ford's reactions may have been similar to those of other scholars who wrote about the enemy in 1917–18. Many academicians who characterized Germany for the CPI had spent time studying there or at least had taken graduate degrees from universities strongly influenced by German scholarship. In addition to Ford, Charles D. Hazen, Elmer E. Stoll, Charles Altschul, and Dana C. Munro had studied in Germany.[22] Their indictment of German autocracy was clearly stated.[23]

Charles D. Hazen had spent two years in Europe in the early 1890s, at Göttingen, Berlin, and Paris, and after he earned a doctorate from Hopkins in 1893 he had returned to Hopkins to lecture. He taught at Smith College before going to Columbia in 1916. Not long after the war broke out in Europe, he had warned of the danger to America of being unprepared to meet Germany, drawing a parallel with France in 1870.[24] After

America entered the conflict, he wrote for *History Teacher's Magazine*, preparing bibliographies on European history, and contributed to the CPI's *War Cyclopedia*.[25] In *World's Work* he discussed "Prussianism in Poland" and the need to return Alsace-Lorraine to France.[26]

Though Hazen apparently did not keep a record of his travels in Europe in the early 1890s, it is clear that he had worried about the growth of militarism in Germany and the undemocratic nature of government there well before the war. In the first edition of *Europe since 1815*, published in 1910, he had contended that Frederick III was "a man of moderation, of liberalism in politics, an admirer of the English constitution"; but when his reign had been cut short by illness and he had been succeeded by his son, William II, the outlook had been quite different. William II pursued an aggressive policy in foreign and colonial affairs, and by 1907 a desire for colonial empire had become government policy and had also captured the popular imagination. William II had a "constant and . . . growing preoccupation" with building a powerful navy. Coupled with this growing militarism was also a lack of political freedom in Germany. "Hundreds of men have, during the past twenty years, been imprisoned for such criticisms of the Government as in other countries are the current coin of discussion." Hazen discussed the unrepresentative nature of the German government and the irresponsible actions of Emperor William. The people, he thought, counted for "less politically in Germany than in the other countries of western Europe." Hazen detected a rising militaristic spirit in Europe and connected it to "the tremendous influence of the Prussian military system." "The Prussian military system, marked by scientific thoroughness and efficiency, has been adopted by all the countries of Europe. Europe is to-day," he wrote four years before the outbreak of fighting, "what she has never been before, literally an armed continent."[27]

Hazen wrote one of the early CPI pamphlets, in which he examined the nature of the German government.[28] He referred to it as "skinning . . . the Kaiser and his system."[29] He had prepared it for the New York *Times*,[30] not the CPI, and it made, although much more forcefully, many of the points of *Europe since 1815*. Waldo G. Leland of the NBHS read the *Times* article and was so impressed that he sent a copy to Ford, suggesting that it be reprinted. Leland declared it "one of the ablest presentations . . . of the political situation in Germany" he had seen.[31] As he had done seven years before, Hazen sketched the workings of the German government and found it undemocratic. The Reichstag was subordinate to the Bundesrat, which was nothing more than a collection of German sovereigns. German princes had a veto over the Reichstag.[32] Not only was this body less powerful than the emperor, the Bundesrat, and the army, but it was unrepresentative, because electoral districts had been laid out in 1871 and never revised. Districts had become grossly unequal. The German government was run by the emperor and the provincial dynasties, with token consent of the Reichstag. If not given voluntarily, consent could be forced, for the Bundesrat had the power of dissolving that body when it wished.[33] Prussia's constitution, Hazen noted, dated to 1850 and had been granted by the king, but did not recognize the sovereignty of the people. The political system gave power to the rich; the poor had little influence. The personal nature of the German government had brought the war. The Prussian army, far from being under popular control, stood outside and above the people, "a kingdom within a kingdom."[34] The cartridge was the real ballot; "the representative of the nation was the army."[35] Attachment to the army did not exemplify patriotism but "the earlier notion of loyalty to a cheiftain," as soldiers served the king and not the fatherland. If civilian authority were ever to control the military, the present government would have to be "debased and disgraced by resounding and disastrous defeats."[36] The CPI printed nearly 1.8 million copies of Hazen's pamphlet in English, and 20,000 or so in German.[37]

Conquest and Kultur, compiled by Wallace Notestein and Elmer E. Stoll, likewise condemned Germany. Notestein at this time was teaching English history at the University of Minnesota. During the war he wrote for *History Teacher's Magazine* and contributed to the *War Cyclopedia*.[38] He helped annotate one of the most popular committee pamphlets, *The President's Flag Day Address with Evidence of Germany's Plans*.[39] He was not enthusiastic about working for Creel, believing that the CPI was badly organized, and he feared that he would be made a scapegoat for the chairman's oversights.[40] In the spring of 1917 he was considering a book that would describe German public opinion toward the United States since 1898. It was his belief that commercial rivalry between Germany and the United States had led to the present troubles and that German opinion had been increasingly envious of and hostile to America since the Spanish-American War.[41] Early in 1918, Ford considered having Notestein write an essay on the "War after the War."[42] Notestein's collaborator in *Conquest and Kultur*, Stoll, was a professor of English at Minnesota, who had studied in Berlin in 1902, taken a doctorate at Munich two years later, and taught at Harvard and Western Reserve. Stoll translated most of the passages in *Conquest and Kultur*.[43]

Notestein did not indiscriminately indict German culture, for he admired aspects of the German economy.[44] The pamphlet he prepared with Stoll—one of the most effective issued during the war—ran to more than 150 pages and focused on those features of German social, political, and philosophical thought emphasizing aggressive, authoritarian government. It used quotations from German writers and leaders to describe a plan for world domination and show the threat of a German victory to American democracy. Germans believed that they were "an original, uncontaminated race." This idea they combined with mystical notions about the state. Unlike the English or Americans, Germans did not view the state as a piece of machinery but "as something living, almost divine" (surely Notestein and Stoll did not fully consider the ideas on America and national loyalty expressed by Lane and Sherman). Once readers accepted this view, it was easy to argue that Germans thought themselves to be a chosen people whose mission was to establish a new, superior culture and impose it on the world.[45]

The two authors contended that Germany demanded, as its literature sometimes stated, "world power or downfall."[46] Germans worshipped power and agreed with Fichte that, if need be, "one single man has the right and duty to compel the whole of mankind."[47] They also agreed with Nietzche that "life is essentially appropriation, injury, conquest of the strange and weak," and with Treitschke that "weakness must always be condemned as the most disastrous and despicable of crimes, the unforgivable sin of politics."[48] War for the Germans was a part of the divine order, "a terrible medicine for mankind diseased." It was the arbiter in international disputes; the goal of perpetual peace was "not only impossible but immoral as well."[49] Germans justified expansion by pointing to economic necessity. They sought to subordinate France, to rule middle Europe, to increase their sea power and colonies.[50] Nearly 1,225,000 copies of this pamphlet were distributed during 1918.

CPI propaganda did not make a sweeping indictment of the German people. President Wilson had said it was not the German people with whom the United States was at war, but the German government, and CPI literature emphasized this distinction, seeking to appeal to the democratic spirit of 1848, the thought of men like Carl Schurz and Francis Lieber.[51]

German Militarism and Its German Critics, by Charles Altschul, attempted to convince the American public that there was opposition to militarism among the German people. The author of this pamphlet was one of the few businessmen to write for the War Information Series. His tract appeared in March 1918, and by the end of the war its circulation had reached four hundred thousand copies.[52] Altschul had been educated in Germany. His father had been Austrian, his mother Prussian. He was anxious to point out to Ford that he was not German, having come to the United States at the age of nineteen and having spent only twelve of his sixty years in Germany. He was not optimistic about changing the minds of many "German-thinking" people, because in time of stress their beliefs, like their religion, were in their blood.[53] The Prussians, he said, should not be singled out for brutish behavior, because the Bavarians had outdone them.[54] Shotwell apparently took interest in Altschul's essay, edited it (as much as the author would allow), and convinced Ford to publish it. Shotwell liked Altschul's enthusiasm and described him to Ford as a man with "a scholar's conscience fortified by business experience in banking."[55]

Altschul's work relied on excerpts from prewar German newspapers. Most passages were taken from the daily *Vörwarts*, the organ of the Social Democratic party, or from the *Berliner Tageblatt*. It rested on a narrow base and focused on two incidents. The first was the trial of the socialist Rosa Luxemburg in 1914, in which testimony supposedly showed the brutality of the German army before the war.[56] The second was the Zabern incident, involving arbitrary treatment of civilians by German army officers.[57] Altschul tried to distinguish between German militarism and American preparedness. Universal military service, a large army and navy, were not dangerous in themselves. Danger arose when military authorities thwarted civil administration.[58] Militarism existed "when education and social custom have for a prolonged period given undue prominence to military training and military glory, and the tendency has developed to magnify the function of the army in the State at the expense of purely civic virtues, until finally civil authority is undermined and no longer resists the encroachment of the military authorities." As long as the United States retained its social and political institutions, industrial and commercial mobilization for war would not result in militarism.[59] The Germans, however, had come to worship authority, and surrendered individual responsibility.[60] Altschul hoped that liberal sentiment might triumph in Germany, for "underneath the cover of patriotic submission to constituted authority there must still be smoldering the embers of individual and humane opinion, which will some day burst into flame and light up the path which Germany will follow in the desire to meet once more as an equal the sister nations she so overbearingly and grievously affronted."[61]

Unfortunately for the historical reputation of the CPI, its pamphlets sometimes placed too much emphasis on fear—on the brutal, depraved nature of the enemy. Despite the efforts of Ford and Creel to avoid sensational accounts of alleged atrocities, some of their publications undoubtedly went too far. The pamphlets by Hazen, Notestein and Stoll, and Altschul argued that the German government was in no sense democratic; that Germany's heritage had led to a perverse respect for authority and military power and a contempt for democratic government; that submerged in Germany was a liberal sentiment opposed to militarism and authoritarian rule. These themes were present in other committee pamphlets and in such publications as *History Teacher's Magazine*. But some of the pamphlets clearly went beyond explaining the German system and sought to instill fear of the enemy.

The CPI's literature of fear was extensive. Frederic C. Walcott's *The Prussian System*, describing brutalities in Poland, was one of the early pamphlets in the Loyalty Leaflet Series and had a circulation of over a half million.[62] Detailing the German drive into Poland in August and September 1916, which left a million people homeless and brought death to as many as four hundred thousand, Walcott told how Germany had required every able-bodied Pole to work in Germany. Neglecting to mention the British blockade of Germany, which had led to widespread distress, he quoted a General von Kries on the military benefit derived from starving the people of East Poland.[63] According to Kries, Germany was destined to rule the world. The German people were but material to build the German state. Other peoples, especially conquered populations, did not matter. "Life, liberty, happiness, human sentiment, family ties, grace and generous impulse, these have no place beside . . . the greatness of the German State."[64] Walcott believed that the German mind welcomed treachery; treaties hindering German aims were scraps of paper; women were the enemy's prey; children were spoils of war; foreign populations were to be enslaved or destroyed. The Prussian system, a "monstrous," "unthinkable" creation, must be destroyed if the world was to be worth inhabiting. Walcott hoped that Germany would experience a rebirth.[65]

Another committee endeavor comprised two pamphlets dealing with German practices toward civilians and conquered territory.[66] Its editors were Dana C. Munro, George C. Sellery, and August Krey. Munro had studied at Strasbourg and Freiburg in 1889 and 1890, had taught at Pennsylvania and Wisconsin, and in 1917 was professor of medieval history at Princeton. Sellery had taken a doctorate from the University of Chicago and taught European history at Wisconsin. Krey taught at Minnesota and also served the CPI's Foreign Language Newspaper Division by reading and reporting on the immigrant press. The first of their two joint pamphlets, *German War Practices*, dealt with enemy treatment of conquered peoples, mainly in Belgium but also in northern France and Poland. It contended that frightfulness was a calculated policy of the German government. So brutal was the government's policy that even the more humane German soldiers revolted. The pamphlet used German and American evidence to document "Prussianism in all its horror."[67] It cited proclamations and other utterances by the German government, and passages from such newspapers as *Vörwarts*. It offered excerpts from diaries supposedly kept by German soldiers, which detailed atrocities. Material was taken from State Department archives, with statements by ambassadors and ministers. Herbert Hoover, Walcott, and Vernon Kellogg made comments for this pamphlet, and so did Brand Whitlock, Ambassador James W. Gerard, and Will Irwin.[68] Readers wishing a more detailed account of atrocities were referred to the Bryce Report of 1915, and to the official *German White Book*, which justified German actions in Belgium but in the editors' view proved the essential depravity of the German military.[69] As with Altschul's account, this pamphlet occasionally cited passages from Germans critical of their government— opposition in the Reichstag by socialists or by laborers was most frequently employed. According to the pamphlet, terrorism and brutality on the part of the German army was not an aberration but was condoned, even encouraged, by the German high command.[70] The contemporary generation of German leaders had been influenced by Clausewitz, Hartmann, Treitschke, and Nietzsche.[71] Brutality, of course, had characterized German conduct of war long before 1914. In 1900 the Kaiser praised the Huns under Attila, and German troops were guilty of criminal behavior in China after the Boxer uprising.[72] In the current war the Germans forced Belgian laborers to leave their families to work in Germany; they raped the young women;[73] they forced wives to watch their husbands being executed; they used civilians as shields for soldiers in combat.[74] The German policy of frightfulness became "exalted into a system with every minute detail worked out in advance."[75]

In the second pamphlet on German war practices, Notestein, Ford, and Harding assisted the editors in an analysis entitled *German Treatment of Conquered Territory*. The focus was Belgium and France, although readers were assured that conditions were far worse in Poland and Serbia.[76] Whereas the preceding publication dealt with civilians, this one dealt with a subject, readers were told, even more serious than murder and enslavement of conquered populations: "systematic exploitation and wanton destruction" of land that led to starvation of the old, the feeble, and the very young.[77] To terrorize inhabitants of occupied countries, and to reduce German expenditures, soldiers were encouraged to pillage; they were allowed to drink, which led to criminal activity. Because of the strict discipline in the German army, such acts would not have taken place had not the military authorities condoned them.[78] German soldiers were modern Huns.[79]

The catalog of the enemy's evil deeds went on and on. German treatment of conquered territory was sinister because it systematically exploited countries like Belgium. Action had been taken to cripple industry and manufacturing in such countries in order to hinder future competition.[80] The policy had grown out of the Rathenau Plan, suggested in early August 1914 by Dr. Walther Rathenau, president of the General Electric Company of Germany, who had called for a Bureau of Raw Materials for the War. His plan tried to do more than make war support war "by the contributions and requisitions forced from the conquered peoples"; it sought to destroy industries in conquered territory so they could not be rebuilt for some years, if at all.[81] In the meantime, Germany would capture those countries' world markets.[82] Even countries gaining freedom from Germany after the war would be in no position to compete.[83] The pamphlet provided lists of articles requisitioned from Belgium, described the destruction of Louvain and the evacuation of northern France, and again used communications, from Whitlock, Kellogg, Hoover, Hugh Gibson, and Ambassadors Sharp and Penfield. There was testimony in diaries of German soldiers.[84] The two pamphlets edited by Munro, Sellery, and Krey had a combined circulation of more than 2,225,000 copies.[85]

Another pamphlet seeking to convince Americans of the brutality of the German army was prepared by George Winfield Scott and James Wilford Garner.[86] Scott was professor of international law and diplomacy at Columbia, and for several years prior to American entry in the war he had been engaged in research on international law and diplomatic claims for indemnity. Garner had taken a doctorate at Columbia and was professor of political science at Illinois. He had been editor-in-chief of the *American Journal of Criminal Law and Criminology* in 1910 and 1911 and was the author of several works on American politics, including *Introduction to Political Science* (1910) and *American Government* (1911). Shortly after the war he published a two-volume study, *International Law and the World War*.[87]

The Scott-Garner pamphlet contrasted German war manuals with those of the United States, Britain, and France. Volunteering his services, Garner had urged Ford to reach the man in the street with pamphlets that would give some idea of the institutions and ideals of the German people. He believed that such publications would show a war of autocracy against democracy, that "the more one studies the German system of government, the less democratic it becomes."[88] Ford apparently suggested comparing German and Allied war manuals, and Garner submitted a manuscript on "German Theory and Practice Affecting the Laws of War."[89] Ford became hesitant about publishing a pamphlet contrasting German and American field regulations (the plan had called for doing so in parallel columns). The more he read American field regulations with their "citations from Moltke and other German writers and their utter confusion of necessity and right," the more doubtful he was about such a venture.[90] The project went ahead, however; the pamphlet was published in February 1918, and better than a half million copies were distributed.

German war manuals undoubtedly were fascinating. Garner and Scott began by discussing the manual *Kriegsbrauch im Landkriege* (1902) and asked readers to consider if "brutality, ruthlessness, terrorism, and violence of the German forces have not been cold-bloodedly programmed for years by the German authorities." The German war code violated the humanitarian restrictions gradually placed on war to prevent mankind from falling back into savagery.[91] The war code violated the Declaration of St. Petersburg (1868), which stated that wars were contests between armies and not peoples. The *Kriegsbrauch* declared that war was not just between armies but was to destroy the material and spiritual power of the enemy. Destruction of private property, terrorization of civilians, and forced labor of enemy populations were permitted. In violation of a Hague convention of 1907, unorganized civilians who resisted German forces might be summarily shot instead of treated as combatants. The German war code violated the Hague rule that goods requisitioned from a country must be paid for. According to the German system, prisoners of war might be killed when their presence created a danger for their captors. The German code emphasized that necessity abolished all restraint upon fighting and authorized every means of war, provided it led to success.[92] It encouraged hatred of the enemy, warned against humanitarianism as a "flabby emotion," and ridiculed rules of war "dictated by chivalry, honor, and generosity to the enemy."[93]

The war manuals of the United States, Britain, and France, the authors claimed, provided "a refreshing contrast." The first American manual, drafted by Francis Lieber, promulgated by Abraham Lincoln in 1863 under the title *Instructions for the Government of the U.S. Armies in the Field*, differed fundamentally from the German code when it said that all measures against an enemy must be in accord with "modern laws and customs of war."[94] Similarly, the American *Rules of Land Warfare* (1914), the British *Manual of Land Warfare* (1914), and the French *Les Lois de la Guerre Continentale* (1913) were enlightened, humane, and in agreement with the Hague regulations.[95] The authors noted that the enemy's rules were the work not of the German people but of the kaiser and his hierarchy. Government power in Germany centered on a reactionary group of wealthy Germans, some with aristocratic backgrounds.[96] Military education upheld "the basest practices" imaginable. Readers were encouraged to look at Clausewitz's Vom Kriege (1832), and at the works of Hartmann, Moltke, von der Goltz, Bernhardi, Hindenburg, Bissing, Treitschke, Leuder, Dahn, and Loening, to see how the German war code had come out of German culture.[97]

Other CPI pamphlets took advantage of German self-criticism, as in the case of Germany's Confession: The Lichnowsky Memorandum. This work was a private statement by Germany's prewar ambassador to England, Prince Karl Max Lichnowsky, which was widely circulated, to the embarrassment of the author. Lichnowsky had blamed Germany for having started the war. The American government distributed 325,000 copies of this publication, and Creel enthusiastically said it was "destined to be the most historical of the internal indictments of Germany."[98]

One of the most controversial pamphlets proved to be Edgar Sisson's The German-Bolshevik Conspiracy, put out late in the war; it was a collection of documents Sisson smuggled out of Russia, which supposedly proved that Lenin was in the pay of the German government. The authenticity of the material was attested by J. Franklin Jameson and Samuel N. Harper, but almost certainly the documents were forgeries.[99]

The Creel committee attempted a variety of tracts warning of German intrigue and espionage in the United States. Late in 1917, Ford asked S. S. McClure to prepare an essay on German intrigue and went so far as to offer McClure space in the Library of Congress to carry out his work. McClure, who had written Obstacles to Peace (1917), was recently returned from the Far East and had been lecturing on China and Japan while at the same time condemning German atrocities in Belgium.[100] He expressed eagerness to help and spent the early months of 1918 in Washington. Although in the beginning he found the task of research "dreary" and "wearisome," his enthusiasm increased, and he expanded his project from collection of material on German espionage in America to preparation of a book tracing German militarism and aggression far enough back in history to "reveal Bismarck's successful policy of destroying liberalism."[101]

The CPI published a few pamphlets on German intrigue. The committee's associate chairman, Harvey O'Higgins, wrote *The German Whisper*, which began by saying that Germany was attacking not just on the western front but in "every community in the United States." Through a "poisonous" propaganda campaign to destroy Allied morale and domestic unity, Germany hoped to bring about the collapse of America.[102] O'Higgins dealt with propaganda arguments that slandered the British, worked on religious prejudice in the United States, appealed to racial problems, and played up troubles confronting farmers. He tried to refute claims that the war was being run by politicians who had been defeated by reform elements in American society.[103] He urged citizens to inform the Department of Justice if "one of these German whispers starts buzzing in your ear."[104] The government printed 437,000 copies of the pamphlet.

O'Higgins probably helped with one of the most widely distributed publications of the CPI—*The Kaiserite in America*— of which more than 5,500,000 copies were printed; this work, designed for the commercial travelers of America, sought to refute "one hundred and one lies" being circulated by German agents.[105] O'Higgins's name was not on this composition, but he most likely was the author. He had been running a newspaper column called the "Daily German Lie," in which he tried to combat German propaganda. *The Kaiserite in America* claimed that the war was not for wealth, especially not for the purpose of gaining foreign markets.[106] This ready reference for the traveling man dealt with such rumors as that Joseph P. Tumulty had been shot for treason, or that the nerves of every new American soldier were tested by placing ground red pepper in his eyes.[107] When such falsehoods could be traced to a source, traveling men were encouraged "to swat the lie" by reporting it to the Department of Justice.[108]

German Plots and Intrigues in the United States during the Period of Our Neutrality, by Earl E. Sperry and Willis Mason West, was published in July 1918 in the Red, White and Blue Series.[109] West had been head of the department of history at the University of Minnesota. Sperry had received a doctorate at Columbia and taught European history at Syracuse University. In the spring of 1917 he had been lecturing on the causes of war and Germany's plan for world domination. He corresponded with Shotwell, sending an article he had published in the Syracuse *Post-Standard* warning of the danger posed by pan-Germanism. He feared that the American public had been "saturated with the rot of the pacifists and the German propagandists" and did not understand the causes of the war.[110] Sperry and West were assisted by Andrew C. McLaughlin, Albert Shaw, and several others. The pamphlet looked at German intrigue in America prior to the summer of 1915, and it included telegrams from the German government to diplomatic representatives in the United States; letters and telegrams between them and their agents; orders to banks for money to pay agents, and their acknowledgments; and evidence from confessions by German agents tried in the United States for criminal acts. The pamphlet related that the German ambassador to the United States, Count Johann von Bernstorff, was the ringleader of German agents. He had been assisted by Constantin Theodor Dumba, the Austro-Hungarian ambassador. Both had been aided by German military, naval, and commercial attachés, as well as German and Austro-Hungarian consuls scattered throughout the country.[111] The agents had tried to prevent the United States from exporting military supplies and had attempted to hinder American industry by strikes. Through German-American voters and such organizations as the National German-American Alliance, they sought to influence Congress.[112] They tried to cause war between the United States and Mexico.[113] American ships and cargoes headed for Entente powers had been destroyed. American passports had been forged to allow German reservists to return to fight. The German ambassador and his assistants had attempted to prevent Canada from aiding England. German agents had tried to use their position in America to aid the Indian Nationalist party in its effort to overthrow the British in India, and they had cooperated with Irish revolutionists in the United States to assist Sir Roger Casement and the Easter Rebellion of 1916.[114]

Have You Met This Kaiserite?

NAIL LIES LIKE THESE!

THAT Red Cross supplies are being sold to shopkeepers by dishonest Red Cross officials.

THAT the Masonic orders have protested against allowing the Knights of Columbus to build recreation huts for soldiers.

THAT interned German prisoners are being fed five meals a day.

THAT this is a rich man's war or a business man's war.

THAT farmers are profiteering.

THAT nine American warships were sunk in a disastrous engagement in the North Sea.

YOU FIND HIM in hotel lobbies, smoking compartments, clubs, offices and even in homes. He thinks it's clever to repeat "inside facts" about the war. He is a scandal-monger of the most dangerous type.

He repeats all the rumors, criticisms and lies he hears about our country's part in the war. He gives you names, places, dates. He is very plausible.

But if you pin him down, if you ask him what he really *knows* at first-hand, he becomes vague, non-committal, slippery. He tries to make you think that the Government can fool you, if you are willing to let it—but it can't fool him. No, siree! He's too smart.

People like that are hurting your country every day. They are playing the Kaiser's game. They are fighting against this country. They are making it harder to win the war.

Through their vanity or curiosity or *treason* they are helping German propagandists to sow the seeds of discontent.

CONTRIBUTED THROUGH DIVISION OF ADVERTISING

For every lie that has been traced originated with a German spy. Don't forget that.

There was the one about the President's Secretary. It was said, and said again, and spread broadcast that Mr. Tumulty was convicted of treason and shot at Fort Leavenworth. That lie was easily scotched by a public statement from Mr. Tumulty himself.

But other lies are more insidious—harder to down. In another paragraph some of them are told. But they are only a few of many.

⊞

They are taken from a publication, issued by the Committee on Public Information, called:

"THE KAISERITE IN AMERICA"

101 GERMAN LIES

This little book describes the methods of Germans here and quotes 101 lies that

have been nailed by a newspaper which took the trouble to run them down. It will be sent to you upon request.

Get the Facts from Washington!

Get in the fight to stamp out this malicious slander. As you travel about the country or even in your social life at home, run down these lies. Call the bluff of any one who says he has "inside information." Tell him that it's his patriotic duty to help you find the source of what he's saying.

If you find a disloyal person in your search, give his name to the Department of Justice in Washington and tell them where to find him. It is your plain and solemn duty to fight the enemy at home by stamping out these lies. Where shall we send your copy of this book? It's free!

COMMITTEE ON
PUBLIC INFORMATION

8 JACKSON PLACE, WASHINGTON, D. C.

U. S. GOV'T COMM. ON PUBLIC INFORMATION

THIS SPACE CONTRIBUTED FOR THE WINNING OF THE WAR BY

5. (Courtesy of the National Archives)

They had financed pro-German publications in America favoring congressional action to prohibit Americans from traveling on ships to belligerent nations, and later had backed a munitions embargo. They had supported a government prohibition on loans to the Allies, a boycott on banks making such loans, and the defeat of President Wilson in the 1916 election. They had encouraged a pacificism that would have kept the United States from defending the property and lives of its citizens from a German attack.[115] German policy toward the United States before the summer of 1915 thus had been characterized by duplicity, by outright attacks on American neutrality and sovereignty.

IN such ways the case was made against German militarism, and by the end of American participation in the war most citizens of the United States were willing to believe it. We now know, of course, that the origins of the Great War were more complex than the CPI led Americans to believe. We also know that all belligerents made wide use of atrocity propaganda and that it was enormously effective in mobilizing opinion. Unquestionably, a large percentage of atrocity stories used during World War I were fabrications, combinations of hyperbole and nonsense, and the effort to track down their truth or falsity leads to a tangled web indeed. The Committee on Public Information did not always resist the temptation to deal in such dubious material. Some of its public speakers and posters—as will be shown—emphasized German atrocities. Some writers were undeniably caught up in the emotions of the period. At least one committee pamphlet probably used forged documents. A part of the CPI's literature drew on such unreliable sources as the Bryce Report and otherwise exaggerated the German threat, oversimplifying the issues surrounding the war.

In admitting these shortcomings one must also grant that Ford did try to hold to standards of documentation. Much of the CPI's indictment of German Kultur was fairly well tempered, especially if compared with some of the propaganda that came from other countries, not to mention the wildly

superpatriotic material put out by unofficial sources in the
United States. It must be remembered that the invasion of
Belgium did result in the deaths of at least five thousand civilians.[116] It is also interesting that a substantial amount of writing
on German history since the end of World War II has come
back to a general position very similar to that taken by Ford
and many of his associates.[117] There is little doubt that many
of the CPI's writers wrote from convictions about the militaristic nature of German society, convictions that sometimes can
be traced to their own experiences before the war. Germany
appeared to them as a country of militarism, a major power
growing in strength, a nation subject to little or no democratic
control. By the time of American entrance into the Great War it
was easy for them to believe that Germans not merely were
capable of admiring the clash of armies, the exhibitions of blood
and iron that already had marked nearly three stalemated years
on the western front. It was possible for them to believe that
Germans reveled in the awful carnage of the trenches. The
scene on the Allied front in France in 1917–18 was dire and frequently desperate, and everywhere the Germans seemed to be
attacking—until the summer of 1918, when the tide of battle at
last turned. The need seemed desperate that Americans should
fear and even hate the enemy. That enemy was German militarism, and the very nature of the adversary seemed to require
that America, for the first time, intervene in a European war.

5

The Literature of the CPI: Justifying Intervention

"Old Glory" knows no alien soil when there is work to do in Freedom's name.[1]

THE UNITED STATES entered the Great War with an unparalleled missionary fervor. The American people, of course, had demonstrated missionary fervor throughout their history, going back to the time of the Puritans.[2] The zeal of the people of the United States in 1917–18 was a manifestation of what has been described as the American mission. That sense of mission traditionally called for providing an example for the rest of the world by a city on a hill, the New World separate from and in contrast to the corruptions of the Old. It became more secular as the United States came to symbolize human freedom and democratic government. Prior to 1917, the doctrine of mission (it was nothing less than that) called for settling a great continent, and only occasionally for intervention outside American borders. It had never required intervention in Europe's political affairs. The United States always had sympathy for the establishment of representative institutions abroad, but not until the administration of Woodrow Wilson did the hope of promoting such institutions seem a realistic goal. Wilson was the first president to urge Americans to become world citizens. He argued that American principles need not be confined to this continent but were applicable worldwide.[3]

The CPI became the champion of these ideas. The committee's writers, sometimes taking their ideas from the president but often arriving at these conclusions on their own, argued that intervention in the European war was not at variance with America's tradition but was a reaffirmation of it. The zeal with which some of these people argued their case no doubt derived from the desire to improve society. The committee's literature argued that isolation was no longer possible, because of modern technology and the German menace.[4] It contended that the idea of two spheres, of a polarity between America and Europe, no longer could apply and that the Monroe Doctrine should be revised, its application perhaps made worldwide.

MUCH of the literature on the German menace assumed that America no longer could be isolated from world affairs because it now faced an enemy threatening its existence. One of the CPI's first pamphlets, *How the War Came to America*, sought to dispel the notion that the United States was isolated from Europe. The essay was mostly the work of Bullard, although Ernest Poole helped put it in popular form and Shotwell and Becker sharpened a few points.[5] Bullard had attacked isolationism in a book published in 1916.[6] Now he argued that America's position toward other countries had been characterized by three ideas. In the Monroe Doctrine the United States had pledged to resist European interference in the New World and made clear that it would not involve itself in any ordinary European conflict. Second, the United States had championed freedom of the seas, arguing "that sea law to be just and worthy of general respect must be based on the consent of the governed." And it had supported arbitration so that international controversies could be settled in the same manner used to resolve disputes in federal courts.[7] Each of these ideas was now challenged by the war. The Germans had violated the Monroe Doctrine by sending spies to the United States, encouraging insurrection in Cuba, Haiti, and Santo Domingo, and promoting unrest and hatred in South America.[8] Freedom of the seas had been challenged by Britain, unwilling to accept the seas as "being distinct from the Old World." (Bullard explained, however, that Britain could not accept a limit on its naval power when neighbors were not willing to limit their land forces.) America hence would have to abandon isolationism and take up world responsibilities, for it could not have freedom of the seas unless it was willing to do its part in maintaining freedom of the land.[9] As for arbitration, the Central Powers had made it impossible. They did not want a peace based on arbitration but desired victory so that they could extend their domination of Europe. Kultur was responsible for the war. Human liberties would not be safe until Germany's leaders were defeated.[10]

According to Bullard, the United States found itself in a new world with expanded responsibilities. Isolation had been destroyed by foreign trade, travel abroad, and modern communication and transportation. These developments, climaxed by the German threat, "made our isolation more and more imaginary." With the entry of Russia in the conflict, the struggle took on the dimension of "a stupendous civil war of all the world." To remain neutral would betray ancestors who had died for freedom.[11]

Some members of the NBHS did not think highly of this pamphlet. Waldo Leland thought it far from adequate, and Charles Haskins felt that it lacked the necessary documentation. It reminded him of the "inspired narratives" Germany produced early in the war. Nevertheless, it was one of the most popular tracts produced by the CPI. Its circulation exceeded 6,250,000 copies.[12]

Disappearance of American isolation was a theme in other CPI pamphlets. Secretary of the Interior Lane's *Why We Are Fighting Germany* described the struggle as self-defense. "The invasion of Belgium, which opened the war, led to the invasion of the United States by slow, steady, logical steps. . . . Our love of fair play ripened into alarm at our own peril." Lane saw a war between feudalism and democracy. It was a struggle against an "ancient, out-worn spirit." It was "the world of Christ . . . come again face to face with the world of Mahomet, who willed to win by force." If the enemy were allowed to have its way, if allowed to defeat England, it would control Canada and "we would live, as France has lived for 40 years, in haunting terror." Lansing's *America's Future at Stake* argued that if Germany had been victorious while America remained neutral, Germany eventually would attack the United States. America owed an even greater debt to the soldiers who were going overseas to fight than it did to those who had fought on American soil: "it calls for more patriotism, more self-denial, and a truer vision to wage war on distant shores than to repel an invader or defend one's home." Former Secretary of State Elihu Root appealed for Americans to enter the war before it was too late. The fighting threatened traditional American protections. German victory would destroy the balance of power in Europe and the British fleet that had supported the Monroe Doctrine and protected the United States. If the mission of American democracy was to succeed, the world to be made free, intervention was imperative. Assistant Secretary of Labor Louis F. Post ended his pamphlet, *The German Attack*, by stating that the problem was "resisting conquest now, in a war in Europe and with allies, or later on in our own country and without allies."[13] The pamphlets by Lane, Lansing, Root, and Post had a combined circulation of almost 2,500,000.[14]

John S. P. Tatlock's *Why America Fights Germany*, published in March 1918, was graphic in showing an America no longer isolated. A professor of English at Stanford, Tatlock was serving as district director of educational work for the War Department. He was paid six dollars a day in February 1918 to work on his pamphlet, which portrayed German frightfulness and warned that Germany meant to dominate not only the Old World but the New. Germany had destroyed American ships and property, killed citizens, insulted the flag. Germany's cruel conduct in Belgium, its method of waging war, threatened mercy and justice throughout the world. Lust for power made it the world's greatest threat to free peoples. The war was a clear-cut struggle between democracies and autocracies. Because Germany's plans called for world domination, the United States should fight while it had allies: otherwise it would have to fight alone. Only two things had to change: the government of Germany, and the spirit of the German people. The latter had led Germans to believe that they possessed a superior civilization, which gave them the right to force themselves on the rest of the world. Plans had "been formed, and printed by men of military rank, for an invasion of America."[15]

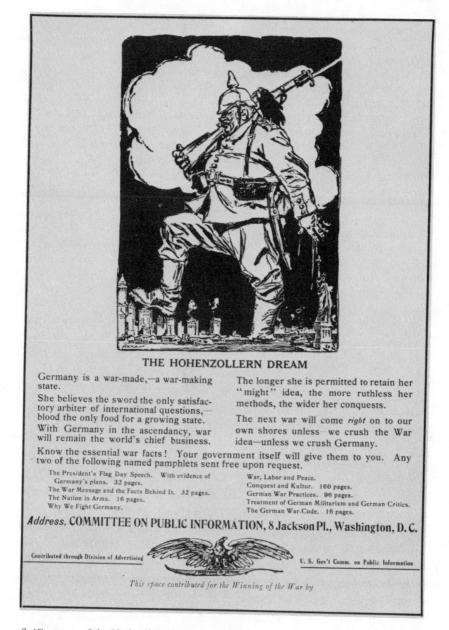

THE HOHENZOLLERN DREAM

Germany is a war-made,—a war-making state.

She believes the sword the only satisfactory arbiter of international questions,—blood the only food for a growing state.

With Germany in the ascendancy, war will remain the world's chief business.

The longer she is permitted to retain her "might" idea, the more ruthless her methods, the wider her conquests.

The next war will come *right* on to our own shores unless we crush the War idea—unless we crush Germany.

Know the essential war facts! Your government itself will give them to you. Any two of the following named pamphlets sent free upon request.

The President's Flag Day Speech. With evidence of Germany's plans. 32 pages.
The War Message and the Facts Behind It. 32 pages.
The Nation in Arms. 16 pages.
Why We Fight Germany.

War, Labor and Peace.
Conquest and Kultur. 160 pages.
German War Practices. 96 pages.
Treatment of German Militarism and German Critics.
The German War-Code. 16 pages.

Address, **COMMITTEE ON PUBLIC INFORMATION, 8 Jackson Pl., Washington, D. C.**

Contributed through Division of Advertising   U. S. Gov't Comm. on Public Information

This space contributed for the Winning of the War by

6. (Courtesy of the National Archives)

Now let us picture what a sudden invasion of the United States by these Germans would mean; sudden, because their settled way is always to attack suddenly. First they set themselves to capture New York City. While their fleet blockades the harbor and shells the city and the forts from far at sea, their troops land somewhere near and advance toward the city in order to cut its rail communications, starve it into surrender, and then plunder it. . . . They pass through Lakewood, a station on the Central Railroad of New Jersey. They first demand wine for the officers and beer for the men. Angered to find that an American town does not contain large quantities of either, they pillage and burn the post-office and most of the hotels and stores. Then they demand $1,000,000 from the residents. One feeble old woman tries to conceal twenty dollars which she had been hoarding in her desk drawer; she is taken out and hanged (to save a cartridge). Some of the teachers in two district schools meet a fate which make them envy her. . . . Robbery, murder and outrage run riot. Fifty leading citizens are lined up against the First National Bank building, and shot. . . .

This is not just a snappy story. It is not fancy. The general plan of campaign against America has been announced repeatedly by German military men. And every horrible detail is just what the German troops have done in Belgium and France. . . .[16]

Nearly three quarters of a million copies of *Why America Fights Germany* were distributed. A related map, "The German Idea," published separately, showed the United States with its cities newly named after a German takeover.

The pamphlet produced by Notestein and Stoll contained a section entitled "Pan-Germanism and America."[17] It quoted an officer of the German general staff as saying in 1901 that the United States could not oppose invading German troops. Germany was the only power that could conquer America. The public was warned of the Germanization of America; within a hundred years, and with aid of the German language, Americans would be conquered by the German spirit.[18] Several passages quoted German writers who commented on the Monroe Doctrine and suggested seizure of such South American countries as Brazil and Uruguay.[19] Readers were warned of a German takeover in New York and Washington. The kaiser was quoted as saying that after the war he would "stand no nonsense from America."[20]

Evarts B. Greene offered a justification for American involvement abroad. Greene had received a doctorate at Harvard

The German Idea

SHALL this war make Germany's word the highest law in the world?

Read what she expects. Here are the words of her own spokesmen.

Then ask yourself where Germany would have the United States stand after the war.

Shall we bow to Germany's wishes—assist German ambition?

No. The German idea must be so completely crushed that it will never again rear its venomous head.

It's a fight, as the President said, "to the last dollar, the last drop of blood."

Americans, know the essential war facts! Your government has itself undertaken to give them to you. The Committee on Public Information has published a series of pamphlets, as follows. Any two sent upon request to the Committee on Public Information, Washington, D. C.

THE AMERICAN IDEA	THE GERMAN IDEA
The President's Flag Day Speech, With Evidence of Germany's Plans. 32 pages.	Conquest and Kultur. 160 Pages.
The War Message and the Facts Behind It. 32 pages.	German War Practices. 96 pages.
The Nation in Arms. 16 pages.	Treatment of German Militarism and German Critics.
Why We Fight Germany.	The German War Code.
War, Labor and Peace.	

COMMITTEE   ON   PUBLIC   INFORMATION
8 JACKSON PLACE, WASHINGTON, D. C.

Contributed through Division of Advertising, United States Gov't Committee on Public Information.

George Creel, Chairman
The Secretary of State
The Secretary of War
The Secretary of the Navy.

This space contributed for the Winning of the War by

The Publisher of

"The German race is called to bind the earth under its control, to exploit the natural resources and the physical powers of man, to use the passive races in subordinate capacity for the development of Kultur."—*Ludwig Woltman, Politische Anthropologie, 1903.*

"Our German Fatherland (to) which I hope it will be granted, through the harmonious coöperation of princes and peoples, of its armies and its citizens, to become in the future as closely united, as powerful and as authoritative as once the Roman world-empire was."—*Kaiser's speech, Imperial Limes Museum, Saalburg, October 11, 1900.*

"Germany's greatness makes it impossible for her to do without the ocean, but the ocean also proves that even in the distance, and on its farther side, without Germany and the German Emperor no great decision dare henceforth be taken."—*Kaiser's speech, Kiel, July 3rd, 1900.*

"If ever the course of world history hastened to bestow upon an undertaking what I might call the historical seal of approval, then this was the case when, directly after the voting of the naval budget, first the Spanish-American war, then the war in South Africa put our oversea interests at such different points in serious embarrassment, and fate proved it all before our eyes. You will understand, gentlemen, that in my official and responsible position, I cannot say much and that I cannot dot all my i's. You will all understand me if I say that fate showed us at more than one point on this globe how urgently necessary was the increase of our navy which took place two years ago, and how wise and patriotic it was of this high assembly to assent to the Government bill of that time (1898)."—*Von Buelow in the Reichstag, 1898.*

7. (Courtesy of the National Archives)

in 1893 and had spent a year studying in Berlin. He was a professor of history at Illinois, where he specialized in the history of the American Revolution. During the war he served on the Inquiry and succeeded Shotwell as chairman of the NBHS.[21] Characterized by a colleague as "thoughtful rather than brilliant," he wrote one of the early pamphlets in the War Information Series, entitled *American Interest in Popular Government Abroad.* It appeared in September 1917, and nearly 600,000 copies of the essay were distributed. Greene argued that from the beginning the United States had shown sympathy toward liberal government in Europe. He cited the eighteenth-century French economist Turgot explaining that the importance of American liberty was not confined to the New World; America was the hope of mankind, a laboratory where a political experiment was being conducted not only for the western hemisphere but for Europe.[22] Greene traced American history from the Farewell Address, which sometimes had been quoted unfairly, he said. The first president had not opposed "temporary alliances for extraordinary emergencies" and had expressed sympathy for popular movements abroad.[23] While rejecting intervention in Europe, James Monroe had expressed sympathy for liberalism abroad, notably the Greek struggle against the Turks. He had commented favorably on reform in Spain and Portugal and had listened to Thomas Jefferson and James Madison as they proposed an alliance with Britain. Albert Gallatin had proposed sending ships to help the Greeks, and so had John C. Calhoun. Henry Clay and Daniel Webster had favored moral support of the Greeks.[24] The United States government had taken interest in popular movements in Germany in the 1830s and 1840s. After failure of the Hungarian revolution in 1851, Congress and President Millard Fillmore had expressed sympathy for Hungarian exiles, and a ship had been dispatched to bring them from Turkey. The government had received Louis Kossuth. A few years later, Lincoln had declared his faith in "the community of democratic interests on both sides of the Atlantic." After the Civil War the United States had recognized such new republican governments as the French Republic and the Russian government of 1917.[25]

Greene contended that the world had undergone a re-markable change during the previous quarter century, with the steamship, ocean cable, airplane, and wireless. People lived on a much smaller planet, interrelated in many ways. Democracies throughout the world were bound not only by sentiment, but by common interest, for protection from militaristic powers. Germany, with its extensive espionage in the New World, sub-marine attacks on American commerce, and the attempt to draw Mexico into the fight, had destroyed our "splendid isola-tion" by threatening to extend a hostile European system into the western hemisphere.[26]

Several historians connected with the NBHS and CPI were interested in rewriting history to show that a cultural and po-litical bond always had existed between the United States and the Old World, especially with Britain and France. Frederick Jackson Turner believed that historians should make the public aware of "new world conditions" in economic, social, political, and military areas, not leaving those points to be made by mili-tary men. He called on historians to demonstrate the propriety of a close connection with England and France. Observing that propagandists would make much of the traditional Anglo-American hostility, he urged historians to stress the new eco-nomic, social, and political conditions in England, which made that country similar to the United States.[27] There also was an effort to show a constant interaction between America and Europe. Many agreed with young Dexter Perkins that for this reason it was impractical for the United States to remain aloof from world affairs. Perkins wrote to Leland that America's entry in the struggle proved "the impossibility of our main-taining our older isolation, and the circumstances which forced action upon us offer clear proof that we have a real stake in the settlement of what we once considered as purely European questions."[28]

CPI pamphlets sought to show the community of interest among the United States, Britain, and France. Sherman's pam-phlet saw American and Allied ideals as one and the same.[29] *The Battle Line of Democracy* contained an essay by James Russell Lowell, "Democracy," which told of the American debt to Britain. It also had a section on France, with smaller segments on Belgium, Russia, and Italy.[30] Ford in his introduction to the Notestein and Stoll pamphlet on German Kultur recommended that "it should never be forgotten that Burke and Chatham and Fox and Barré in England and Lafayette and Turgot and Beaumarchais in France held political ideas which made them the supporters of the American colonies and the intellectual comrades of Washington, Franklin, and Jefferson."[31]

History Teacher's Magazine, put out by the NBHS, contained articles on ancient, modern, English, and American history suggesting episodes of interest in light of the entry into the struggle. One of the themes in this publication was the interaction between American and European history. Many people in the CPI wrote for the magazine. Greene was chairman of the committee on American history for the NBHS and was responsible for articles on American history. His responsibility expanded as members of the publication's editorial board left for the army, and he came to exercise much influence over the periodical.[32] Articles for *History Teacher's Magazine* generally ran to about a thousand words, and Greene contributed several.[33] In an essay entitled "The American Revolution and the British Empire," he stated that the break with England was more than just the appearance of a new nation; it was the start of American foreign policy. In another article he argued that European blood formed American society. He also contended that the United States was much closer to Europe physically. "America can no longer be regarded as a world apart. . . . Less and less can we feel ourselves a peculiar people; more and more we are enjoying the gains and bearing the burdens of a common civilization."[34]

In letters to contributors to the magazine, Greene repeatedly urged highlighting instances of contact or cooperation between America and Europe. St. George L. Sioussat wrote "English Foundations of American Institutional Life," and Arthur Cross traced the origins of local government to Tudor England.[35] Greene asked Cross to include some transatlantic endeavors of the English people. He urged James Sullivan, writing on American military and diplomatic policy between 1775 and 1783, to emphasize the French Alliance of 1778.[36] Theodore C. Smith of Williams College was asked to write on "The Relation of the United States to World Politics from 1792 to 1815," pointing out incidents in foreign relations that would illuminate contemporary events. Green requested Albert Bushnell Hart to write on "The European System and the Monroe Doctrine," with emphasis on the years 1815 to 1823, not neglecting subsequent events in development of the doctrine. E. D. Adams of the University of Michigan was asked to write on "Our International Relations during the Civil War Period," mentioning Lincoln's attempt to stress democratic interests on both shores of the Atlantic. Sometimes the strain of drawing lessons from the past was too much. Tenny Frank, a student of ancient history from Bryn Mawr, told Greene that though he had been able to get the facts out of ancient history for his article, he did not "seem to be able to combine that job with *drawing the lessons*."[37]

In showing how intervention was essential to the war in Europe, it was one thing to demonstrate how the mission of America made intervention necessary. It was something else to take that other primeval doctrine of American history, the Monroe Doctrine, and show it as requiring two million Americans in France. The problem of what to do with the doctrine concerned many people, from Arthur W. Dunn of the Bureau of Education to members of the NBHS and CPI.[38] The doctrine had declared that America and Europe contained antagonistic political traditions: the United States would not tolerate European interference in the western hemisphere, and in return, the United States would not interfere with Europe.

Of all the writers connected with the CPI it was probably Carl Becker who was most interested in revising the Monroe Doctrine. He was impressed by a statement President Wilson had made on January 22, 1917, urging that Monroe's policy be made "the doctrine of the world."[39] Becker had written to Turner that the war was not a break with American tradition. The Monroe Doctrine had been inspired by a desire not to be left alone but to make the western hemisphere "safe for democracy" or "at least safe for the experiment." Wilson had not abandoned the doctrine but was only expanding it.[40]

Becker wrote about the Monroe Doctrine in a notable article for the *Minnesota History Bulletin* published in May 1917. When Greene was unable to convince Hart to write "The European System and the Monroe Doctrine," Becker's article was reprinted in *History Teacher's Magazine*.[41] American independence, he contended, had been won on the principle of government deriving its sanction from consent of the governed. Political and social life was grounded in the idea that people have the right to govern and to be assured of equal opporutnity—"the United States has stood for this or it has stood for nothing."[42] Neither Washington nor Monroe believed that America and Europe should have nothing to do with one another. The concern had been that the United States not enter the European system of alliances, and they opposed any effort to extend that system to this continent. Even though the Monroe Doctrine may have been partly an expression of material interest, the policy's major function had been to oppose the extension of the European political system, because it would "endanger our institutions as well as our interests."[43] The doctrine had been an "expression of that most deep-seated of American instincts, the attachment to free government and democratic social institutions." Becker argued that when the doctrine had been formed, the powers of Europe were reactionary. During the nineteenth century some European nations became more democratic, to the point where the traditional division between New World democracy and Old World reaction was no longer valid. The Germany of 1917 threatened the experiment in free government more than the Holy Alliance ever did, and other European countries were struggling to preserve the very ideals the United States professed. President Wilson was "not renouncing but only extending the Monroe Doctrine."[44]

At Ford's request, Becker prepared another essay on this subject, aimed at Latin America. It was finished by early October 1918, and emphasized that the doctrine had been to protect democracy not only in the United States but throughout the hemisphere. Again Becker contended that European countries had become more democratic, and he believed America should not hesitate to align itself with them. Critics had argued that the doctrine existed only to protect the self-interest of the United States, citing the Mexican War. Becker replied that the smaller states in the hemisphere had little to fear when they compared such historical events with the protection the United States offered. Some contended that the doctrine existed to make the hemisphere safe for American capitalism. Becker responded that all nations were free to invest in the Americas so long as investors did not become "advance agents of foreign aggression." It was only "these more subtle forms of acquisition" that the United States opposed.[45]

Whether the Monroe Doctrine and intervention abroad would be used to protect democracy or capitalism greatly concerned Becker. In *United States: An Experiment in Democracy*, he wrote that Ameria needed to be certain that in entering the war and attempting to preserve peace it was for "*democracy* and not *capitalistic imperialism.*" America needed to be careful that it was not imposing its own style of democracy on the world.[46]

Becker was not the only writer associated with the CPI and the NBHS who discussed the meaning of the Monroe Doctrine. Andrew C. McLaughlin of the University of Chicago argued against isolation and tried to persuade the public of the necessity of expanding the doctrine. "The Great War: From Spectator to Participant" was published in the June 1917 issue of *History Teacher's Magazine* and reprinted by the CPI in its War Information Series in 1.5 million copies.[47] It emphasized German aggression, arguing that America faced danger from a victorious Germany. The conflict went deeper than forms of government, as German policy was formed "within a wall of psychological superiority and inculcated obedience as the great end of being." He emphasized the development of liberalism in the British government, which made it more compatible with the United States, and he held that American entry into the war was to help "establish democracy, humanity, and a sense of national duty without profit."[48]

McLaughlin undertook a speaking tour in England for the

NBHS in 1918 and lectured at the University of London on the Monroe Doctrine.[49] In the past fifty years more nations had become democratic, he then said. The idea of two spheres of political principles had broken down.[50] He denied that the doctrine existed for expansion of American capital in Latin America or sought aggrandizement of the United States in any other way.[51] "Until . . . every nation of the world adopts the principles of democracy in its internal organization, there can be little hope for peace between nations."[52] He discussed President Wilson's call for making the Monroe Doctrine worldwide. The old Monroe Doctrine meant that the United States must be free from European political influence. The new doctrine proposed "that we win assured freedom by going across the water to help in destroying the whole system of force, suspicion and intrigue to which Germany still clings, and to set up in its place an appeal to the tribunal of public intelligence."[53]

Had there been more public discussion about the doctrine and its contravention by entry into the war, the CPI was prepared to publish even more on the topic. Ford expressed surprise in the autumn of 1917 that there was not more interest in the problem.[54] Other writers for the committee touched the subject, including Bullard, Creel, and Ford himself, who wrote that "a new Monroe Doctrine must be defended on the pathways of the seas and in the fields of Flanders if the Western World is to be preserved as the citadel of a free-developing, forward-looking democracy."[55] Scholars volunteered to write on the doctrine, including I. J. Cox of the University of Cincinnati and George G. Wilson of Harvard. Wilson was on the CPI's payroll and had prepared an essay, "The Monroe Doctrine after the War." Ford did not feel that his division could use it, and it was published under other auspices. George Wilson believed it would take some doing to reconcile the president's stand with the attitude toward the doctrine in many European countries, and he sought to "facilitate a world-wide recognition" of its principles.[56] Shotwell asked Sperry to go through German sources and write "German Comment on the Monroe Doctrine."[57] The *War Cyclopedia*, the combined effort of many writers, contained entries on the Monroe Doctrine in addition

to others on the United States as champion of free government, American interference in European affairs, America as a
world power, and United States isolation.[58]

IN this manner the CPI redefined America's
mission to support intervention. It sought to convince Americans that isolation was no longer a realistic policy and that the
spirit of the Monroe Doctrine called for the United States to
participate in a European war. Many committee writers did
not see a clash between America's national principles, rightly
understood, and internationalism.[59] Becker and McLaughlin
believed (as had Sherman) that American ideals, rooted in
democratic principles, formed a basis for a new international
order. Greene, who tried hard to demonstrate the historical
interaction between America and Europe, wanted more attention to "the positive values of nationalism" and believed the liberal spirit important in any international order.[60] Most writers
thus believed, as an article of faith, that the American system
was a model for the world. In this sense internationalism as
expressed through the CPI was a manifestation of American
nationalism.[61]

6

"To Create a Nation of Noble Men"—The *National School Service*

> The Committee on Public Information and the schools have a great common war task to make an Americanized, nationalized American nation. If we, working with all other agencies, fail, then America will fail.
> —Guy Stanton Ford[1]

LOYALTY TO ONE'S COUNTRY is not instinctive but rather is learned or otherwise acquired, and though there are many ways to instill such a sentiment, one of the most convenient has been through the public schools.[2] European countries long have used the schools to inculcate loyalty.[3] The United States government has been no exception in this regard. Beginning in the autumn of 1918 and continuing well into 1919, at first through the Committee on Public Information, the government published a bulletin, the *National School Service* (*NSS*), to promote national unity by emphasizing the obligations of citizenship. This concern owed much to the fighting in Europe, for modern war required the support of the entire population. But, as with so much of the CPI literature, more than the war inspired this concern over loyalty. It was related to the desire, so ardent at the time, to improve society, to alleviate the evils that afflicted modern life.[4]

DURING the Great War there were many attempts to promote patriotism in the public schools by private organizations, such as the National Security League, or by agen-

cies that worked with or were part of the federal government—
the National Board for Historical Service, the Committee on
Public Information, the Student Army Training Corps.[5] By
spring of 1918, a lack of patriotism was not at issue; the problem was that patriotic demands on the teachers had become so
great, with advice coming from so many quarters and in such
volume, that the teachers were almost overwhelmed. One member of the Bureau of Education estimated that the educational
activities of the government were "scattered among half a hundred different agencies in twenty-three distinct departments,
bureaus, or commissions."[6] Teachers had neither the time nor
the inclination to sort through the patriotic information offered
them, and much of the material went unread.

The problem of how best to use public schools to promote
patriotism had interested Guy Stanton Ford from almost the
beginning of the war. Ford lamented the lack of national organization and observed that every governmental department that
tried to present its views to the teacher had to rely on the county
superintendent. Particularly in rural areas, the county superintendent linked the teacher to the state superintendent and
ultimately to the national government. It was at the county level
that the effort to mobilize the schools had too frequently broken
down.[7] Ford favored something like a ministry of education to
get the government's message to teachers and pupils.[8]

The United States Commissioner of Education, Philander P.
Claxton, was similarly concerned. A meeting in his office in
mid-February 1918 recommended that the Committee on Public Information prepare a school bulletin. Such a publication
would circumvent the county superintendent and reach not
only students but adults with the government's message.[9] The
National Education Association's Commission on the National
Emergency in Education at its meeting in April 1918 passed a
resolution asking the National Council of Defense and other
agencies to create a clearinghouse for school propaganda.[10]
Ford drew up a plan and asked for names of educators to serve
as an Advisory Editorial Board to help put it in operation. The
National School Service was published first under the auspices of
the CPI and then, beginning in January 1919, under the direc-

tion of the Division of Educational Extension of the Department of the Interior.

Although Ford was director of the *NSS* and often wrote for the publication, he delegated much of his authority to a young professor of English then studying at Columbia, J. W. Searson. Searson did most of the work of putting the bulletin together and served as its managing editor for thirty-five dollars a week. One of his first tasks was to write each state superintendent, asking him to appoint a five-man state consulting editorial board. The purpose of the board, of which the state superintendent was to be chairman, was to offer advice based on classroom experience to the central advisory editorial board in Washington.[11] State boards would promote "the harmony of national with local programs of procedure" in adapting war service material to the needs of the schools. It was planned that a bulletin would be ready for summer school sessions. Searson in early May sent letters to public schools, colleges, and universities asking for summer school dates and anticipated enrollments. Perhaps because there were not enough summer students to justify the cost, the first issue of the bulletin did not appear until September 1918.[12]

It is interesting to note the response to the bulletin from educational leaders across the country. In May and June, Searson requested advice on how to make the publication effective. The response was enthusiastic. Several hundred teachers and administrators replied, half expressing approval, the other half going further and sending in suggestions about what the paper should contain.[13] William H. Kilpatrick of Columbia Teachers College eagerly offered advice. Kilpatrick urged against a "parochial patriotism," in favor of loyalty to the nation that was "broader, more intelligent," than before the war. His colleague E. S. Evenden wanted the bulletin to set standards "to avoid extremes in thought and action," to remedy a "lack of balance" in American society.[14]

These letters give fascinating insight into how nationalistic concerns permeated the thought of many teachers in 1918. The success of the federal government in using schools to teach patriotism and citizenship owed much to the enthusiasm of the teachers. Many letters called for making the public school system an arm of the state. The government did not have to launch a campaign to make schools into engines of patriotism. Claxton observed confidently that "there is no other group in our population so strategically situated for direct patriotic service as the teachers."[15] He might have added that few groups were apparently more eager to give such service.

During the life of the *NSS* the editorial staff remained virtually unchanged. Ford directed the bulletin, sometimes contributing material, while it was under the CPI's control. Beginning in January 1919, when the Department of the Interior began publishing the *NSS*, J. J. Pettijohn replaced Ford, who returned to Minnesota. Searson served the entire period as the publication's managing editor, and William C. Bagley of Columbia Teachers College was editor-in-chief.

Bagley evidently had considerable influence on the *NSS*. A well-known figure in educational circles, he had received a doctorate from Cornell in 1900 and had taught in public and normal schools. He had been vice-president and director of training at Montana State Normal College, before becoming professor of education at the University of Illinois in 1908.[16] In 1917 he went to Columbia. By 1918 he had written a half-dozen books, including *Educative Process* (1905), *Educational Values* (1911), and *Human Behavior* (with S. S. Colvin, 1913). *The History of the American People*, with Charles A. Beard, appeared in 1918.[17] The theme of social responsibility, so important in the *NSS*, was part of his theory of education. His first book (1905) had proclaimed that the goal of education was development of "the socially efficient individual" who would not only "pull his own weight" but "sacrifice his own pleasure . . . when its gratification will not directly or indirectly lead to social achievement."[18] Bagley opposed what he believed to be a trend to emphasize self-centeredness and individualism as the ultimate goal of education.[19] In his view, democratic government was challenged perhaps as much by prosperity as by external enemies, and in order to function democracy required an educated citizenry instructed in "the more virile virtues of duty and effort and sacrifice." For both the nation and the individual, "real freedom, the only kind of freedom that does not sink one in hopeless individualism, is not the kind that comes as a gift, but the kind that comes as a conquest—the freedom that has been bought at the price of sacrifice and effort." Each individual, each generation, had to win freedom.[20] Bagley believed that the teacher had a special civic duty because, ideally, democracy was not direct government by the people but government of experts responsible to the people. The teacher was important in developing civic virtues that, if firmly implanted in pupils' minds, would facilitate reform both in government and in business.[21] The volume written with Beard that appeared in 1918 was dominated by "one great motive": the preparation of children for "citizenship through an understanding of the ideals, institutions, achievements, and problems of our country."[22]

Bagley wanted the federal government to upgrade education in local and rural schools. He believed that local autonomy in education needed "very radical modification," in view of the deficiencies uncovered by army testing. There was no official channel through which the nation could satisfactorily meet its educational needs. The war had brought a "marvelous awakening of the national consciousness" and provided educational leaders a "golden hour" of opportunity to establish a national program of education. All this work could be done, he felt, without excessive bureaucratic control.[23]

Samuel B. Harding assisted Bagley and Searson as head of the bulletin's historical section. Mabel Carney was responsible for rural schools and was assisted by Fannie W. Dunn, who had been in charge of intermediate grades. Alberta Walker eventually took over the latter work. Lula McNally Cain looked after the material for primary grades; and the seventh through twelfth grades were the responsibility of Charles A. Coulomb, who earlier had helped prepare a publication for teaching patriotism in elementary schools.[24]

The typical bulletin devoted its opening pages to stories on the war, and this was true even after the Armistice. Subsequent pages would tell of war work or Americanization efforts undertaken by pupils across the country and would suggest how pupils could contribute to victory or to Americanizing the country. Messages from government officials and short, snappy entries contrasted American ideals with those of Germany. Pictures, maps, and diagrams illustrated points. In the last five or six pages were sections for rural schools, primary grades, intermediate grades, upper grades, and high schools. Programs to promote national loyalty were outlined for teachers. Occasional issues of the *NSS* would be devoted to such themes as Americanization and good citizenship, the Red Cross, or food conservation.

Distribution of the *NSS* was based on the national school building address list compiled by the Bureau of Education. The bulletin was mailed not to teachers but to the school buildings. An attempt was made to supply copies to the State Consulting Advisory Boards.[25] It is doubtful that many copies were distributed to schoolchildren, for funds were limited. Had it been possible to supply each student with a copy of the paper, as many as twenty million homes might have been reached directly.[26] The bulletin's mail list probably never exceeded six hundred thousand, and Searson had to deny hundreds of requests from superintendents.[27] The extent to which the bulletin's message entered American homes depended on the clarity with which each teacher presented it. Teachers were told that few people had "a more serious responsibility for clear vision and straight thinking," and that "the ideals of America past and future were never more clearly committed into [their] hands than they are today. . . ." They were urged to become "expert" on issues of the war and form every message "intelligently and intelligibly," so that children could carry it to their families.[28]

In this manner the *National School Service* sought to influence public school instruction from primary grades through high school, educating children to "unswerving loyalty." This sixteen-page paper issued twice monthly tried "to keep up the proper patriotic morale behind the lines" by making "every school pupil a messenger for Uncle Sam."[29] It used the teacher "as an officer of the state."[30]

After the Armistice, the emphasis of the *National School Service* shifted to domestic problems, but themes still ran through each issue. Material fell into several categories. First were articles to define American democracy, or Americanism, and the good citizen. During the war these qualities were often reduced to willingness to make immediate sacrifices. After the Armistice the qualities became more explicit, becoming the desirable traits of citizens. Because community service was important in citizenship, the activities of the Red Cross and Junior Red Cross were emphasized, as were such practical activities as boys' and girls' clubs and school gardens. Second were articles dealing with the war—origins, progress, consequences. Items of this sort appeared in virtually every issue up to the bulletin's demise in May 1919. A third theme was thrift, the economical production and conservation of food, fuel, and other commodities. Fourth was public health and sanitation. Fifth, an effort was made to reach the rural schools, to link them effectively with the national government. Sixth, after the Armistice the *National School Service* attempted to instruct teachers and pupils in America's international responsibilities through a "League-of-Nations attitude of mind."[31] In the first weeks of the bulletin—September 1918 through early November—the most important issue was winning the war. Domestic problems were submerged in the drive toward victory. After the Armistice the emphasis became American society and international responsibilities.

American democracy, or often simply Americanism, was the ideological cement for the *National School Service*. The term referred to all values and ideals that made up the American way of life. One of the earliest attempts to give it definition was "The American's Creed," by William Tyler Page, who had gained national attention after winning a patriotic contest in Baltimore. The creed brought together quotations from the Constitution, *Federalist* No. 10, Daniel Webster's speech to the Senate in January 1830, and the Gettysburg Address:

I believe in the United States of America as a government of the people, by the people, for the people, whose just powers are derived from the consent of the governed; a democracy in a Republic; a sovereign nation of many sovereign states; a perfect Union, one and inseparable; established upon the principles of freedom, equality, justice, and humanity for which American patriots sacrificed their lives and fortunes.

I therefore believe it my duty to my country to love it, to support its

Constitution, to obey its laws, to respect its flag, and to defend it against all enemies.[32]

In the course of its activities the NSS attempted a sort of spiritual renaissance. Native Americans needed "to be born again in the faith of their fathers." The NSS listed distinctive American ideals, including equal opportunity for all, together with "a socialization of all the best things that have come to any one."[33] Religious toleration and universal education were on the list, along with labor's right to adequate wages; majority rule with respect for minority rights; respect for women, children, and the aged; and deep "respect for the home as the social unit." The list was rounded out with freedom of speech and the press; "the abolition of social, industrial, commercial, or religious caste"; and "national idealism, or the exercise of a national conscience in international relationships."[34]

The NSS contended that Americanism developed "only in a crusade against common difficulties." The frontier Americanized newcomers. The national army during the war served as the great Americanizer. For the postwar period, pioneers, frontiersmen, and crusaders could fight poverty, disease, ignorance, and injustice. Domestic tyranny and greed would replace foreign autocracy as democracy's enemy.[35]

Citizenship was defined within the framework of American democracy, or Americanism, and was bound up with duties called forth by the war. It was connected with social problems, notably the assimilation of immigrants. The NSS observed that at least thirteen million persons of foreign birth and thirty-three million with at least one parent of foreign birth lived in the United States, then a country of about one hundred million. More than a hundred languages and dialects were spoken; nearly sixteen hundred foreign-language newspapers appeared, with a circulation of almost eleven million. Five million persons were unable to speak English, and 40 percent of these people were illiterate. Three million unnaturalized persons of military age were in the country. About half a million foreign-born registrants between the ages of twenty-one and thirty-one could not understand military orders in English.[36]

The basis of the effort to Americanize the immigrant, according to the *NSS*, was therefore the English language, learning to speak and read English. Teachers were to work for "clear, clean, beautiful speech." The slogan was "one language and that the best!"[37]

Illiteracy increasingly became a target of the *NSS*. After the war the publication mounted a stay-in-school drive. Teachers were urged to make certain that children attended classes. The bulletin recommended intelligence tests for classification of students, similar to those given by the army. The *NSS* strove to give the best education to rich and poor alike. It opposed a "cultural" education for the well-to-do and a "practical" education for the less wealthy. Both types of education should be presented, so "that all should learn to work efficiently in some necessary, productive occupation, and that all should have the stimulus and inspiration which may come from an acquaintance with the best that the world has thought and felt and dreamed."[38]

In later years it would be remarked that many of the "new" immigrants brought a system of political ethics much different from the Yankee-Protestant tradition. Old-stock, native-born, middle-class Americans "assumed and demanded the constant, disinterested activity of the citizen in public affairs, argued that political life ought to be run, to a greater degree than it was, in accordance with general principles and abstract laws apart from [and] superior to personal needs." In this view the government sought to make individuals more moral, whereas economic life sought to develop character. Many immigrants were not accustomed to independent political action, being more familiar with a system that emphasized authority and hierarchy. They assumed that the individual's politics would come out of family needs, "interpreted political and civic relations chiefly in terms of personal obligations, and placed personal loyalties above allegiance to abstract codes of law and morals." These attitudes were understandable when one considered the struggle of immigrants merely to survive. Disinterested community service must have been difficult for newcomers to appreciate.[39] It was perhaps in this respect that the *NSS* contended that the two "sterling ideals" of true Americanism were "equality of opportunity and the spirit of obligation and service."[40]

It was hoped that assimilation would be facilitated by the abolition of immigrant colonies in America. Immigrants were expected to shed many of their Old World ways in order to fit into American life. Yet teachers were to show compassion for new arrivals and attempt to encourage love and respect for America and its institutions, so that the immigrant would want to settle here.[41] The *NSS* advocated welcoming the stranger, showing patience when immigrants mispronounced American words, taking time to escort immigrant children on walking trips to public buildings and other institutions of American life. Teachers were to educate the native born for "a more sympathetic and tolerant treatment of the foreign-born and their problems, for greater courtesy in dealing with them, and for the elimination of nicknames."[42] The *NSS* did not encourage hatred of the foreign born but tried to convert the newcomer to the American way.[43]

Community responsibility was a major feature of citizenship as defined by the *National School Service*. The bulletin attempted to submerge the individual within the community, defining freedom in terms of larger political and social obligation. The war would bring "a new consciousness of the meaning of citizenship," realization that "citizenship of the highest type is governed by good will and expressed in service." Ford in the first issue of the *NSS* emphasized service and the view that education in a democracy should never teach "private gain and individual excellence" as the measure of either education or success. He said that "only as each of us becomes part of a greater community can we expect success in war as in peace." Service presented the opportunity to become part of greater things.[44] After the Armistice teachers were told that peace did not mean victory for democracy, and education must continue to emphasize responsibilities of democratic government. "We are each of us going to have our victory over selfishness, over individualism," the first issue declared. "We must recognize . . . that getting out of the way of the Government and putting our lives, our means, and our power at the disposal of the Government, is now the duty that rests on every one of us." Every student was a part of a larger whole. If need be, the citizen must sacrifice his life.[45] "Wherever a child may live, however rich or poor his parents may be, whatever the occupation that he will enter, he is still a child of the Nation, a voter in embryo, a potential element of strength or of weakness in the future life of the Nation." An individual's duty to society, his obligation to the common good, increased in proportion to his resources and abilities.[46]

Part of the bulletin was given over to recommendations of activities that would teach community responsibility. Young children, it was noted, expressed citizenship primarily in service. During the war programs of collecting fruit pits for gas masks and buying war savings stamps were measures for victory. When peace returned, practical endeavors were to secure a worthy peace. Such activities acquainted children with American institutions, instilling respect, giving an idea of the duties of citizenship. Such activities were not intrusions on school work, Ford explained, but "unique opportunities" for service. During the war the Red Cross provided assistance to both American and Allied troops, and teachers were urged to instill this spirit of service. The *NSS* encouraged Junior Red Cross activities, such as making comfort kits, selling tinfoil to raise money, and knitting.[47] The Red Cross continued to provide much help. A special issue of the *Four Minute Men Bulletin* supplemented the *NSS* in November and sought to employ Junior Four Minute Men in behalf of the Red Cross Christmas Roll Call Contest. The contest tried for 100 percent membership in the Red Cross. The spirit of the Red Cross and the Christmas spirit were one and the same, teachers learned, and they were asked to teach this spirit as "a form of national service." Practical endeavors were suggested by the *NSS*: one issue listed more than forty good citizenship activities, from keeping the school grounds clean, to a campaign for clean speech, to helping save trees by exterminating the Tussoch moth.[48]

A further aspect of this discussion that deserves mention was the contrast drawn between Americanism and German authoritarianism. Articles on the latter were few, but made their point. German educational institutions were "nurseries of autocracy." German education prepared only the privileged for leadership—most people were educated to become "efficient, docile, and contented." Teachers were to reject this approach, to abandon the narrow, selfish variety of nationalism against which the war had been fought.[49] After the war ended the *NSS* showed similarities between German autocracy and Russian bolshevism. Both fed on hatred. "Clearly anything that smacks of terrorism must be banished from American methods of dealing with troublesome problems," the bulletin concluded.[50]

William Bagley had been interested in relating education to current events, and nearly every issue of *National School Service* started with an article on the war or, after the Armistice, the consequences of the war.[51] The opening issue began with "American Marines in France," detailing how German attacks had been repelled, machine gun nests cleared. It ended by describing the effect the presence of American occupation troops had on the enemy. Subsequent issues contained a "Personal Narrative of a Submarine Sinking" and articles explaining how "American Aviators Bomb Hun Airdromes" and how Germans used poison gas.[52]

The staff of the bulletin was aware of opportunities for using the war for patriotic instruction, especially in primary grades. "Here we have the children at the most impressionable age. . . . It is during these first years that right habits of thinking and acting are begun." It was a time when the bond between home and school was strongest.[53] Teachers of primary grades were to use the natural interest in the war. The sand table, it was observed, was one of the best ways of teaching the war spirit. Teachers were to let the war interest run its course and, if possible, give students ways for fuller expression. Many lessons could be taught by using the soldier as an example, as he was thought to be the child's ideal.[54]

Interest in the war allowed more sophisticated study among high school students. Geography was related to fighting. Maps prepared by the National Geographic Society encouraged students to connect the war to the geography of Europe. Students were asked to name Paris's eight natural defenses, or to describe the Paris basin.[55]

At the beginning of 1919, when the *National School Service* moved from the CPI to the Department of the Interior, teachers were asked to concentrate more on peace and reconstruction. Subsequent issues still offered lessons on "Why Great Britain Entered the War," "The War in 1915," "The Great War in 1916," and the war in 1917 and 1918.[56] These topics now were interspersed with articles on reconstructing society or on the League of Nations and the increase of international feeling.

There were lessons important to both wartime and postwar success, such as the need for thrift or the production and conservation of food and fuel. Use of resources with maximum efficiency was essential to a nation in a life-and-death struggle. F. A. Vanderlip, chairman of the War Savings Committee, argued that thrift was at the foundation of civilization. Thrift would strengthen the nation's character.[57] Making do with less would provide more money for the federal government. Students were asked to buy thrift stamps, war savings stamps, and war bonds and to encourage their parents to do the same.

The thirft theme continued after the war, and an entire issue of the *NSS* was devoted to it in March 1919. Whereas thrift during the war had the purpose of supplying money for victory, the aim after the fighting was "to change the United States from one of the greatest spendthrift nations into one of the greatest saving nations in the world, for the immediate benefit of every man, woman, and child in the country, and for the prospective benefit of future generations." Intelligent saving of money, wise expenditure, elimination of harmful waste—such would achieve the goal.[58]

Related to frugality was conservation and economical production of food, fuel, clothing, paper—even time. The Food and Fuel Administrations used the *NSS*. Teachers were told that conservation could be linked with the study of geography, in addition to composition, arithmetic, civics, history, industrial arts, and homemaking. The *NSS* promoted "Victory Mixed Flour," containing a 20 percent substitute for wheat. Sugar conservation was emphasized, because the war had drastically reduced the availability of that commodity in England, France, and Italy.[59] The Fuel Administration supplied the *National School Service* with ways to conserve coal and gas: cooking with a clean range, wearing warmer clothing, and keeping rooms at lower temperature and higher humidity.[60]

Food conservation continued in the postwar period—the December 1 issue of the *NSS* was devoted to the theme "Food will win the world." America was obligated to save Europe, including the peoples of the Central Powers, from famine. As President Wilson told Congress on November 11, 1918, "Hunger does not breed reform: it breeds madness and all the ugly distempers that make an ordered life impossible."[61]

The connection among health, community sanitation, and winning the war was obvious. A nation of healthy individuals stood a better chance of victory. The *National School Service* recognized the importance of public health, brought home by the many physical defects discovered among men called to military service. The bulletin championed physical improvement as an essential of national defense. Taking health "out of the field of merely personal concern" and making it "a duty one owes to the nation" would aid the effort to create hygienic habits. Health care would instill pride in young pupils and provide a chance to "lift the pettiest detail into dignity." It would have permanent effects upon conduct.[62] High school and college instructors were informed that the War Department approved of athletic competition during the war, provided it did not involve practice and trips that would interfere with academic and military training.[63] The *NSS* also tried to check the outbreak of Spanish influenza in the autumn of 1918. Taking advantage of nationwide interest in the disease, it told teachers to make the most of this exceptional opportunity to inform students how other illnesses were spread in a similar manner—tuberculosis, diphtheria, whooping cough, the common cold.[64]

Hygienic habits had been part of Bagley's theory of education. In 1905 he had argued that they were "the balance wheels of civilization." He contended that "there is no sterner duty laid upon the teacher than the development of these habits and ideals." The task required vigilance on the part of the instructor. Filth produced filth, materially and mentally. Poor standards of health, coupled with the sexual impulse in developing youth, threatened civilization.[65] Only the school and education stood as guardians. Public health was increasingly important in the postwar period, and teachers and pupils were encouraged to become "modern health crusaders."[66] Thrift, conservation, and concern over public health would aid in winning the war, and once fighting stopped they would promote a better world.

One part of society drew the special interest of the *National School Service*: rural America, still relatively isolated in 1918 and 1919, the illiteracy rate high, its teachers poorly prepared. It was estimated that more than half of the country's children attended village or rural schools. Through the *NSS*, Bagley hoped to change "these lonely outposts of culture" into "strategic centers of national life and national idealism."[67] Alice Florer, the rural school inspector and assistant superintendent in Lincoln, Nebraska, showed early interest in developing a program of rural education. She had proposed "a National rural school course of study" in August 1918 and was appointed to the bulletin's editorial advisory board in hope that she would offer advice.[68] From the beginning the *NSS* attempted more than the organization of rural life for war; it also sought the "permanent upbuilding of country life."[69] The *National School Service* set out a plan that sought to draw rural America into national life, and the community council was the instrument through which such development was to occur.

The Council of National Defense recommended local community councils of defense as the best way of organizing country communities and, through the *NSS*, suggested ways to establish the councils. The most thorough way to organize local rural communities was on a county basis. A county war conference of county officials and heads of county organizations should be called, and the county superintendent of schools and the chairman of the county council of defense were to take the initiative. The conference would divide the county into subdistricts that might, though were not required to, coincide with school districts. As many as four persons, usually including the rural schoolteacher, would serve as a local organization committee. After the county organization, a committee in each locality would set up a war conference, perhaps at the schoolhouse. Such a meeting would bring results if it considered some large issue, such as the Liberty Loan campaign. The conference would encourage a patriotic spirit among children and adults. For communities already organized, the *NSS* recommended a federation of their clubs into a community council.

There followed a detailed plan for the organizational meeting. It was suggested that some prominent local official address the local community council meetings on the war responsibilities of rural areas. The audience should elect a community council of defense, composed of three officers—chairman, vice-chairman, and secretary-treasurer. The rural teacher, preferably, would serve as secretary-treasurer and would submit reports to the county council and county women's division. The secretary-treasurer would receive literature from the CPI and other agencies, serving as a contact between rural areas and the federal government. Further committees were to be avoided. Community councils were to plan a yearly program of war-related activities. Themes for rural America were "food production, food conservation, thrift and bonds, Red Cross work, fuel conservation, child welfare, and patriotism and Americanization." Good health habits were also to be emphasized. Women should head at least three of these campaigns—food conservation, child welfare, and Red Cross work. Each leader would be responsible for informing community councils of progress. Community councils were to meet perhaps every two weeks and during busy periods once a month. Though the rural social structure was simple, through a single organization like the community council war enthusiasm could be given purpose and perhaps contribute to the permanent improvement of rural life.[70] President Wilson was enthusiastic about the creation of community councils, believing that when carried out they would weld the nation together "as no nation of great size has ever been welded before." Each citizen would be "touched with the inspiration of the common cause."[71]

In the postwar period the *National School Service* tried to promote the League of Nations. Internationalism based on "the continuance of national states" now had a greater chance for success than had any previous effort at European or world unity. The reason was the breakdown of national isolation, which had resulted from new social and economic conditions. Every nation was part of world order, even though political organization had not kept pace. Railroads, telegraph lines, and national interdependence in industry and commerce were drawing nations together. A League of Nations would ensure peace; it was the only sure way to prevent an arms race that would result in development of weapons to the point where, the *NSS* added prophetically, "the present war will be only a pale image of the yet more terrible struggles to come." An international frame of mind did not mean repudiation of Americanism. "The establishment of the League of Nations will not lessen in any degree the duty of the school to inculcate sound American ideals." As Secretary of the Interior Lane explained, America's international value would depend on unity, national strength, vision.[72] Americans were a model for the world. There was a world trend toward self-government and democracy, and Americans were "privileged to live under a government that most nearly approaches the ideal."[73]

IN the final analysis the *National School Service* should not be judged by later standards. It came out of an educational system in which national loyalty was fashionable. Shortly after the war, Ford said that "no group more loyally responded to the call from Washington" than did the public schoolteachers, and "their effort was no small part in the unanimity of national feeling."[74] Teachers and their administrators willingly embraced the national cause, and although one has no way of knowing the extent to which they used the *NSS*, given the enthusiastic approval it received from educational leaders one is probably safe in assuming that its use was widespread. Had teachers and administrators been more restrained in their enthusiasm, the ability of the federal government to use public schools for its own ends would have been impaired.

The bulletin sought to organize the enthusiasm already

present in the schools, and it also presented a blueprint for using public education to nationalize American life. Such a plan no doubt improved the quality of education, particularly in rural and isolated schools, thereby helping to create a better-educated citizenry, an essential element in a democratic society. The *NSS* also sought to promote community service, teaching that in a modern, complex society the political freedom inherent in democratic government required turning away from the laissez faire individualism of the frontier. The publication's goal was perhaps best summarized by Carl Becker, who wrote for the CPI in another capacity, when he said that "the chief purpose of free education in a democratic society is to make good citizens rather than good scholars."[75]

However well intentioned these ideas may have been, though, they had disturbing implications for democracy. By defining political freedom in terms of community service, by promoting Americanism as a national ideology, the bulletin perhaps lost sight of democratic individualism and opened the possibility of submerging the individual in the will of the state. Within the bulletin's efforts to protect democracy were attitudes potentially capable of undermining individual liberty.[76]

Nationalism's darker side and its implications for democracy had not, however, been fully seen. If there was danger in such a publication as the *National School Service*, with its glorification of the nation and its championing of a martial spirit (especially in the autumn of 1918), the bulletin did have a constructive side. The concern for defining citizenship in terms of community service, for creating "a nation of noble men" as one educator urged,[77] derived not just from the war but from the problems of immigration, from the other social injustices of modern life, from a vague awareness of the challenges already being made against democratic theory.[78] The *National School Service* tried to offer a program to meet these problems and must be considered not only as war propaganda but as part of the reform literature of its day.

7

Public Speakers and the CPI

> Men and nations are at their worst or at best in any great
> struggle. The spoken word may light the fires of passion
> or it may inspire to highest action and noblest sacrifice a
> nation of free men.
>   —Woodrow Wilson[1]

THE SPOKEN WORD has always been a powerful
means of arousing emotion, and the Committee on Public
Information used it to mobilize the nation in 1917–18. The
CPI recognized that there were tens of thousands—perhaps
millions—of Americans who either could not or would not
read. How to reach those "vacant minds"?[2] If only the CPI
could have advanced the clock just a few short years, into the
early twenties, it could have used that marvelous channel for
public wisdom, the radio. There was no radio in 1917–18, and
so it was necessary to set up a network of speakers to cover
the country, to talk in halls and auditoriums and, generally,
wherever audiences could be collected.

By the end of the war the CPI had sent speakers into the
remotest regions, and hardly an American of adult age, or any
age, had not heard them. An organization known as the Four
Minute Men grew so rapidly that Creel likened it to a prairie
fire. From 2,500 speakers in July 1917, it increased to 15,000
by November; by September 1918, there were 40,000. By the
end of the year, when it disbanded, the figure was 74,500.[3] In
Illinois alone, at the time of the Armistice, 2,800 Four Minute
Men were speaking each week to 800,000 people. In Chicago
during the war, 451 speakers gave 50,000 talks to an estimated
25 million Americans.[4] By the end of 1918, Four Minute Men
had reached into all the states and Alaska, the Canal Zone,

Guam, Hawaii, Puerto Rico, and even Samoa.[5] In all, nearly a million four-minute speeches were given to perhaps 400 million people. And the speeches were "no haphazard talks by nondescripts, but the careful, studied, and rehearsed efforts of the *best* men in each community, each speech aimed as a rifle is aimed, and driving to its mark with the precision of a bullet."[6]

A second group of speakers, organized in what was called the Speaking Division, sometimes referred to as the "Four Hour Men," was less centrally controlled but provided the country with many inspiring speakers. It arranged speaking tours for such diverse people as Jane Addams, Charles Edward Russell, and a young French lieutenant, Paul Périgord. The influence this bureau exercised over its speakers came mainly through the state councils of defense.[7]

THE idea of the Four Minute Men originated in Chicago, where in March 1917 a group of young businessmen, following a suggestion by Senator Medill McCormick, formed a patriotic committee. They proposed to send speakers, preferably young men aged nineteen or twenty, into the city's motion-picture theaters to explain the Chamberlain bill, which called for universal military training. Donald Ryerson was president of this organization, which on April 28, 1917, incorporated under a state charter as the Four Minute Men of Illinois. The name was taken in part from the minutemen of the Revolutionary War, and in part from the time limit imposed on the speakers. Ryerson gave the first speech at the city's Strand Theater in early April.[8]

After the declaration of war, Ryerson went to Washington to gain information about the details of the Selective Service law and saw officials of the Committee on Public Information. At this time the CPI was in cramped quarters in the Department of the Navy's library. It was there that Ryerson met Creel, or, more accurately, cornered him in a crowded hallway and told him of the volunteer organization in Chicago. Within ten minutes, Creel decided to create a national program based on the Chicago plan and appointed Ryerson director. The latter returned to Chicago to set up headquarters. For each campaign his speakers undertook for the CPI, he agreed to prepare an illustrated speech and submit it to Creel for approval.[9]

The chairman of the CPI was aware of the danger of sending out large numbers of speakers to exhort their fellow citizens on behalf of the government. He realized that control over their utterances would be difficult, and he determined to ensure that the government's message was presented accurately. He managed to do it in two ways—through organization and through bulletins from the division's headquarters.

During the war the national organization of the Four Minute Men passed through a series of changes.[10] Headquarters moved to Washington in May 1917.[11] Shortly thereafter, Ryerson resigned as director to enter the navy and was succeeded by William McCormick Blair, also of Chicago. Blair directed the Four Minute Men for fourteen months and oversaw the division's major development. William H. Ingersoll replaced Blair as national director when the latter entered the army.[12]

As the organization expanded, Ernest T. Gundlach of Chicago became assistant director and editor of bulletins. In late January 1918, W. Curtis Nicholson took charge of the Four Minute Men in the South. Thomas J. Meek of Chicago headed the central states. Philip Lyndon Dodge, in mid-February 1918, took over the East. Bertram S. Nelson served as associate national director, resigning in the spring of 1918; he continued to serve as a member of the Four Minute Men Advisory Council. Nelson had made a specialty of the four-minute address and spent nearly all his time visiting local organizations. He held classes in every state east of the Mississippi River. Blair estimated that he met more Four Minute Men than anyone else connected with the division.[13] Nelson believed that an important function of the organization was to serve as a large correspondence school, and according to his own appraisal it was the greatest force for direct and effective public speaking this country had ever known.[14]

Beginning in December 1917, the division had a National Advisory Council, of which a notable member was Solomon H. Clark, head of the department of public speaking at the University of Chicago. Clark had helped coach the city's four-minute speakers. He was a believer in the speaking programs undertaken by the CPI—two sons were in France—and did much speaking both for the Four Minute Men and for the Speaking Division, especially in the western United States. He was a forceful talker; people who heard him in California compared him with Hiram Johnson. In the spring of 1918, he spoke in almost every state west of the Mississippi—108 speeches in 40 cities in 16 states. He sent frank reports on local Four Minute Men leaders.[15] Clark was enthusiastic about the program: its influence, he believed, was greater than that of the newspaper press. The primary purpose was educational, but it could help the government with the Liberty Loan, the Red Cross, and food conservation.[16]

The original plan for Four Minute Men had called for a regional organization according to the federal reserve districts, but the CPI eventually organized speakers by states. Blair appointed several state chairmen, who cooperated with state councils of defense, chambers of commerce, and public safety committees. Where chairmen were not appointed, the CPI worked through state councils of defense. Usually governors were asked to nominate directors, and the organization of speakers was combined with the work of the state councils.[17]

The state chairman appointed leaders at county, city, or town levels. To set up a local unit at first required three prominent citizens (a lawyer, a businessman, and a banker). Using their own stationery, the three would submit the name of a chairman to the national director.[18] Eventually, chairmen of states or even counties did the nominating. Local chairmen were registered in Washington, took an oath, and obtained documents confirming their appointments. Many local chairmen were given the privilege of using a government frank—about one third of the nearly seventy-five hundred local chairmen were considered trustworthy enough to have this privilege.[19] Chairmen chose speakers, drew up schedules, and generally took responsibility for arrangements. Occasionally a chairman would have a staff—the St. Louis chairman had a staff of nine.[20]

In addition to the staff of a county or city or town unit, an executive committee helped with the planning and a speaker's committee evaluated speakers. There usually was a theater committee that included a theater manager. Some units, especially in larger cities, had other committees; the Chicago organization had committees on public schools, publicity, and speakers' conferences and subcommittees on labor unions, amusement parks, conventions, and churches.[21] Many units had women's auxiliaries, to furnish speakers at women's clubs and theater matinees. Several units had black departments. There were language sections; in New York City ten men specialized in Yiddish and seven in Italian. In New York about one hundred speakers were expert in Four Minute singing.[22] New York City had nearly sixteen hundred Four Minute Men, and it was estimated that they spoke to almost a half million people each week.[23] Generally, expenses incurred by local units were borne by the speakers, and Creel estimated that the total cost for all local units, including travel, was only about two million dollars.[24]

The Four Minute Men proved extraordinarily successful for perhaps three reasons—the use of voluntary local speakers, the ability to use ready-made audiences, and a tight control from national headquarters in Washington. Nearly every one of the Four Minute Men was chosen from his own area, although there were a few national figures, such as President Wilson, who prepared a four-minute speech for the Fourth of July 1918, to be given by proxy by some thirty-five thousand speakers across the United States.[25] Former President Roosevelt, Secretary of the Interior Lane, and Secretary of the Treasury William G. McAdoo were Four Minute Men. Honus Wagner, the baseball player, spoke in Carnegie, Pennsylvania.[26] As a rule, though, the Four Minute Men spoke in their localities. The truly important work of the division's organization was the selection, preparation, and control of these individuals. A rigorous effort was made to find the best speakers. Local chairmen were told to select men who above all else were good speakers but who also would obey instructions from national headquarters. A poor speaker was considered worse than none.

8. Woodrow Wilson Delivering Address at Mount Vernon, July 4, 1918. To Wilson's immediate left, George Creel; to Creel's left, Mrs. Wilson; to Wilson's right, in the white suit, Secretary of State Robert Lansing
(Courtesy of the Library of Congress)

9. Four Minute Men in New York for Liberty Loan Drive
(Courtesy of the National Archives, photo no. 165-WW-134-42)

Local chairmen were urged to check Four Minute Men regularly on delivery, message, and observance of the four-minute time limit.[27]

The backgrounds of Four Minute Men were diverse, for it was decided to seek out not so much a cross-section of a community as its leaders. Business and professional men were likely to be chosen. The speaker's greatest asset was sincerity—a sincerity highlighted by the fact that he usually was unpaid. Early in the war, when Ryerson was seeking to have his speakers explain universal military service, it was thought best to have young men. As the program expanded, age became less important, and ages ranged from seventeen to eighty, with most of the speakers being between forty and fifty.[28]

If picking volunteer local speakers was important, so was the existence of ready-made audiences. The division relied on motion-picture theaters across the country. The government secured an endorsement from the national organization of theater owners, making the Four Minute Men the only authorized agents to speak for the government in the theaters. Creel opposed allowing individuals not associated with the division to give four-minute talks, lest they confuse the government's message.[29] Theaters provided the largest single audience for the Four Minute Men, as millions of people undoubtedly attended movies each week even in 1917 and 1918. Four Minute Men spoke at the changing of reels or after the film, whichever time was deemed best.[30]

The third factor in the success of the Four Minute Men was that each speech was closely controlled by Washington.[31] Speakers were expected to follow instructions. Talks were to take four minutes and no longer, and chairmen were told to remove speakers who did not observe the limit.[32] Holding the stage for a longer period was a breach of the contract with the theater managers. Speakers were expected to arrive at the theater in ample time, to take the platform promptly, and to leave it as promptly. Analysis of the local audience would determine the best moment for the speaker. Chairmen were urged not to keep assigning the same man to the same theater—he should speak no more than twice in the same theater on the same subject each week. When questions came from the audience, speakers were instructed either to ignore them or to respond that they did not have time to answer. Contention with theater managers was to be avoided, even if it meant canceling a speech. Bulletins from division headquarters covering campaign topics were sent to local chairmen several days in advance and were to be distributed to each speaker; he was expected to read them and prepare his speech from them. Chairmen were expected to inform speakers of other publications from the CPI, so that material could be incorporated. Finally, speakers were especially encouraged to write out or memorize their concluding remarks, so that each speech contained a suitable peroration.[33]

Four Minute Men Bulletins from Washington standardized the talks so that each speaker across the country would cover the same topic at the same time. More than forty bulletins were published, nearly all edited by Ford, each covering a topic and giving information from which the speaker was to prepare his talk.[34] The bulletins included sample speeches. *Four Minute Men News*, also put out by the division, supplemented information in the bulletins.

Though ideas found in the bulletins varied from campaign to campaign, many of them complemented the themes found in other CPI literature. Bulletins were devoted to "The Danger to Democracy" or "The Danger to America," or discussed the Monroe Doctrine, or otherwise justified intervention abroad. Speakers were referred to Notestein and Stoll's *Conquest and Kultur* and were told that isolation was an illusion; America either fought Germany with allies or would have to fight later on the enemy's terms.[35] The American past was "the beacon light" for mankind. By sending an army to Europe the United States was "living true to this country's traditions."[36] Concerning the Monroe Doctrine, it was pointed out that German actions had challenged it. Americans would tolerate "no further extension of that system of government which so essentially differs from that of free countries." Speakers spread the message that President Wilson was seeking a Monroe Doctrine for the world.[37]

Four Minute Men Bulletins not merely justified intervention but sought to define the meaning of the war. "The Meaning of America," used during the first weeks of July 1918, explained what Blair referred to as "vital truths."[38] It tried to give speakers more than the usual "avalanche of platitudes" about patriotism, furnishing them with "striking facts" and "fresh viewpoints." Speakers were urged to use tact in referring to wartime allies. America was not the leader of the allies, nor anything more than a comrade in arms.[39] Speakers were not only to trace America's history to English sources, but to tell how France had been a leader of civilization—how, say, Montesquieu's ideas had been the basis for the Constitution.[40] They were to emphasize that democracy depended on education to equalize opportunity. They also supported universal suffrage. Whatever restrictions the war might have placed on individual freedom, it was "laying foundations for greater, better democracy," with "new conceptions of property rights and communal duties."[41]

Speakers were warned about dealing with the foreign born. They were to avoid patronizing attitudes: any appeal to "new Americans," any call to meet responsibilities as citizens, was to be balanced by a similar appeal to native Americans. The oath of loyalty, however, meant giving up allegiance to any former country. Inward loyalty was wanted—"America must come first in your inner heart." The United States required "courageous devotion" and "a spirit of self-sacrifice."[42]

Appeals were made to win the support of blacks. Liberia had declared war on Germany. The bulletin pointed out that Germany was no place for blacks, because the kaiser favored slavery. Ministers of black churches were asked to remind their parishioners that every American "must be especially loyal, especially obedient to the laws, and especially orderly."[43] The American army provided opportunity for blacks—more than a thousand men had won commissions. The bulletin proclaimed, somewhat optimistically, that "a result of this war will be a wonderful amalgamation of the races within America."[44]

Occasionally, bulletins would explain new legislation in Washington. In March 1918 the division arranged for thousands of speakers to talk on "The Income Tax: An Answer to the Question: Is This a Capitalists' War?" Blair asserted in a bulletin that rather than making money on the war, the rich and the big industries were losing, and willingly so because America's future was at stake. The bulletin explained how the tax worked. It was not to drain the rich but was "a new concept of society," founded on the "copartnership of mankind, a certain vague sense of the brotherhood of man."[45]

Late in the war the division sent out a bulletin about fire prevention. Loss from fire was many times higher in the United States than in any other country—some fifteen hundred buildings were damaged every day, and more than three out of four fire losses were preventable. Speakers were to discuss the danger of spontaneous combustion and to stress that every American had to exercise "personal responsibility." Increased care would safeguard natural and acquired resources, dollars and lives that could be used for war service.[46]

The variety of subjects treated in the bulletins, and dealt with by the speakers, was extraordinary. The initial bulletin, written by Waldo P. Warren and printed in Chicago, concerned the First Liberty Loan, oversubscribed by more than half, thanks in part to the Four Minute Men. Later issues concerned subsequent loan drives. For the Third Liberty Loan a short sermon was suggested for clergymen.[47] Bulletins were for the Red Cross, food conservation, "morals and morale," war savings stamps, binoculars for the navy, registering men under Selective Service, and so on. One bulletin, "Where Did You Get Your Facts?" emphasized the use of reliable information in the four-minute talks.[48]

One fascinating aspect of the division's work was the manner in which it instructed speakers not only in what to say but in how to say it. Creel denied that the CPI ever made an appeal to the emotions; but speakers were told that if appeals were made to emotion they must be based on truth, and emotional appeals were an important part of the Four Minute Man's strategy.[49] Unsubstantiated atrocity stories were discouraged, as were appeals to hatred. "Words evaporate" but "facts remain," speakers were told, and they were urged to "inspire, not inflame."[50] As the war continued, however, the division encouraged atrocity stories through the *Four Minute Men Bulletin*. Four Minute Men were told to appeal to fear, "an important element to be bred in the civilian population. It is difficult to unite a people by talking only on the highest ethical plane. To fight for an ideal, perhaps, must be coupled with thoughts of self-preservation." In the drive to sell war savings stamps, Four Minute Men were given a speech about Prussian brutality:

Prussian "Schrecklichkeit" (the deliberate policy of terrorism) leads to almost unbelievable besotten brutality. The German soldiers—their letters are reprinted—were often forced against their wills, they themselves weeping, to carry out unspeakable orders against defenseless old men, women, and children, so that "*respect*" might grow for German "efficiency." For instance, at Dinant the wives and children of 40 men were forced to witness the execution of their husbands and fathers.

Now, then, do you want to take the *slightest* chance of meeting Prussianism here in America?[51]

Appeals were made to idealism, with the claim that it was a war to end war. A proposed speech for the Fourth Liberty Loan drew on the Biblical verse "For what doth it profit a man to gain the whole world and lose his soul?" (Mark viii, 36):

At this supreme moment in the world's history when all that men have dreamed or dared for the building of Christian civilization is put to the jeopard, our Government is saying to us: "Take your money and buy honor and chivalry, liberty and love." Which do you want most, things which can be measured and marketed and will pass away with the using, or the unseen things which are the eternal values? Which will you feed, the body or the soul?[52]

Never was there any doubt as to the justice of America's cause:

Every now and then I hear a man say, "Sure, I am for the war." And he adds, "Our country, right or wrong."

That man does not seem to understand that in the great struggle our country *is* right, supremely right, overwhelmingly right, sacredly right.[53]

So many people wished to speak about the war—people other than the 74,500 Four Minute Men—that it proved necessary to organize the volunteers in a Speaking Division of the CPI, and so this second division was created on September 25,

1917.[54] Arthur E. Bestor, president of the Chautauqua Institution, was put in charge.[55] Bestor believed that the Great War was different from previous conflicts because it involved more than armies—it engulfed nations. The mobilization of public opinion, he believed, required an awkward change in the pattern of individual lives. "In a democracy like ours, steeped in a *laissez faire* individualism, it necessitates a complete reorganization of our life and putting aside some ideals and many controversies which have always seemed to us supremely important."[56]

Bestor retained his Chautauqua position, maintaining a secretary at his own expense to care for that institution's business.[57] During the summer of 1917, when he also was secretary of the Committee on Patriotism through Education of the National Security League, he had hoped to turn the Chautauqua into a "dynamo" of patriotic propaganda.[58] Chautauqua, he thought, had "made no larger contribution than to patriotic nationalism." He was proud that Chautauqua had helped unify America and had always seemed slightly ahead of public opinion in regard to "new plans of social amelioration, religious tolerance, and the socialization of the state." The United States needed "a moral and spiritual dynamic," and he felt that Chautauqua could help "in making up the mind and actuating the effort of the nation."[59]

Bestor received assistance from Byron W. Shimp, who as secretary handled much of the new division's correspondence. J. J. Pettijohn became associate director of the division in May 1918. Bestor was head of the Speaking Division until it merged with the Four Minute Men on September 1, 1918, but was absent during the summer of 1918, and Pettijohn took charge. After the merger with the Four Minute Men, Pettijohn became associate director of that division. Thomas F. Moran of Purdue University assisted the Speaking Division between January and April 1918, editing bulletins and delivering thirty-four addresses. He was particularly effective in speaking before southern war conferences.[60]

An Advisory Committee from government and nongovernment organizations assisted Bestor. Members pledged to put the war above any other goal, agreeing that they would make a national effort to carry on speaking campaigns or obtain audiences for such campaigns.[61]

The Speaking Division sought to fulfill requests for speakers of broad reputation and attempted to route these speakers through the country as representatives of government departments or allied countries. It sought to be a clearinghouse for campaigns, avoiding overlapping of territory and duplication of effort, and standing as the arbiter when more than one organization made demands on a speaker's time.[62] Speakers as a rule were not paid. The division took care only of traveling expense, usually ten dollars per day. Many times the expense was borne by the state or local organization to which the speech was given.

Bestor himself gave more than fifty addresses. He viewed the war as a struggle against the idea of divine right of kings, against militarism, against the idea that might makes right.[63] He believed that the country's educational institutions should help mobilize public opinion, and his speeches almost always dealt with the CPI's effort in this direction: his usual topic was "America and the War" or "The War and the Making of Public Opinion." A moderate orator, he often would end somewhat unoriginally, if effectively, by paraphrasing Lincoln: "With malice toward none, with charity for all, with firmness in the right, as God gives us to see the right, let us continue the work that has been given us to do."[64]

Prominent officials were sent out by the division. Vice-President Thomas R. Marshall, a noted wit and reconteur, headed the list, together with Secretaries Baker, McAdoo, David Houston, Lane, and William C. Redfield. Bestor was reluctant to bother cabinet members, saving his influence to secure their services for such occasions as war conferences.[65] Other figures included Senators William S. Kenyon and Knute Nelson; Carl Vrooman, assistant secretary of agriculture; Joseph E. Grew and Wesley Frost of the State Department; Vernon Kellogg and Frederic C. Walcott of the Food Administration; and Anna Shaw and Ida Tarbell of the Woman's Committee of the Council of National Defense.

Solomon Clark was a regular speaker for Bestor's division; he was probably an effective talker, certainly an opinionated one. He delivered nearly twenty speeches in four western states in conjunction with the Four Minute Men. Clark wanted the CPI to refute the antiwar ideas of Senator Robert M. La Follette, and was even willing to debate the senator "to drive him out of his present position." He was convinced that the public schools had failed to present war propaganda to students, and he offered an elaborate plan to improve the situation. He wanted to make CPI pamphlets compulsory reading for teachers and principals, with teachers required to take exams on their reading. Pupils should be tested on war-related material, with nothing less than a grade of 80 percent acceptable for passing. Speaker training was another of Clark's projects, and he urged the CPI to exercise a careful control over speakers.[66] On a speaking tour of the West he watched the work of the Four Minute Men, and by the time he reached California he was bored with the typical war speech, "tired of the 'Hun' stuff, and the Lusitania, and the raping of the Belgium women." He recommended a different approach, with emphasis on reasons for American entry into the war, legal and otherwise, and on Germany's goal of world domination. Greater use should be made of documentary evidence. German cruelty should be discussed, but not for its own sake.[67]

Despite her opposition to the war, Jane Addams spoke under the division's auspices, undertaking a tour for the Food Administration in early 1918. After President Wilson's speech on the Fourteen Points, on January 8, 1918, she wrote Bestor that she was "quite eager" to accept an invitation. Bestor had heard her speak for the Food Administration in Long Beach, New York, the previous May, and recommended her to Creel. In February she spoke at Cornell University and in early March to the City Club of Cleveland. A few days later she was addressing Food Administration representatives in New Orleans; from there she traveled to El Paso and then on to California.[68] She thought that by speaking for the Food Administration, stressing the need for conservation so as to feed the world's hungry, she might help the cause of world organization. Attempts at internationalism in the past had failed, she said, because "there was nothing upon which to focus scattered moral energies and to make operative a new moral ideal." The work had centered on the negative ideal of preventing war. Her efforts for the Food Administration, in behalf of economic and social needs, could in some way provide a positive incentive.[69]

The noted socialist Charles Edward Russell gave fifty-eight addresses for the Speaking Division between October 1917 and February 1918. He was particularly effective before labor audiences. A member of the President's Commission to Russia, he had urged Creel to make a much greater propaganda effort there.[70] His speeches exhibited an intense nationalism. Before the Union League Club of New York, on August 15, 1917, he spoke of disloyalty in Congress and called for "absolute union, absolute standing together, and absolute spirit of sacrifice to the last drop of blood if . . . necessary." The American Republic was more than a geographic expression—it was "a living creed."[71] He had been expelled from the Socialist party because of his support of the war. He did not consider war service a betrayal of socialist principles, however, but saw the possibility of reform as a result of the struggle.[72] Early in 1918, he attacked German socialists for having supported their country so enthusiastically. He believed that the war was bringing a great spiritual uprising to the world but that, if socialism were to make headway in the United States, it would have to be stripped of its German garb. The war had broken a way through barriers that had blocked social reform and had shown that industrial democracy was "a nearly attainable goal."[73]

Some of Russell's utterances were among the most inflammatory of those of any speaker associated with the CPI. Before a mass meeting of the American Alliance for Labor and Democracy he charged that traitors and pacifists, aided by Senators A. J. Gronna, William J. Stone, and Robert M. La Follette, and by German propaganda, had ended the Russian government's participation in the war.[74] In a speech in Madison, Wisconsin, he suggested a petition to remove La Follette.[75] Before the Union League Club in New York City he accused one senator of treason:

Disloyal American, disloyal American that disgraces the Congress of the United States, traitor in disguise that has taken the oath of allegiance and goes to the Senate of the United States to do the dirty work of the Kaiser, oh, could I have taken you by the throat, and dragged you to Petrograd to put you up there in the Field of Mars on a Sunday afternoon and let you see the results of your work! For then you would have seen the miserable, fawning, slimy creatures that take the dirty money of Germany, some of them—ashamed I am to tell you of it, some of them with American passports in their pockets. You would have seen them going from crowd to crowd upon that field and repeating your words of treason, quoting you, quoting what you say in the Senate of the United States; when you introduce a resolution in Congress looking towards a peace conference, within three weeks those words will be repeated upon the Field of Mars, and they will be quoted in this way.[76]

Russell's speeches seem to have received a mixed reaction. In Cleveland he spoke to one of the largest crowds in the history of the Cleveland Advertising Club and made a good impression. He accompanied some visiting French speakers, the Marquis and Marquise de Courtivron and the Marquis and Marquise de Polignac, on an extensive tour of the South. In Paducah, Kentucky, he spoke to overflow crowds, and at least one observer reported that his talk "was in no way overdrawn." An observer in Des Moines was more enthusiastic, comparing Russell's "forceful stage presence and dramatic instinct" with that of the Reverend Billy Sunday. CPI authorities seem to have been pleased. But some residents of Nashville, Tennessee, urged Bestor not to send him out, and Creel on one occasion considered disapproving a speaking engagement for Russell in Bismarck, North Dakota. His attacks on members of Congress may have been one of the reasons why the House eventually cut the CPI's appropriation.[77]

The former American consul at Queenstown, Wesley Frost, was particularly impressive as a speaker for Bestor's division. In his official capacity he had reported eighty-one submarine sinkings. He spoke in twenty-nine states and delivered more than sixty speeches, usually before Chambers of Commerce and Rotary clubs. He was effective in describing the sinking of the *Lusitania*. It was almost as if he had been there:

It was quite black out there on the Atlantic, and in the blackness the lifeboats alternately rose on the crests of the waves and sank into the black valley between. The boats carried women and children whose hair hung in icicles over their shoulders and their half-frozen bodies yielded to the rolling and pitching of the frail boats. Now and then a half-dead passenger uttered a shriek of pain or of anguish as she realized that a friend or relative had died in her arms. Meanwhile, in the dark hull of the German submarine, the captain watching through the periscope finally turned his head away. Even this man, agent of Prussian cruelty, had witnessed a scene upon which he did not care to gaze.[78]

The Speaking Division arranged tours for notable foreigners, such as members of the British War Mission, the French High Commission, and the Italian Embassy in Washington. Bestor believed that men in uniform could be effective speakers and sought to secure British and French combat soldiers. He insisted that the British officers be still in military service, but in the case of wounded British soldiers this proved impossible: British custom was that they be honorably discharged and no longer draw pay. The British soldiers generally charged high fees. Sergeant Guy Empey, who had written the best-selling novel *Over the Top*, asked for half the admission receipts, which guaranteed him $750 an address, or else a flat $1,000— his fee was far above what representatives of the Speaking Division usually obtained. The division scheduled such military groups as the French Blue Devils and some 344 Belgian soldiers returning from Russia.[79]

By most accounts, one of the most inspiring and magnetic of all the war speakers was the young French Lieutenant Paul Périgord. Creel described him as having been "blessed with a voice like an organ" and told General Pershing that of all the speakers associated with the CPI, Périgord was the most effective.[80] The lieutenant was a Roman Catholic priest. He had studied at several American universities, including Columbia and Harvard, and had taken a masters' degree at the University of Chicago. His teacher at Chicago, Albion W. Small, met Périgord in the summer of 1910 and was immediately impressed— the only word he could think of to describe the face of this priest-soldier was "spectral." It was a face Small associated with Savonarola and Francis of Assisi.[81] Périgord was lent to the United States by the French High Commission and in seven months made 152 addresses under the auspices of the Speaking Division.[82]

Most people who heard Périgord were moved by such stories as that of the French boys at Verdun. Some six thousand young men, aged eighteen to twenty-four, he said, defended the fortress against the armies of the German crown prince, who wanted to capture it on Bastille Day. Fortunately, before the young men went into battle they received a blessing from Périgord.

About nine o'clock on the morning of July 13 the first unit of the German attack charged up the hill of Verdun; but we charged down on them and drove them back. At noon a new unit charged; and the boys drove them back also. At three o'clock a fresh unit charged; and the boys were so tired that an entire German company entered the ditches of the fort. Then our General sent for me, and he said, "What shall we do? The reserves cannot come until five o'clock, and the Germans are in the ditches of the fort." I said: "You come see the boys, General; they are all ready to die for France, and France can ask no more of her sons. Let us charge once more."

So we charged down the hill, and we took the German company prisoners, those whom we did not kill; and at five o'clock the reserves came, and the city of Verdun was forever saved.

So the Crown Prince, who had his mail sent to Verdun, had to have it sent back again, with the notice, "Has not yet arrived!" But of the six thousand boys who received my blessing that morning only fifteen hundred were left; and the first thing they did was to ask for a thanksgiving service, kneeling down there, because their lives had been spared. And yet people sometimes say that France is a faithless nation![83]

Few individuals did more than Périgord to create a bond between France and the United States. The imagery of his speeches was vivid. France, he told Americans, had mobilized seven million men; had the United States equally mobilized its men, almost eighteen million would have been called. Of those seven million Frenchmen, fourteen hundred thousand had been killed. "Should these dead pass across the stage, four abreast, and marching at regular military gait, it would take them twelve days and twelve nights to pass by."[84]

Controlling speakers was a serious problem, and there were efforts to provide speakers with information in the hope of unifying them with a sense of national purpose. The division put out bulletins early in 1918 but abandoned the practice because they duplicated the *Four Minute Men Bulletins*.[85] The division sometimes urged speakers to use the CPI's *War Cyclopedia*. Bestor opposed having his division take responsibility for addresses, believing it would be "exceedingly dangerous." He maintained that it was easy to control what was said in a four-minute speech but that when a person spoke for between a half hour and two hours, as was often the case, control was next to impossible. He hoped the bulletins would provide some uniformity, yet he only suggested their use. Government officials speaking under his direction were the responsibility of their respective departments, and the Speaking Division refused to censor their material or take responsibility for their utterances.[86]

Control of speakers was partly solved by operating through the state councils of defense. Bestor tried to avoid an elaborate organization for his division, preferring to work through existing institutions at both the national and the state level. He sought to organize speaking forces in every state and place them under the state councils, which provided the link between the Speaking Division and the state and local level.[87] As George F. Porter, chief of the State Councils Section of the National Council of Defense, observed, the councils offered an excellent means of spreading information that for one reason or another was not to be connected officially with the government. The councils lent semiofficial support to patriotic messages.[88]

Each state was expected to organize a speakers' bureau. The director of a bureau was to canvass the state, gathering information about all available audiences, determining where speaking was needed, collecting and grading speakers, arranging for talks. In some states, such as Iowa, the chairman of the State Council of Defense was urged to gather one or two hundred of the best speakers for a training camp. Having nationally known speakers at such camps would ensure concerted action by orators throughout the state.[89]

One of the most important functions of the Speaking Division was arranging war conferences in every state, and the first responsibility of each state speakers' bureau was to arrange a two-day conference in either the capital or the state's principal city. Bestor considered the war conferences, which brought together representatives of various state agencies, the most important work carried on by his division.[90] Each conference was to be attended by the chairman of the state council of defense and by as many members as possible of county and city or town councils, particularly people with speaking ability. A large public meeting was suggested during the first evening, well advertised so that it would be an "event of the first magnitude" for both the city and the state. The CPI's Speaking Division tried to send two speakers to these initial meetings, one of national reputation and the other either a foreigner or an American who had recently been to Europe. The public meeting was to emphasize the importance of a state campaign that would spread information about the war, especially to groups such as laborers or farmers, who might otherwise be isolated and not hear the government's message. The second day of the conference was to be devoted to smaller sessions, organizing the statewide campaign and discussing state problems related to the war. At the smaller meetings a representative of the state speakers' bureau was expected to report on information collected by his office.[91]

State councils of defense were to extend their organizations by creating county and local community councils. Most states were organized along county lines or their equivalent. School districts were thought the best means for setting up community councils. As we have seen, President Wilson believed the creation of community councils to be of great significance, because they would help unite the country as no large country had ever been united before.[92]

The Connecticut State Council of Defense was particularly well organized and illustrates the work of the Speaking Division within the states. The state chairman was Richard M. Bissell of Hartford, and George B. Chandler was chairman of the committee on publicity. Chandler was apparently a good speaker and spoke at war conferences in several other states.

In Connecticut the state council was able to control speakers

more closely than the CPI, often successfully resisting establishment of committee administrative machinery.[93] There, much
effort went into providing speakers with instruction about the
message they were to deliver. As Chandler explained, the state
council did not want speakers to use their old Fourth of July
orations. There was no plan to abridge free speech, but the
council did follow the policy that "if a speaker was not willing to
deliver the right kind of a message, he or she would not be
invited to speak a second time."[94] Chandler invited about four
hundred speakers to a conference at the state capital. Nearly
three hundred persons showed up; no reporters were allowed.
In an hour and a half he explained what was expected, what
the council deemed important.[95] The council provided speech
outlines, such as "The Workman's Stake in the World War,"
which related that workingmen had an interest in the American
cause and that their standard of living depended on victory.
In an hour-long speech about workingmen, it was suggested,
no more than thirty to forty minutes should compare living
standards under the kaiser and under the American government, lest workmen become bored. The council recommended
that the last twenty minutes or so be used for discussing war
themes. The Connecticut outline for workingmen observed
that "somehow people do love to see the flag waved." Speakers
were warned that no one grasped an idea until he heard it at
least eight times.[96]

In Connecticut several methods were employed to control
speakers. Town chairmen received printed instruction on how
to conduct war rallies. They were to have an observer evaluate
speakers, and the state council provided a printed form. If a
speaker injected "partisan politics, Pacifism, Socialism, anti-
Englishism, or any other controversial prejudice or issue," the
council asked that it be reported. Much of this problem seems
to have been resolved by December 1917, but Chandler was not
satisfied with the evaluations: they were much more lavish with
praise than with criticism.[97]

War rallies in Connecticut were carefully advertised. Hand-
bills headed "War Rally Tonight," with names of speakers, were
distributed by schoolchildren. Posters showed why the world

was not yet ready for peace. A state council bulletin board went up in nearly every town, and knock-down bulletin boards for posters were supplied to town officials at cost. The council made arrangements with the New Haven Railroad to have posters in every station. Standard news releases with blanks filled in by local chairmen were sent to local newspapers. Many state councils maintained news services, and Connecticut specialized in interviewing distinguished people who discussed the war. Connecticut was one of eight states to put out a bulletin; an eight-page biweekly, the *Connecticut Bulletin*, carried "Made in Connecticut War Interviews." Each newspaper had on its staff an official representative of the state council, commissioned by the governor to see that the paper printed council news. The state council's committee on publicity maintained a clipping bureau that kept an eye on the press.[98]

The state council had a department of "liberty choruses" under the direction of James S. Stevens. There were some sixty-eight liberty choruses in the state, and in towns in which none existed citizens were asked to improvise them for war rallies. Liberty Song Sheets were printed and given to town committees.[99]

Local expenses of each rally were paid by the local committee. Usually the hall was donated. Many times speakers paid their expenses, but when necessary the local committee provided payment. All speakers spoke without fee, and so the cost of the council of defense was surprisingly small.[100]

Speaker organization in Connecticut seems to have been among the best in the country. Control in Indiana was good, where Pettijohn directed the state speakers' bureau. Pennsylvania was well organized. County organization in Ohio was poor, as the state council's work had been taken over by the Food Administration. No state war conference was held.[101] In Minnesota the CPI's effort to schedule speakers through certain local organizations was hindered by the state's Public Safety Commission.[102] The state of Washington had difficulty setting up a speakers' bureau because of lack of money to pay travel expenses.[103] As late as March 1918, Bestor was informed that there were no bureaus in Arizona, Delaware, Florida, Georgia,

Maine, Massachusetts, New York, West Virginia, Wyoming, and the District of Columbia.[104] At war's end there had been forty-five war conferences in thirty-seven states, with local conferences in five cities in Utah and four cities in Arizona.[105]

The state war conference was the climax of each state's attempt to arouse its citizenry through the national Speaking Division, and it perhaps is useful in this respect to look at the conference held in Indianapolis in mid-December 1917, which was illustrative of how such patriotic gatherings were intended to proceed. The assembly was in Tomlinson Hall and Vice-President Marshall, a native Hoosier, was the featured speaker. Unfortunately, on the first day of the conference the weather was bad and delayed the vice-president's train, so that he did not arrive in time. But there was an impressive array of orators, including Creel, Bestor, McCormick, James Scherer, Périgord, and former Indiana governor Samuel M. Ralston, who was acting chairman. Nearly eleven hundred members of the state's county councils of defense had made reservations for the evening meeting. The weather prevented many from attending, but an hour before the doors opened several thousand people had arrived along Market and Delaware streets. They all but overwhelmed the police, and when the hall was opened there was a crush of people filling the building to overflow—those who could not get seats stood around the edges of the hall and filled the outside corridors.

To arouse the crowd, local businessmen had hired the 250-piece band from the Great Lakes Naval Training Station, directed by John Philip Sousa. The band cost the city more than four thousand dollars, but no one complained once it began the stirring marches, played as only a Sousa band could play.[106] Then the music ended, and Governor Goodrich introduced a local Baptist minister to give the invocation. He asked divine blessing for the president, Congress, the army, the navy, and soldiers holding the front in France and Italy. He looked forward to the day when war would end.

Ralston was first to speak and praised President Wilson as "the master mind of the world." His address was loudly applauded. He was followed by the others, who received enthusiastic responses. To climax the evening, Lieutenant Périgord stepped to the rostrum, dressed in uniform. "I am sorry that I have been introduced as an orator," he began. "I am not an orator. I am only a soldier. I shall speak to you from my heart. After three years of war I have left only my heart and my sword. My heart goes out to France. My sword," and he raised it aloft, "I am proud to give to the service of the United States."

The soldier-orator continued: "I shall only rehearse a speech made in France, by a great American who[m] you all love—General Pershing. When General Pershing arrived in France the first pilgrimage he made was to the tomb of General Lafayette. He knelt over the tomb of Lafayette and said softly: 'Lafayette, we are here.' That was all. It was all there was to be said. But those words rang through France and through the world, and I know I may say to France tonight that the people of Indiana echo that speech, 'Lafayette, we are here.'"

He concluded with a touching tribute to American mothers whose sons were fighting in France: "Some of your boys will stay in France. How many will stay depends on the people of this country. May the number be small. It may be many. But the mothers of France, whose hearts are empty, will take your places in keeping their memory green. The little children in France will pick the sweetest flowers and place them on the graves of French and Americans alike. For both will fall, side by side, fighting for the same cause—the cause of liberty."[107]

THROUGH the spoken word, the Committee on Public Information sent its message to millions of Americans. Working through state, county, and community councils, it brought nearly every citizen, no matter how isolated, into touch with the war. The Four Minute Men proved extraordinarily successful. National headquarters used volunteer speakers, made use of ready-made audiences, and tried—though often without succeeding—to control the speakers rigidly. The Speaking Division was less centrally controlled. Bestor tried to work through the state councils of defense and was unable to organize many of the states. The division nonetheless provided inspiring orators.

There were interesting consequences from the committee's use of orators. The CPI served as a great correspondence school in public speaking: tens of thousands of speakers received experience that would not have been possible otherwise, and most of them undoubtedly gained a sense of participation in the work of the national government.

Although the CPI's use of speakers increased citizen participation in public affairs, there was one disturbing result from their activity. Emotional appeals to audiences, whether calculated in Washington or the result of rhetorical flights by individual speakers, helped raise the wartime level of emotion. Intolerance toward anything or anyone remotely opposing the war may have assisted national unity, but it also assailed civil rights and liberties. Some of this intense emotion probably carried over into the postwar period. Public speakers, though, were not the only ones to inflame such emotion.

8

Advertising America—
and Advertising

> For Advertising has been called to the colors. Inscribed
> in our banner even above the legend Truth is the noblest
> of all mottoes—"We serve."   —William C. D'Arcy[1]

AMONG THE POWERFUL FORCES in human affairs
in the twentieth century have been nationalism and advertising.
Nationalism has been described as "the most significant emotional factor in public life." Advertising's influence has been
compared to that of the school and the church.[2] It is interesting, therefore, that these two phenomena came together
during the World War in 1917 and 1918, the one aiding and
abetting the other, to mobilize American public opinion. The
Committee on Public Information linked these two forces. Indeed, the CPI enlisted some of the best advertising men in
America to stimulate the country's patriotism.[3]

In a characteristic statement, Creel described the CPI as
"a vast enterprise in salesmanship, the world's greatest ad-
venture in advertising." The work of the committee required
such evangelical activity, he said, that "almost instinctively" he
had turned to the advertising profession for help.[4] The committee attracted many prominent advertising men, including
William H. Ingersoll and Edward L. Bernays. Ingersoll was a
former president of the New York Advertising Club. Bernays,
later a leader in public relations, worked for the CPI in Latin
America and found the experience a turning point in his career.[5] The Division of Advertising enlisted such individuals as
William H. Johns, Herbert S. Houston, William Rankin, and
William C. D'Arcy. Their work heightened patriotic pride and

drove the nation to greater levels of unity and achievement. It also assisted the profession of advertising. The work of the CPI proved a "Golden Gate of opportunity" to demonstrate advertising's power.[6] The success of the Division of Advertising and of a sister bureau, the Division of Pictorial Publicity, helped produce a veritable new industry in the 1920s. Old-time salesmanship was transformed, its crudities sublimated. There arose a feeling that with proper advertising (its enemies described the process as scientific misrepresentation) one could sell anything.

IF the Division of Advertising was not established until more than nine months after the United States entered the war, events leading to its creation, together with the work of the division, show that from the outset the government had not neglected advertising men. Shortly after the United States severed diplomatic relations with Germany, the Associated Advertising Clubs of the World (AACW), which represented about 180 clubs with a membership of seventeen thousand, formed the National Advertising Advisory Board. The purpose was to provide advice to Washington leaders in their work during 1917, notably to sell the First and Second Liberty Loans and the Red Cross drives.

The leading spirit in forming the National Advertising Advisory Board was Herbert S. Houston, who before and during his presidency of the AACW had opposed what he described as fraudulent advertising.[7] Such organizations as the AACW, he believed, could enforce a code of morality on advertisers, while at the same time making advertising more efficient. He hoped the AACW would standardize and "purify" advertising. He also thought advertising could help democracy, which was "the creed of the Gospel"—"applied righteousness," he called it. In utterances before and during 1917, Houston expressed his hope of educating the public about the value of advertising. Not only could advertising help protect democracy, it could also aid business by lowering the cost of distribution. Commercial development stimulated the democratic idea. Houston helped to link advertisers with the government during

1917, and after the Division of Advertising was created he served as a member of that section of the CPI.[8]

William H. Rankin assisted Houston as vice-chairman of the National Advertising Advisory Board. President of a firm in Chicago that bore his name, he was chairman of the newspaper committee of the American Association of Advertising Agencies. In Chicago he had helped enlist volunteers for the Red Cross. He was a source of ideas, such as the Chicago Plan, in which businessmen bought and donated advertising space to such causes as the Liberty Loan and the Red Cross. In the Red Cross drive, Rankin persuaded Chicago businessmen to pay for thirty-five full-page advertisements. He secured every dollar membership in the Red Cross at an expense of two and one half cents, compared with twenty-three cents per dollar membership in New York.[9] Rankin argued in June 1917 that the war could put advertising "on a firm, unshakable, business foundation." Speaking before the AACW convention in St. Louis in August, he pointed to Britain's use of advertising as a weapon. He urged much greater effort to use advertising and called for a new cabinet post, a secretary of advertising.[10]

Advertising men, however patriotic, soon found themselves in a controversy over whether the federal government during the bond drives should pay for advertising or rely on donated space. Some members of the AACW advisory board, notably Houston, Rankin, and William C. D'Arcy, who succeeded Houston as president of the AACW, thought the government should pay.[11] When a New York *Times* editorial argued that the government should not have to pay, Houston argued to the contrary.[12] Advertising, he contended, had moved out of the dark ages and was no longer guesswork. England in its Victory Loan campaign had saved fifty million dollars by a plan of paid advertising, at a cost of probably not over two million dollars. The Treasury Department argued that if it paid for advertising it would have to advertise in all newspapers and magazines, lest it be accused of discrimination. Houston said the government always discriminated, buying shoes, clothes, and ammunition from some manufacturers and not from others. It should not be expected to buy advertising from everyone. He called for an efficient, coordinated effort that would leave little to chance, and argued that the advisory board's plan of using advertising men who had nothing to sell the government would assure fairness in choosing publications.[13]

Rankin, who was an equally strong advocate of paid advertising, viewed the government's policy as a great disappointment, for it represented an enormous waste that stood in contrast to Washington leaders' call for thrift. He was nothing if not persistent. After the First Liberty Loan campaign he filed a report with the chairman of the Seventh Federal Reserve Bank District, arguing that wherever a campaign of paid advertising had occurred there was oversubscription. He thought it a mistake to fail to adopt a similar businesslike policy in the Second Liberty Loan drive. The government had no more right to demand that newspapers donate space, he believed, than to require merchants to donate clothing, food, and ammunition.[14] Even though the second drive was more successful, Rankin argued that paid advertising could be more efficient. Central advertising could be two to three times as effective as scattering the same money through local communities. He estimated that for three million dollars, and probably for considerably less, the government could reach every newspaper in the country.[15]

D'Arcy made the same arguments. He viewed advertising as educational, a way to unify the "national mind," moving it to "quick, all-powerful action" on such issues as the Liberty Loan, the Red Cross, or food conservation. He believed that the services of advertising men should be voluntary but that the government should buy advertising space. Spending to advertise Liberty bonds would be an excellent investment, because it gave the bond owner a corporate interest in his government. Government advertising, D'Arcy said, should exhibit the same characteristics as a merchandising campaign.[16]

Houston, Rankin, and D'Arcy, together with Thomas Cusack of Chicago, John E. Shoemaker of Washington, and Frank H. Sisson, Collin Armstrong, George W. Hopkins, Courtland Smith, and William A. Thomason—all of New York—in August 1917 presented a plan to Secretary McAdoo calling for from $1 million to $2.5 million on advertising for the Second Liberty Loan campaign.[17] The government rejected the plan. McAdoo argued that the cost would exceed the money appropriated by Congress for the Second Liberty Loan.[18] As Creel explained, "voluntary" was a magic word in those days, and the government wanted nothing that hinted of profit. Creel did not doubt the economic waste in relying on voluntary contributions, but at the time he and others thought of advertising "as a business, not a profession" and regarded advertising men only as "plausible pirates" to be viewed with suspicion.[19]

The argument over paid advertising escalated in the autumn of 1917, and the National Advertising Advisory Board's position led to a good deal of contention. Leaders in Washington did not have to look far for offers of assistance from advertisers. By late November and December 1917, such groups as the Association of National Advertisers (ANA), the Agricultural Publishers Association, and the Six Point League were proposing their services.[20] At its eighth annual convention in early December, in New York, the ANA appointed four members to make up a committee to advise the government on advertising: O. C. Harn, chairman, who had been chairman of the Committee on Plan and Scope of the AACW's advisory board; together with George W. Hopkins, Edward Hungerford, and Lewis B. Jones. The committee was supposed to work with the Food Commission, the Fuel Administration, and the Treasury Department. Eula McClary helped the ANA set up the group.[21] John Sullivan, secretary-treasurer of the ANA, invited Creel and the associate chairman of the CPI, Carl Byoir, to the organization's annual dinner, explaining that the meeting would present an excellent opportunity for "inspirational mobilization of the forces of advertising for practical co-operation with the government."[22] Byoir went to New York, conferred with the committee, and named a board of directors for what was to be the CPI's Division of Advertising.[23]

According to *Advertising News*, the effort of Houston and others in behalf of having the government pay for advertising reached its height late in 1917. Apparently the advisory board of the AACW tried to push the issue, and hard feeling resulted.

When the ANA came along with its offer of cooperation the government accepted.[24]

The new Division of Advertising was headed by William H. Johns, then president of the American Association of Advertising Agents (AAAA), an organization representing about 115 firms that was formed in June 1917 at the St. Louis convention of the AACW.[25] Johns started his career as an employee of Funk and Wagnalls and had worked for the banking firm of Blair and Company. In 1892 he helped George Batten start the advertising firm of George Batten Company, Incorporated, and upon Batten's death in 1918 he became the agency's president.[26]

Johns was assisted on the division's board of directors by Houston, Harn, D'Arcy, and Lewis B. Jones, the latter being president of the ANA. Jones was advertising manager of Eastman Kodak in Rochester, New York, and a popular figure in advertising circles. In the Division of Advertising he became known as "Blue Pencil" Jones because of his editorial zeal.[27] Helping Jones and the others on the board of directors were Thomas Cusack, a leader in the painted bulletin and poster industry; and Jesse H. Neal, executive secretary of the Associated Business Papers, composed of five hundred leading technical trade publications.[28]

Division offices were in the Metropolitan Tower in New York City, but close connection was maintained with the CPI offices in Washington, partly through Byoir and Carl E. Walberg. Byoir took special interest in the advertising activities of the federal government and in the Division of Advertising, and attempted to standardize the work.[29] After the creation of the division he suggested that if advertisers and publishers still felt strongly about paid advertising, they and not the division "should solicit the government as they would any other organization that had goods to sell them."[30] Walberg, Byoir's collaborator in the Division of Advertising, had been employed by the William H. Rankin Company in Chicago and was a source of many suggestions for the division's copy and procedures. In the early days of the division he helped organize the division so that it could run in the same manner as a well-organized advertising agency. He was interested in having the government

exploit the great possibilities of a national advertising campaign, something he thought leaders in Washington had failed
to do.[31]

The Division of Advertising was established on January 20,
1918, when President Wilson's executive order placed it under
the jurisdiction of the CPI "for the purpose of receiving and
directing through the proper channels the generous offers of
advertising forces of the nation" in the effort to "inform public
opinion properly and adequately."[32] The division was to prepare copy, art, plans, and designs and to address, distribute,
and mail literature—in short, to handle everything connected
with advertising except defraying the cost of printing, purchasing advertising space, or furnishing editorials and news
publicity.[33] As Creel explained to Secretary of Labor William B.
Wilson, he hoped that every periodical or newspaper advertisement would have at least a portion of its space devoted to the
war. He expected some thirty million dollars in advertising to
be donated during 1918.[34]

One of the division's goals was to make free government
advertising more efficient. Johns explained that the purpose
was not to replace any of the publicity sections or advertising
agencies of any government department. Rather, it was to improve coordination and to suggest ways in which space might
be used best. The division was to "act as a national advertising
agency," a "clearing house," to assist the departments of government just as an advertising agent would advise a client.[35] At the
outset the division undertook contacts with the departments of
the government, and letters went to department heads asking
them to appoint representatives.[36] Nearly all the country's
advertising firms and associations volunteered their services to
the government through the division, including the AACW, the
ANA, the AAAA, the Associated Business Papers, the Periodical Publishers Association, the National Advertising Advisory
Board, the Agricultural Publishers Association, the Six Point
League, the Bureau of Advertising of the American Newspaper
Publishers Association, and many leaders in paint, posters, and
streetcar card advertising.[37]

Johns, Byoir, Lebair, and Creel asserted that the Division

of Advertising did not solicit advertising space, a claim that was
technically true, inasmuch as the division was prohibited by law
from asking or paying for advertising.[38] Still, relations with
publishers' associations and advertising clubs were put to advantage, and such organizations often encouraged their members to contribute time and space. On many occasions space
would be donated by a firm to one of the advertising clubs—
such as the AACW—which would forward it to the CPI. The
War Advertising Committee of the AAAA wrote members of its
New York Council urging cooperation with the Division of
Advertising. In the interest of efficiency the committee suggested that, rather than having the entire association contribute
copy to each and every program the government wished advertised, from three to five agencies should devote themselves to
one activity. Agencies interested in the Food Administration's
message were to apply to the Frank Seaman Company, a firm
that had devoted considerable time to such endeavors. Agencies interested in the Red Cross or Thrift campaigns were told
to get in touch with companies working in those areas. Concentrating on one campaign, agencies could become expert.
Agencies were requested to state the amount of service they
would give.[39]

   Firms contributing space to the government usually received letters of appreciation from Johns. Often contributors
would request that their offers be placed in certain journals, to
appeal to particular types of readers. Records were kept on
these journals and their readerships. Usually businesses donating space were allowed to print their names at the bottom of
displays: beneath the seal of the CPI and Division of Advertising was a legend, "This space contributed for the Winning of
the War by," followed by the name of the firm. It was probably
good business to associate a product with the national cause.
Johns often encouraged businesses to link their products to a
message from the government. The Central Oil and Gas Stove
Company helped the Fuel Administration conserve coal by
advertising the advantages of oil heat. The same firm later
offered space to the Food Administration in its drive to convince Americans to can and dry vegetables and fruit, and Johns

sought a statement from the Food Administration that would once again help the company tie its product to government directives.[40]

Perhaps the most memorable part of propaganda during the war was the vivid posters in support of the cause—when "art put on khaki and went into action."[41] It is sometimes difficult to know which posters were the work of the CPI, since the committee was but one of many organizations putting out propaganda in 1917 and 1918. Usually posters of the Division of Advertising were so labeled. The division had little to do with the drawing of posters, for that task fell to the Division of Pictorial Publicity, which had appeared on April 22, 1917.

The latter division was the brainchild of a group of artists known as the Vigilantes, which included Jack Sheridan, C. B. Falls, and James Montgomery Flagg. Charles Dana Gibson, who had made the Gibson Girls a part of American culture, was the leader of the Vigilantes, and he headed that CPI section.[42] From the start in January 1918, the Division of Advertising worked closely with Gibson's division, and the two sections' efforts must be considered together.[43] Whenever illustrations or sketches were needed, the Division of Advertising, lacking funds, looked to the Division of Pictorial Publicity. Though the advertising division might offer suggestions on subject and layout, Gibson's division did the drawing.[44]

The primary work of the artists and advertisers was mobilization of public opinion, and the means many of them employed provide an interesting commentary on public opinion theory during 1917–18. Creel believed in the rationality of public opinion and contended that the CPI merely sought to "inform" the public. Ford thought of his division as educational, and even though some of its literature overplayed the German menace, its writers were concerned about making democracy function. The correspondence that remains from the Divisions of Advertising and Pictorial Publicity, however, reflects little awareness of the complexities confronting democratic society. These men—most of whom were trying to aid the country in its hour of crisis—worried about results, about what appeal would increase public support. Though the claim that Creel and Ford were engaged only in educational work is questionable, the work of the CPI's artists and advertisers seems even more clearly aimed at manipulating opinion. The work of these two divisions anticipated more sinister uses of propaganda in the postwar years.

One has only to consider the effect of working with such a person as Gibson, whose pen, it was said, was often dripping with venom. Such was Gibson's zeal that for some time he paid his expenses and those of his entire division out of his own pocket.[45] He believed that America, separated from Europe, was too far removed to understand the war. Until Americans were made to feel the war's horrors, they would not be aroused. In the initial months, American war art concentrated on material things, showing ammunition, clothing, and the necessities of war. Gibson said such subjects would hardly inspire the imagination of the lethargic "thousands who clutter our streets." The government, he thought, appealed to opinion as if the United States was composed of people interested only in practical things. Nothing was more remote from the psychology of the public. Gibson said: "One cannot create enthusiasm for war on the basis of practical appeal. The spirit that will lead a man to put away the things of his accustomed life and go forth to all the hardships of war is not kindled by showing him the facts. . . ."[46] War art must "appeal to the heart" and imagination.[47] To rouse the public, he suggested that paintings, old and new, illustrate the appeals of the day. Displays could be set up in show windows on Fifth Avenue in New York. Aisles in the busiest streets in large cities could display replicas of Mac-Monnies's "Nathan Hale" or Saint-Gaudens's statue of General William T. Sherman atop his charger. Gibson appealed to fellow artists to "see more of the spiritual side of the conflict."[48] Americans must see the Belgian child dying of hunger, the American soldier killed because he lacked ammunition to defend himself.

Frank De Sales Casey was Gibson's most important assistant in the Division of Pictorial Publicity and served as the section's vice-chairman and secretary. Casey had been art director of *Collier's* and knew nearly all the leading artists who might be available to the government.[49] At the division's weekly meetings

10. Charles Dana Gibson
(Courtesy of the National Archives, photo no. 165-WW-134-17)

11. Division of Pictorial Publicity. Left to right: J. E. Seridan, Wallace Morgan, G. Devitt Welsh, H. D. Adams, Charles Dana Gibson, Chairman, F. D. Casey, F. J. Sheridan, Jr., Adolph Treidler, Harry Townsend, and C. B. Falls. (Courtesy of the National Archives, photo no. 165-WW-134-41)

at Keene's Chop House in New York, orders were received from Washington for designs, and then it was usually Casey who would choose artists best qualified to handle the proposed project.[50]

Gibson drew on some of the country's leading landscape painters, illustrators, mural decorators, architects, and sculptors. Assisting him were Herbert Adams, president of the National Academy of Design; E. H. Blashfield, former president of the Society of American Artists; the former president of the Architectural League, Cass Gilbert; and Joseph Pennell, who had drawn the official pictures of the Panama Canal.[51]

In association with Gibson's section, the Division of Advertising moved swiftly into operation and had copy for the March 1918 issues of most monthly periodicals.[52] As it picked up momentum, publications increased. There were long lists of names and addresses of magazines, farm papers, house organs, newspapers, college papers, trade publications. Detailed records were kept on periodicals, insertions, circulation, and value of advertisements. Johns submitted monthly records to Creel.

The division helped the campaigns of several agencies, including the Shipping Board, United States Employment Service, War Department, War Savings and Liberty Loan drives of the Treasury Department, Red Cross, Young Men's Christian Association, Food and Fuel Administrations, and Department of Agriculture.[53]

The first large campaign by the Division of Advertising, assisted by Gibson's artists, was to raise 250,000 shipyard volunteers. Concentrating on magazines and trade papers, it used a poster entitled *U.S. Shipyard Volunteers*, largely the work of C. T. Adams, who considered it the foundation of a whole series of illustrations to enlist shipyward workers. In designing the poster he attempted "to reduce the entire proposition to the simplest and most easily understood terms." The advertisement's "lead" contained a "sentimental or patriotic appeal" and was followed by what advertisers called "standard detail," made up of "hard and fast informative copy" calling for volunteers. Adams recommended that subsequent posters in the campaign vary in openings, basing leads upon "patriotism, sentiment, the desire for gain, safety of life and limb, and other more or less emotional appeals." These would attract the reader and focus interest on the standard details that in every case would be identical. Though there was but one proposition to offer many people, they must be reached in different fashions. Adams suggested that the most successful appeal to workers would be one emphasizing comfort or the desire for gain by showing how the worker would get high wages, exemption from the draft and meatless Tuesdays, and comfortable working conditions.[54] In the first five months of the campaign some eighty advertisements were used, having a total circulation of approximately eight million, and a space value of twenty thousand dollars.[55]

Other appeals were to enlist the support of labor. Thanks to men like Hubert L. Towle of the J. H. Cross Company in Philadelphia, the division was furnished with a long list of periodicals of interest to labor.[56] Advertisements for workingmen were drawn for these publications.

Some advertising by the division sought to appeal to both workers and employers—such as the campaign on behalf of the United States Employment Service (USES), a branch of the Department of Labor. USES sought central control of employment, the "federalization of the labor supply." It had about five hundred branch offices and was organized in thirteen districts, each with a superintendent. The organization was divided into sections that concentrated on skilled labor, common labor, farm service, women, an information and education service, and a public service reserve. Secretary of Labor Wilson hoped that the USES would stop the rapid turnover of men that had afflicted many plants and would thereby make it possible to increase production by 15 percent. Carl Walberg had a major part in this drive and was responsible for a sixteen-page publication, *United States Employment Service Bulletin*. About sixty thousand copies of this publication were distributed to the press, advertisers, and manufacturers. The Department of Labor received more than eleven thousand advertisements, which showed the extent to which the bulletin had been copied. A typical poster in this campaign was *The Right Men in the Right Jobs Will Win the War*. It emphasized "a stirring note of patriotism" and tried to convince employers that the USES was the best way to secure trained labor. It asserted that employers who procured labor by private means were interfering with the government's work, placing personal interest over national well-being. There was an appeal to the worker to register with the Public Service Reserve and stick with his job until the government recommended that he change: "The war worker ranks with the fighter in the trenches. He will help beat the Hun."[57]

Another effort sought to have employers encourage employees to register under the Selective Service Act. Merchants were asked to use store bulletin boards, pay envelopes, package wrappings, special meetings, and so on to tell every man between eighteen and forty-five about the law. (It was estimated that there were thirteen million men of draft age.) With help from the Division of Pictorial Publicity, the *Advertising Service Bulletin* was published. The *Selective Service Register*, a regular newspaper, used messages from President Wilson, Secretary of War Baker, General E. H. Crowder, and Secretary of the Navy Daniels to inform men of their duty to register. A special mailing card was produced and sent to forty-three thousand rural free delivery routes, to reach individuals who did not regularly read newspapers.[58]

Through the Division of Advertising the CPI sought the support of businessmen.[59] Houston was highly vocal in appealing to this group. Rather than asking for democratic idealism, his messages usually stressed material gain from supporting the war. When the AACW held its annual convention in July 1918 in San Francisco, he described its objects as "helping the Government and helping business." He hoped to have A. Mitchell Palmer address the convention on "The Menace of German Business, Both in the United States and outside of the United States."[60] He sought to make business more efficient and urged that it be allowed to operate with as few handicaps and restrictions as possible during the war.[61] Even if Germany were defeated, he thought German business would present a threat to Allied and American industry.[62] He proposed a league of nations that would prevent war by using economic pressure.[63]

Houston's appeal was not exceptional, as businessmen were often reminded that German industry had been unharmed by the war and that especially in South America it threatened American supremacy.

One of the posters most frequently requested by businesses donating advertising space was *Spies and Lies*, used in literary magazines to appeal to suspicion. "German agents are everywhere," it began. Citizens were to report to the Department of Justice the name of any person "who spreads pessimistic stories, divulges—or seeks—confidential military information, cries for peace, or belittles our effort to win the war." Lewis Jones felt that the *Spies and Lies* campaign reached "the educated, though thoughtless person," but not the uneducated, those who read only the yellow journals. He urged that through Thomas Cusack the division appeal to the latter people by billboard illustrations.[64]

There were, of course, many attempts to persuade citizens to invest their money in America. During the Division of Advertising's first months, an attempt was made to use virtually every sort of publication to sell war savings stamps (WSS) and Liberty Loan bonds. It was estimated that the WSS drive used 1,130 advertisements (with a value of $132,000) to reach fifty-five million people. Because the Division of Advertising had not been established in time to put its full weight behind the Third Liberty Loan, the Fourth Loan became the first bond drive to receive an all-out effort.[65] Nevertheless, the effort on behalf of the Third Liberty Loan used 177 advertisements (total value about $53,600) to reach an estimated sixteen million persons.[66] In the Third Liberty Loan drive, such themes as love of country, devotion to liberty, and desire to destroy an enemy who threatened home and nation were employed.[67]

The campaigns for war savings stamps and Liberty Loan bonds that were undertaken for the Treasury Department unquestionably produced some of the war's most striking—and gory—posters. The responsibility for these productions is especially important in light of Creel's contention that his agency tried to avoid using atrocity material and the assumption or implication in virtually all literature on the committee that nearly every war poster in support of bond drives was the work of the CPI.[68]

Poster contests were held for both the stamp and bond campaigns. In the spring of 1918, the war savings stamps' committee announced such a competition; Gibson chaired the committee of judges, which offered a one thousand dollar first prize.[69] The winner was Adolph Treidler of New York City, whose drawing showed a German soldier slouching across a devastated landscape, a destroyed church in the background, and also a woman obviously wounded. In one hand the soldier carried a rifle, in the other a bloody knife. The poster's caption read: *Help Stop This—Buy W.S.S. and Keep Him Out of America*. In second place was a drawing by Coles Phillips showing a German soldier using his rifle as a club. M. Leone Bracker of New York took first prize for the best newspaper advertisement, and G. B. Inwood, also from New York, won the award for the best "car or window card." Bracker's drawing, entitled *Behold Your Enemy*, showed German soldiers abusing Belgian children, women, and old men. Inwood's work pictured a soldier going into battle; the caption read, *Meanwhile You Save!* Gibson's committee received twenty-two hundred entries, many of which were displayed at the New York Public Library.[70]

Similarly—as it was thought that each campaign required new posters—a competition was held for the Fourth Liberty Loan drive. The appeal for the Fourth Loan was to be even more dramatic than that for the Third, and was summarized by one writer as teaching the people of America "what sort of bestiality we are fighting when we fight the Hun."[71] Although Gibson was not on the committee judging these drawings, it was not surprising that when the contest ended all designs accepted were by members of the Division of Pictorial Publicity.[72] Among the most popular posters were Walter Whitehead's *Come On!* showing a soldier with rifle, standing over a dead German, defiantly awaiting the assault; F. Strothman's *Beat Back the Hun with Liberty Bonds*, which revealed a green-eyed Hun, bloody bayonet fixed, looking over the edge of Europe toward the United States; and Joseph Pennell's *That Liberty Shall Not Perish from the Earth, Buy Liberty Bonds*, which pictured the Statue of Liberty crumbling under German fire, with the burning ruins of New York City silhouetted against the background.[73]

Whether the Division of Advertising used these drawings is unclear.[74] Posters from the CPI were usually labeled as such. Undoubtedly, the Committee on Public Information was not responsible for scores of drawings turned out by zealous artists, even though some of them may have been used by various government departments. Until evidence is presented that the committee used posters without the CPI's imprint, it is only fair to assume that such material was not circulated by Creel and his associates. But exercising such caution does not absolve the CPI or leave unanswered the question whether the committee used inflammatory drawings. It is clear that the committee did use other posters in the Fourth Liberty Loan drive that emphasized German atrocities. Creel admitted that atrocity material, "posters showing 'bloody boots,' trampled children and mutilated women," appeared in the Liberty Loan campaigns, but he contended that the CPI had no control over such developments.[75] Whatever Creel's feelings about such material —whether it was forced on the committee by the Treasury Department or from elsewhere—it is very probable that Gibson favored using it, and there is no doubt that some members of the Division of Advertising were enthusiastic about such pictures. Clarence A. Hope, the division's secretary, was especially impressed with one drawing, which he thought could be used in the *Ladies' Home Journal*; it showed "a street scene in which brutal German officers are chopping off the hands of a boy, and in the background another group of officers is choking a woman."[76] The division did put out such a poster, entitled *This is Kultur*. It claimed that a wide gulf existed between the way German Kultur and American civilization treated women and children. The poster went on to say that "Kultur in Belgium . . . is a tale so terrible that never yet has one dared more than whisper fragments of it. Yet the wrongs of Belgium, as a State outraged, pale beside the wrongs inflicted in savage, bestial revenge upon its defenceless women and children." "Such a civilization," readers were told, "is not fit to live." The fight against Germany was "a Crusade, not merely to re-win the tomb of Christ, but to bring back to earth the rule of right, the peace, good will to men and gentleness He taught." Americans were urged to "sacrifice, that our Crusaders may save us and our children from the horrors that have come to the little ones of Belgium and of France."

There were other posters of this kind circulated by the Division of Advertising in support of the Fourth Liberty Loan. *Remember Belgium* pictured a German soldier bayoneting a fallen woman and another soldier apparently ready to rape his victim, both against a background of burning buildings and German plunder. Readers were informed that they could "hit the Hun the hardest by putting every possible dollar in this critical bond issue" and were asked to make it their business to see that every person "understands the importance of buying bonds to the limit. The enemy has developed a world-distribution on brutalities that bear the Berlin shipping-tag. . . . You can crack Kultur on the head by volunteering *more* of your money than the Government asks for." The *Bachelor of Atrocities*, obviously aimed at college publications, also showed German soldiers plundering and abusing women against a picture of a burning university. In the upper right hand corner was the kaiser. Readers were asked: "Are you going to let the Prussian Python strike at your Alma Mater, as it struck at the University of Louvain? The Hohenzollern fang strikes at every element of decency and culture and taste that your college stands for. It leaves a track so terrible that only whispered fragments may be recounted. It has ripped all world-old romance out of war, and reduced it to the dead, black depths of muck, and hate, and bitterness. . . . It is sometimes harder to live nobly than to die nobly. . . . You are called to exercise stern self-discipline. . . . Kill every wasteful impulse, that America may live. Every bond you buy fires point-blank at Prussian Terrorism." It was hoped that ten million posters would be used during the Fourth Liberty Loan drive.[77]

The Liberty Loan posters were among the most blatant efforts to create fear and hatred of the enemy; many other drawings, however, were more reserved. Several posters were

12–41. (Courtesy of the National Archives)

To Employers and Important Executives—

𝔄 Government Proclamation

The Army Needs Your Influence in an Emergency—

This is a man-to-man appeal for you to help the Government grasp a great opportunity, and for you to discharge a grave responsibility.

The Allied program to speed up the war and quickly bring about the final overthrow of the German Armies calls for an immediate mustering of America's final contribution of man-power. We must raise our army to 5,000,000 men at once!

Nearly 3,000,000 of the needed 5,000,000 are already under arms—but Class 1 of the Draft will be exhausted by October 1. To go into the deferred classifications and take men essential to industries, and men with dependent families, is unwise.

A new Class 1 must be created at once. Laws are being framed calling upon men within certain ages to register (the War Department's recommendation is for 18 to 21 and 32 to 45 years as the age limits), and the President will appoint a Registration Day early in September.

Thirteen million men must register in a single day. Later these men will be classified. Industries will not lose men who are absolutely essential to them, and families will not lose their bread-winners. But every man must register.

You are a center of influence

As an employer or an important executive you are a center of influence, and the Government needs your active co-operation in putting through this gigantic task without confusion or delay. Thirteen million men must be *told* of the law between now and Registration Day (watch newspapers for date); and they must understand the *why* of it, and just *where* and *how* they are to register. For these details ask your

Local Board, or your city or county clerk.

You can reach the men in your employ more effectively than they can be reached from the outside. We earnestly urge, therefore, that you make definite plans, in the interest of a speedy VICTORY, and in the interest of your own business, to see that all of your men are properly informed, so that they can be promptly and correctly registered when the day comes.

Every man between the ages to be specified in the President's Proclamation must register.

How you can help

Start at once to get in touch with your men. Bring to their attention the *need* for the registration and the *facts about it.* Get in touch with your Local Registration officials and co-operate with them.

Here are a few suggestions:

Arrange for talks to your men; place inspirational and informative bulletins on bulletin-boards; establish Selective Service Information Bureaus; inclose slips in your men's pay envelopes.

Arrange for definite hours when the men in the different departments or sub-divisions of your business shall be allowed time to go and register. Post full lists of the men in your employ between the specified ages, the men to check off their names after they have registered.

Many other ideas, applicable to your own business, will doubtless occur to you.

This is an emergency such as this country has never faced before, and the Government must depend upon you to bring all of your influence and inspiration and ingenuity to bear out this problem, that this crisis in the war may be met in a way that shall avoid hardship to the businesses and families of the Nation.

Signed:

E. H. CROWDER
PROVOST MARSHAL GENERAL

Approved:

NEWTON D. BAKER
SECRETARY OF WAR

Watch the newspapers for the date and further details

Contributed through Division of Advertising — United States Govt. Comm. on Public Information

This space contributed for the Winning of the War by The Publisher

To the Boy who thinks he was born too late

EVERY time a fellow hears about the fighting going on "over there" or on the sea he feels "it's tough to be young!"

Get over that! The battles are not only on the battlefields. The war is fought by saving behind the lines.

And there is one job-of-work you can do that is 100 per cent. man's size. Don't doubt it for a minute!

If you were in a trench out there at the front right now and Private Longlegs needed more ammunition quick, would you hustle a few clips of cartridges to him—and wouldn't that be man's work?

Yes. And if you were behind the sector held by our own United States troops and Private Shorty needed a shoulder at the mired wheel of his gun caisson, would you go to it—and wouldn't that be man's work?

Well, then, what's the difference whether you hoist away alongside of Shorty or scout around here way behind the fighting lines and help Shorty's government to keep this thing going?

What you do now, the work you do, the saving you will make this world and this nation

a safer and better place to live in when you are twenty-one.

And here's how you do it. You buy United States War Savings Stamps. They cost $4.17 in June and a cent more each month thereafter. They will be worth $5.00 on January 1, 1923. The interest accumulates just by your keeping them, until the five-dollar period is reached. They are the best and safest investment in the world—the finest saving.

If you can't go right out and save as much as $4.17 all at one time you still can do your part for America and give your country the aid it must have. You can buy United States Thrift Stamps—little brothers to the War Savings Stamps. They cost 25 cents each. When you have bought sixteen of them, you can add 17 cents or 18 cents according to the month and exchange them at any bank, postoffice or store selling War Savings Stamps for a United States War Savings Stamp.

It's a man's work to go "over the top." It's a man's size job to help other men "over the top," outfitted and fed and equipped as they should be.

And that's your job. Stick out your chest and tell your father that here's where you get in the game with your money for War Savings Stamps.

W.S.S.
WAR SAVINGS STAMPS
ISSUED BY THE
UNITED STATES
GOVERNMENT

Contributed through Division of Advertising

U. S. Gov't Comm. on Public Information

This space contributed for the Winning of the War by

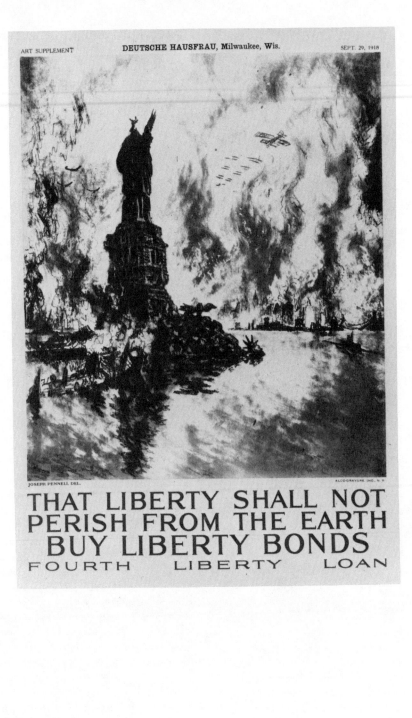

FROM A LITHOGRAPH, DRAWN ON THE STONE BY GEORGE BELLOWS

This is Kultur

T HERE is no sharper contrast between German Kultur and the
civilization that our forefathers died for, than the difference in the
attitude of the two civilizations towards women and children.

Kultur in Belgium, and other devastated
countries, is a tale so terrible that never
yet has one dared more than whisper fragments of it. Yet the wrongs of Belgium, as
a State outraged, pale beside the wrongs
inflicted in savage, bestial revenge upon its
defenceless women and children.

Such a civilization is not fit to live. And,
God willing, it shall be mended or ended.
To this task America summons every loyal
heart and hand. It is a Crusade, not merely
to re-win the tomb of Christ, but to bring
back to earth the rule of right, the peace,
good will to men and gentleness He taught.

To carry on this crusade of modern
righteousness means not merely that our
young men shall cross the seas to fight the
Hun. It means that we at home shall up-
hold them. It means that we shall back
them with all things spiritual and material.
It means that we shall lend, not merely
from our plenty, but that we shall save and
serve. It means that we shall give up many
things that are dear to us; sacrifice, that
our Crusaders may save us and our children
from the horrors that have come to the little
ones of Belgium and of France.

BUY U. S. GOVERNMENT BONDS FOURTH LIBERTY LOAN

Contributed through Division of Advertising   United States Govt. Comm. on Public Information

This space contributed for the Winning of the War by

The Publisher of

Remember Belgium

YOU can floor an Uhlan with lead, but only gold can floor Berlin—the gold of a world aroused.

You can hit the Hun the hardest by putting every possible dollar into this critical bond issue. Make it your business to see that every man and woman in your establishment understands the importance of buying bonds to the limit.

The enemy has developed a world-distribution on brutalities that bear the Berlin shipping-tag. How long shall this obscene commerce in brutality continue?

Your answer is required, now. Your money talks. You can crack Kultur on the head by volunteering *more of* your money than the Government asks for. You can overwhelm the mad Wolf of Wilhelmstrasse with the crushing wrath of billions.

How long do you want to receive news of U-boat sinkings, casualty lists, and maimed sons, marked F. O. B. Berlin?

Gentlemen, your answer?

Put your answer in writing—on a check. Now is the time to hurl Wilhelm II against the fence, and make him face a firing squad of 100,000,000 Americans—with dollars for bullets.

Buy U. S. Gov't Bonds Fourth Liberty Loan

Contributed through
Division of Advertising

United States Govt. Comm.
on Public Information

This space contributed for the Winning of the War by

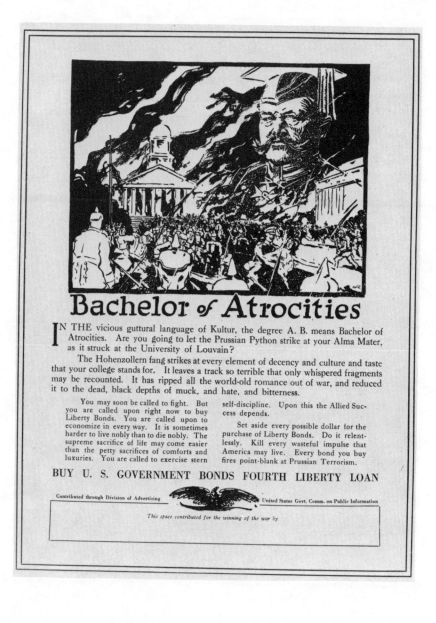

Bachelor *of* Atrocities

IN THE vicious guttural language of Kultur, the degree A. B. means Bachelor of Atrocities. Are you going to let the Prussian Python strike at your Alma Mater, as it struck at the University of Louvain?

The Hohenzollern fang strikes at every element of decency and culture and taste that your college stands for. It leaves a track so terrible that only whispered fragments may be recounted. It has ripped all the world-old romance out of war, and reduced it to the dead, black depths of muck, and hate, and bitterness.

You may soon be called to fight. But you are called upon right now to buy Liberty Bonds. You are called upon to economize in every way. It is sometimes harder to live nobly than to die nobly. The supreme sacrifice of life may come easier than the petty sacrifices of comforts and luxuries. You are called to exercise stern self-discipline. Upon this the Allied Success depends.

Set aside every possible dollar for the purchase of Liberty Bonds. Do it relentlessly. Kill every wasteful impulse that America may live. Every bond you buy fires point-blank at Prussian Terrorism.

BUY U. S. GOVERNMENT BONDS FOURTH LIBERTY LOAN

Contributed through Division of Advertising   United States Govt. Comm. on Public Information

This space contributed for the winning of the war by

I Am Public Opinion

All men fear me!

I declare that Uncle Sam shall not go to his knees to beg you to buy his bonds. That is no position for a fighting man. But if you have the money to buy and do not buy, I will make this No Man's Land for you!

I will judge you not by an allegiance expressed in mere words.

I will judge you not by your mad cheers as our boys march away to whatever fate may have in store for them.

I will judge you not by the warmth of the tears you shed over the lists of the dead and the injured that come to us from time to time.

I will judge you not by your uncovered head and solemn mien as our maimed in battle return to our shores for loving care.

But, as wise as I am just, I will judge you by the material aid you give to the fighting men who are facing death that you may live and move and have your being in a world made safe.

I warn you—don't talk patriotism over here unless your money is talking victory Over There.

I am Public Opinion!
As I judge, all men stand or fall!

Buy U. S. Gov't Bonds Fourth Liberty Loan

Contributed through Division of Advertising   United States Govt. Comm. on Public Information

This space contributed for the Winning of the War by

Ad E 4

"What you can do to make life cheerful in camp and trench"

THE letter from home—what a wealth of sentiment it contains. Far removed from what has been most dear to him from his childhood days, up through the years of boyhood, his school days, his play and work days, and now in the most noble days of all, the young soldier is fighting for his country.

In his lonesomeness and possible homesickness, a cheering word helps him to "carry on" and gives him new determination to fight for your protection and for those ideals which we all hold dear.

If he be a son, brother, cousin, husband, friend or acquaintance a letter will be most welcome to him. A spirit backed up by a loving thought from home cannot lose.

The battle line may mean stubborn drudgery, but the home-ties must never be severed. In the darkness of the night he dreams a loving picture of those dear ones "back home" who are thinking of him. Make that letter a letter of good cheer—a letter with a smile.

Write him today

COMMITTEE ON PUBLIC INFORMATION, Washington, D. C.

Contributed through
Division of Advertising
U. S. Gov't Comm.
on Public Information

George Creelman, Chairman
The Secretary of State
The Secretary of War
The Secretary of the Navy

This space contributed for the Winning of the War by

Write him cheerful letters

THE man you love is fighting for your security and happiness. He is helping to bring this war to an early end — and to make another war like this impossible. He is doing something that HAS to be done for your sake. The *more hopefully* you write, the *easier* for him — and the *quicker* he comes back.

Of course his life is no bed of roses. Yet his discomforts are the discomforts of a red-blooded life in the open—the sort of life enjoyed by the cowboy of Arizona, by the mounted police of Canada, and by the adventurous spirits of all the world and of all times.

He has good, wholesome food, well cooked, in great abundance and variety—hot from the camp kitchen, wherever he is stationed in camp or trench. He has comfortable shoes and warm clothing. He lives under conditions of healthfulness maintained by sanitary experts. His health is constantly looked after by capable physicians—who bend every effort towards keeping him well, instead of waiting to cure him after he becomes ill.

His fighting equipment, his bayonet, gas mask and ammunition embody every known advantage and improvement—American ingenuity has profited by all the past experiences of our allies and the enemy as well. He has every possible advantage over the enemy in both defense and aggression. In all the history of the world no soldier has been so well equipped, so well taken care of as the American soldier.

As a result, even with battle losses included, the death rate in the American Army is not materially greater than in most American cities. The great majority of American soldiers will return stronger and more vigorous in body and in mind than when they joined the army.

Every conceivable condition contributes to his safety, comfort and happiness EXCEPT ONE—The strong arm of Uncle Sam can do everything in the world for him—*except control his thoughts of you.*

That one condition is entirely within *your* control.

His fighting power, his health, his chance of *winning* and *living* depend in the *end* upon WHAT YOU WRITE TO HIM.

If you let him feel that you are discouraged, that you are afraid for *yourself* or for *him*, then he will be downcast and heavy-hearted.

If you let him feel that you are happy, that you are getting along well, that you are full of hope and courage, then he will be happy and stout-hearted—a mighty fighter in attack or defense.

So write him newsy, cheerful letters. Tell him the pleasant, treasured bits of gossip from home.

That is the one thing that *you* must do for him—and for your country.

That is one thing above all others that you *can* do to hasten the end of the war and victory for America and the right.

That is the one thing that we ask of your wisdom, your loyalty—that no one else can do.

For it is the high spirit, the dauntless courage, of the American soldier that is winning this war—for you.

Do your part to maintain this spirit, this courage!

And by your bravery, by your gameness, help to KEEP THE KAISER ON THE RUN.

COMMITTEE ON PUBLIC INFORMATION
8 JACKSON PLACE, WASHINGTON, D. C.

George Creel, Chairman
The Secretary of State

Contributed through Division of Advertising

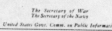

The Secretary of War
The Secretary of the Navy

United States Govt. Comm. on Public Information

This space contributed for the Winning of the War by

One member in a family is not enough

EVERY man and woman in the country, not in khaki or navy blue, should answer "present" to the Red Cross Christmas Roll Call the week of December 16—23.

A message of good cheer will be sent overseas this coming Christmas Eve, to hearten our fighting boys and our Allies.

That message must be complete —there must be no room for doubt that we stand behind them—it must bear the word that there is *Universal Membership* in the Red Cross— *their Red Cross.*

Let us make our second Christmas at war a Red Cross Christmas— with full membership in every American home.

All you need is a Heart and a Dollar
RED CROSS CHRISTMAS ROLL CALL
December 16—23

Contributed Through
Division of Advertising

This space contributed for the Winning of the War by

United States Gov't Comm.
on Public Information

Make this a Red Cross Christmas

America's second war-time Christmas is almost here. Our thoughts, our interests, our hearts are not in the trivial things now—they are with the boys in France and our war-tried Allies.

Their thoughts, their interests, their hopes are in the Red Cross and the knowledge that it is ever present and ready to lend them aid most needed.

Let our Christmas message to those loved ones be that we stand solidly behind the American Red Cross—that there is full membership in every American home. No other word we can send will give them greater encouragement, or fortitude for that which must be accomplished.

+ All you need is a heart and a dollar +
Red Cross Christmas Roll Call, December 16-23

Contributed through Division of Advertising   United States Gov't Comm. on Public Information

This space contributed for the Winning of the War by

The Spirit of the Red Cross Should Enter Every Home

THROUGH the Red Cross all the love of kindred and country, which gives our National soul its greatness, finds expression.

Those who love America, believe in humanity, and have faith in God, must count themselves proud to answer "present" at the Red Cross Christmas Roll Call, December 16th to 23rd, during which period the privilege of membership is to be extended to every loyal American.

Let us grasp this opportunity to make this a Red Cross Christmas.

Let us be able to tell our boys at the front, when we send them our Christmas greetings, that America stands solidly behind the Red Cross—*their Red Cross* —with full membership in every home.

Let us tell them that this beautiful spirit of love, and compassion, and generosity, and unselfish service, has entered every home in our land—from the smallest farm in Maine to the largest ranch in California.

No other message we can send will give them greater courage or encouragement. They know what the Red Cross means to them.

Join the Red Cross
All you need is a heart and a dollar

Contributed through
Division of Advertising

U. S. Govt. Comm.
on Public Information

This space contributed for the Winning of the War by

Wear Your Button

Fly Your Flag

The GREATEST MOTHER *in the* WORLD

holds a sacred place of honor within our homes and in our hearts

THE message that the American people stand as one behind our brave boys and gallant Allies, is the most cheerful "Merry Christmas" we can send them.

Let us make this a Red Cross Christmas—let us see to it that every member of every family joins the Red Cross. She is warming thousands, feeding thousands, healing thousands from her store—the Greatest Mother in the World.

All you need is a Heart and a Dollar

RED CROSS CHRISTMAS ROLL CALL

December 16—23

Contributed Through Division of Advertising   United States Gov't Comm. on Public Information

This space contributed for the Winning of the War by

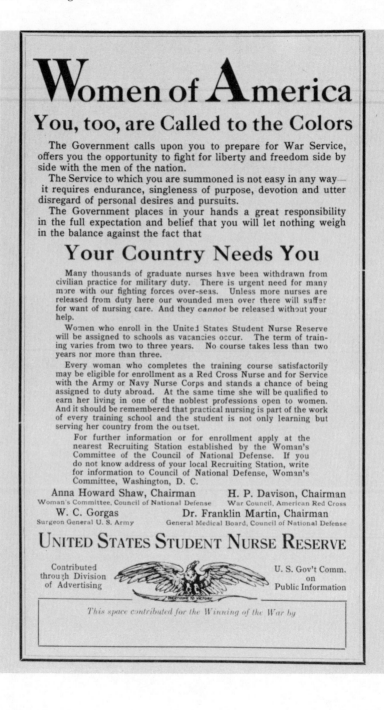

Women of America
You, too, are Called to the Colors

The Government calls upon you to prepare for War Service, offers you the opportunity to fight for liberty and freedom side by side with the men of the nation.

The Service to which you are summoned is not easy in any way— it requires endurance, singleness of purpose, devotion and utter disregard of personal desires and pursuits.

The Government places in your hands a great responsibility in the full expectation and belief that you will let nothing weigh in the balance against the fact that

Your Country Needs You

Many thousands of graduate nurses have been withdrawn from civilian practice for military duty. There is urgent need for many more with our fighting forces over-seas. Unless more nurses are released from duty here our wounded men over there will suffer for want of nursing care. And they *cannot* be released without your help.

Women who enroll in the United States Student Nurse Reserve will be assigned to schools as vacancies occur. The term of training varies from two to three years. No course takes less than two years nor more than three.

Every woman who completes the training course satisfactorily may be eligible for enrollment as a Red Cross Nurse and for Service with the Army or Navy Nurse Corps and stands a chance of being assigned to duty abroad. At the same time she will be qualified to earn her living in one of the noblest professions open to women. And it should be remembered that practical nursing is part of the work of every training school and the student is not only learning but serving her country from the outset.

For further information or for enrollment apply at the nearest Recruiting Station established by the Woman's Committee of the Council of National Defense. If you do not know address of your local Recruiting Station, write for information to Council of National Defense, Woman's Committee, Washington, D. C.

Anna Howard Shaw, Chairman
Woman's Committee, Council of National Defense

H. P. Davison, Chairman
War Council, American Red Cross

W. C. Gorgas
Surgeon General U. S. Army

Dr. Franklin Martin, Chairman
General Medical Board, Council of National Defense

United States Student Nurse Reserve

Contributed
through Division
of Advertising

U. S. Gov't Comm.
on
Public Information

This space contributed for the Winning of the War by

He *Must Not* Overstay His Leave!

Save trouble for him by
keeping your eye on the clock

YOU loving wives and sweethearts! You fond parents and devoted friends! We know just how you feel when *HIS* leave is almost up, and it is about time for him to start back to camp.

A few minutes more means *so* much to you—and *seems* to mean so little to Uncle Sam.

Surely, you think, there is no great harm if *one* soldier is a few minutes, or even hours, late, getting back. How could an innocent and well-meaning soldier be punished for so trifling a transgression?

But such thoughts do *HIM* and Uncle Sam—and yourself as well—more harm than you can possibly realize.

An army must be run by the clock!

When you stop to think that the army is made up of millions of individuals, each with his own little circle of friends and acquaintants, just like your soldier boy, you can see how vitally important it is for *every* man to be in the appointed *place* at the appointed *time.*

The slightest laxity of discipline here means hope-

less confusion. Without absolute regularity, uniformity, orderliness, an army would be helpless. That is why all breaches of discipline are punished severely.

And since ABSENCE WITHOUT LEAVE is one of the most dangerous offences of all, it is one of the MOST SEVERELY PUNISHED.

The regrettable part about this is, that the soldier's friends are nearly always more to blame than he is.

Nine times out of ten the soldier overstays his leave because his loving friends cling to him—tempt him —encourage his tardiness.

HE has to pay for *YOUR* unwise kindness— *YOUR* thoughtless hospitality. He has to pay for his own politeness in accepting the attentions you thrust upon him through your love and patriotism *improperly directed.*

For his sake, for Uncle Sam's sake, and to help lick the Kaiser, ask him when his leave expires— "send him away with a smile" *BEFORE* HIS TIME IS UP.

COMMITTEE ON PUBLIC INFORMATION, *8 Jackson Place, Washington, D. C.*

GEORGE CREEL, *Chairman*
THE SECRETARY OF STATE

THE SECRETARY OF WAR
THE SECRETARY OF THE NAVY

Contributed through Division of Advertising

U. S. Gov't Committee on Public Information

This space contributed for the Winning of the War by

He Will
Come Back a Better Man!

*Uncle Sam is giving him a newer and better equipment,
in mind and body — fitting him for a bigger, finer life*

WHEN that boy of yours comes marching home a Victorious Crusader he will be a very different person from the lad you bravely sent away with a kiss, a tear and a smile.

He will be strong in body, quick and sure in action, alert and keen in mind, firm and resolute in character, calm and even-tempered.

Self-control and self-reliance — ability to think and act in emergencies — coolness and courage in time of stress and danger — such will be the product of his training and experience.

Neatness, precision in detail without fuss and worry, promptness, reliability,

scrupulous integrity, thoughtfulness and courtesy — these things come from army comradeship and discipline.

A broad-shouldered, deep-chested, square-jawed YOUNG MAN with flashing eyes and a happy smile — that's who will throw himself into your arms when "Johnny Comes Marching Home Again."

That's who is coming back to live his life in happiness with you.

And in his hands — and yours — lies the future of America.

Help him, keep him happy NOW — by cheerful, newsy letters — for your sake — and for Uncle Sam.

COMMITTEE ON PUBLIC INFORMATION, *8 Jackson Place, Washington, D. C.*

GEORGE CREEL, *Chairman*
THE SECRETARY OF STATE

THE SECRETARY OF WAR
THE SECRETARY OF THE NAVY

Contributed through Division of Advertising

U. S. Gov't Committee on Public Information

This space contributed for the Winning of the War by

Germany Has Not Yet Invented a Substitute for the American Spirit

POISON GAS, the flame thrower, the tear bomb, the saw-tooth bayonet—these are the contributions of Germany's scientists to modern warfare.

But that peculiar combination of high spirits and vigor called "pep" is a distinctive American invention. "Pep" will win the war. Let's cultivate it.

Never will it be necessary to chain American gunners to their pieces and station the officers <u>behind</u> our men to shoot them if they waver.

The especial field of Y. M. C. A. work is the conservation of "pep." Like a high-bred animal, the soldier is temperamental; he has his ups and downs. The "Y" increases the percentage of "ups."

Send the Boys Over the Top Cheering

The "Y" huts are on all fronts where our boys are fighting. Wherever they are, is a welcome for any American soldier of whatever creed. There he will find home papers, free writing paper, music, free entertainments to cure the blues. He may see movies of American life that will make him think of the home folks. He can get free instruction in French, Italian or in reading and writ-ing English if need be. He can attend religious service. He can buy there at less than cost the little necessities of life. Thanks to the Y. M. C. A., he is able to take part in active athletics and manly games which keep mind and body fit. And these things will make him think better, fight harder and shoot straighter.

This is what you are giving the boys when you donate to the Y. M. C. A. Are these little comforts and advantages, to which the poorest in this country are accustomed, too good for those who are fighting for you? If you do not think so—and, of course, you don't—stint yourself to the utmost to give to the Y. M. C. A.

YMCA   Four allied activities, all endorsed by the Government, are combined in the United War Work Campaign, with the budgets distributed as follows: Y.M.C.A., $100,000,000, Y.W.C.A., $15,000,000, War Camp Community Service, $15,000,000, American Library Association, $3,500,000.   YMCA

Contributed through Division of Advertising   U. S. Govt. Comm. on Public Information

This space contributed for the Winning of the War by

Mary Garden, Maxine Adams, Julia Marlowe, Elsie Janis, Jane Cowl, Otis Skinner, Marie Doro, Weber and Fields, E. H. Sothern and many other American actors and singers have been bringing cheer and encouragement to the boys in khaki who patronize the Y. M. C. A. "flashlight circuit" in France.

Shakespeare under fire—

IT was in a Y. M. C. A. hut in a "little hole in France." E. H. Sothern, the famous actor, was doing a scene from Hamlet, before a soldier audience.

"Oh, what a rash and bloody deed was this!" he was saying.

Like an echo to his words came the piercing call of the bugle as a signal of an air raid. The lights flashed out.

From the dark, the colonel's voice rang out, "Let's have a light! We can have an air raid every evening, but we can't often hear Mr. Sothern. If he doesn't mind, we should like to have him go on."

Of course Mr. Sothern did not mind. One small light was snapped on, and the actor continued to the end.

THEY GIVE UP BOTH TIME AND MONEY, FOR THIS GREAT WORK

Mr. Sothern or other players like him get little or no salary for working the great Y. M. C. A. circuit in France. Yet there is a large and increasing number of our best known artists who are cheerfully undergo-ing unusual hardships in order to bring wholesome cheer and amusement to our boys in khaki wherever they go.

But the "flashlight circuit" of the Y. M. C. A. is only a small part of the work done by this organization. One of the dispatches from Europe recently tells of boys in khaki seen playing billiards in gas masks in a Y. M. C. A. hut. The secretary in charge of the hut was on the job, of course, and overhead the big shells whining through the air as they were hurled from the German heavies.

At these huts the man with the Red Tri-angle on his sleeve meets the troops march-ing to and from the trenches with hot cof-fee and food and cigarettes at the moment when these comforts make life bright once more. No matter how thick the barrage overhead the steaming pot of coffee is forth-coming. When the battle is hottest and the wounded begin to filter back through the lines, some of them—hit by a shell splinter or shot through an arm or a shoulder—are able to stumble back alone toward the near dressing stations between the lines. Here the Y. M. C. A. man comes to his aid; a sip of coffee, a careful arm under his shoulder to help him, a renewal of his first aid bandage. In this way the Red Triangle has saved the lives of thousands of men who would have died of exhaustion.

Whether you think of the Y. M. C. A. man as helping the "walking wounded," supply-ing entertainment, shows, baseballs and punching bags, or as the man who runs the post exchange or store, or just as the man who helps keep things going in the huts and supplies paper and ink for writing home, you must get behind his work.

General Pershing has officially designated the Y. M. C. A. to operate the post ex-changes for the entire army. It is also the only organization authorized to exhibit "movies" to the soldiers.

This splendid work that the Y. M. C. A. is doing is just as important as the actual transportation of men and supplies to the front.

Lord Northcliffe recently said: "Without the Y. M. C. A. we could not win the war." whatever it costs to maintain this import-ant work, it must not fail for lack of sup-port by those who stay behind.

Picture yourself stumbling in from a hot battle—a minor wound from a piece of shrapnel has put you out for the moment. Think what it means to meet a friend—a Y. M. C. A. man who gives you coffee and a sandwich to back you up, puts an arm under your shoulder and helps you back.

Where are the college coaches? Working in France, helping to keep the boys in condition for a rattling good scrap. Quimby of Yale, Magee of Houston, Saver of Princeton, Fults of Brown, Stagg of Chi-cago, are some of the men who now wear the Red Triangle.

When the boys in France are playing a game of billiards in a Y. M. C. A. hut and the gas signals come, you wouldn't expect them to quit, would you? No. On go the gas masks and the game proceeds.

YMCA Seven allied activities, all endorsed by the Government are combined in the United War Work Campaign, with the budgets dis-tributed as follows: Young Mens Christian Association $100,000,000, Y. W. C. A., $15,000,000, National Catholic War Council (including the work of the Knights of Columbus) and special war activities for women) $30,000,000, Jewish Welfare Board, $3,500,000, American Library Association, $3,500,000, War Camp Community Service $15,000,000, Salvation Army $3,500,000. **YMCA**

Contributed through Division of Advertising.   United States Govt. Comm. on Public Information

This space contributed for the Winning of the War by

Out of the Mouth of Hell

our boys come, nerve-racked, tense, exhausted by their sleepless vigil and harassed with tragic memories.

Rest they will have, but rest is not re-creation.   Mind must relax as well as body.   They must forget awhile, must turn their thoughts into their normal course before facing anew the horrors of the first-line trenches.

Courage they have always, but we can put fresh heart into them; we can restore the high spirits of youth and send them singing into the fray.

They Are Fighting for You—Show Your Appreciation

When you give them arms, you give them only the instruments of your own defense; when you give for the wounded, you give only in common humanity; but when you give to the Y. M. C. A., you are extending to the boys the warm hand of gratitude, the last token of your appreciation of what they are doing for you. You are doing this by showing your interest in their welfare.

The Y. M. C. A. furnishes to the boys, not only in its own "huts"—which are often close to the firing line—but in the trenches, the material and intangible comforts which mean much to morale. It furnishes free entertainment back of the lines. It supplies free writing paper and reading matter. It conducts all post exchanges, selling general merchandise without profit. It has charge of and encourages athletics, and conducts a "khaki college" for liberal education. Its religious work is non-sectarian and non-propagandist. It keeps alive in the boys "over there" the life and the spirit of "over here."

GIVE NOW—BEFORE THEIR SACRIFICE IS MADE

Seven allied activities, all endorsed by the Government, are combined in the United War Campaign, with the budgets distributed as follows: Y. M. C. A. $100,000,000; Y. W. C. A. $15,000,000; National Catholic War Council (including the work of the Knights of Columbus and special war activities for women), $30,000,000; Jewish Welfare Board, $3,500,000; American Library Association, $3,500,000; War Camp Community Service, $15,000,000; Salvation Army, $3,500,000.

Contributed through Division of Advertising   United States Gov't. Comm. on Public Information

This space contributed for the Winning of the War by

— R-M-BRINKERHOFF —

Bring a Little Bit of Home
to the Boys at the Front

"KEEP THE HOME FIRES BURNING" in their hearts as well as on our hearths. Don't let them forget that over here a hundred million loyal backers are with them heart and soul. Don't let them feel they are forgotten; strengthen the bonds between them and their home country.

You can help do this for a million, two million boys who have gone to fight in a strange land. Give to them freely through the Y. M. C. A. and you will be giving them the little comforts that look ten times as big over there—free books and magazines, free writing paper, and a hundred of the lesser necessities—shaving materials, foot powder, needles and thread, etc.—at less than cost. You will be giving them entertainment of a wholesome, clean sort—music, "movies," lec-

tures on instructive and interesting topics. You will be giving them the means of engaging in athletic sports, invaluable in keeping men in good physical and mental condition. You will be giving them instruction in French, Italian, English, if needed, history, geography, etc. You will be giving them the opportunity to attend religious services of a broad, non-sectarian character.

These things are more than comforts—they are *necessities* to men engaged in exhausting and nerve-racking warfare. They keep hearts strong and courage high. And by giving them these simple pleasures and lesser essentials, you show your gratitude for those who are giving their lives. Open your heart and purse freely and pay, in so far as you can, your debt to them.

YMCA   *Seven allied activities, all endorsed by the Government, are combined in the United War Campaign, with the budgets distributed as follows: Y. M. C. A., $100,000,000; Y. W. C. A., $15,000,000; National Catholic War Council (including the work of the Knights of Columbus and special war activities for women), $30,000,000; Jewish Welfare Board, $3,500,000; American Library Association, $3,500,000; War Camp Community Service, $15,000,000; Salvation Army, $3,500,000.*   **YMCA**

Contributed through Division of Advertising   United States Gov't Comm. on Public Information

This Space contributed for the Winning of the War by

How your soldier's every need is served

YOUR boy has just come back from a front-line trench. His nerves are stretched to the snapping point. He has brushed against death. He has felt the fury of plunging on to kill or be killed. The crash of guns has beat into his brain.

Then, suddenly, comes his rest period. He staggers back to his billet. He is whole in body, but how can he rest? His whole system is keyed up to high tension. He has forgotten how to rest.

That is the danger point—as dangerous in its way as any phase of fighting—unless there is a hand to steady him.

Wherever your man in uniform goes, on the trains, in camp, on transports, in foreign cities and villages, in rest billets, even in the fire trenches—there, standing beside him, are the strong, splendid, helpful men of the Y. M. C. A.

It is the task of the "Y" to be father, mother, friend, to be club, amusement place, library, corner grocery store, hotel, college, church, to our millions who are so far away among strange people in strange lands.

From merely furnishing a sheet of paper to reserving every hotel in a resort town for our men on leave, the Y. M. C. A. does its utmost to provide for the wholesome pleasure, the comfort, well being and moral safety of your soldier and over two million others.

It sends out for its workers, thousands of splendid men *beyond the active service age*—famous business executives, college presidents, actors, popular coaches, leaders among men—to carry on this great task.

The cost of erecting and equipping thousands of huts, the cost of providing food and cheer to millions of men, of transporting shiploads of supplies, of buying amusement places and offering a high grade of entertainment, the cost of merely keeping thousands of the huts warm this coming winter in a land where coal is $80 a ton, is a vast undertaking. It is so vast that it will require all the help that the entire nation can give.

But the work must be done.

Already Commanders of the French and Italian Armies as well as General Pershing are asking for more huts.

If this work is to go forward the Y. M. C. A. and the organizations allied with it in our United War Fund Campaign, must have at once no less than $170,500,000.

This seems a huge sum. Yet it means only about 10 cents a day to spend for each soldier and sailor.

On this money depends to a great extent the morale of our army—on which rests the future of our country and the winning of the war. Lord Northcliffe says, "Without the Y. M. C. A., the war could not be won."

Give fully, greatly; give till you feel the pinch.

A PLACE TO ATTEND THE SERVICES OF HIS OWN FAITH

After he has been in action, after he has met danger and seen death, many a boy who never before gave much thought to religion, longs for the services of his own church. He longs to hear of God and immortality. He craves the peace and comfort of the services in which he was reared. In the Y. M. C. A. for every kind of service is held, Protestant, Catholic, Hebrew, etc. There your boy may worship in the faith of his own people. This is what our boys want. This is what they ask. Surely we cannot deny them a place in which to pray!

A BIT OF PLEASURE MAKES LIFE BEARABLE

Gas attacks are more regular than meals in some of the huts close to the front. But in the "Y" huts, even when they must wear their gas masks, a game will make the boy forget trouble and danger. They can stand any amount of shelling, but they MUST have a bit of fun.

ON LEAVE!

When your sailor or soldier has a few days leave trained "Y" girls and men, the finest kind of Americans, are their hosts. Providing our boys on leave with some place to go, giving them wholesome good times, is one of the biggest tasks the Y. M. C. A. has undertaken. Just for them it is running all the big hotels in Aix les Bains, the finest resort in France. For their entertainment, it runs great huts and hotels in the big cities. For them it provides guides for every kind of pleasure and relaxation.

Seven allied activities, all endorsed by the Government, are combined in the United War Work Campaign, with the budgets distributed as follows: Young Men's Christian Association, $100,000,000; Y. W. C. A., $15,000,000; National Catholic War Council (including the work of the Knights of Columbus and special war activities for women), $30,000,000; Jewish Welfare Board, $3,500,000; American Library Association, $3,500,000; War Camp Community Service, $15,000,000; Salvation Army, $3,500,000.

Contributed through Division of Advertising   United States Government Committee on Public Information

This space contributed for the Winning of the War by
THE DELINEATOR

WANTED
3,000 Red-Blooded Men

"There is no Railroad President—no Corporation Director in America too big for the job of handling one of our huts in France," cables one of America's best known business men from "over there." Here is a chance for you men whom war has skipped.

Men of the "skipped generation," men whose fathers were in the Civil War and whose sons are in this war—"regular fellows," of the in-between age, men who have made good in business, made good in times of peace, men whose success has come to them through knowing how to handle other men—three thousand of you are wanted.

There's a need in France right now for such as you to take charge of Y. M. C. A. huts. These are the unarmed soldiers, nerve-proof under a shower of shells, willing to sleep where they can, eat when there's a chance, able to work 16 hours a day, good mixers, ready to be preachers or friends—yes, and at need, game to the core.

Three thousand such jobs are waiting—at nothing per year—for those who can fill them. Nothing per year—nothing but the thrill that comes to the man who does his part, nothing but the tingle of blood that squares his shoulders and makes him say to himself: "It was my part and I did it."

Write, giving full details, to Y. M. C. A. Overseas' Headquarters
E. D. POUCH, 347 Madison Avenue, New York

Y.   M.   C.   A.

Contributed through Division of Advertising.   United States Gov't Comm. on Public Information

This space contributed for the Winning of the War by

Guess What They're Reading

"Zippy stories or trashy trifles?"

No.

"Well, some kind of a man's story. You know —full of blood and thunder and everything?"

Perhaps. But it's a little better than an even chance, as borne out by Camp Library records, that these men are reading *technical books*— books that will help them better their positions in their former jobs when they get back into tweeds and blue serge again after the war.

That may surprise you. It startled us. Because in the Public Library System of the United States, 70% of the books asked for are fiction. In the camps, *less than 50% of the demand is for fiction!*

Facts show that our men in the service—here as well as overseas—are eager for books that will help them, first, to be better soldiers; second, to be better Americans; third, to progress faster when they get back to civil life.

Why, if they were yelling for cheap, trashy novels, we fathers and mothers would send them fast enough. But they don't want trash. They want *the real thing*—the kind of reading that, fortunately, will bring them back to us stronger

in purpose and better trained than when they went out.

It's because the men want technical books and business books that funds are needed. The public has donated millions of books, mostly novels. We must buy (at a liberal discount from the publisher) the educational works they are so anxious for—books that will make them better soldiers today—better soldiers tomorrow. Is the cause big enough? Then, give and give freely.

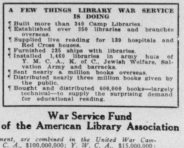

A FEW THINGS LIBRARY WAR SERVICE IS DOING
¶ Built more than 340 Camp Libraries.
¶ Established over 350 libraries and branches overseas.
¶ Supplied live reading for 139 hospitals and Red Cross houses.
¶ Furnished 235 ships with libraries.
¶ Installed 1,460 libraries in army huts of Y. M. C. A., K. of C., Jewish Welfare, Salvation Army and barracks.
¶ Sent nearly a million books overseas.
¶ Distributed nearly three million books given by the public.
¶ Bought and distributed 600,000 books—largely technical—to supply the surprising demand for educational reading.

War Service Fund
of the American Library Association

Seven allied activities, all endorsed by the Government, are combined in the United War Campaign, with the budgets distributed, as follows: Y. M. C. A., $100,000,000; Y. W. C. A., $15,000,000; National Catholic War Council (including the work of the Knights of Columbus and special war activities for women), $30,000,000; Jewish Welfare Board, $3,500,000; American Library Association, $3,500,000; War Camp Community Service, $15,000,000; Salvation Army, $3,500,000.

Contributed through Division of Advertising   United States Gov't Comm. on Public Information

This Space Contributed for the Winning of the War by

"Gee!
I wish there was something I could do!"

WHEN you think of what the boys "over there" are doing to help the great cause of freedom, wouldn't you just give anything to be there and help them? Wouldn't you fairly jump at the chance to do anything in the world to back up the men that are fighting?

You can't be there yet, of course, but there is a place for a boy who wants to help our country, a place where he can show the stuff he is made of as well as he could over in France.

There is a new opportunity for boys who want to do their share toward winning the war. It is called the *Victory Boys*. Its motto is, "A million boys behind a million fighters."

The organizations for which the *Victory Boys* are working provide the soldier with his movie theatre, his church, his club, his store where he buys the little everyday things he needs. When he is hungry, they feed him; when he is tired, they comfort him.

When you enroll with the *Victory Boys*, you pledge yourself to go out and earn money for this great work that the soldier needs so much. Ask your neighbors for odd jobs. Tell them of the great cause you are working for. If you can pledge yourself to earn $20, remember that for five months you are giving all that these mean to some lonely soldier.

Wear the *Victory Boys* button—It is a badge of honor. It means that you are doing everything in your power to help your country to victory.

**For further information inquire at the Victory Boys Division of your local
UNITED WAR WORK CAMPAIGN COMMITTEE**

Seven Allied activities, all endorsed by the Government, are combined in the United War Campaign, with the budgets distributed as follows: Y. M. C. A., $100,000,000; Y. W. C. A., $15,000,000; National Catholic War Council (including the work of the Knights of Columbus and special war activities for women), $30,000,000; Jewish Welfare Board, $3,500,000; American Library Association, $3,500,000; War Camp Community Service, $15,000,000; Salvation Army, $3,500,000.

Contributed through Division
of Advertising

United States Gov't Comm. on
Public Information

This space contributed for the Winning of the War by

More Shells—Fewer Casualties

BACK of every war activity lies—coal. Ships, shells, guns, transportation. For all these we must have—coal.

The more coal, the more shells with which to destroy the machine-gun nests of our enemies—and thereby save the lives of our own boys.

The larger the supply of coal—the shorter the war and fewer casualties.

Our annual output of coal has increased a hundred million tons since we went into the war, while no other nation has even been able to maintain its output during the war.

Another fifty million badly needed tons can be saved—to help shorten the war.

Save coal.

Close up the unused rooms and turn off the heat. Put on storm doors and windows—put them on early. See to it that the weather strips fit.

Don't heat your home above 68°. A higher temperature is unhealthy, anyway.

Burn wood where you can.

Keep an eye on the furnace—don't leave it all to "the man."

If you feel that one shovelful of coal won't make any difference—think of it as a shell for the boys over there.

If you find yourself burning two lights when one will do—turn one out.

You, who have bought bonds and thrift stamps, you who have given of your money for war charities, given until you have felt the pinch, you whose sons and neighbors' sons are over there, will you not give up, too, just a bit of lazy, enervating comfort to help hurry along the job those brave boys have tackled?

Save light and heat, save coal.

To learn to operate your furnace efficiently, get from your local fuel administrator a leaflet entitled "Save Coal in the Home."

UNITED STATES FUEL ADMINISTRATION

Contributed through Division of Advertising   United States Gov't Comm. on Public Information

This space contributed for the Winning of the War by

directed at women. Byoir suggested that ads in women's magazines should encourage cheerful letters to American soldiers.[78]
Illustrations such as *What You Can Do to Make Life Cheerful in
Camp and Trench* and *Write Him Cheerful Letters* urged the fighting spirit, so as "to keep the Kaiser on the run." Posters encouraged women to avoid letting their sons or husbands overstay
leaves and offered assurance that sons or husbands would come
back as better men. An effort was considered to use magazines
such as *Ladies' Home Journal* to impress on women the need for
silence about war information.

The drive for the Red Cross looked carefully to wives and
mothers: *When Distress Calls the Red Cross Answers "Here":—
Join the Red Cross, One Member of a Family Is Not Enough*, and
Make This a Red Cross Christmas. Red Cross advertising generally
sought to base its message on "heart appeal." It was believed
that this approach would be most productive, as other themes
had been worked to the limit by other campaigns. But before
the appeal was made to sentiment and generosity, an effort was
made to acquaint the public with Red Cross work. The poster
What Your Red Cross Dollars Do detailed how the money for the
First Red Cross Fund had been spent. Other advertisements informed of the 3,350 Red Cross chapters, the 11,000 branches,
the more than 2 million adult members. The most appealing
copy was designed "to stir the emotions and unloosen the
strings around people's pocketbooks." Illustrations sought to
make people "glow with feeling," to quicken the heartbeat and
bring tears to the eyes.[79] Perhaps the most famous Red Cross
poster, certainly one of the most powerful, was A. E. Foringer's
The Greatest Mother in the World, a matron dressed as a Red Cross
nurse, holding a miniature hospital stretcher with a wounded
soldier. The attitude reflected that of a mother caring for a
child.[80]

It is interesting to observe parenthetically the treatment of
women in CPI posters. Women were frequently pictured as
devoted wives and mothers who stood firmly behind their men
as they went off to war. The nursing figure was also prominent,
and such posters as *Women of America You, Too, Are Called to
the Colors!* encouraged women to serve their country as nurses.

Sometimes this figure was combined with the mother image to produce—as in the Foringer drawing—very effective results. Women were portrayed in other ways, too. Often, as in *Remember Belgium* or *This Is Kultur*, they were shown as victims of German brutality. And women were used symbolically to represent Public Opinion or Democracy.[81]

Like the Red Cross, the YMCA and YWCA received help from the Division of Advertising. Some posters also appealed to the mother instinct, asking *How Great Is Your Mother Love?* and remarking that "the most you can give them is less than they are giving you." Another illustration, *The "Y" and the War*, told the public how the YMCA was helping to win the war. One poster quoted an army officer saying to a YMCA entertainer, "You have kept my men from thinking of tomorrow's battle; they will fight better because of tonight." Another drawing credited the YMCA with fighting spirit and called for aid for the "Y" by saying, *Send the Boys over the Top Cheering*. Posters for the "Y" were entitled *Shakespeare under Fire*, which portrayed the actor E. H. Southern performing *Hamlet* in a YMCA hut that was under attack; *Out of the Mouth of Hell—They are Fighting for You—Show Your Appreciation*; *Bring a Little Bit of Home to the Boys at the Front*; *Wanted: 3,000 Red-Blooded Men*; and *How the Y.M.C.A. Invested Fifty Millions*.

As mentioned, the Division of Advertising served the Food and Fuel Administrations and the Department of Agriculture. An ad for the Fuel Administration—*More Shells—Fewer Casualties*—urged conservation of coal, appealing to citizens to read the Fuel Administration leaflet *Save Coal in the Home*, to learn how to operate furnaces efficiently. One of the first drives for the Department of Agriculture was the War Garden Campaign— also the responsibility of the Department of the Interior, as Secretary Lane had been directed to organize a War Garden Army. The Division of Advertising was notified too late to reach many magazines, but did inaugurate a department store campaign that sought to combine the stores' advertisements for garden tools and implements with the government's message. It tried to organize public schools. Distribution was handled by the AACW, and the war committees of each of its nearly 180

clubs worked on the project.[82] Other messages relating to agriculture called for a Liberty Wheat Harvest entailing a 7 percent
increase in planting of winter wheat. An effort was made to destroy rats; posters such as *Kill Every Rat* described how rodents
endangered health and annually destroyed $200 million worth
of property. "Organize to exterminate rats. Stir up your Grange
to give prizes in a rat-tail contest. . . . Let none escape."

The Division of Advertising used about $1.6 million of
donated advertising space ($2.25 million had been contributed),
about 9,400 insertions in periodicals, with a combined circulation of nearly 550 million. More than 800 publishers of weekly
and monthly publications gave space, in addition to space donated by advertisers of merchandise.[83] Creel estimated that the
work of the division normally would have cost the government
at least $5 million.[84]

ADVERTISING proved extremely important in
mobilizing patriotism during 1917 and 1918. The appeals by
advertisers fed the flames of national enthusiasm manifest during this time. Sales of bonds and savings stamps, which these
appeals helped stimulate, strengthened the attachment to the
nation because they gave citizens a vested interest in their government. Participation in such activities as war gardens, the
Red Cross, and even the conservation of coal doubtless stirred a
sense of community.

The work of the Division of Advertising and of Gibson's
Division of Pictorial Publicity proved indeed an enormous success, and its success helped weaken the idea of the rational
citizen. Creel had believed in the rational nature of public
opinion and held the CPI's function to be educational. Gibson
and others did not even pay lip service to this idea, with their
attempt to arouse enthusiasm.[85] The success of advertising in
the war lent strength to those who questioned the rationality
of public opinion. Many writers who in the 1920s were to become critics of the rational nature of man—people like Walter
Lippmann and Bernays—learned much from the study of such
war propaganda.[86]

The Division of Advertising also enhanced the prestige of

advertising men. Advertising men sought recognition of their work through having the government pay for advertising, and although the attempt failed, the Division of Advertising accomplished essentially the same thing. D'Arcy proclaimed that "advertising's hour of opportunity has struck."[87] Creel, who early in the war had thought of advertising men as "plausible pirates," came to believe that if his committee had done nothing else, its use of advertising men gave advertising "the dignity of a profession" and incorporated "its dynamic abilities in American team-play."[88] The advertising division ably demonstrated the possibility of national campaigns.[89]

9

News as Propaganda

Public opinion is a factor in victory no less than ships and guns, and the creation and stimulation of a healthy, ardent national sentiment is the kind of fighting that the press can do.[1]

ALEXIS DE TOCQUEVILLE once wrote that only a newspaper could "drop the same thought into a thousand minds at the same moment."[2] Because many members of the CPI came from journalism, and had been using the press for many years to support one cause or another, there was an almost instinctive recognition of Tocqueville's point. Some years before the war, Will Irwin commented on the great increase in newspaper readers in the late nineteenth and early twentieth centuries, noting that he believed "no other extra-judicial force, except religion, . . . half so powerful" as the American press.[3] Equally convinced of the press's importance, Creel called it the greatest power on earth. The importance of the press was profound, he thought, "for we know only what it tells us."[4]

It is not surprising that from the outset the Committee on Public Information sought to influence the news. The Division of News was one of the first sections established by the committee. The CPI published the country's first government daily, the *Official Bulletin*, and influenced the hundreds of foreign-language newspapers in the country through the Foreign Language Newspaper Division, which monitored virtually all such publications. The Bureau of Cartoons provided visual commentaries on events. The Division of Films, with its subsidiary departments, captured the war by photography. No wonder Creel after the war could boast that even his critics took "a daily diet of our material."[5]

President Wilson once said that "the particular thing you have to surrender to is facts."[6] The CPI discovered in 1917–18 that one of the best means of controlling news was flooding news channels with "facts," or what amounted to official information. Nearly all government departments had their information bureaus—it was estimated that there were as many as forty-five or fifty.[7] News from the bureaus reached such a volume that by the end of 1917, every newspaper in California received on the average of six pounds of publicity from the government each day, enough to fill more than twelve hundred columns.[8] The CPI's Division of News hoped to impose order on these chaotic releases, especially those by the army and navy. Eventually, the division's work expanded, and it became the sole medium for official war information, not only that put out by the army and navy but also that from the White House, the Department of Labor, the Department of Justice, the National War Labor Board, the War Industries Board, the Council of National Defense, the Alien Property Custodian, and the War Trade Board.[9] The division maintained representatives in many government departments and with their assistance prepared news statements and made them available for daily newspapers and trade papers. Articles were submitted to the chief of each department for approval.[10] President Wilson seems to have exercised considerable control over the division, often determining if and when items from one of the government departments would be released.[11]

During the war years the "handout" became an institution in Washington, and the Division of News helped in its development.[12] Daily interviews of Secretary of War Baker, communiqués from General Pershing, press interviews of General March, lists of American casualties—all were released through the Division of News. The division published a *War News Digest*, sent to country weeklies and dailies requesting it. More than twelve thousand rural dailies used the service. Toward the end of the war the division prepared a nightly review of world news, transmitted by wireless to all navy vessels as well as to other ships at sea.[13] The news division stopped issuing releases to the press on December 1, 1918, although arrangements to continue operating were made with the liaison offices of the committee in the War and Navy Departments.[14] Up to that time the division had put out perhaps six thousand releases, and by one estimate the bureau's material appeared in at least twenty thousand newspaper columns each week.[15] These figures are the more interesting when one considers that the Division of News could not command publication, but only presented material to the press to use or discard at its own discretion.[16]

The division directed a voluntary censorship, although Creel maintained that it made no effort "to prevent independent news-gathering or to interfere with individual contacts." When writers had an idea for a story, the news division sought to provide facts and statistics or to arrange interviews.[17] Creel contended that the division sought "to present the facts without the slightest trace of color or bias, either in the selection of news or the manner in which it was presented."[18]

Some people believed the Division of News was staffed by men of radical social views, who were even sympathetic to bolshevism. The Military Intelligence, whose reports on CPI personnel were often founded on hearsay, arrived at this conclusion. The evaluation may have had some basis in fact, although it surely was exaggerated. Edgar Sisson helped establish the division and organize voluntary censorship, in addition to setting up an apparatus to collect and distribute news. L. Ames Brown was the division's first director, although he soon left to head the CPI's Division of Syndicated Features.[19] J. W. McConaughy succeeded Brown as director and was followed in this post in June 1918 by Leigh Reilly.[20] Ranking assistants were Marlen E. Pew and Arthur W. Crawford.[21] Kenneth Durant and Maurice Strunsky were associated with the division, the latter serving as a caption writer in the Pictures Division.[22]

The critics liked to show that the second director of the division, McConaughy, had been an editorial writer for *Munsey's Magazine* and had worked for the New York *Evening Mail* after S. S. McClure gained control. While working in the New York press he was considered to have "extreme socialistic views." Military Intelligence thought him an admirer of Trotsky and Lenin, and he was supposedly convinced that the war had inspired a great social revolution. Some people expressed fear that his views colored the work of the news division.[23] Both Creel and Will Irwin admitted McConaughy's radical views but argued that he was absolutely loyal.[24] His articles for *Munsey's Magazine* before entry in the war do not reveal such a radical bias. They show him as an early advocate of the airplane as an instrument of war and commerce. He championed the right of neutral blockade runners to carry cargo and wrote about how the war in Britain tended to reduce the country's nobility, because all men were equal in the trenches.[25] He showed knowledge of the economic plight of South America and of the political situation in the Balkans and China.[26] He urged women to take a greater part in the Red Cross. He saw that modern war was far more destructive than previous conflicts: "The very breath of modern war is a destroying fire," a conflagration leaving "scars that can never be effaced."[27]

Other members of the division, such as Durant, Pew, and Strunsky, all idealistic reformers, were thought to have harbored radical views. Durant had worked with the English Propaganda Bureau, representing the British government in the United States and preparing a weekly digest of public opinion for the British cabinet. Creel took him into the CPI on the recommendation of Sir Gilbert Parker. To some conservatives he appeared as a radical and "a wild eyed visionary." Creel defended him, admitting that, like many others in the government, Durant believed in "the idea of Bolsheviki sincerity."[28] Pew was Secretary Baker's personal representative in charge of army publicity. Creel called him "every inch a progressive, with an insistent belief in the right of the people to have the facts." Before American entry in the war he had written approvingly about mobilization of young boys under military age to do war work at home, stressing the social value of such effort.[29] On recommendation of a motion-picture company, Creel had hired Strunsky to write captions and lectures for still photographs in the Division of Pictures. A socialist and former editor of the New York *Call*, Strunsky was suspected of pro-German views.[30] He left the CPI in April 1918, and Creel accepted (no doubt he had requested) the resignation—not, as he later said, because

Strunsky was disloyal but because "an excess of loyalty . . . led him to give his captions too much color and feeling."[31]

A news service was set up between the Division of News and the American Expeditionary Force, with Maximilian Foster representing the CPI in France.[32] Over the objection of General Pershing, Creel managed to have American correspondents visit war zones in Europe.[33] Through such branches as the Foreign Press Bureau, headed by Ernest Poole, the CPI maintained an impressive news network throughout not merely Europe but most of the world.[34]

In addition, the CPI published the first official daily newspaper to appear in the United States. Nearly a decade earlier, Woodrow Wilson had lamented the absence of a "national newspaper" to counter the provincialism he felt characterized local newspapers.[35] Beginning in May 1917, the *Official Bulletin* appeared each day, except Sundays, through March 31, 1919. The 9" × 11" paper varied in length. In May 1917 it ran about eight pages, but by 1918, when casualty lists increased, it went as high as forty or more pages. Daily circulation varied from 60,000 in May 1917 to a high of 115,031 in October 1918. By March the following year circulation had dropped to about 33,000.[36] The bulletin went free to public officials, newspapers, and other agencies equipped to spread its information.[37] A copy was posted in nearly every military camp and in some fifty-four thousand post offices across the United States, supplementing the Post Office Department's *Postal Bulletin*. Individual subscriptions were five dollars a year, a substantial cost for that time, but purposely so because the government wished to assure other newspapers that it was not attempting to take business. Paid subscriptions were not especially important—at the end of 1918 its editor estimated them at eighty thousand dollars, equivalent to about sixteen thousand subscribers.[38]

The *Official Bulletin* apparently originated as a result of a letter of April 18, 1917, from the president to Creel, signed by members of the War Trade Committee—the assistant attorney general, the solicitor of the Department of State, and the chief of the Bureau of Foreign and Domestic Commerce of the Department of Commerce. They recommended a "national bulletin" to publish notices of the federal government that might affect the rights and actions of American citizens and that would reduce correspondence resulting from inquiries by the public concerning government policy.[39] The first issue of the bulletin appeared on May 10.

In the early weeks there was misunderstanding of the bulletin's function. A statement explained that it was not a newspaper in the usual sense but the "full and legal printing of the official announcements of the Government heads in connection with government business." Nearly all material in the bulletin related to the government and the war. It denied any intent of exclusive publication or scooping other newspapers or in any other way hindering the legitimate functions of the press.[40]

The *Official Bulletin* tried to give the public "acts and proceedings vitally affecting their legal rights and obligations," a record that would inform of the government's objectives and its reasons. The bulletin sought to provide an accurate record of the government's part in the war.[41] It served as a means of communication between branches of government, between the government and businesses with which Washington had contracts, and between Washington and governments abroad and their representatives in the United States. It also informed American representatives abroad. Creel at first opposed the idea of such a publication, but eventually he came to feel that the bulletin "justified itself a thousandfold."[42]

The bulletin's content included a range of government activities. As mentioned, it published all pronouncements, addresses, statements, state papers, executive orders, and proclamations issued by the president after the United States entered the war. It listed the name of virtually every casualty released by the American army and navy, as well as names of men taken prisoner, wounded, or cited for bravery. The bulletin helped link the departments and bureaus of the executive branch with industry, the Red Cross, and other organizations. It tried to publish every pronouncement, order, or regulation put out by major government departments and also the War Industries Board; the Alien Property Custodian; the War Labor Board; the War Trade Board; the Telephone, Telegraph, and Cable

Systems; and the Food and Fuel Administrations. The Council
of National Defense relied on the bulletin to maintain contact
with its thousands of cooperating agencies. The Railroad Administration used the *Official Bulletin* because government assumption of control over the railroads left the director general
of railroads no other medium with which to reach the nearly
two million railroad employees. The War and Navy Departments extensively used the bulletin; Secretaries Baker and Daniels made a large effort to see that it was available for officers
and enlisted men.[43]

Edward S. Rochester, the publication's editor, saw the bulletin as a clearinghouse for government departments, which
were estimated to have nearly fifty publicity bureaus. He believed that if forty of them could be eliminated, "a rational
system of publicity" could be established.[44]

Rochester noted that other countries—Germany, France,
Britain—had such publications. He became convinced of the
"necessity for some governmental organ or mouthpiece—an
institution maintained by the Government through which the
Government might speak to the people in its own language and
in its own way." He regretted that the American public depended upon daily newspapers, that such papers did not have
space for "purely governmental textual statements" but gave
out such information piecemeal.

> Conjecture, speculation, personal analysis and interpretation of every
> hue are indulged in by editors in an effort to tell what the Government is
> doing, why it is doing it, and how it is doing it. The Government is unable to
> give its own interpretation of its own decrees, to tell in its own way why it is
> doing this or that. And the result—not in one State, but throughout the
> land—dissention, distrust, disturbed minds—unrest that imperils the very
> foundations of the Government. . . . There is no attempt to guide the minds
> of the masses.

Rochester believed the *Official Bulletin* essential "if ever the
Government hoped to work in harmonious partnership with
its people."[45]

Both Creel and Rochester maintained that news in the *Official Bulletin* was "official, without color or bias."[46] Denying that
the bulletin reflected editorial comment, Rochester acknowl-

edged that it took government advertising.[47] Some material did have propaganda value, such as the State Department's release of the Belgian government's report of German brutalities.[48] In late November 1918 the bulletin warned of the Retail Grocers' Syndicate of Worcester, Massachusetts, which lost its license to deal in sugar because of fraudulent use of sugar certificates. Such a story warned other sugar dealers of penalties for disobeying government regulations.[49]

Despite the claim that the bulletin's news was without color or bias, the publication, and indeed most of the work of the news division, was colored by nationalistic assumptions. It was, after all, the national government that was at the center of this effort to disseminate news. If nothing else, the national government received publicity from publications like the *Official Bulletin* and was increasingly able to penetrate the consciousness of the average citizen.[50]

The *Official Bulletin* was not the only effort to overcome provincialism in the local press. During 1917–18 several hundred foreign-language newspapers were published on a regular basis in the United States. The Division of Work with the Foreign Born set up bureaus to deal with several foreign-language groups. The CPI estimated that at least 865 foreign-language newspapers were published for these groups. Most of the papers appeared regularly and were received by the division's bureaus. Beginning in the spring of 1918, the bureaus began sending news releases, and by the war's end twenty-three hundred had been sent. It was estimated that 96 percent of the 745 regularly published foreign-language papers used these releases and often would carry as many as two or three columns of bureau material on their front pages. Nearly all releases were based on information given out by governmental departments, mostly the Departments of War, Labor, Internal Revenue, and Agriculture.[51]

More than two hundred CPI volunteers translated foreign-language papers and made reports on them.[52] The Foreign Language Newspaper Division, established in April 1917 and directed by William Churchill, followed almost every foreign-language paper in the country, watching for violations of the

Trading-with-the-Enemy Act. Section Nineteen of this law said that no one could mail a newspaper or magazine with editorials or articles on the United States government, or any nation in the war, or their conduct relating to the war, without filing a sworn translation with the postmaster. The president could lift restrictions on publications that were loyal.[53] The division also translated committee pamphlets and other CPI materials. It merged with the Division of Work with the Foreign Born in early 1918.[54]

In the discussion of the CPI's use of news, it is necessary to turn to the Bureau of Cartoons, established on May 28, 1918.[55] George J. Hecht supervised it, although Alfred M. Saperston was the bureau's official director. When Saperston enlisted in Marine Aviation in August, he was replaced by Gretchen Leicht. The work of the bureau was to produce the weekly *Bulletin for Cartoonists*. It maintained relations with thirty-seven government agencies, which provided material that made up the bulletin. The material went to more than 750 cartoonists across the country.

The purpose of the bulletin was to direct cartoonists' attention to important subjects. Creel believed that "the value of a unified cartoon power, which will result in centering the minds of every community on the same subject, is inestimable." Cartoonists were told that their constituency would be virtually every reader of their newspapers. The cartoonist could expose injustice, furnish humor in a dark hour, and "excite to patriotic emulation" those persons who viewed their work. "Your appeal is irresistible," they were told, "and if your subject is wisely selected and handled with skill and force your success is instantaneous."[56]

The bureau secured cartoons to be syndicated during a campaign. Unsolicited cartoons were given to interested government departments, and when departments wanted cartoons the bureau would channel their requests to some of the more qualified cartoonists. In special campaigns rush orders were often supplied.[57]

Beginning in June and running to the end of the war in November, the bureau turned out at least twenty-five bulletins.

The Woman's Committee of the Council of National Defense urged that cartoonists assist the Red Cross in obtaining nurses not just to attend wounded soldiers but to meet domestic needs as well: "There is the appeal of the sick and helpless of our crowded cities, our factory centers, our rural communities, which is no less real. It is the duty of every American woman who can be spared and who meets the requirements to see that both of these appeals are answered."[58] Another bulletin called on cartoonists to show that "the woman's sphere is now larger than the home. . . . In these times it is not right for any woman to live without working, no matter how wealthy she is."[59]

The Department of Labor realized that one of the best ways to appeal to workers was through cartoons. Cartoonists encouraged workers not to strike and to equate the striker with the army deserter.[60] A bulletin called for cartoons that would stress a "new era of partnership" among employees, employers, and the government.[61] For Labor Day, cartoons were to emphasize that "it is the privilege of youth and young manhood to fight. It is the duty of those who by reason of age or circumstances are denied that opportunity, to work." Labor Day was to celebrate "a new enfranchisement that strikes from our hands the shackles of selfishness and makes us soldiers in the greatest battle ever fought against brutality, greed, and autocracy, for freedom and justice to all lands and peoples."[62]

The Shipping Board used the Bureau of Cartoons to publicize a new steamship line between the United States and South America, a step toward giving America first-rate shipping service and assuring that "the opportunities of South American trade may be open to this country."[63] The board wished to strengthen bonds of friendship with China, but its appeal was mainly to emphasize the importance of shipbuilding in the defeat of Germany.[64]

There was a disturbing aspect to the bureau's work, in that some government departments used it for questionable ends. The Bureau of Internal Revenue wanted cartoons that would equate the tax evader with the draft dodger. "Let our fellow citizens know that the man who reports his neighbor who fails to file an income tax statement is a real patriot. Be sure and picture the idea that the real way to keep down income tax rates is to make every man file an honest return."[65] Similarly, the Department of Justice wanted cartoons that would encourage citizens to report anyone spreading German propaganda.[66] A. Mitchell Palmer, then Alien Property Custodian, sought to use cartoons to "kick German interests out of America." A bulletin boasted that the Alien Property Custodian had taken over, "body and soul," at least 140 German-owned corporations. The problem then was "to round up all smaller estates and property of every conceivable form owned by Germans who are over in Germany. Cartoonists, ask every loyal American to aid in the task of rooting German interests out of America, by reporting any knowledge concerning German ownership of property in this country."[67]

By far the largest volume of material in the *Bulletin for Cartoonists* was put out for the Food and Fuel Administrations in behalf of conservation and other related measures. Food and fuel conservation were especially strong themes during the summer of 1918. During the autumn of 1918 conservation took a back seat to information put out for the Treasury Department in behalf of the Fourth Liberty Loan.[68] In terms of entries in each bulletin, thrift and food and fuel conservation, together with the Liberty Loan, made up nearly a third of the material.

Another way to present news was through film.[69] The CPI recognized the importance of the motion-picture theater and used it extensively in the Four Minute Man campaigns. The CPI also was quick to realize the importance of photography, particularly the relatively new and exciting art of motion pictures. In addition to the written and spoken word, Creel considered it one of the three means of mobilization. Before the war ended there were several departments in the CPI centering around the camera.

During the first months of the war—April, May, and June 1917—the committee was not involved officially in the film industry, although privately produced motion pictures sounded patriotic themes.[70] As with many other groups, lack of loyalty was not a problem with most of the film producers.[71]

William A. Brady, president of the National Association of the Motion Picture Industry, conferred with Creel, who suggested a plan whereby Brady and his industry's War Cooperating Committee would place a delegate in each government department to discover how the film industry might cooperate.[72] The War Cooperating Committee, which included D. W. Griffith, Cecil B. De Mille, William Fox, and others, accepted this plan.[73]

The CPI, on September 25, 1917, established the Division of Films, with Charles S. Hart as director. Hart, who had been advertising manager for *Hearst's Magazine*, was responsible for putting the CPI's film division together and within eight months had built an organization of some forty-five persons.

At first the division limited itself to distributing Signal Corps material. The CPI hoped to use commercial producers to record the war on film, but the War Department ruled that only photographers who were members of the armed forces could take pictures at the front or in military camps. Secretary Baker thereupon recognized the CPI as the authorized distributor of Signal Corps films. Kendall Banning, former editor of *System*, and Lawrence E. Rubel, a Chicago businessman, were responsible for helping the Signal Corps build its staff. Rubel concentrated on distributing still pictures, and Louis B. Mack, a Chicago lawyer, and Walter Niebuhr dealt with motion pictures. Negatives of Signal Corps film were delivered to the chief of staff for transmission to the War College. Pictures deemed suitable for public consumption were given to the CPI in duplicate negatives, from which the committee made prints. As the service developed, feature films were made for distribution to patriotic societies and state councils of defense; distribution was carried out in such a manner as to avoid competition with the film industry.[74] Hart hoped to put the best of the Signal Corps film into features that would provide the American public with a war record.[75]

Early Signal Corps film distributed by the CPI was not sent to motion-picture theaters except for some war benefits. Unless shown at such benefits, the early pictures were free. This method of distribution soon proved to be inefficient and a financial drain, and the division was reorganized under Hart.

Within the Division of Films, a Bureau of Distribution was set up, with the domestic end of the operation directed by Denis J. Sullivan and his assistant, George Meeker. Sullivan and Meeker sought the widest possible distribution of government pictures in the shortest time and were responsible for the proportionate selling plan under which the rental on a film charged a movie house was based on the average income of that house. A small theater hence was charged less for government film than larger theaters. Distribution was taken care of by contracts with film-distributing organizations, on a percentage basis.[76] The Domestic Distribution Department had some seventeen field representatives in large cities, which served as distribution centers. Representatives supervised the distributors and appealed to exhibitors to use the films. Of the twelve thousand motion-picture theaters in America, the division's films played in more than half (a booking of 40 percent was considered 100 percent distribution, because of the proximity of theaters). The distribution department furnished a weekly quota of five hundred feet of topical film to the four film news weeklies—Gaumont, Universal, Mutual, and Pathé. This war film was to be combined into their respective motion-picture news weeklies.[77]

Most, perhaps virtually all, films put out by or distributed by the CPI were documentaries or newsreels showing phases of the war or the "latest" news from the front. Some of the films associated with the committee included *Pershing's Crusaders*, *America's Answer*, and *Official War Review*. *Pershing's Crusaders* was one of the best-known pictures; it opened in several larger cities in late April and early May 1918. The seven-reel feature film, which ran about fifty-six minutes, was photographed by the Signal Corps and the navy. It was distributed by the First National Exhibitors Circuit, Incorporated, and advertised as "the very latest news of what our boys are doing in the front line trenches and all over France," the first film "to show the true conditions now prevailing where Americans are on the fighting line."[78] Newspapers were asked to give it "unusual publicity" so that Hun propaganda might be hit "in the solar plexus."[79] The film had been entitled *Pershing Carries On*, but the title had little meaning in the Middle West and became the more colorful *Pershing's Crusaders*. The opening scene showed a crusader from the Middle Ages standing between two American soldiers. The subtitle informed the audience that

the world conflict takes upon itself the nature of a Crusade. . . . We go forth in the same spirit in which the knights of old went forth to do battle with the Saracens. Notwithstanding the sacrifices, we shall gain from it a nobler manhood and a deeper sense of America's mission in the world. . . . The young men of America are going out to rescue Civilization. They are going to fight for one definite thing, to save Democracy from death. They are marching on to give America's freedom to the oppressed multitudes of the earth. The mighty exodus of America's manhood to the plains of Europe may well be called "The Eighth Crusade."[80]

Scenes showed German soldiers crawling through woods—then pictures of a devastated, burning Belgium. One subtitle read, "Cold steel scares the Boche to death, but *sharp* steel *keeps* him dead."[81] Frames showed the French "Blue Devils," German POWs being interrogated, Secretary Baker drawing draft numbers, and draftees training. Hart hoped this film would inform the public and arouse patriotism. In the New York opening he wanted it on the same program with Douglas Fairbank's *Swat the Kaiser*, a picture produced outside the auspices of the CPI.[82] *Pershing's Crusaders* played to large crowds of people who paid from twenty-five to fifty cents each.[83]

A similar feature distributed by the committee, through the World Film Corporation, was *America's Answer*, likewise by the Signal Corps. The nine-reel film (later cut to five) focused on American activities in the war up to mid-1918 and was employed in behalf of the Liberty Loan campaign.[84] It showed President Wilson and General Pershing, a destroyer-escorted convoy, and engineers dredging a marsh and building wharves at Brest. Camouflaged troops appeared in the field, infantrymen trudged through the mud toward the front, artillery convoys passed through destroyed villages, Memorial Day services were held in a cemetery, and Major Theodore Roosevelt, Jr., decorated troops.

The *Official War Review* resulted from combined efforts of the United States, Britain, France, and Italy and carried the story of each nation's war effort by presenting fighting on nearly every front. Issued weekly and distributed by Pathé, the *Official War Review* appeared in nearly half the movie theaters in America. One week's picture focused on Allied offensives. It showed German and Austrian prisoners and President Poincaré reviewing the Polish artillery and cavalry units. Pershing was shown decorating American soldiers.[85]

An effort was made to supply films for black audiences. In some of these pictures, blacks were stereotyped. One of the films showed four blacks tap-dancing in France, with the caption indicating that they had "rhythm" in France no less than under the southern sun. The CPI Produced *Our Colored Fighters*, which was distributed by the Downing Films Company. The secretary of the film division perhaps reflected the attitude of many committee members toward blacks when she wrote that "the education of the colored race and development of citizenship among them is very important."[86]

The CPI did much to publicize its films. It published a biweekly entitled *Official Film News*, describing war films put out by the government as well as telling what was happening within the film division. Publicity was given to periodicals and newspapers and press sheets were passed out to film exhibitors in the hope of stimulating bookings in the remotest communities. The government publicized major feature films "to take them out of the class of ordinary motion-picture productions in the minds of the general public," and to impress persons whose influence was important in securing showings for such films. Three films—*Pershing's Crusaders, America's Answer,* and *Under Four Flags*—received such presentations. Each official showing lasted a week or more and was presented in municipal halls or central theaters. Schools, churches, political and social clubs, and chambers of commerce were encouraged to help publicize the openings. On some evenings theater seats might be sold just to organizations attending en masse. Each of the three films was shown in New York City, preceded by a press campaign that lasted nearly two weeks. Thousands of window cards were displayed, and invitations were sent to nearly all local dignitaries, as well as to representatives of the British, French, and Italian High Commissions. When the films were shown in Washington, the president, his cabinet, members of Congress, and other officials attended. *Pershing's Crusaders* opened in twenty-four cities, *America's Answer* was shown in thirty-four, and *Under Four Flags* played in nine. Beginning with *America's Answer*, a clause was inserted in the contract with exhibitors stating that no increase in admission would result when a government film was shown. Theaters that played government films were given certificates indicating service rendered the federal government.[87]

The Educational Department headed by Clare de Lissa Berg was one of the first sections created in the Division of Films; its function was to provide film to patriotic organizations, educational institutions, base hospitals, and training camps. Usually such material was free, except for transportation charges. Other individuals and organizations were charged a dollar a reel for each day of use. The fee barely covered the cost of producing the film and was less than leading theaters might pay for a feature film (in New York a privately produced feature might cost as much as three thousand dollars per week).

Prior to June 1918, government departments contracted for propaganda films and had to make additional contracts to gain circulation of the motion pictures. Many exhibitors felt that propaganda pictures or documentaries such as the CPI wanted had slight audience appeal. As a result, a Scenario Department under Rufus Steele was established on June 1, in the belief that such films could be interesting if skillfully made. Producers were persuaded to make one-reel pictures for which the Division of Films would provide the scenario, locations, and camera permits for filming, without charge. The finished product became the property of the producer, who, after the film division approved, was required only to give the picture the widest possible circulation. At least eighteen one-reel films were produced in cooperation with the Scenario Department. Paramount-Bray Pictograph made four *Says Uncle Sam* films, including ones that showed the program of vocal training in the army and navy and the work of the War Risk Insurance Bureau and the United States Employment Service. The Pathé Company turned out *Solving the Farm Problem of the Nation*, which described the work of the United States Boys' Working Reserve, and *Feeding the Fighters*, which showed how food was supplied to the army. The Universal Company made *Reclaiming the Soldiers' Duds*, which dealt with the salvage work of the War Department, and *The American Indian Gets into the War Game*, which showed the Indians' part in both the military and food production. C. L. Chester produced ten films, including *There Shall Be No Cripples*, detailing the work of the surgeon general's office; *Colored Americans*, which showed blacks in the army and navy as well as participating in war activities at home; *Waging War in Washington*, which dealt with the way the government in the nation's capital operated; *All the Comforts of Home*, showing the War Department's effort to provide necessities and conveniences for soldiers; *Railless Railroads*, which dealt with the work of the Highway Transport Committee; and *The College for Camp Cooks*, showing the training of army cooks.[88]

The Scenario Department turned out films of more than one reel, and C. L. Chester made a six-reel picture, *The Miracle of the Ships*, which showed in great detail the construction of the vessles at Hog Island, beginning with the mining of iron and cutting of lumber. The W. W. Hodkinson Corporation spent more than forty thousand dollars on *Made in America*, an eight-reel film "telling the full story of the Liberty Army." The picture followed the soldier from his draft through training to combat abroad. The Morale Branch of the War Department wanted such a film, and production costs were taken up by the Hodkinson Corporation. The film was only half completed when the war ended, but production continued and in February 1919 it was shown in Washington to the War College, and then to Secretary Baker, his associates, and other government officials. Upon request a copy was sent to Pershing.[89]

Many films were scheduled and would have been turned out by other producers had the Armistice not halted them. In late summer 1918 the Division of Films undertook to produce its own pictures; scenarios were prepared and six two-reel films made. *Our Wings of Victory* showed the production and operation of airplanes. *Our Horses of War* showed training of mounts used by the cavalry and artillery. *If Your Soldier's Hit* revealed how a field hospital worked to save soldiers at the front. *Making the Nation Fit* portrayed training in the army and navy. *The Bath of Bullets* showed the development and employment of the machine gun, and *The Storm of Steel* detailed how Liberty Loan money went into constructing munitions; scenes were from gun plants across America and from proving grounds. The first four of these motion pictures were released at two-week intervals beginning December 23, 1918. The last two—*Bath of Bullets* and *The Storm of Steel*—were never shown, as they dealt only with war subjects. Another series of six two-reel films had been planned but was canceled after the Armistice.[90]

Many privately produced movies had the war as a central theme. Griffith's *Hearts of the World* was one such movie.[91] Brady wanted to produce a movie on the war and aims of the United States and apparently had Augustus Thomas prepare a scenario.[92] Charlie Chaplin's *Shoulder Arms* became something of a classic. Occasionally such films might be recommended by the CPI. There were "hate" films, such as *To Hell with the Kaiser*, *Wolves of Kultur*, and *The Kaiser, the Beast of Berlin*. Members of the film division sometimes objected to these pictures; the division's secretary condemned *The Kaiser, the Beast of Berlin*, perhaps the best known of the hate movies.[93]

The film division came close to paying its way. The expenditure of the division was $1,077,730.59, and better than $850,000 was recovered from sales. *Pershing's Crusaders* and *America's Answer* had more than four thousand bookings. The thirty-one weekly films in the *Official War Review* had almost seven thousand bookings. The Division of Films also cooperated with the Foreign Film Section of the CPI. More than sixty-two hundred reels of film went abroad, and money taken in by the Division of Films helped meet the expense of distributing film in neutral countries.[94] Brady boasted that at the beginning of the war, London had been the center of the film market, but that by the summer of 1918, New York had become the center and 85 percent of the motion pictures used throughout the world were exported from the United States.[95]

The CPI's Division of Pictures had been separate from the

Division of Films when the two were created by executive order on September 25, 1917. Because their work often coincided, they were combined in March 1918, and the Bureau of War Photographs of the film division took over the picture division. A voluntary agreement was worked out whereby all still photographs and motion pictures that dealt with the war were submitted to the CPI for censorship. The CPI also agreed to investigate applications for camera permits. Lawrence Rubel was in charge of permits, and the Military and Naval Intelligence had a veto over his actions. Creel felt this voluntary censorship was more successful than any other effort in belligerent countries and claimed that "no request was ever ignored" and that, "while thousands of permits were issued, none was ever abused."[96]

Another function of the division, in addition to censorship, was the distribution of Signal Corps film. A plan was developed to work with the Photographic Association, whose members included Underwood and Underwood, International Film Service, Brown Brothers, Paul Thompson, Kadel and Herbert, Harris and Ewing, Western Newspaper Union, News Enterprise Association, and others. Signal Corps film received both national and international circulation as pictures were placed in daily newspapers, periodicals, and technical publications. To speed production and delivery, the Signal Corps operated a laboratory in New York in conjunction with Columbia University. Prices for this service were nominal—prints usually sold for ten cents—and covered only expenses.

This division supplied still photographs publicizing motion pictures by the film division; publicity shots were often reproduced in newspapers and reached millions of people. Photographs were supplied to universities, historical societies, libraries. Pictures were supplied to families with members directly involved in the war. The division provided photographs for the Foreign Service Section, to be used in propaganda in Allied and neutral countries.[97] Cost of the Bureau of War Photographs totaled about $400,000, with about $100,000 resulting from work in the United States and the remainder spent on the effort abroad. About $70,000 was made on sales of photographs, nearly all of which were purchased in the United States.[98]

The Department of Slides, another department in the Division of Films, offered slides to schoolteachers, lecturers, and ministers, for about fifteen cents each, or about 50 to 80 percent below what they would normally cost. At first dependent on the Signal Corps laboratory in Washington, the CPI built its own lab in the city to have facilities to keep up with demand. Catalogs were produced, listing slides and illustrated lectures.[99] John Tatlock wrote one of the CPI pamphlets and prepared a slide lecture on "The Ruined Churches of France" (fifty slides). George F. Zook, professor of modern European history at Pennsylvania State College, prepared nine slide lectures, including "The Call to Arms" (fifty-eight slides), "Airplanes and How Made" (sixty-one slides), "Flying for America" (fifty-four slides), "The American Navy" (fifty-one slides), "Transporting the Army to France" (sixty-three slides), and "Carrying the Home to the Camp" (sixty-one slides). Nine hundred of Zook's lectures were ordered by schools, churches, and patriotic organizations. In about a year the department distributed approximately two hundred thousand slides. After the war the department's files were turned over to the War and Navy Departments.[100]

THE accuracy of the CPI's news releases later was defended by Creel and other commentators. Of the six thousand releases only three were ever questioned; in two cases the committee was vindicated and in the third the fault rested with an official not a member of the CPI.[101] The latter charge involved the claim that the CPI gave false information regarding American-made aircraft sent to France. The information originated with Colonel Edward A. Deeds, who early in 1918 gave four photographs of airplane bodies and engines to Rubel of the picture division. Rubel sent them to the caption writer, Strunsky, who prepared a caption stating that hundreds of planes had been shipped to France, with thousands more on the way. When Senator James Wadsworth of the Military Affairs Committee called this error to Rubel's attention, Rubel sought to recall the pictures but was unable to prevent them and their captions from appearing in the *Official Bulletin*.[102] A dispute over airplane photographs arose again in July, when Senator James A. Reed of Missouri asserted that the CPI had issued a statement that Secretary Baker during a visit to France had seen "one thousand American airplanes in the air." Creel denied that the CPI was responsible for the story and claimed that it originated in the Paris *Herald*.[103] Privately he seems to have told a different story: when Ben Lindsey asked him in August what to say to people who asked why more airplanes had not been sent abroad, he referred Lindsey to the morning paper and said that "over 1,000 battle planes have already been shipped and a steady stream is being kept up."[104]

Beyond the question of the accuracy of news was a contention by Creel, Rochester, and others that cannot go unchallenged—that the CPI provided news without bias or color. There was an intention to report only facts, and it cannot be denied that Creel and the committee surely helped convince the military to increase the news given out, including information on casualties, conditions in camps, and other sometimes unfavorable matters. But there was a bias in news provided by the CPI, whether in newspapers and periodicals or on film. The news not only informed the public about war-related subjects but publicized virtually every department of the national government from the president on down. The Division of News served the government departments that chose to use it. The *Official Bulletin* provided a record of government actions. The *Bulletin for Cartoonists* took its lead from bureaus within the federal government. The Division of Films showed the actions of the federal government in winning the war. Such an avalanche of publicity increased the public's awareness of government and instilled a certain reverence. It therefore helped to mobilize opinion and nationalize the American mind.

10

The CPI and Censorship

> Never at any time did it occur to the press to provide its
> own discipline for the punishment of dishonor.
> —George Creel[1]

EVEN IN THE CALMEST OF TIMES, individual
freedom is fragile—constantly threatened by human passion
and economic privation, it has probably been most effectively
extinguished throughout the world in this century by organized
authority, this is, by government. Our understanding of how
civil liberties fared in the United States during the Great War
could be enhanced by more information on how those rights
were treated in other countries. Although our knowledge is
sketchy, we do know that other belligerents often imposed
severe restrictions. In Germany censorship was controlled by
deputy commanding generals placed at the head of every army
corps district. These officers were the emperor's agents, responsible to him only, and they wielded great power. There was
often little coordination among districts, and censorship questions were frequently handled in a capricious fashion. The
government used the generals to restrict debate. Strikers were
sometimes threatened with up to ten years in prison, or even
death. In Austria-Hungary military officials were given authority to determine civilian conditions even to the extent of
nullifying existing laws. They could stop the circulation of
minority publications, compel workers to put in longer days,
and halt travel to many areas of the empire. In France newspapers were censored daily, and both civil and military correspondence, coming in and going out of the country, was subject
to restrictions. The government sought to limit discussion on a
range of subjects—many of a nonmilitary nature—that might

demoralize the civilian population. It should be mentioned parenthetically that early in the war the French tried to instill discipline in the army by setting up court-martials or "special councils of war," and more than eighty soldiers were executed, often summarily, for a variety of reasons. In Great Britain, a Joint Consultative Committee of Admiralty, War Office, and Press was established a year before the war for the purpose of planning censorship, and this committee was replaced in August 1916 by the Press Bureau, which was strongly influenced by military and naval censors operating under instructions from the Admiralty and War Office. Censorship also was imposed by the Defence of the Realm Act. The act set up controls over statements designed "to prejudice His Majesty's relations with foreign powers." By means of this act and subsequent regulations the government acquired large powers to legislate by virtual decree on nearly every phase of life. Authorities could enter establishments suspected of being used to publish or distribute disloyal literature, and the result sometimes was raids on pacifist premises, where sizable quantities of material were seized. In addition, the government acquiesced in allowing public opinion to silence dissenters. Conscientious objectors were often treated harshly and more than 1,000 of them were given repeated prison sentences ranging up to three years at hard labor.[2]

It has been said that in the United States during 1917–18 nearly every right guaranteed under the Constitution was either abridged or nullified, especially freedom of the press and freedom of speech. Much of the literature on civil liberties in the United States has been highly critical of the actions taken by the federal government during this period, and indeed the reader is often left with the impression that under no circumstances was the government justified in limiting the expression of ideas. At the national level a combination of federal statutes and executive orders sharply limited freedom of expression. The Espionage Act, which became law on June 15, 1917; the Trading-with-the-Enemy Act, which went into effect on October 6, 1917; and the Sedition Act of May 1918 provided the federal government with a formidable power to limit public utterances. President Wilson issued an executive order on April 28, 1917, that gave the government control of cable and land telegraph lines out of the country. Some months later, on October 12, another order, stemming from the Trading-with-the-Enemy Act, provided a Censorship Board to coordinate censorship and make recommendations regarding such matters for the rest of the war. And in exercising these powers the government surely was not without blame in the abuse of American freedoms. Postmaster General Albert S. Burleson often acted indiscriminately in denying publications access to the mails. Altogether, almost 2,200 people were prosecuted under the Espionage and Sedition Acts, although less than half (1,055) were convicted.[3]

Still, it is worth observing that some of the most severe repression of civil liberties came on the state and local level. Several of the state laws remained on the books long after the war ended.[4] Especially important in restricting freedom of expression were the state councils of defense and their county and local auxiliaries. Our knowledge of American civil liberties will most likely remain incomplete until we have a good history of those agencies.[5] The state councils, along with such extra-governmental organizations as the National Security League and the American Defense Society, were powerful forces in establishing conformity.[6]

There is no simple explanation for state and local repression. One must remember that not only was the United States involved in a war of unprecedented dimension—one that to many Americans seemed a fight for survival itself—but the country had also been experiencing major social and economic changes resulting from the growth of industry, urbanization, and immigration. Undoubtedly these developments helped to create uncertainty about America's future and increased nativist sentiment, especially fear of aliens and radicals.[7] Often tensions such as those between some German-Americans and the native born traced back to the nineteenth century and were merely brought to a crisis by the war.[8]

As for repression on the national level, how does one interpret it? How much blame should go to the Wilson administration? Many intelligent Americans in 1917–18 believed that the government faced an unprecedented crisis and that something had to be done. They were proud that the American Constitution—with all its imperfections—guaranteed a degree of political freedom unknown in most countries. To them it was of the highest priority that the Constitution and its system of government be defended even if that meant *temporarily* suspending many of the freedoms normally guaranteed to citizens. It was entirely understandable that in a country with a strong tradition of freedom of the press and speech this position subsequently was strongly criticized. The line separating acceptable expression from the unacceptable is difficult to draw; the power to make such distinctions will always be subject to abuse. Reasonable individuals disagreed during the war, as well as after, about whether the government was in fact gravely threatened in 1917–18. It does seem clear, though, that many persons associated with the government and the CPI believed in the existence of such a crisis.

Where did the Committee on Public Information stand on the terribly awkward problem of censorship? President Wilson had created the CPI at the outset of the war, and, as mentioned, the secretaries of war, the navy, and state in their joint letter to the president had recommended that the committee combine censorship and publicity.[9] Was the combination in favor of censorship?

ONE of the hopes for the CPI was that the United States could avoid a rigid censorship. Arthur Bullard, important in the early days of the committee, who stated his views on First Amendment liberties in early 1917 more clearly than did Creel, urged the Wilson administration to avoid the blunders of the European belligerents.[10] He opposed the strict proposal of the War Department. Bullard's friend Ernest Poole, who also helped put the CPI together, had similar views. He opposed an early version of the Espionage Act that would have imposed life imprisonment on any private person who gave out military information or otherwise interfered with American military forces.[11]

Creel objected to rigid censorship and suggested to President Wilson in early April 1917 that *"expression*, not *suppression*, was the real need."[12] After the Armistice he insisted that he had always opposed any legislation involving censorship—with the exception of cable censorship—preferring voluntary measures. An agreement was worked out with the press, which he asserted was the CPI's "one and only connection with censorship of any kind. At no time did the Committee exercise or seek authorities under the war measures that limited the peace-time freedom of individuals or professions."[13]

Although it is technically true that the Committee on Public Information had no power of censorship, and Creel did attempt to promote voluntary measures, it is misleading to say that the CPI did not engage in censorship of a serious sort. Early in the war, on May 28, 1917, the CPI issued a "Preliminary Statement to the Press of the United States."[14] The statement was probably the work of Creel, Bullard, and Edgar Sisson.[15] It explained that modern war necessitated a readjustment in the way news was gathered and distributed. Acknowledging difficulty in "hard-and-fast rules," admitting that mistakes would be made, it hoped that most of the errors of the European belligerents could be avoided. Speed in transmission of news was less important than in Europe, where German spies in Switzerland or Holland could read French or British papers within twenty-four hours. American newspapers usually did not reach neutral countries in Europe for at least ten days. The statement assured the press that the only news it wished to keep from the German authorities was "the kind which would be of tangible help to them in their military operations." It argued that censorship should be at a minimum, because repressing articles critical of the allies, or of military officials, or of unfavorable conditions in American camps would help spread rumors and German propaganda. As Bullard had argued, the statement claimed that censorship worked to protect dishonest or incompetent officials and demonstrated a "distrust of democratic common sense."

The statement divided news into three categories: dangerous, questionable, and routine. Dangerous news consisted of stories on military or naval operations currently in progress, threats against the life of the president, movement of official missions, and other sensitive matters. Questionable material was to be published with caution and only after approval of the CPI. Most news items fell into the routine category, and editors and writers were encouraged to submit such stories to the CPI if there was any question about publication. A subsequent effort was made to evaluate such material quickly and, if approved, label it "Passed by the Committee on Public Information" (meaning that the material was safe though not necessarily accurate) or "Authorized by the Committee on Public Information" (meaning that the information had been investigated and approved). Though these regulations were to be voluntary, the statement emphasized the responsibility of editors to prevent publication of dangerous news and to report people who broke the rules.[16] "Reckless journalism, regrettable enough in times of peace, is a positive menace when the Nation is at war. . . . In this day of high emotionalism and mental confusion, the printed word has immeasurable power, and the term traitor is not too harsh in application to the publisher, editor, or writer who wields this power without full and even solemn recognition of responsibilities." The American press, as well as the American people, was on trial. The statement attempted to end on a positive note, by indicating that the CPI dealt with information rather than censorship. The committee hoped to open every government department to the widest inspection and to provide news in no way colored by favoritism regarding policies or individuals.[17]

Some officials of the Wilson administration felt that voluntary censorship left much to be desired. Robert Lansing wanted a tight control over the press similar to that imposed in Britain. Breckinridge Long, then third assistant secretary of state, complained to the president that news from the front was not handled properly. Such information when first published had its greatest emotional effect on opinion, and Long wanted an advisory committee in Washington, with branches in other cities, to censor news before its release in order to create a favorable psychological reaction. Such a committee would centralize responsibility for censorship. Long cited a Washington *Post* headline: "Germans Raid Trench, Kill 3, Wound 5." A better headline, he thought, would have read: "Americans Fight Fiercely; Beaten by Superior Force, All Traditions of U.S. Army Upheld against Picked German Shock-Troops—Bravery Recorded."[18]

Wilson believed proper cooperation with newspapers impossible because of "the small but powerful lawless elements among them who observe no rules, regard no understandings as binding, and act always as they please." The president pointed out that Creel had been chosen for a function similar to that recommended by Long, but coordination and central management were difficult because of lack of cooperation from some executive departments, notably the Department of State.[19]

Unimpressed with Long's plan for an advisory committee, Creel believed that anything other than voluntary censorship of the press was impossible. The press, he complained, was the only profession "without an organization of any kind." It had no central body to speak for it or to impose discipline. Any advisory committee would have to include almost every metropolitan editor, and then the only certainty would be disunity. The management of such control would be beyond any man. What was needed was a different approach, "involving changes in training, aims, ideals and ambitions. *News* itself must be given a new definition."[20] Creel thus placed his hope in voluntary censorship.

In speeches to newspaper editors across the country, Creel denied that he was a censor and emphasized the voluntary nature of the CPI's regulations.[21] He encouraged editors to unite in order to discipline their profession. In Indianapolis in December 1917, he pointed to the difficulty, indeed impossibility, of effectively penalizing newspapers that had violated the rules of the CPI. Such papers should be disciplined by the profession, but the press had no organization to speak for it or to enforce a code of ethics. He urged the press to be patient, explaining that he was caught between generals and admirals who wanted silence, and reporters who suspected concealment.[22] This message of self-discipline and restraint he repeated in late January 1918 and also at the annual convention of the North Carolina Press Association in August. Disloyalty and disunity destroyed a nation's courage, but

suppression is not a wise remedy. . . . I was not in favor of a censorship law in the beginning, nor am I now in favor of the enactment of any legislation. Aside from the physical difficulties of enforcement, the enormous cost, the overwhelming irritation, and the inevitable tendency of such laws to operate solely against the weak and powerless, I have always had the conviction that our hope must lie in the aroused patriotism, the nobler consciences, of the men who make the papers of America.[23]

Creel's association with censorship went beyond statements and speeches, for he was a member of the Censorship Board, an advisory body overseeing and coordinating the government's censoring agencies. In addition to Creel, who represented the CPI, the board was composed of representatives of the postmaster general, the secretaries of war and the navy, and the War Trade Board.[24] This position, together with the support and close cooperation he enjoyed with Military and Naval Intelligence and the Department of Justice, placed Creel and the CPI in a strategic position for influence over censorship.[25] Although undoubtedly more liberal than some of his board associates, Creel diminished his reputation as a defender of civil liberties by being on the board. As Guy Stanton Ford later suggested, Creel's opposition to censorship might have been better served had he not been a member.[26]

Creel's work on the Censorship Board reflected the dilemma confronting most liberals involved in restricting First Amendment liberties. In December he wrote the board's chairman, Robert L. Maddox, expressing concern that it might become "a secret service organization for the detection of crimes." He believed that a censor had a duty to report any clear-cut crime to the authorities. He opposed using the board as a secret agency for exposure of criminal activity.[27] There were instances when he used his influence to limit the censor's authority: he protested to Maddox in June 1918 that censors had exceeded their authority in tearing out pages of magazines, and in October of that year he complained that there was too much concern for hidden messages in second-class mail.[28]

The CPI's chairman became involved in a controversy in April 1918 over whether the Censorship Board or the post office should censor mail. The executive order had charged the board with "the Executive Administration" of censoring all communications, authority "to take all such measures as may be necessary or expedient to administer the powers conferred." The board delegated telegraph and telephone censorship to the War Department and cable censorship to the Navy Department. Wilson had given instructions to the board to set up mail censorship where the public safety required, and a judgment was made that public safety required censoring mail between the United States and foreign countries not already subject to censorship by allied governments. An office was set up in New York to administer censorship, but because Congress did not appropriate sufficient funds for this task, mail censorship fell to the Post Office Department, which paid the persons engaged in censoring mail. The question of who controlled mail censorship—the board or the postmaster general—came to a crisis in April. Creel, along with two other members of the board, Paul Fuller and David Todd, drafted a report expressing majority sentiment that funds should be given the bureau to conduct mail censorship. The report was submitted to Wilson. Maddox, also the chief postal censor, prepared a minority report that postal authorities should continue mail censorship (they would be more efficient, he argued) and submitted his report to Wilson. In late May 1918, Wilson agreed with Maddox's view, explaining that postal censorship under control of the postmaster general was more nearly in accord with his intentions.[29] It is interesting to speculate what might have been the effect if Creel had won, because his views of censorship were probably less stringent than those of Albert S. Burleson.[30]

Whatever his intentions, whatever hesitancy he may have had about censorship legislation, Creel, the record indicates, was active in the board's discussions and involved in attempts to suppress certain kinds of literature. The minutes of the board

42. George Creel (Courtesy of the Library of Congress)

43. Edward S. Corwin (Reprinted by permission of Princeton University Library)

from April 3, 1918, indicate a long discussion on the problem of press restrictions and show that Creel received full authority to deal with newspaper censorship. It was agreed that all magazines in the United States had to submit articles to the Censorship Board several weeks prior to publication.[31] Acting under the Trading-with-the-Enemy Act, Creel was interested in printed material exported from or imported to the United States. Even if a periodical or newspaper did not fall under the act, there were other ways of bringing it into line. He might suggest to the Department of Justice that its editor be prosecuted or that the publication be barred from the mails. Through contact with the War Trade Board, whose representative was on the Censorship Board, he could even stop the publication's supply of newsprint.[32]

Creel requested a list of magazines that were sent abroad, and the board asked for a plan to deal with such printed material. A group of publishers represented by John Macrae, vice-president of E. P. Dutton and Company, appeared before the board on September 5, 1918; Macrae complained that the reduction in books sent to England and other allied countries worried publishers, stating that he spoke for several publishers and would guarantee to the satisfaction of the Censorship Board that no books other than those that were pro-American would go out of the country. The publishers agreed to submit lists, even the books, provided that the flow abroad could increase.[33] Creel drew up a publishers' agreement on material allowed to leave the country. A copy of each book was to be submitted to Military Intelligence. A list of reliable publishers exporting books was prepared, along with a list of approved consignees in foreign countries. The lists were submitted to each censorship station, and all printed matter shipped from a publisher on the list to a consignee on the list was passed without censorship. Creel submitted a resolution, which the board passed, calling on the chairman to ask Military Intelligence, the War Trade Board, the solicitor of the Post Office Department, and the Committee on Public Information to cooperate in preparing lists of magazine and book publishers whose publications were not to be passed by the authorities.[34]

As a member of the board, the CPI's chairman was asked to comment about or pass judgment on much material. Technical journals were watched to prevent deliberate or inadvertent leakage of information about military hardware, and Creel commented on such periodicals as *Motor Age* and *Air Service Journal*.[35] There was concern that military and naval textbooks might give valuable information to the enemy, and the board asked Creel to investigate such material.[36]

Creel sought to repress material that either presented the United States in an unfavorable light or contained opinions or ideas he felt too dangerous for the American public. He asked Maddox in March 1918 to instruct censors to watch for material put out by the Bolsheviks and prevent it from coming into the country. He urged that Scandinavian publications be screened because they might contain pro-German material.[37] He watched material leaving the country, and when issues of *Mid-Week Pictorial* and *Current History* were held up by a Military Intelligence censor, he complained that the decision (and the censor's qualifications) should be reexamined because the publications were good propaganda for the United States. He praised a decision to hold back books "laudatory of Germany" and urged Maddox to instruct censors to watch for them.[38] Philip Powers's *America among Nations* was one book Creel believed harmful to American interests, and he urged the Censorship Board to consider ways to prevent its circulation in South America.[39] *The Menace*, published by the Free Press Defense League of Aurora, Missouri, was another, and Creel sought to have it "barred absolutely" from leaving the United States.[40]

Creel maintained a steady correspondence with the chief Canadian press censor, Colonel Ernest J. Chambers, who appears to have been the more eager censor of the two; but both men worked to suppress what they considered "dangerous" material. Some American publications either were barred by or raised concern among Canadian authorities, and in early April 1918, Chambers approached Creel to ask whether banning Albert Shaw's *Review of Reviews* would create a bad impression in the United States. Chambers was disturbed by what he thought an anti-British bias. Creel informed Shaw of Chambers's concern and was able to persuade the editor to omit subsequent offensive material, to the apparent satisfaction of the Canadian censor.[41] Other publications were less fortunate. For a time all Hearst-owned newspapers were barred from Canada and Britain. The Hearst press had not always followed the CPI's regulations, and William Randolph Hearst openly opposed Canadian and British censors. He told Creel he would shut down his papers before allowing such authorities to dictate to him.[42]

The content of motion pictures was a concern. Colonel Chambers warned Creel that many films had titles that damned the Germans but had story lines that were sympathetic to the enemy. Such films, Chambers believed, were effective before audiences that did not have a good command of English. Creel recommended careful attention to censoring motion pictures. Indeed, by this time—early 1918—he had come to have a higher regard for censorship in general. Not only had he worried about enemy films, but he wanted to suppress criticism from the floor of Congress by senators he believed to be giving a misleading view of the war.[43]

When Chambers complained that some New England publications had offended French-Canadians, Creel tried to persuade New England newspapers to stop articles critical of this group.[44] Chambers complained of George R. Kirkpatrick's *War— What For?* and argued that it was "an excitement to the extreme Pacifist element" in North America. He recommended that the book be prohibited in Canada. Creel did not have the legal authority of Chambers, but he wrote to the Librarian of Congress, Herbert Putnam, and asked that the book be removed and that names of people who had asked for it be sent to him.[45]

By putting together bits and pieces of Creel's correspondence it is possible to see consistency between his public statements and his actions. Neither Creel nor many other workers for the CPI believed freedom of speech to be an absolute right. Creel dealt with the problem in May 1918 at the forum of the Church of the Ascension in New York. Asked if he thought "absolute freedom of speech" possible in time of war, he replied: "We have never had absolute freedom of speech. In war, more

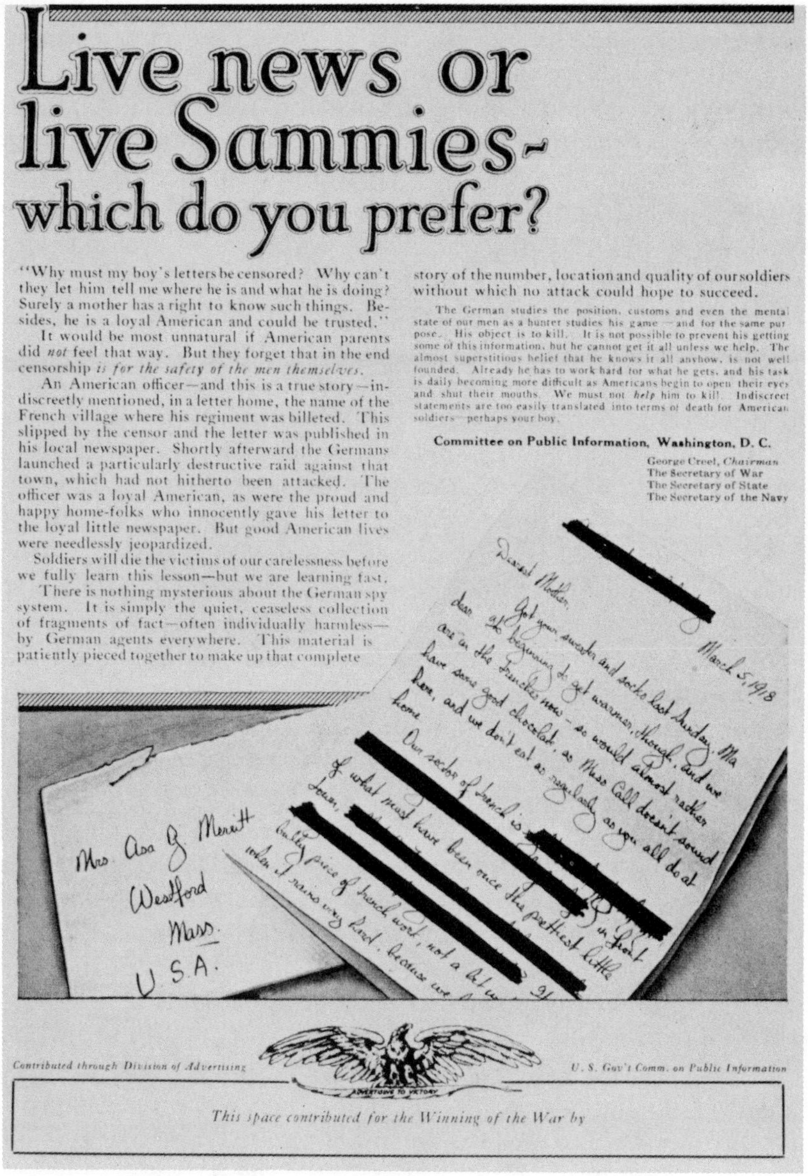

44. (Courtesy of the National Archives)

than at any other time, it is necessary to have free speech because of the necessity for criticism." But, he continued, "there is a difference between free speech and seditious speech. Just as there is a law against indecent speech so is there a law against seditious speech and offenders may be apprehended." Asked if legislation limiting free speech were compatible with "free public opinion," he responded that Congress was the voice of the people. "The right of habeas corpus is a safeguard of free speech, and we have no right to kick against a law after Congress passes it."[46]

The opinions on free speech in wartime championed by the CPI's chairman may have reflected the views of most Americans, and they certainly mirrored the positions of several writers for the committee. Associate chairman Harvey O'Higgins echoed Creel's argument. The war, he contended, presented a clear-cut issue for the American public: "Be German or be killed."[47] The right of free speech was not absolute. Asserting that the United States had "preserved our peace-time right to say what we please," he advocated that persons be held responsible for their utterances. People who spoke loudest for free speech and free press, he said, were the very ones guilty of abusing their First Amendment privileges. Such persons "cry not for liberty, but for immunity from the responsibilities of liberty."[48]

A similar view of free speech was revealed in some of the CPI pamphlets. Even though the committee lacked the power of censorship, it publicized arguments for the restriction of free speech and press. Statements opposing a premature peace, and advocating suspension of free discussion during the war, came from interesting sources. Part of an address by the well-known civil libertarian Clarence Darrow was reprinted in *The War for Peace*; Darrow argued that pacifists used the arguments of German sympathizers.[49] He said he had never been neutral about the war, because "the German criminal military machine invaded Belgium. I did not stop to think," he stated, "I only felt. In a great crisis like that I would be ashamed to think." Condemning pacifists for neutrality during and after the invasion of Belgium, Darrow said, "When I hear a man advising the

American people to state the terms of peace, I know he is working for Germany."[50] Rules of war and peace were different. He urged suspension of debate over divisive issues until the crisis passed. William Jennings Bryan, Darrow's later antagonist, also desired suspending free discussion during the war. It was proper to discuss the wisdom of fighting before war was declared, "but the discusion is closed when Congress acts." After a declaration of war, no one should be allowed to attack the government or aid the enemy in the name of free speech.[51] Freedom of expression during war was secondary to concern for obedience to law; duty was sometimes more urgent than rights; the citizen should express his concerns to elected officials who would discuss them in Congress, and there was no reason for the citizen to discuss public questions in any other manner. When final action was taken by Congress, "acquiescence on the part of the citizen becomes a duty."[52]

Probably the most substantial figure associated with the CPI to write about First Amendment liberties was Edward S. Corwin of Princeton, already widely recognized in 1917–18 as an authority on the Constitution. Corwin was one of the editors of the *War Cyclopedia* and probably was responsible for the entry "Freedom of the Press."[53] His publications had included *National Supremacy* (1913) and *The President's Control of Foreign Relations* (1917).[54] In his subsequent writings, he opposed the interpretation later given to the First Amendment by Oliver Wendell Holmes, Jr., and Zechariah Chafee, Jr., favoring instead a nationalistic interpretation of the Constitution similar to that taken a century earlier by John Marshall—Corwin believed that the Constitution had resulted from social disorders in the Confederation period.[55] He attempted to define First Amendment liberties "in relation to the powers of government" and maintained that "a republican form of government must rest upon an agreement regarding certain fundamentals."[56] He did not think the First Amendment released the press from "the restraints imposed by the common law doctrine of seditious libel, which condemned as criminal all publications having a tendency to bring Church or State, or the officers of the Government, or the administration of the law into contempt."[57]

Unlike Holmes, who contended in late 1919 that it was necessary to show a "clear and present danger" in order to punish an utterance, Corwin argued that it was necessary only to show a "bad tendency." The "tendency" doctrine, he asserted, underlay the common law tradition of seditious libel. In the *Abrams* case (1919), where the Supreme Court first passed on the Sedition Act, Corwin supported the majority decision, arguing that it rested "on secure ground."[58]

Acknowledging that freedom was essential to a republican form of government, Corwin later said that "*freedom* of utterance is not *license* of utterance." Only the former was covered by the First Amendment.[59] "Freedom of the press in war time rests," he wrote for the CPI, "largely with the discretion of Congress."[60] Congress's ability to impose censorship derived from authority to pass laws "necessary and proper for carrying into execution" the powers of the national government, which in this case meant the successful prosecution of a declared war.[61] Corwin maintained that "the subjection of the press to the powers given Congress by the Constitution can hardly be said to *abridge* the freedom there recognized."[62] Congress could restrict publications designed to promote sedition, obstruct execution of the laws, or aid the enemy. Admitting that ours was a "government by discussion," he argued that the object of discussion was decision, and that once the majority had registered its decision in accord with the Constitution it had a right to act on that decision.[63] Whatever restrictions might be imposed on the press during the war, they would not severely limit responsible discussion of important public questions—"it seems extremely unlikely . . . that any widespread conviction of the American people could long be denied effective expression."[64] After the war he wrote that "amid the uncomplicated conditions of frontier life it was entirely feasible to assure each individual a certain quantum of 'inalienable rights,' but to-day the pursuit of happiness has become a joint-stock enterprise in which the welfare of all is embarked."[65] He believed that freedom in modern society did not mean individual license.

Spies and Lies

German agents are everywhere, eager to gather scraps of news about our men, our ships, our munitions. It is still possible to get such information through to Germany, where thousands of these fragments—often individually harmless—are patiently pieced together into a whole which spells death to American soldiers and danger to American homes.

But while the enemy is most industrious in trying to collect information, and his systems elaborate, he is *not* superhuman—indeed he is often very stupid, and would fail to get what he wants were it not deliberately handed to him by the carelessness of loyal Americans.

Do not discuss in public, or with strangers, any news of troop and transport movements, of bits of gossip as to our military preparations, which come into your possession.

Do not permit your friends in service to tell you—or write you—"inside" facts about where they are, what they are doing and seeing.

Do not become a tool of the Hun by passing on the malicious, disheartening rumors which he so eagerly sows. Remember he asks no better service than to have you spread his lies of disasters to our soldiers and sailors, gross scandals in the Red Cross, cruelties, neglect and wholesale executions in our camps, drunkenness and vice in the Expeditionary Force, and other tales certain to disturb American patriots and to bring anxiety and grief to American parents.

And do not wait until you catch someone putting a bomb under a factory. Report the man who spreads pessimistic stories, divulges—or seeks—confidential military information, cries for peace, or belittles our efforts to win the war.

Send the names of such persons, even if they are in uniform, to the Department of Justice, Washington. Give all the details you can, with names of witnesses if possible—show the Hun that we can beat him at his own game of collecting scattered information and putting it to work. The fact that you made the report will not become public.

You are in contact with the enemy *today*, just as truly as if you faced him across No Man's Land. In your hands are two powerful weapons with which to meet him—discretion and vigilance. *Use them.*

COMMITTEE ON PUBLIC INFORMATION

8 JACKSON PLACE, WASHINGTON, D. C.

George Creel, Chairman
The Secretary of State
The Secretary of War
The Secretary of the Navy

Contributed through Division of Advertising   *United States Gov't Comm. on Public Information*

This space contributed for the Winning of the War by

The Publisher of

45. (Courtesy of the National Archives)

THE Committee on Public Information thus dealt with censorship. Although it possessed no statutory authority, and although Creel was more liberal than many persons associated with the government at this time, the CPI did work to suppress ideas considered threatening to the American war effort. The committee emphasized publicity and released a tremendous volume of news. Yet the news promoted national unity, and the very process of selecting it involved a subtle censorship. Moreover, the CPI occupied a strategic position from which it could influence public opinion. Creel attempted to keep out "dangerous" material, whether pro-German or Bolshevik. He stopped publications from leaving the country that would give the enemy information or present the United States in an unfavorable way. Through Military Intelligence, the Department of Justice, and the postmaster general, he could bring pressure on editors. The CPI also publicized the idea that free discussion was not an absolute right in wartime and that the fate of First Amendment liberties rested with legislatures. One need only read the tracts by Darrow and Bryan to see the intolerance of minority opinions—indeed, what some have called the tyranny of the majority.

11

Conclusion

> There is a spiritual exaltation in 100,000,000 Americans
> united in a sacred cause, ready for any labor, anxious to
> serve, eager to take the places assigned them.[1]

THE COMMITTEE ON PUBLIC INFORMATION tried
to reach all Americans, to penetrate their lives, to draw citizens
closer to their government. No channel of communication was
neglected. The pamphlets of the CPI numbered in the millions.
Using public education to spread the government's message,
the CPI circumvented county superintendents by sending bulletins directly to school buildings. Community councils linked
local areas to the federal government. Through the Four Minute Men the CPI created a national network of local speakers,
each supposedly talking on the same topic at approximately the
same time—subjects controlled by the national government.
The country's leading advertising men and artists tried to sell
the American war effort to the public. News releases from
Washington flooded the papers, from metropolitan dailies to
rural weeklies. Criticism of the war and of the American system was discouraged. A later writer has remarked that "the
nation and nationalism developed because the government . . .
increasingly penetrated the lives of people, because people
increasingly participated in the national affairs and identified
themselves and their political and cultural interests with those of
their respective nations . . . [and] once established nationalism
fed upon itself and grew."[2] Clearly the CPI was a nationalizing
agent greatly enhancing nationalism during 1917–18.

Perhaps because the Committee on Public Information so
encouraged nationalism, many writers have assumed that the
CPI actually worked at cross-purposes with democratic govern-

ment. Certainly a portion of the committee's endeavors did have this effect, as loyalty to the nation was promoted in ways that were antithetical to the functioning of democracy. But the CPI's legacy for democracy is more complex, for American nationalism has often been founded on the idea of democracy, of government with individual liberty and human equality before the law.[3] Some people associated with the committee believed that nationalism could work to strengthen democratic government, and several writers sought to redefine democracy to meet the problems of the twentieth century.

To be sure, the CPI's work had dangerous implications for democracy. The committee often promoted a negative form of nationalism. As a national ideology, American democracy, or Americanism, with its emphasis on citizen reponsibility, provided opportunity for abuse. Whereas CPI writers commendably attacked chauvinistic nationalism and militarism, the writings of men like Sherman and Lane described America in almost mystical terms, subordinating the individual to the country's broader needs. Such writings raised the possibility that the free individual might be submerged in the will of the state. President Wilson defined Americanism as "utterly believing in the principles of America and putting them first as above anything that may come into competition with them."[4] From such arguments it was easy for the popular mind to associate Americanism with loyalty to the nation, rather than with loyalty to democratic individualism.

The committee was too ready to suspend freedom of speech and the press. Although Creel was anxious to see that civil liberties were not abused, and warned against allowing censorship to be used as an instrument of a secret police, he was a member of the Censorship Board and became involved in attempting to keep material from the public. The CPI engaged in a subtle censorship, too, when it filled the country with official news. Committee pamphlets tried to convince Americans to limit dissent about the war and publicized the idea that the fate of First Amendment liberties rested with legislatures. The tracts by Darrow and Bryan reflected intolerance of anyone critical of the war and called for suspension of public discussion.

Another unfortunate aspect of the committee's work was its representation of women and blacks. It is true that Creel worked behind the scenes to promote woman's suffrage, but CPI posters most frequently pictured women in traditional roles or as idealized symbols depicting democratic virtue or the victims of German brutality. Blacks, especially in CPI films, were often stereotyped.

There were other negative sides to the CPI. The committee not only publicized the national government but helped bring about what would be known as the imperial presidency. The widest publicity was given the utterances of President Wilson, whether in pamphlets, the *Four Minute Men Bulletins*, the *National School Service*, or the *Official Bulletin*. Wilson asked Americans to think of him as a symbol "of the power and dignity and hope of the United States." Creel, himself, saw Wilson in these terms and did his best to promote this idea among his fellow Americans.[5] He often expressed impatience with Congress and once said that "a President of the United States, in time of war, is either a *dictator* or a *traitor*, for dictatorship in war is the Constitution's direct intent."[6] Whatever the constitutional merits of Creel's argument, he presided over an organization that left behind a larger image of the presidency.

The CPI had an unfortunate effect on public opinion theory. Participation in the World War of 1917–18 has often been described as a dividing line in American thought about the formation of opinion. Prior to the war, theorists held that one should inform the public; afterwards, they were more inclined to manipulate opinion.[7] The propaganda of the Great War demonstrated and suggested ways to manipulate opinion. Creel had faith in mass democracy, believing that the average man, if informed, was capable of rational judgment. Much of his life as a journalist and public official before 1917 had been based on this belief. In his attempt to rouse opinion to a "white-hot" intensity, however, he went against this position.[8] He presided over several CPI divisions with an approach to public opinion different from his own stated views. The Divisions of Four Minute Men, Speakers, Advertising, and Pictorial Publicity were successful because they made a calculated appeal to emotion. When the war was over, the sensational phase of the CPI's work caught public attention, and whatever the challenges to mass democracy before 1917, whatever the argument that public opinion was rational, the idea of irrationality was strengthened.[9] Such ideas assisted the position of those persons who wished to inculcate an unthinking loyalty to the state. It was Adolf Hitler who attributed the success of Allied propaganda to its emotional portrayal of the enemy as barbaric.[10]

One must keep in mind that the CPI was but one of many governmental and nongovernmental agencies filling the country with propaganda during the war, and that in an evaluation of its effect it is sometimes easy to confuse its work with that of other organizations.[11] The CPI came into existence partly to organize the propaganda agencies of the government and to serve as a clearinghouse. The major criticism of the committee in 1917–18 came from groups and individuals who felt that the CPI was not patriotic enough and who even accused it of "treasonable moderation."[12] The success with which the committee's message reached citizens depended on local cooperation. Public schoolteachers could have refused to use the pamphlet literature or the *National School Service*. Communities could have refused to set up Four Minute Men organizations or community councils. Newspapers could have ignored committee releases. They did not, and usually if there was variance from Washington's policies at the state and local level it was in the direction of whipping patriotic fervor ever higher.

If there was a negative side to the CPI's operations, one must be prepared to acknowledge that the committee's work also had positive qualities. Most workers for the CPI were dedicated to the preservation, if necessary the revitalization, and indeed the expansion of democratic government. Their concern with democratic government antedated the war and was highly important in the CPI's operations. To mobilize opinion and promote unity behind the war was their immediate goal. But there was a forward-looking, progressive aspect to the work of the committee that has often been overlooked. Such people as Bullard, Creel, Ford, Becker, Commons, and Simons, to mention only a few, retained their liberal attitudes and tried, insofar as possible, to use the committee to further the reform of society. They feared Prussian militarism but at the same time were concerned about the other forces challenging democracy —immigration, social injustice brought by the spread of industry and cities, ideas (philosophical, literary, social) thought to undermine traditional American values.[13] The committee's work in the United States has been described as "holding fast the inner lines," a statement implying more than a defense against an external enemy, Germany. Creel and his associates were trying to reinforce a traditional way of life in a country where "old landmarks were losing their familiar contours."[14] They saw intervention as an extension of domestic reform, an opportunity to expand the crusade for democracy. Because of the war their ideas reached a much larger and perhaps different public than before.

Some CPI writers believed that democratic principles could flourish only in a society united by national spirit. They often intentionally associated democracy with the nation. Sherman argued that national cultures offered the best way to advance civilization and individual liberty. Hazen believed nationalism far more powerful than internationalism and held that democracy's survival depended on nationalistic energies. Bagley thought democracy needed a national program of education that would overcome deficiencies resulting from local autonomy. Ingersoll hoped the national network of Four Minute Men would continue after the war as an updated version of the town meeting, thereby satisfying one of America's needs— greater citizen interest in public questions.[15]

To the extent that Ford, Becker, and other writers attempted to understand the problems of industrial and city life and of expanded world responsibilities, and to redefine democracy so that it might meet these realities—while at the same time promoting national unity—the CPI can be said to have encouraged a variety of nationalism that assisted democracy. Ideology was central to the committee's effort to create national unity and redefine democracy. Promoting the ideas of American democracy, or often simply Americanism, vaguely defined as the essence of the American democratic system, the committee sought a spiritual awakening, almost an "ideological renaissance."[16] Many of the CPI's writers had a deep emotional commitment to this ideology. American democracy, or Americanism, was to be the common denominator, the ideological cement, a secular religion, to unify an increasingly pluralistic society. Committee writers feared laissez-faire individualism and believed that the anarchy resulting from license was the basis of authoritarian or autocratic government. Opposition to authoritarianism was implicit in the CPI's discussions of American democracy. It was assumed that democracy at home, with its political liberty, required personal responsibility. Freedom required a sense of obligation to the community, inner restraint of natural impulse. If democracy was to work, all citizens were obliged to adopt such responsible attitudes.

Much of the Committee on Public Information's work was well intentioned, and much was worthwhile. For the most part the committee stressed antimilitarism, antiauthoritarianism, and the defense of democratic government. Its record was flawed by the crusading zeal of the time.

Notes

PREFACE

1. Some writers have placed the committee only in the context of the war and compared its work to the propaganda bureaus of other countries, emphasizing their similarities. See Harold D. Lasswell, *Propaganda Technique in World War I* (Cambridge, Mass., 1927, 1971); George G. Bruntz, *Allied Propaganda and the Collapse of the German Empire in 1918* (Stanford, Calif., 1938); Terence H. Qualter, *Propaganda and Psychological Warfare* (New York, 1962), 63; and Charles Roetter, *Art of Psychological Warfare, 1914–1945* (New York, 1974), 72. For other propaganda studies that place the Committee on Public Information only in the context of the war, see Harold J. Tobin and Percy W. Bidwell, *Mobilizing Civilian America* (New York, 1940), 75–82; Wilson P. Dizard, *Strategy of Truth: The Story of the U.S. Information Service* (Washington, D.C., 1961), 30–31; Ronald I. Rubin, *Objectives of the U.S. Information Agency: Controversies and Analysis* (New York, 1966), 96–97; Robert E. Elder, *Information Machine: The United States Information Agency and American Foreign Policy* (Syracuse, 1968), 34; Thomas C. Sorensen, *Word War: The Story of American Propaganda* (New York, 1968), 5–8; and John W. Henderson, *United States Information Agency* (New York, 1969), 23–28.

2. Marbury Bladen Ogle, Jr., *Public Opinion and Political Dynamics* (Boston, 1950), 227–29.

CHAPTER ONE

1. Albert Edwards [Arthur Bullard], "An Essay on the Beneficence of Fallacious Ideas," p. 6, Arthur Bullard Papers, Box 3, Seeley G. Mudd Library, Princeton University, Princeton, N.J.

2. Carl Wittke, *German-Language Press in America* (Lexington, Ky., 1957), 235; Frederick C. Luebke, *Bonds of Loyalty: German-Americans and World War I* (DeKalb, Ill., 1974), 29.

3. Although the number of German-language newspapers declined between 1914 and 1917, by the latter year there were approximately five hundred such publications in the United States, almost half the total number of foreign-language newspapers in this country. About fifty of these German-language publications were dailies whose circulation had increased since 1914 to perhaps as much as 950,000 by 1917. See Luebke, *Bonds of Loyalty*, 45; and Wittke, *German-Language Press in America*, 243–44. On the attitude of the German-language press prior to the American declaration of war, see ibid., 236–61; and Luebke, *Bonds of Loyalty*, 88–89, 91–93, 205.

4. For the opposition to war in America see Merle Curti, *Peace or War: The American Struggle, 1636–1936* (Boston, 1936, 1959), 228–61; David S. Patterson, *Toward a Warless World: The Travail of the American Peace Movement, 1887–1914* (Bloomington, Ind., 1976); Charles Chatfield, *For Peace and Justice: Pacifism in America, 1914–1941* (Knoxville, Tenn., 1971), 15–87; Blanche Wiesen Cook, "Democracy in Wartime: Antimilitarism in England and the United States, 1914–1918," Charles Chatfield, ed., *Peace Movements in America* (New York, 1973), 39–56; H. C. Peterson and Gilbert C. Fite, *Opponents of War: 1917–1918* (Madison, Wis., 1957); and Frederick C. Giffin, *Six Who Protested: Radical Opposition to the First World War* (Port Washington, N.Y., 1977). For a discussion of the antiwar faction in the United States Senate, see Thomas W. Ryley, *A Little Group of Willful Men: A Study of Congressional-Presidential Authority* (Port Washington, N.Y., 1975).

5. George Creel, *Rebel at Large: Recollections of Fifty Crowded Years* (New York, 1947), 157.

6. Quoted in United States Committee on Public Information, *National Service Handbook*, Red, White and Blue Series, No. 2 (Washington, D.C., 1917), title page.

7. For the association between Lippmann and Wilson see David Elliott Weingast, *Walter Lippmann: A Study in Personal Journalism* (Westport, Conn., 1949, 1970), 14–15.

8. Walter Lippmann to Woodrow Wilson, Feb. 6, 1917, and Lippmann to Wilson, Apr. 13, 1917, Woodrow Wilson Papers, Library of Congress Annex, Washington, D.C., Reel 86.

9. Lippmann to Wilson, Feb. 6, 1917, ibid.

10. The memorandum was attached to Lippmann's letter to Wilson. See Lippmann to Wilson, Mar. 11, 1917, ibid.

11. Edward M. House asked Lippmann to contact Henry Canby of Yale in preparing plans for the publicity bureau. *Diary of Colonel Edward M. House* (Apr. 11, 1917), 10: 105. See also Walter Lippmann to Edward M. House, Apr. 12, 1917, quoted in Francine Curro Cary, *Influence of War on Walter Lippmann, 1914–1944* (Madison, Wis., 1967), 37–38.

12. David Lawrence to Woodrow Wilson, Mar. 31, 1917, Wilson papers, Reel 86.

13. David Lawrence to Robert Lansing, Apr. 7, 1917, ibid., Reel 87;

David Lawrence to Woodrow Wilson, Apr. 8, 1917, ibid. A copy of Lawrence's letter to Lansing was enclosed in his correspondence with Wilson.

14. Interestingly, throughout the remainder of the war, the CPI sought to do what Lawrence suggested, and not just in Latin America but in more than thirty countries. Though not attempting to maintain complete secrecy, the task of the committee's Foreign Section was to project abroad the most favorable image possible of the United States. The CPI used news releases, films, and American business concerns in this effort. For treatment of the CPI's Foreign Section, see James R. Mock and Cedric Larson, *Words That Won the War: The Story of the Committee on Public Information, 1917–1919* (Princeton, 1939), 235–334; and George Creel, *How We Advertised America: The First Telling of the Amazing Story of the Committee on Public Information That Carried the Gospel of Americanism to Every Corner of the Globe* (New York, 1920), 237–398.

15. Historians have neglected Arthur Bullard in discussing the origins of the Committee on Public Information. The only full-scale scholarly treatment of the CPI is Mock and Larson, *Words That Won the War*. According to Mock and Larson—who were relying on a letter written to them by the CPI chairman in 1939—shortly after the United States declared war, George Creel wrote to Woodrow Wilson protesting reports that the government planned rigid censorship. He urged that the Wilson administration publicize its war aims rather than suppress news. On Apr. 13, 1917, Secretary of State Robert Lansing, Secretary of War Newton Baker, and Secretary of the Navy Josephus Daniels wrote Wilson saying that America's greatest needs were "confidence, enthusiasm, and service" and recommending the creation of a "committee on public information" that would combine the two functions of censorship and publicity. The cabinet members thus presented the "germ" of the idea for the CPI, according to Mock and Larson, and Creel then took the idea and created "a vast and complex organization." Ibid., 10–11, 48. For Creel's account of his influence on the creation of the CPI, see Creel, *Rebel at Large*, 156–58. For a fuller account of the cabinet letter to Wilson than is found in the Mock and Larson study, see New York *Times*, Apr. 15, 1917, p. 1. Also, for the original letter and an attached memorandum stating that Wilson's immediate decision to create the CPI was based on the cabinet communication, see Wilson papers, Reel 355.

It has been argued that Henry Canby was responsible for the idea behind the CPI, although this claim has not been sufficiently documented. See Edward L. Schapsmeier and Frederick H. Schapsmeier, *Walter Lippmann: Philosopher-Journalist* (Washington, D.C., 1969), 29. For others who may have offered advice on publicity and censorship before the CPI was created, see James R. Mock, *Censorship, 1917* (Princeton, N.J., 1941), 44–45.

16. For Bullard's family background see Bullard papers, Box 1, Folder: "Biographical Material."

17. Albert Edwards, *Comrade Yetta* (New York, 1913), 5. This novel deals with the experiences of a Russian Jewish immigrant girl in New York.

18. Arthur Bullard, "The Only Possibilism," 1, 3, Bullard papers, Box 3. Bullard's association with socialism caused concern among not only conservatives but also the Military Intelligence unit that made a security check on CPI personnel. See Military Intelligence Branch, Executive Division, "Report on the Committee on Public Information" (May 1918), 15. Records of the Committee on Public Information, Record Group 63, National Archives (hereafter cited as CPI papers), CPI 1–A1. Bullard was apparently never a member of the Socialist party, and George Kennan argued that his views were "liberal rather than socialistic." George F. Kennan, *Soviet-American Relations, 1917–1920: Russia Leaves the War* (Princeton, 1956), 46.

19. Bullard traveled to Russia during the abortive Russian revolution of 1905–6; among his writings on those events are Arthur Bullard, "The St. Petersburg Massacre and the Russian East Side," *Independent* 58 (Feb. 2, 1905): 252–56; Albert Edwards, "An Eye-witness's Story of the Russian Revolution," *Harper's Weekly* 50 (Feb. 17 and 24 and Mar. 3, 1906): 228–29, 232, 258–61, 294–96; Edwards, "The Death and Resurrection of the Russian Press," ibid. (Mar. 24, 1906): 424; Edwards, "The Opening of the Duma," *Independent* 60 (June 14, 1906): 1412–15; Edwards, "The Peasant's Union," ibid. 61 (July 19, 1906): 147–52; Edwards, "Rise of the Russian Proletariat and the Russian Revolution," *International Socialist Review* 8 (July, Aug., Sept., and Oct. 1907): 20–32, 76–87, 155–76, 193–203; and Edwards, "Vox Populi," *Outlook* 91 (Apr. 3, 1909): 789–91. For other material on Bullard and the revolution of 1905–6, see Bullard papers, Box 12.

Bullard's writings on the Russian revolution of 1917 include Bullard, *Russian Pendulum: Autocracy—Democracy—Bolshivism* (New York, 1919); and Bullard, "The Wrong Side of the Looking-Glass: Impressions of Topsy-Turvy Russia," *Harper's Magazine* 139 (Aug. 1919): 408–13.

20. Bullard's writings on the war include Bullard, "National Defense," *Century* 89 (Feb. 1915): 489–91; Bullard, "Clausewitz and This War," *Outlook* 109 (Feb. 24, 1915): 433–36; Bullard, "The British War Machine," ibid. (Mar. 24, 1915): 683–86; Bullard, "The War and Workingmen," ibid. (Mar. 31, 1915): 770, 779–82; Bullard, "Business and the War," ibid. (Apr. 7, 1915): 832–35; Bullard, "English View-Points on the War," ibid. (June 9, 1915): 327–34; Bullard, "Are We a World Power?" *Century* 91 (Nov. 1915): 114–19; Bullard, "Our Relations with Great Britain," *Atlantic Monthly* 118 (Oct. 1916): 451–61; Bullard, "How Strong Are the Germans?" *Outlook* 114 (Oct. 18, 1916): 380–84; Bullard, "England and the Future of Democracy," ibid. (Oct. 25, 1916): 416–19; and Bullard, "Our Relations with France," *Atlantic Monthly* 118 (Nov. 1916): 634–40.

Also early in the war, Bullard tried unsuccessfully to enlist in the French army and air service. Ethel Bullard to Malcolm [Davis], Jan. 17, 1931, Bullard papers, Box 14.

21. House told Bullard that this was so. For example, Colonel Edward M. House to Arthur Bullard, June 10, 1916, Bullard papers, Box 12.

22. For excerpts from Douglas MacArthur's statement, see *New York Times*, July 7, 1916, p. 6. MacArthur's biographers say little about his position in the War Department in 1916, and they portray his relations with the press as having been exceptionally good, citing a letter signed by twenty-nine correspondents that praised him for his dealing with the press. See D. Clayton James, *Years of MacArthur: Volume I, 1880–1941* (Boston, 1970), 130–32; Frazier Hunt, *Untold Story of Douglas MacArthur* (New York, 1954), 61–64; and Gavin Long, *MacArthur as Military Commander* (New York, 1969), 13. MacArthur devotes little space to his role as press censor. [Douglas MacArthur], *Reminiscences: General of the Army Douglas MacArthur* (New York, 1964), 43–44. Also giving only slight attention to MacArthur's position in the War Department in 1916 is Clark Lee and Richard Henschel, *Douglas MacArthur* (New York, 1952), 32.

It must be said in fairness to MacArthur that once war was declared and censorship legislation was proposed by members of President Wilson's cabinet, MacArthur sought to moderate the penalties for publishing unauthorized military information. Whereas persons in the Army War College apparently favored a penalty of up to three years in prison and up to a ten thousand dollar fine or both, MacArthur felt that such punishment went "beyond the point of helping enforcement . . . and tend[ed] to intimidation, especially of the smaller and less powerful papers." He favored a penalty of no more than a one thousand dollar fine and no more than six months in jail or both for such violations. See Josephus Daniels to Woodrow Wilson, Apr. 1917, Josephus Daniels Papers, Library of Congress Annex, Washington, D.C., Box 109, Folder: "Wilson, Woodrow Correspondence with JD April–May 1917"; and Douglas MacArthur to Secretary of War, Apr. 18, 1917, ibid., Box 60, Folder: "Baker, Newton D. April–May 1917."

23. Arthur Bullard, [Memorandum on Censorship], [July 1916], p. 1; Papers of Colonel E. M. House: *Domestic and International Questions 1911–1918*, Yale University Library, New Haven, Conn., Group No. 466, Series No. III, Box No. 185, Folder No. 1/220.

24. Ibid.   25. Ibid., 9.

26. Ibid., 11.   27. Ibid.

28. Ibid.

29. See Bullard to House, July 18, 1916, Bullard papers, Box 12. In a subsequent article he attacked English censors, declaring that censorship of the press and enlightened public opinion were mutually exclusive. See Bullard, "Our Relations with Great Britain," 459.

30. Bullard to House, July 18, 1916, Bullard papers, Box 12.

31. Bullard to House, May 23, 1916, ibid.; Arthur Bullard, "Democracy and Diplomacy," *Atlantic Monthly* 119 (Apr. 1917): 496.

32. Bullard to House, July 18, 1916, Bullard papers, Box 12.

33. Ibid. Bullard, incidentally, was not in favor of an automatic alliance with England in the event that the United States entered the war—especially if England was controlled by the Tories. He described himself as "pro-Liberal"

rather than "pro-English" (Bullard, "Our Relations with Great Britain," 452–53); advocated an alliance with France, hopefully to move England in a more liberal direction and to avoid an Anglo-Saxon imperialism (Bullard, "Our Relations with France," 638, 640); and wrote to House that "a Pan-Anglo-Saxonism would be quite as dangerous to democracy as Pan-Germanism or Pan-Slavism," stating that he "would vote against any European entanglement which was not obviously Pan-Liberalism." (Bullard to House, July 16, 1916, Bullard papers, Box 12). Bullard feared that liberalism would not do well in England, but he did write that "the worst I can say against Great Britain is that I fear it will be reactionary. Germany already is." Bullard to House, May 23, 1916, ibid.

34. House to Bullard and Ernest Poole, July 21, 1916, Bullard papers, Box 12.

35. Bullard to House, Aug. 8, 1916, ibid., Box 20.

36. House to Bullard, Aug. 9, 1916, ibid.

37. Bullard, "Democracy and Diplomacy," 491. The substance of this article appeared in Bullard's letters to House of July 16 and 18, 1916. Bullard did write an article for the November issue of *Atlantic Monthly*, although it was on U.S. relations with France: Bullard, "Our Relations with France."

38. Bullard, "Democracy and Diplomacy," 492.

39. Ibid., 499.

40. Ibid.

41. Ibid., 491.

42. Bullard to House, July 18, 1916, Bullard papers, Box 12.

43. Bullard, "Democracy and Diplomacy," 497.

44. In correspondence with House he had urged "the diplomatic use of newspapers." In this regard, Russia, Germany, and Britain had been more imaginative. Bullard to House, July 18, 1916, Bullard papers, Box 12. See also Bullard to House, Feb. 23, 1917, ibid., Box 20. He suggested that stories the American government wished to have printed in the British press be first published in Montreal and Toronto papers, as these publications were generally not altered for the reading public in England. Bullard to House, July 18, 1916, ibid., Box 12.

45. Bullard, "Democracy and Diplomacy," 497.

46. Bullard to House, Feb. 23, 1917, Bullard papers, Box 20.

47. Bullard to House, Mar. 15, 1917, ibid.

48. House asked Bullard to call him to make such an appointment. House to Bullard, Mar. 17, 1917, ibid. See also Bullard to House, Mar. 20, 1917, ibid.; the memorandum was attached to this letter.

49. Arthur Bullard, *Mobilising America* (New York, 1917). Bullard's book was published on or about Mar. 26, 1917 (the date in the preface), six days after the above memorandum was sent to House.

50. For Bullard, the call for emotional fervor was not entirely new. The previous year he had published *Diplomacy of the Great War*, in which he had

contended that entrance into the war would require "some motive of sufficient force to completely revolutionize our habits and our attitude towards
life." If we decided to go to war we should not do so halfheartedly, he argued,
but should "fight to the limit." Arthur Bullard, *Diplomacy of the Great War* (New
York, 1916), 303, 304.

51. Bullard, *Mobilising America*, 25.

52. Ibid., 41, 10.

53. Ibid., 16–17. Chapter 2 is entitled "Democracies as Fighting Machines."

54. Ibid., 24, 26.   55. Ibid., 24.

56. Ibid., 26.   57. Ibid., 45.

58. Ibid., 40. See also 37–40.

59. Ibid., 42–43. The CPI supplied "Army stories" to the American public through the Division of Syndicated Features, headed by L. Ames Brown.
The CPI's Division of Advertising resembled a corps of press agents.

60. Ibid., 60–61. The CPI issued news bulletins on a much larger scale.
Some six thousand releases were put out by the committee's Division of News.

61. Ibid., 59. The CPI also tried to utilize public schools by issuing a
sixteen-page paper, *National School Service*, which was sent without charge to
all public schools.

62. Kennan, *Russia Leaves the War*, 49–50. House to Bullard, Apr. 13,
1917, Bullard papers, Box 20.

63. Bullard to House, Apr. 1917, Bullard papers, Box 20; see also Bullard
to House, May 3, 1917, ibid.

64. George Creel to Marlborough Churchill, July 8, 1918, CPI papers,
CPI 1–A1, Box 5. Creel apparently confirmed to William English Walling
that it was Bullard who had suggested the idea for the CPI. Ibid. Creel called
Mobilising America "a clarion call to the Nation." George Creel to Ralph M.
Easley, July 9, 1918, ibid., Box 9, Folder 194. Heber Blankenhorn, Bullard's
friend and fellow journalist, also stated that it was Bullard's ideas that led to
the creation of the CPI. "Reminiscences of Heber Blankenhorn" (1956), 1:
75, Columbia Oral History Collection, Columbia University, New York.

In addition to Bullard, others also helped organize the CPI in the early
weeks of its existence, including Ernest Poole, Edgar Sisson, Charles Hart,
Harvey O'Higgins, and W. L. Chenery. MacArthur helped Creel choose a
building to serve as committee headquarters. Creel, *Rebel at Large*, 160.

65. [Arthur Bullard and Ernest Poole], *How the War Came to America*, Red,
White and Blue Series, No. 1 (Washington, D.C., 1917).

66. Creel recommended Bullard for service in Russia. See George Creel
to Woodrow Wilson, May 10, 1917, George Creel Papers, Library of Congress
Annex, Washington, D.C.; and Woodrow Wilson to "Mr. Secretary," May 14,
1917, Bullard papers, Box 20.

67. New York *Times*, Apr. 15, 1917, p. 1. The CPI was first funded by
money from the president's National Security and Defense Fund. Congress

appropriated $1,250,000 to the committee for the year 1918–19 ($5,600,000 came from the president's fund). Another $2,825,000 resulted from earnings on film rentals, sales of publications, and similar transactions. In all, the CPI received over $9,675,000. See Mock and Larson, *Words That Won the War*, 67.

68. See Josephus Daniels, *Wilson Era: Years of War and After, 1917–1923* (Chapel Hill, N.C., 1946), 221–22; and E. David Cronon, ed., *Cabinet Diaries of Josephus Daniels, 1913–1921* (Lincoln, Nebr., 1963), 115–16, 127, 128. See also Newton D. Baker to Josephus Daniels, Jan. 12, 1917, Newton Diehl Baker Papers, Library of Congress Annex, Washington, D.C., Ac. 9676, Container 1; Newton D. Baker to Gilson Gardner (Newspaper Enterprise Association), Mar. 27, 1917, Daniels papers, Box 60, Folder: "Baker, Newton D., Jan.–March 1917"; and "Press Notice," ibid., Box 573, Folder: "Censorship Mar. 1914–Mar. 1917."

69. For an account of Daniels's work editing the Raleigh *News and Observer* and his connection with progressivism, see Joseph L. Morrison, *Josephus Daniels Says . . .: An Editor's Political Odyssey from Bryan to F.D.R., 1894–1913* (Chapel Hill, N.C., 1962), 3–35, 149–86. Incidentally, when Daniels came under fire as secretary of the navy, it was Creel who came to his defense. George Creel, *Wilson and the Issues* (New York, 1916), 37–46.

70. Josephus Daniels to James Mock and Cedric Larson, quoted in Mock and Larson, *Words That Won the War*, 50; Daniels, *Wilson Era: Years of War and After, 1917–1923*, 222. Further substantiation of Baker's slight role in the CPI is found in Baker's remarks in the "Foreword" of Creel, *How We Advertised America*, xi.

71. Daniels to Mock and Larson, quoted in *Words That Won the War*, 50; George Creel to James Mock and Cedric Larson, quoted in ibid., 11.

72. Creel, *Rebel at Large*, 101, 153; Creel to Mock and Larson, in *Words That Won the War*, 11. Creel's friendship with Wilson was also aided by the close friendship between Creel's wife, the actress Blanche Bates, and Margaret Wilson.

73. Creel, *Rebel at Large*, 156.

74. George Creel to Josephus Daniels, Mar. 19, 1917, Daniels papers, Box 73, Folder: "Creel, George 1917."

75. Creel to Daniels, Mar. 28, 1917, ibid.

76. Creel to Daniels, Apr. 4, 1917, ibid.; Creel to Daniels, Apr. 4, 1917, ibid.; Creel to Daniels, [Apr. 8, 1917], ibid. For Creel's memorandum see Daniels papers, Box 109, Folder: "Wilson, Woodrow Correspondence with JD April–May 1917."

77. The proposed censorship legislation dealt with publishing unauthorized information of a military nature, including "referring to the armed forces of the Government, materials or implements of war, or the means and measures that may be contemplated for the defense of the country. . . ." Violations of these regulations by individuals would have resulted in either a fine of up to ten thousand dollars or three years in prison or both. Interestingly, Wilson favored inserting a section which stated that nothing in this

proposed legislation would be construed as limiting or restricting discussion or criticism of government actions or policies, providing it did not reveal such unauthorized information. See Cronon, ed., *Cabinet Diaries of Josephus Daniels*, 131; Josephus Daniels to Woodrow Wilson, Apr. 11, 1917, Daniels papers, Box 109, Folder: "Wilson, Woodrow Correspondence with JD April–May 1917" (Creel's memorandum and the proposed censorship legislation were attached to this letter). See also Wilson to Daniels, Apr. 12, 1917, ibid.

78. The original draft of the executive order omitted mention of the secretary of state, and only later was his name penned in, as if by after-thought. Creel apparently took the letter drafted by Daniels and Baker to Lansing to sign on Apr. 13. Lansing insisted, according to Daniels, that the letter be on State Department stationery and that Lansing's name appear first. The secretary of state was considerably more conservative in outlook than the CPI's chairman. Lansing desired a strict regulation of the press modeled after England's efforts. He wished to have England send over to the United States someone experienced in censorship matters to guide American efforts in the beginning. Wilson, who according to Daniels wanted to keep censorship at a minimum, vetoed this idea. Lansing also wanted the United States to subsidize South American papers, in order to counteract German influence there. Throughout the war the secretary of state had little to do with the CPI and got along poorly with Creel. In fact, there was bad feeling between the two men. Lansing was bothered by what he thought to be Creel's "socialistic tendencies" and his "radicalism." He also thought Creel to be a publicity hound. In his autobiography, Creel expresses disdain for Lansing. See Wilson papers, Reel 87; Cronon, ed., *Cabinet Diaries of Josephus Daniels*, 133–34, 136; Daniels, *Wilson Era: Years of War and After, 1917–1923*, 221–22; Robert Lansing, *War Memoirs of Robert Lansing, Secretary of State* (Westport, Conn., 1935), 322–23; and Creel, *Rebel at Large*, 160.

79. Frank Luther Mott, *History of American Magazines, 1885–1905* (5 vols., Cambridge, Mass., 1957), 4: 97–98. Creel gave up the weekly in Jan. 1909 to Clara Kellogg and Katherine Baxter.

80. Robert L. Perkin, *First Hundred Years: An Informal History of Denver and the "Rocky Mountain News"* (Garden City, N.Y., 1959), 414–17; and Gene Fowler, *Timber Line: A Story of Bonfils and Tammen* (New York, 1933), 319–28.

81. Creel, *Wilson and the Issues*, 71.

82. Creel, *Rebel at Large*, 50; Edwin Markham, Benjamin B. Lindsey, and George Creel, *Children in Bondage: A Complete and Careful Presentation of the Anxious Problem of Child Labor—Its Causes, Its Crimes, and Its Cure* (New York, 1914); George Creel and Benjamin Barr Lindsey, "Measuring Up Equal Suffrage in Colorado," *Delinquent* 77 (Feb. 1911): 85–86; George Creel, *Measuring Up Equal Suffrage: An Authoritative Estimate of Results in Colorado* (New York, [1912]); Creel, *Chivalry versus Justice: Why the Women of the Nation Demand the Right to Vote* (New York, 1915); and Creel, *What Have Women Done With the Vote?* (New York, [1915]).

83. Creel, *Rebel at Large*, 45, 47.

84. George Creel, "Our 'Visionary' President: An Interpretation of Woodrow Wilson," *Century* 89 (Dec. 1914): 200; Creel, "Can a Democratic Government Control Prices? An Interview with Joseph E. Davies of the Federal Trade Commission," ibid. 93 (Feb. 1917): 611.

85. In 1914, Creel argued that "preparedness for war" had encouraged militarism and had resulted in war. By early 1917, however, he appears to have altered his views. In two articles written before he was appointed chairman of the CPI, Creel argued that universal military training was more democratic than the volunteer system and that it would offer a chance to further public health and teach civic virtues, in addition to providing the country with defense. He also emphasized the need for more scientific organization of industry so that it could be employed efficiently during the war. See George Creel, "The Ghastly Swindle," *Harper's Weekly* 59 (Aug. 29, 1914): 196–97; Creel, "Four Million Citizen Defenders: What Universal Training Means in Dollars, Duty, and Defense," *Everybody's Magazine* 36 (May 1917): 545–54; and Creel, "The Sweat of War: What It Means to Put One Million Men in the Field," ibid. (June 1917): 708–17.

86. George Creel, "Public Opinion in War Time," *Annals of the American Academy of Political and Social Science* 78 (July 1918): 185.

87. United States Committee on Public Information, *Creel Report: Complete Report of the Chairman of the Committee on Public Information, 1917, 1918, 1919* (New York, 1920, 1972), 1. Hereafter cited as *Creel Report*.

88. Creel, *How We Advertised America*, 4–5. Creel's faith in the rational nature of opinion was no doubt genuine, even if he failed to recognize the implications of the CPI's work. In his desire to inform the public, he was markedly different from later successful propagandists in such countries as Nazi Germany, who were openly contemptuous of opinion. One need only compare Creel's writing on this subject with that of Adolf Hitler or of Joseph Goebbels's one-time deputy Eugen Hadamovsky. See Adolf Hitler, *Mein Kampf*, (translated by Ralph Manheim) (Boston, 1925, 1971), 180, 183; and Eugen Hadamovsky, *Propaganda and National Power* (New York, 1933, 1972).

89. Creel, *How We Advertised America*, 5.

90. Creel maintained, incorrectly, that the CPI never appealed to the emotions; the work of the committee was "educational and informative throughout," he said. The Speakers' Bureau and the Divisions of Four Minute Men, Pictorial Publicity, and Advertising were especially guilty of making strong emotional appeals. See ibid., 4; and Creel, "Public Opinion in War Time," 185.

91. Editorial, New York *Times*, Apr. 16, 1917, p. 12.

92. George Creel, "The 'Lash' of Public Opinion," *Collier's* 74 (Nov. 22, 1924): 46.

93. On Creel's "slumming" remark see Mock and Larson, *Words That Won the War*, 61. He also said that Congress was the one place in America where "the mouth is above the law." Creel, *How We Advertised America*, 52.

Creel called Congressman Knutson of Minnesota a "petty malignant" because
Knutson had accused CPI publications of being propaganda for the Democratic party. Ibid., 55–56. Creel also called Lodge "an exceedingly dull man"
and "very vain." Ibid., 59–60. Creel usually had better access to Wilson than
most officials, and he apparently found that one of the most effective ways of
seeing the president was to enter the White House cursing Senator Lodge.
See Walter F. Willcox to Carl Becker, Aug. 15, 1940, Carl Becker Papers,
Cornell University Libraries, Department of Manuscripts and Archives, Box
14. Creel's comments regarding Lansing are found in a statement by Creel
attached to a letter from Woodrow Wilson to Lansing, Creel papers, Container
1. See also Creel, *Rebel at Large*, 160. Walton Bean has an amusing discussion
on Creel's use of the zoological metaphor. See Walton E. Bean, "George Creel
and His Critics: A Study of the Attacks on the Committee on Public Information, 1917–1919" (doctoral dissertation, University of California Berkeley,
1941), 10–11.

94. George Creel to George Bates Creel, Mar. 21, 1931, Creel papers,
Container 3.

95. John Dos Passos, *Mr. Wilson's War* (Garden City, N.Y., 1962), 300;
Tattler, "National Miniatures: George Creel," *Nation* 105 (Nov. 22, 1917):
573; Jonathan Daniels, *End of Innocence* (New York, 1954), 226. Creel learned
to take most of these descriptions philosophically and confided to Albert
Shaw that his face was something for which he should not be blamed. George
Creel to Albert Shaw, Nov. 1, 1917, Albert Shaw Papers, New York Public
Library Annex, Personalities and Groups, Box 3.

96. "Reminiscences of Guy Stanton Ford" (1954–55), 401, Columbia
Oral History Collection, Columbia University, New York.

97. "Reminiscences of James T. Shotwell" (1964), 73–74, ibid.

98. Mark Sullivan, *Our Times: The United States, 1900–1925*, Vol. 5, *Over
Here, 1914–1918* (New York, 1933), 425; "Reminiscences of Heber Blankenhorn," 79.

Chapter Two

1. From the text of a speech delivered at Madison Square Garden, Sept.
15, 1917, in Charles Edward Russell Papers, Library of Congress Annex,
Container 8. See also New York *Times*, Sept. 16, 1917, pp. 1, 3. This remark
was not reprinted in the *Times*'s coverage of Russell's speech.

2. Louis Filler, *Appointment at Armageddon: Muckraking and Progressivism in
the American Tradition* (Westport, Conn., 1976), 64; Richard Hofstadter, *Age of
Reform: From Bryan to F.D.R.* (New York, 1955), 275 (see also p. 278).

3. The fact that intellectuals—academicians and others—wrote in support of the national cause was not unique to the United States. Such people
in Britain, France, and Germany were also ardent propagandists and important in defining their countries' positions during the war. See James Duane

Squires, *British Propaganda at Home and in the United States from 1914 to 1917* (Cambridge, Mass., 1935), 17–19; H. C. Peterson, *Propaganda for War: The Campaign against American Neutrality, 1914–1917* (Norman, Okla., 1939), 17–18, especially note 22; Klaus Schwabe, "Zur politischen Haltung der deutschen Professoren im ersten Weltkrieg," *Historische Zeitschrift* 193 (Dec. 1961): 601–34; Fritz Klein, "Gli storici tedeschi di fronte alla prima guerra mondiale," *Studi Storici* 3 (No. 4, 1962): 730–56; Abraham Ascher, "Professors as Propagandists: The Politics of the Kathedersozialisten," *Journal of Central European Affairs* 23 (Oct. 1963): 282–302; and Klaus Schwabe, "Ursprung und Verbreitung des alldeutschen Annexionismus in der deutschen Professorenschaft im ersten Weltkrieg," *Vierteljahrshefte für Zeitgeschichte* 14 (Apr. 1966): 105–38.

4. J. A. Thompson, after studying a somewhat different group of progressive publicists, has observed that this "heightened social spirit," more than the appeal of physical valor, attracted many progressives to the war. J. A. Thompson, "American Progressive Publicists and the First World War, 1914–1917," *Journal of American History* 58 (Sept. 1971): 380.

5. The Committee on Public Information provides a further chapter in the story of reform during the war. Hofstadter contended that "the war put an end to the Progressive movement," and C. C. Regier argued that whatever fragments of the muckraking movement remained in 1917 were "crushed" by American entry in the World War. See Hofstadter, *Age of Reform*, 275; and C. C. Regier, *Era of the Muckrakers* (Gloucester, Mass., 1932, 1957), 194–95. It has been well documented, however, that many reformers saw the war as an opportunity for further reform of society. See Walter I. Trattner, "Progressivism and World War I: A Re-appraisal," *Mid-America* 44 (July 1962): 131–45; Charles Hirschfeld, "Nationalist Progressivism and World War I," ibid. 45 (July 1963): 139–56; Allen F. Davis, "Welfare, Reform, and World War I," *American Quarterly* 19 (Fall 1967): 516–33; James Weinstein, *Corporate Ideal and the Liberal State: 1900–1918* (Boston, 1968), 214–15; and Stanley Shapiro, "The Great War and Reform: Liberals and Labor, 1917–19," *Labor History* 11 (Summer 1971): 323–44.

It has been noted that the problems plaguing democracy in the early twentieth century were not confined by national boundaries. It also has been observed that many reformers saw American intervention in the war as an "extension of domestic progressivism," an opportunity to make reform international. See Russel B. Nye, *This Almost Chosen People: Essays in the History of American Ideas* (East Lansing, Mich., 1966), 84; and Filler, *Appointment at Armageddon*, 394. See also Robert Endicott Osgood, *Ideals and Self-Interest in America's Foreign Relations: The Great Transformation of the Twentieth Century* (Chicago, 1953), 275.

Other historians have pointed out that the CPI attracted a substantial number of reformers to its ranks, but they have not explored this connection, nor have they suggested that the CPI was interested in reform in addition to the defeat of Germany. See Hofstadter, *Age of Reform*, 275–76; and Louis Filler, *Muckrakers: Crusaders for American Liberalism* (Yellow Springs, Ohio, 1950), 374–75.

It also has been asserted by both Creel and Walton Bean that the CPI was an entirely nonpartisan operation—Creel contending that the committee was divided among Democrats, Republicans, and Independents. To be sure, membership cut across party lines. It is hoped that this chapter will make clear, however, that much of the membership of the committee came from a reforming background and that important committee members more often than not had been involved in supporting reforms that antedated the war. This fact perhaps helps to explain why in 1918 the CPI was sometimes accused of harboring "radicals" and "bolsheviki." For example, see [Ralph M. Easley?] to George Creel, Jan. 19, 1918, National Civic Federation Papers, New York Public Library Annex, Gen. Correspondence, 1918, Box 55. See also Creel, *How We Advertised America*, 14–15; and Bean, "George Creel and His Critics," 24–62.

6. Although this study focuses only on the CPI's Domestic Section, the Foreign Section is treated in *Creel Report*, 108–290, and in the studies by Creel and Mock and Larson mentioned above (note 14, Chapter 1).

7. The task of many subdivisions was to impose order on situations that had become chaotic. The CPI sought a high degree of centralization. Its operation, according to Robert Wiebe, fell within a design that had been sketched by progressive legislation. See Robert H. Wiebe, *Search for Order, 1877–1920* (New York, 1967), 298–99; and Creel, *How We Advertised America*, 13.

8. For a list of the subdivisions of the Committee on Public Information, see Mock and Larson, *Words That Won the War*, 66–74. Both the Mock and Larson study and Creel's *How We Advertised America* are organized around the committee's subdivisions.

Payroll records of the CPI are located in the National Personnel Records Center, St. Louis, Mo.

9. Creel, *Rebel at Large*, 161; Creel, *Wilson and the Issues*, 62.

10. Quoted in Bean, "George Creel and His Critics," 257.

11. From a statement drafted by Creel for President Wilson commending the *National School Service*, Creel Papers, Vol. 3. Wilson did not use this passage, however.

12. Creel, *How We Advertised America*, 105. This statement and indeed the entire chapter in which it appears were probably written by Guy Stanton Ford. For a draft of this chapter see Guy Stanton Ford Papers, University of Minnesota Archives, Minneapolis, Folder 163. See also George Creel to Guy Stanton Ford, Aug. 18, 1919, ibid., Folder 32.

13. Creel was paid $8,000 a year; O'Higgins and Sisson received $6,000; Byoir drew $5,200. Mock and Larson, *Words That Won the War*, 67.

14. Some of O'Higgins's early works included O'Higgins, *Smoke Eaters:*

The Story of a Fire Crew (New York, 1905); O'Higgins, *Grand Army Man* (New York, 1908); O'Higgins and Benjamin B. Lindsey, *The Beast* (New York, 1910); and O'Higgins and Frank J. Cannon, *Under the Prophet in Utah: The National Menace of a Political Priesthood* (Boston, 1911).

15. Harvey O'Higgins, "Judge Ben Lindsey: Advance Agent of the New Freedom," *Cosmopolitan* 66 (Jan. 1919): 70–71.

16. Ben B. Lindsey in collaboration with Harvey O'Higgins, "The Doughboy's Religion," ibid. (Mar. 1919): 126, 127.

17. Ben B. Lindsey in collaboration with Harvey O'Higgins, "Our National Faith Cure," ibid. (Apr. 1919): 30–33, 123–26.

O'Higgins supported increased maternity and child care benefits, urged a greater effort to educate the public about venereal disease, and argued that criminal prosecution was not the answer to illegitimate children. Ben B. Lindsey in collaboration with Harvey O'Higgins, "Horses' Rights for Women," ibid. (May 1919): 71–75, 166, 168.

18. William Randolph Hearst to George Creel, May 21, 1917, CPI papers, CPI 1–A1, Box 4, Folder: "Censorship, Mail."

19. Kennan, *Russia Leaves the War*, 51–52. Sisson helped produce one of the CPI's most controversial pamphlets, *The German-Bolshevik Conspiracy*, War Information Series, No. 20 (Washington, D.C., 1918).

20. Sisson registered as a member of the Progressive party in 1912 and 1916, after which time he registered as a Republican. Sisson's remarks were quoted by Creel in a letter to Marlborough Churchill, head of Military Intelligence. George Creel to Marlborough Churchill, July 8, 1918, CPI papers, CPI 1–A1, Box 5. In a Military Intelligence report on the backgrounds of CPI members—one, incidentally, that relied heavily on hearsay information and that reveals the primitive nature of American intelligence gathering at this time—someone had accused Sisson of having been a socialist. Sisson denied to Creel that he had ever voted a socialist ticket. Military Intelligence Branch, Executive Division, General Staff, "Report on the Committee on Public Information" (May 1918), 8, CPI papers, CPI 1–A1, Box 5.

21. See Carl Byoir, "The Presentation of Montessori Material," *National Education Association of the United States: Journal of Proceedings and Addresses* (1912), 613–18. See also Mock and Larson, *Words That Won the War*, 66.

22. George Creel to Bronson Winthrop (local Selective Service Board chairman), June 27, 1918, CPI papers, CPI 1–A1, Folder 89. See also *Editor and Publisher* 51 (July 13, 1918): 24.

23. Mock and Larson, *Words That Won the War*, 66. More will be said of Byoir in connection with the Division of Advertising.

24. For example, the Service Bureau was established by executive order on Mar. 19, 1918, to answer citizens' questions about the work of various government agencies. Frederick W. McReynolds of Dartmouth was director. He was followed in this post by former congressman and later Civil Service commissioner Martin A. Morrison, and by Mary A. Schick.

25. Mock and Larson, *Words That Won the War*, 48.

26. Chapters 3 through 5 below examine the people who wrote for Ford and the themes present in the literature of his division.

27. Guy Stanton Ford, "America's Fight for Public Opinion," *Minnesota History Bulletin* 3 (Feb. 1919): 24–25.

28. [Roger W. Babson], *Actions and Reactions: An Autobiography of Roger W. Babson* (New York, 1935), 38–47, 231–41.

29. See Roger W. Babson, "The South American Plan," *Sagamore Sociological Conference* (Eighth Year) (Sagamore Beach, Mass., June 30–July 2, 1914), 35–36; and Babson, *Future of South America* (Boston, 1915).

30. Roger W. Babson, "Eliminating the Economic Causes of War," George H. Blakeslee, ed., *Problems and Lessons of the War: Clark University Addresses December 16, 17, and 18, 1915* (New York, 1916), 155–62. For Babson and the Society to Eliminate the Economic Causes of War, see Curti, *Peace or War*, 230.

31. [Babson], *Actions and Reactions*, 234–42; Mock and Larson, *Words That Won the War*, 191, 193, 195. For Babson's account of his war work with the government, see [Babson], *Actions and Reactions*, 242–49.

32. Mock and Larson, *Words that Won the War*, 70–71. The prowar alliance was created to win the support of labor away from the antiwar People's Council of America for Democracy and Terms of Peace. It also worked for continued labor reforms for the American Federation of Labor from Congress and the Wilson administration. Frank L. Grubbs contends, and CPI records verify his contention, that the CPI helped finance the alliance and that Creel exerted a strong influence over that organization. See Frank L. Grubbs, Jr., *Struggle for Labor Loyalty: Gompers, the A. F. of L., and the Pacifists, 1917–1920* (Durham, N.C., 1968), vii–viii, 43–45. James Weinstein and Ronald Radosh also argue that Creel controlled the American Alliance for Labor and Democracy. Weinstein, *Corporate Ideal and the Liberal State*, 240; Ronald Radosh, *American Labor and United States Foreign Policy* (New York, 1969), 60. For money given to the alliance by the CPI, see ibid., 69; and Lewis L. Lorwin, with the assistance of Jean Atherton Flexner, *American Federation of Labor: History, Policies, and Prospects* (Washington, D.C., 1933), 152–53.

33. Grubbs, *Struggle for Labor Loyalty*, 36–37. Questions about Maisel's loyalty and socialism were raised in Military Intelligence Branch, "Report on the Committee on Public Information," 41. Creel's defense of Maisel is found in Creel to Churchill, July 8, 1918.

34. This organization tried to bring together prowar socialists and progressives from minor party movements to further industrial and political democracy. Stokes served as treasurer for both the American Alliance for Labor and Democracy and the Social Democratic League of America. As early as Mar. 29, 1917, Stokes and other members of the Socialist party, including Russell and Walling, drew up a manifesto in opposition to the Socialist party's stand on national defense as "contrary to the interests of

democracy and . . . the hitherto accepted views of the International Socialist movement." See James G. Phelps Stokes Papers, Butler Library, Columbia University, New York, Box 20, Folder: "The 'Manifesto' of March 29, 1917." See also Kenneth E. Hendrickson, Jr., "The Pro-War Socialists, the Social Democratic League and the Ill-Fated Drive for Industrial Democracy in America, 1917–1920," *Labor History* 11 (Summer 1970): 304–22, especially 310, 313; Grubbs, *Struggle for Labor Loyalty*, 20, 40–42; Radosh, *American Labor and United States Foreign Policy*, 34–43; and Lorwin, *American Federation of Labor*, 148–49.

Literature on American socialism sometimes has accused Stokes of advocating the shooting of antiwar senators and congressmen guilty of treasonable activity. It has been recently shown, however, that such remarks were incorrectly attributed to Stokes, having actually been made by his uncle, William Earl Doge Stokes. See Robert D. Reynolds, Jr., "Pro-War Socialists: Intolerant or Bloodthirsty?" *Labor History* 17 (Summer 1976): 413–15.

35. Mock and Larson, *Words That Won the War*, 191.

36. See Chapter 3 below.

37. *Creel Report*, 75; Mock and Larson, *Words That Won the War*, 110; Perkin, *First Hundred Years*, 415. Associate chairman O'Higgins was interested in and worked closely with this bureau. Unfortunately, most of the records of this division were either misplaced or destroyed. It is for this reason that the present study does not treat this section of the CPI more thoroughly.

38. Brown defended Wilson's policy toward Mexico and Huerta. L. Ames Brown, "President Wilson's Mexican Policy," *Atlantic Monthly* 117 (June 1916): 732–44. In an earlier article, Brown also wrote about Wilson's policies toward Central and South America: "A New Era of Good Feeling," ibid. 115 (Jan. 1915): 99–110. He described Wilson's personal qualifications and his relation to the independent voter in "Wilson the Candidate," *American Review of Reviews* 54 (July 1916): 41–45, and in "The President on the Independent Voter," *World's Work* 32 (Sept. 1916): 494–98. And he discussed Wilson's plans for helping business take the lead in cornering international markets once the war ended in "Preparedness for Peace: An Authorized Statement of President Wilson's Plans," *Collier's* 58 (Sept. 16, 1916): 12–13.

39. See L. Ames Brown, "Nation-Wide Prohibition," *Atlantic Monthly* 115 (June 1915): 735–47; Brown, "Prohibition," *North American Review* 202 (Nov. 1915): 702–29; Brown, "Suffrage and Prohibition," ibid. 203 (Jan. 1916): 93–100; Brown, "Economics of Prohibition," ibid. (Feb. 1916): 256–64; Brown, "Is Prohibition American?" ibid. (Mar. 1916): 413–19 (for his remark on the survival of the fittest, see p. 418); Brown, "Prohibition or Temperance?" ibid. (Apr. 1916): 564–71; Brown, "Prohibition's Legislative Efforts," ibid. 204 (Oct. 1916): 589–93; and Brown, "The Election and Prohibition," ibid. (Dec. 1916): 850–56.

Shortly after American entry in the war he also called for a "scientific reorganization" of the General Staff, with training for the officers to become staff members. Brown, "The General Staff," ibid. 206 (Aug. 1917): 239.

40. Mock and Larson, *Words That Won the War*, 110.

41. Harvey O'Higgins to George Creel, undated, CPI papers, CPI 1–A1, Box 20, Folder 24. For other writers working for the Division of Syndicated Features, see *Creel Report*, 74–75. Before becoming associated with the CPI, many of these writers had done similar work in a private group known as the Vigilantes. Mock and Larson, *Words That Won the War*, 110.

42. Samuel Hopkins Adams, *Common Cause: A Novel of the War in America* (Boston, 1918). It is unclear if this book was written for the Division of Syndicated Features. Adams also played an important part in the Division of Four Minute Men (see Chapter 7 below).

Works by Booth Tarkington written during the war included " 'Middle Western Apathy,' " *American Magazine* 83 (June 1917): 31–32, 118–22; "Using the Kaiser," ibid. 84 (Aug. 1918): 44–45, 83–84, 87; and *Great German Bluff about America* (London, 1918). This latter pamphlet, apparently written for the CPI, was distributed by the British government in summer 1918 in an edition of about 850,000 copies. See Creel papers, Container 23. For other works by Tarkington written during the war, see Dorothy Ritter Russo and Thelma L. Sullivan, *Bibliography of Booth Tarkington, 1869–1946* (Indianapolis, 1949).

43. *Creel Report*, 75.

44. Mock and Larson, *Words That Won the War*, 111; L. Ames Brown to "Editors," Aug. 8, 1917, Wilson papers, Reel 355.

45. *Creel Report*, 75. Creel estimated that the stories reached a monthly circulation of about twelve million. If two people read each paper, then perhaps 25 percent of the population had access to the division's material. Ibid.

46. Creel, *How We Advertised America*, 155; *Creel Report*, 39–40.

47. Ida Tarbell's efforts during the war were not confined to public speaking. Shortly after the Armistice she published a novel about the war's impact on a small Ohio town. Though its citizens had favored isolationism and laissez faire individualism in 1914, by the war's end they had come to develop a sense of community and to realize the worldwide implications of the conflict. Ida M. Tarbell, *Rising of the Tide: The Story of Sabinsport* (New York, 1919). See also Mary E. Tomkins, *Ida M. Tarbell* (New York, 1974), 117–21.

48. For more about Jane Addams and Charles Edward Russell, see Chapter 7.

49. *Creel Report*, 38.

50. Herbert S. Houston, "The New Morals of Advertising," *World's Work* 28 (Aug. 1914): 384–88.

51. Captain Joseph H. Hittinger of the War Department headed the CPI's efforts with the Bureau of State Fair Exhibits, working in cooperation with the Joint Committee on Government Exhibits. Frank Lamson-Scribner of the Department of Agriculture was chairman of this committee. Mock and Larson, *Words That Won the War*, 70. See also *Creel Report*, 59–60.

52. Ibid., 68, 89–90.

53. Maurice Strunsky served with the Division of Pictures.

54. For an annotated list of films put out by the Signal Corps during World War I, see K. Jack Bauer, comp., *List of World War I Signal Corps Films* (Record Group 111) (Washington, D.C., 1957). This publication was put out by the National Archives and Records Service, General Services Administration.

55. See Chapter 9 below.

56. William A. Brady, "Have the Movies Ideals?" *Forum* 59 (Mar. 1918): 307–15. See also Lary May, "D. W. Griffith and the Aesthetics of Progressive Reform, 1908–1920" (paper presented at convention of the Organization of American Historians, St. Louis, 1976).

57. See Division of Pictures, United States Committee on Public Information, *Catalogue of Photographs and Stereopticon Slides* (Oct. 25, 1917 to Jan. 31, 1918) (Washington, D.C., 1918). A copy is located in CPI papers, CPI 14–A3, Folder: (Dec. 1917–Feb. 1918).

58. One pamphlet issued in Apr. 1918 for the newspaper press was United States Committee on Public Information, *War Work of Women in Colleges*, No. 2 (Washington, D.C., 1918).

59. Clara Sears Taylor was helped by Mrs. William A. Mundell ("Caroline Singer"), who was the division's assistant director and who specialized in covering the War Department.

60. For a summary of the activities of the Division of Women's War Work, see *Creel Report*, 75–76; and Mock and Larson, *Words That Won the War*, 72–73. As with the Division of Syndicated Features, most of the records of this section of the CPI no longer exist.

61. Perkin, *First Hundred Years*, 415.

62. Creel, *Rebel at Large*, 101.

63. After the war, Roche was to continue a distinguished career. She was director of the Foreign Language Information Service between 1918 and 1923. She also became assistant secretary of the Treasury, chairperson of the executive committee of the National Youth Administration, president of the Rocky Mountain Fuel Company, and, in 1934, Democratic candidate for governor of Colorado.

64. Mock and Larson say the CPI maintained contact with twenty-three foreign groups; the *Creel Report* (p. 80) says Roche worked with fourteen "racial groups." Mock and Larson, *Words That Won the War*, 219. Most of the records of this division are no longer in the papers of the Committee on Public Information. The CPI's attempt to ensure the loyalty of foreign-born Americans is treated in ibid., 213–32, and Roche's division is also discussed in *Creel Report*, 78–103.

The Division of Work with the Foreign Born eventually turned into the Foreign Language Information Service after the war. This agency is treated in Daniel E. Weinberg, "The Ethnic Technician and the Foreign-Born: Another Look at Americanization Ideology and Goals," *Societas* 7 (Summer 1977): 209–27.

65. A. M. Simons, "Pacifism vs. Revolution," *New Republic* 10 (Mar. 24, 1917): 221.

66. For discussion of Algie Simons's efforts for the Wisconsin Defense League and the Wisconsin Loyalty League, for his efforts not only to inculcate patriotism but also to suppress "unpatriotic" dissent, see Kent Kreuter and Gretchen Kreuter, *An American Dissenter: The Life of Algie Martin Simons, 1870–1950* (Lexington, Ky., 1969), 165–67. In June 1918 he was chosen chairman of the American Socialist and Labor Mission, to travel to Europe (with the approval of Secretary of State Lansing) to win European socialists for Wilson's war aims. While on this tour he took notes for a book finished in December of that year, *The Vision for Which We Fought.* For an account of this mission see Kreuter and Kreuter, *American Dissenter*, 178–91, and Marian Simons Leuck, "The American Socialist and Labor Mission to Europe, 1918, Background, Activities and Significance: An Experiment in Democratic Diplomacy" (doctoral dissertation, Northwestern University, 1941) (the author was Simons's daughter). For Simons's book see Simons, *Vision for Which We Fought: A Study in Reconstruction* (New York, 1919); and Kreuter and Kreuter, *American Dissenter*, 184–88, 192, 198–99.

67. Quoted by Samuel Haber, *Efficiency and Uplift: Scientific Management in the Progressive Era, 1890–1920* (Chicago, 1964), 153.

68. Kreuter and Kreuter, *American Dissenter*, 172–73. Also see Sally M. Miller, "Victor L. Berger and the Promise of Constructive Socialism, 1910–1920" (doctoral dissertation, University of Toronto, 1966), 207–8; A. M. Simons, "The Future of the Socialist Party," *New Republic* 9 (Dec. 2, 1916): 119; and Sally M. Miller, *Victor Berger and the Promise of Constructive Socialism, 1910–1920* (Westport, Conn., 1973).

69. Simons, "Pacifism vs. Revolution," 220–21.

70. Miller, "Victor L. Berger and the Promise of Constructive Socialism, 1910–1920," 240.

71. A. M. Simons, "Memorandum on Cyclopedia," CPI papers, CPI 3–A11, Box 654970 (old numbering), Folder 11.

72. A. M. Simons to May Simons, Aug. 10, 1918, quoted in Kreuter and Kreuter, *American Dissenter*, 187; ibid., 191.

73. Ibid., 179; Grubbs, *Struggle for Labor Loyalty*, 40–41 (as mentioned, Spargo along with Stokes and others hoped to create a separate prowar socialist movement); Bean, "George Creel and His Critics," 258. Creel did refuse to publish a pamphlet by Spargo, recommended by Maisel, entitled "The Allied Cause Is the Cause of Socialist Internationalism." Robert Maisel to George Creel, May 8, 1918, CPI papers, CPI 1–A1, Box 17, Folder 3; Creel to Maisel, May 15, 1918, ibid.

74. Bean, "George Creel and His Critics," 258–60. Upton Sinclair to George Creel, undated, Upton Sinclair Papers, Lilly Library, Indiana University. This letter suggests that Sinclair was concerned to express his loyalty. See also Creel to Sinclair, Oct. 2, 1918, ibid.

75. Will Irwin became managing editor of *McClure's Magazine* during

1906–7 and the following year was a columnist for *Collier's Weekly*. From then until the outbreak of the war he wrote for a variety of magazines, and one of his most serious pieces of investigative reporting was a study of American newspapers, which appeared in *Collier's* between Jan. and July 1911. This series of articles is reprinted in Will Irwin, *American Newspaper* (with comments by Clifford F. Weigle and David G. Clark) (Ames, Iowa, 1969). For biographical information on Irwin see ibid., ix–x; David Mark Chalmers, *Social and Political Ideas of the Muckrakers* (Freeport, N.Y., 1964), 37–41; and Will Irwin, *Making of a Reporter* (New York, 1942).

Among Irwin's writings on war is *Babes of Belgium: The Splendid Story of the Battle of Ypres* (London, 1915), in condensed form in "An American War Correspondent," *Literary Digest* 50 (Apr. 24, 1915): 954–55. Other books are Irwin, *Men, Women and War* (New York, 1915); Irwin, *Latin at War* (New York, 1917); Irwin, *Reporter at Armageddon: Letters from the Front and behind the Lines of the Great War* (New York, 1918); Irwin, *"The Next War": An Appeal to Common Sense* (New York, 1921); and Irwin, *Christ or Mars?* (New York, 1923).

For Irwin's views on the war and the transformation of capitalism, see Irwin, *Latin at War*, 8–9; for Irwin's pessimistic views on the ability of war to purify society, see Will Irwin, "The 'Glory' of War," *American Magazine* 78 (Dec. 1914): 53–54, 72–75.

76. Irwin, "An American War Correspondent," 955; Irwin, *"The Next War."*

77. George Creel, "Makers of Opinion," *Collier's* 65 (May 15, 1920): 20. Military Intelligence believed that Irwin held "radical social views." For this opinion and MI's estimate of Irwin's value to the CPI, see Military Intelligence Branch, "Report on the Committee on Public Information," 23. For the accusation that Irwin was a socialist and his wife an IWW sympathizer, see Ralph Easley to George Creel, July 3, 1918, CPI papers, CPI 1–A1, Box 9, Folder 194. For Creel's defense of Irwin see Creel to Easley, July 8, 1918, ibid.

78. During 1914 and 1915, Irwin was a member of the executive committee of the Commission for Relief in Belgium. Between 1916 and 1918, before joining the CPI, he covered the American, British, and Italian armies for the *Saturday Evening Post*. In addition to his *Post* stories, other war articles by Irwin included "Wreckage of War: Flashlight Pictures Taken on the Trail of the German Army," *American Magazine* 78 (Nov. 1914): 49, 70–73, 76–78; "Hats Off to France!" ibid. 79 (Jan. 1915): 62–65; "England: The Puzzle: Are Her People Cool—or Asleep? Brave—or Blind?" ibid. (Feb. 1915): 40–41, 78–83. See also Irwin, "The 'Glory' of War."

79. Ernest Poole, "Why I Am No Longer a Pacifist," *McClure's Magazine* 49 (Aug. 1917): 19, 67. Poole discussed the manner in which war called forth great sacrifices in spite of various creeds and self-interests. Poole, *Bridge: My Own Story* (New York, 1940), 250. He also argued against making hate a central theme of the war effort. Poole, "The Fighters and the Haters," *McClure's Magazine* 49 (Sept. 1917): 19.

80. Ernest Poole to George Creel, Feb. 15, 1918, CPI papers, CPI 1–A1, Box 22, Folder 9; Poole to Creel, May 6, 1918, ibid.; George Creel to Byron Newton, May 8, 1918, ibid. Shortly after the war, Poole published a novel, *Blind: A Story of These Times* (New York, 1921).

Poole was concerned with educating American soldiers in France, especially those who might remain there after the Armistice, and he suggested a weekly nonpartisan paper somewhat different from *Stars and Stripes* that would prepare these men for the problems of reconstruction. Creel, however, did not think the idea possible. Poole to Creel, Oct. 28, 1918, CPI papers, CPI 1–A1, Box 22, Folder 9; Creel to Poole, Oct. 30, 1918, ibid.

81. On Charles E. Merriam during the war, see Barry D. Karl, *Charles E. Merriam and the Study of Politics* (Chicago, 1974), 84–99. For Merriam's account of his wartime work, see Charles E. Merriam, "American Publicity in Italy," *American Political Science Review* 13 (Nov. 1919): 541–55.

Whitehouse's account of her CPI work is Vira B. Whitehouse, *Year as a Government Agent* (New York, 1920). There is also a considerable volume of correspondence to and from Whitehouse in the Schwimmer-Lloyd Papers, New York Public Library Annex.

For Creel's comment on Bohn, see George Creel to Marlborough Churchill, July 8, 1918, CPI papers, CPI 1–A1, Box 5. After the war, Bohn worked for the New York *Times*.

After the war, James Kerney wrote *Political Education of Woodrow Wilson* (New York, 1926).

Lindsey received more than fourteen hundred dollars from the CPI for this trip. George Creel to Ben B. Lindsey, Oct. 30, 1918, Ben B. Lindsey Papers, Library of Congress Annex, Washington, D.C., Corresp. (Carded Series) 1897–1931, Aug.–Nov. 1918, Container 59. Also see Lindsey to Creel, Nov. 4, 1918, ibid.; Lindsey to Creel, Nov. 29, 1918, ibid.

The list of liberals working for the CPI abroad can be expanded to include Fiorello LaGuardia, Arthur Woods, and Robert Murray. Heber Blankenhorn, Charles Merz, and Walter Lippmann were associated with CPI propaganda in Europe during the summer and autumn of 1918 as officers in a Military Intelligence unit responsible for directing American propaganda behind enemy lines. Merz wrote one of the CPI's pamphlets.

82. The work of the CPI could be illuminated further by more studies of individual members of the committee. Though biographies exist for Simons, McClure, Tarbell, and Merriam, there are none for most of the committee members. No adequate studies exist of the CPI's chairman, Creel, or of Guy Stanton Ford, for example.

Also, people like Irwin, Bullard, and Poole had left for Europe once the war began and gained experience about that conflict before the United States declared war. Bullard and Poole had been interested in reform abroad for more than a decade before 1917. The effect of such journalists on American neutrality deserves further treatment.

83. Attitudes toward religion may have been a factor in explaining the positions taken by some CPI members, although such influences are difficult to assess. The evidence is sketchy, but most who chose to discuss their religious beliefs were raised as Protestants. They maintained a commitment to the emotional, spiritual side of religion; they disliked restricting religion by denominations. Men like O'Higgins championed a secular ethic and were concerned with making this world a better place, with little emphasis on preparing for an afterlife. Most of them believed in a Supreme Being, one who was benevolent rather than wrathful.

Creel may have been typical. His mother was a devout Episcopalian and his father a nominal Catholic. If we are to believe his autobiography, his mother had the greater influence on him. Yet the son refused to be confirmed in his mother's church and claimed to have been repelled by the savagery of the Old Testament. He rejected denominationalism and only in the early 1930s, when writing a biography of Thomas Paine, did he realize he was a deist. Ernest Poole is perhaps another example. He came from a religious home where his mother and grandmother stressed weekly attendance of religious services. Yet at Princeton, Poole found his religious faith slipping away and says he came to find in Lincoln's Gettysburg Address "the creed of a grand religion" he was to retain the rest of his life. Was it possible that Americanism, or a more general attachment to American democracy and the national cause, in some way acted as a surrogate for religion? Or did attachment to reform prior to the war in some ways fill a vacuum that might have been created by rejection of doctrinaire religious attitudes? For Creel's view of religion see his *Rebel at Large*, 21–23; for Poole's see Poole, *Bridge*, 7–10, 16, 57–58, 62–63. Will Irwin's and Ida Tarbell's attitudes toward religion are found in Will Irwin, "'My Religion,'" as told by Will Irwin et al., *They Believe* (New York, 1928), 81–86; and Ida M. Tarbell, "'My Religion,'" ibid., 29–38. Russell discusses his religious training and subsequent preference for Henry George as "the apostle of a new gospel" in Charles Edward Russell, *Bare Hands and Stone Walls: Some Recollections of a Side-Line Reformer* (New York, 1933), 10–25. An indication of the religious views of O'Higgins can be found in the works cited above, especially those listed in note 16. For Stuart P. Sherman, who is discussed in Chapter 3 of this study, see J. David Hoeveler, Jr., *New Humanism: A Critique of Modern America, 1900–1940* (Charlottesville, Va., 1977), 157–59. For Carl Becker, see Michael Kammen, "Introduction," Michael Kammen, ed., *"What Is the Good of History?" Selected Letters of Carl L. Becker, 1900–1945* (Ithaca, N.Y., 1973), xviii.

CHAPTER THREE

1. Samuel Hopkins Adams, "Invaded America: Making Over the Alien," *Everybody's Magazine*, 38 (Mar. 1918): 64.

2. "CPI literature" as used in this and subsequent chapters of course

refers to material published by the committee. But it also has a slightly broader meaning. Many pamphlets were the result of the writer's own ideas rather than closely controlled conclusions dictated by the CPI. Therefore, I have attempted to draw, when possible, on other writings by the same individuals during this period in order to place their thoughts in the broadest possible context.

There has been no adequate analysis of the pamphlet literature put out by the CPI. Studies of the committee sometimes have treated its literature selectively or have provided only a brief description of the pamphlets' contents. See Mock and Larson, *Words That Won the War*, 158–77; George T. Blakey, *Historians on the Homefront: American Propagandists for the Great War* (Lexington, Ky., 1970), 34–56; and Carol S. Gruber, *Mars and Minerva: World War I and the Uses of the Higher Learning in America* (Baton Rouge, La., 1975), 146–57.

3. Newton D. Baker, "Foreword,"in Creel, *How We Advertised America*, xvi.

4. Guy Stanton Ford, "A New Educational Agency," National Education Association of the United States, *Addresses and Proceedings of the Fifty-Sixth Annual Meeting Pittsburgh, Pennsylvania, June 29–July 6* 56 (1918): 207. Carol Gruber points out, and correctly so, that despite Ford's claim that his division's work was purely informational, his selection of pamphlets often was motivated more by propagandistic considerations than by purely educational objectives. Gruber, *Mars and Minerva*, 141–57.

Creel, of course, was interested in the content of the pamphlets, but he did not play as important a role in selecting them as did Ford. See Mock and Larson, *Words That Won the War*, 185.

5. Creel, *How We Advertised America*, 101.

6. Ibid. See also "Reminiscences of Guy Stanton Ford," 371–72; Guy Stanton Ford to James Mock and Cedric Larson, quoted in Mock and Larson, *Words That Won the War*, 158–59.

7. Guy Stanton Ford, *Hanover and Prussia, 1795–1803: A Study in Neutrality* (New York, 1903).

8. Samuel B. Harding to Waldo G. Leland, June 20, 1917, Papers of the National Board for Historical Service, Library of Congress Annex, Washington, D.C., Ac. 3699, Box 3, Folder: "Samuel B. Harding." (Hereafter cited as NBHS papers.) See also Creel, *How We Advertised America*, 111.

Ford received about the same salary for this work on the CPI as he had received at Minnesota—$5,200 a year. Harding was paid about half as much. Other writers, who were on and off the committee's payroll, were usually paid by the week. Frederic L. Paxson received $50 a week, and Wallace Notestein and Dana C. Munro were paid $35. A. M. Simons, who aided the CPI in Wisconsin and who also contributed his services as a writer, was paid a nominal wage of $12 a year. The division's total cost was $568,306.08, most expenses resulting from the bureau's publication schedule. "Reminiscences of Guy Stanton Ford," 552; Division of Civic and Educational Publications,

"Report on Personnel and Projects" (May 28, 1918), 1, CPI papers, CPI
3–A1, Box 63, Folder 3; Guy Stanton Ford to Mr. Claffey, Aug. 28, 1917,
ibid., L–1–234, Folder 3; Mock and Larson, *Words That Won the War*, 160.

9. The list of assistants was impressive. Among those who wrote for the
committee were Carl Becker of Cornell; Edward S. Corwin and Dana C.
Munro of Princeton; Sidney B. Fay of Smith College; Evarts B. Greene,
Laurence M. Larson, and Stuart P. Sherman of the University of Illinois;
Samuel B. Harding of Indiana, J. Franklin Jameson, editor of the *American
Historical Review*; Andrew C. McLaughlin of the University of Chicago, also
president of the Mississippi Valley Historical Association; Monroe Smith,
Wallace Notestein, and Charles A. Beard of Columbia; Frederic L. Paxson,
Carl Russell Fish, and John R. Commons of the University of Wisconsin;
George H. Sabine of Missouri; Albert Shaw, editor of the *Review of Reviews*;
and S. S. McClure. Many of these men served Ford's division in more than
one capacity. Sabine was employed to read German newspapers in Missouri
with an eye toward spotting sedition. Larson performed a similar task in
Illinois (as well as being asked to write for the *War Cyclopedia*). And, as impres-
sive as this list is, it could have been easily expanded. Ford corresponded with
other scholars, such as Ulbrich Philips, who was working with the YMCA, and
Arthur O. Lovejoy, who served with the Maryland State Council of Defense.
Ralph Barton Perry of Harvard and Frederick E. Bolton of the University of
Washington eagerly offered their services to Ford. Ralph Barton Perry to Guy
Stanton Ford, May 17, 1918, CPI papers, CPI 3–Al, Box 74, L–l–1469,
Folder: "L–2–26 to L–2–50"; Frederick E. Bolton to Guy Stanton Ford,
Sept. 3, 1918, ibid., Box 69, L–1–1099. For correspondence with Ulbrich
Philips see ibid., Box 67, Folder 3. Also see Guy Stanton Ford to George
Sabine, Oct. 4, 1917, ibid., Box 75, L–3–5; Sabine to Ford, Mar. 25, 1918,
ibid., Box 69, L–1–1214; Guy Stanton Ford to Laurence M. Larson, July 12,
July 25, Aug. 14, Sept. 13, Sept. 26, 1917, Laurence M. Larson Papers,
University of Illinois Archives, Urbana, Box 1; and Frederic L. Paxson to
Laurence M. Larson, Aug. 29, 1917, ibid.

10. "Reminiscences of James T. Shotwell" (Feb. 27, 1951), 69, 72–73.

11. As the NBHS demonstrated, historians were by far the best organized of scholarly groups, although Ford hoped that political scientists and
economists would form agencies to cooperate with the CPI. Guy Stanton
Ford to Charles H. Haskins, June 11, 1917, CPI papers, CPI 3–A1, Box 62,
L–1–63.

12. *Creel Report*, 15–18.

13. *Century Magazine* sometimes received such articles.

14. *Creel Report*, 18; Creel, *How We Advertised America*, 114.

15. Robert Wiebe has linked progressivism to the process of moderniza-
tion, and this perspective may be useful in viewing a portion of the CPI's
literature. Robert H. Wiebe, "The Progressive Years, 1900–1917," William H.
Cartwright and Richard L. Watson, eds., *Reinterpretation of American History
and Culture* (Washington, D.C., 1973), 425–42.

16. As early as 1899, when Ford was a graduate student at the University of Wisconsin, he had written on "faithfulness to ideals": "The ideal is real, life is real only as it knows and has correspondence with ideals above and beyond the material." Guy Stanton Ford, "My Year Abroad" (Diary) (1899), Ford papers, legal folder 4(l). During the war, Ford considered the definition of American ideals "both to ourselves and to the world" to be the most important goal of the CPI. "I cannot believe that the millions of pamphlets that went forth instinct with America's message had no other effect . . . than to arouse the spirit of armed combat. I can not but believe that in the years of civic striving still before us the spirit of service and sacrifice for common human rights which these publications embodied will serve to make a better America in the days of readjustment and reconstruction. . . ." From the draft of a chapter (p. 7), written by Ford, that was to appear in Creel's *How We Advertised America*. See Ford papers, Folder 163.

17. United States Committee on Public Information, *The War Message and Facts behind It: Annotated Text of President Wilson's Message, April 2, 1917*, War Information Series, No. 1 (Washington, D.C., 1917). William Stearns Davis of the University of Minnesota did much of the work of annotating this speech, with the assistance of C. D. Allin and William Anderson, also of Minnesota. The government printed 2,499,903 copies. United States Committee on Public Information, *The President's Flag Day Address: With Evidence of Germany's Plans*, Red, White and Blue Series, No. 4 (Washington, D.C., 1917). This work was annotated by Wallace Notestein, Elmer Stoll, August C. Krey, and Anderson of the University of Minnesota and Professor Guernsey Jones of the University of Nebraska. Over 6,800,000 copies were printed.

18. For example, see United States Committee on Public Information, *War, Labor and Peace: Some Recent Addresses and Writings of President Wilson*, Red, White and Blue Series, No. 9 (Washington, D.C., 1918). This pamphlet included the president's reply to the pope's peace proposals (Aug. 27, 1917); an address before the American Federation of Labor in Buffalo, N.Y., Nov. 12, 1917; the Annual Message to Congress, Dec. 4, 1917, asking for a declaration of war with Austria-Hungary and recommending additional war legislation; an address to Congress (Jan. 8, 1918), dealing with the Brest-Litovsk negotiations and putting forth a peace program based on the Fourteen Points; and a reply to Chancellor von Hertling and Count Czernin (Feb. 11, 1918).

Other addresses or communications from President Wilson were included in *Labor's Red, White and Blue Book: The Official Record of the Organized Labor Movement of America in Relation to the World War* (New York, 1918?), published for the American Alliance for Labor and Democracy; United States Committee on Public Information, *A War Message to the Farmer*, Loyalty Leaflets, No. 4 (Washington, D.C., 1918); United States Committee on Public Information, *Labor and the War: President Wilson's Address to the American Federation of Labor, Delivered at Buffalo, N.Y., November 12, 1917*, Loyalty Leaflets, No. 3 (Washington, D.C., 1917?); and United States Committee on Public Information, *Ways to Serve the Nation: A Proclamation by the President, April 16, 1917,* Loyalty Leaflets, No. 6 (Washington, D.C., 1917?).

19. [Bullard and Poole], *How the War Came to America,* 17–31. Speeches by Wilson included those given on Jan. 22, 1917, Apr. 2, 1917, and June 14, 1917.

20. Carl L. Becker, comp., *America's War Aims and Peace Program,* War Information Series, No. 21 (Washington, D.C., 1918), 7–11, 14–16, 20–22, 25–31, 36–37, 43. Becker compiled statements tracing America's war aims from the German note of Dec. 12, 1916, through the Armistice and the discussion over the League of Nations.

21. Wilson's Fourteen Points were printed in ibid., 20–22; Samuel B. Harding, *Study of the Great War: A Topical Outline, with Extensive Quotations and Reading References,* War Information Series, No. 16 (Washington, D.C., 1918), 87–89; and *War, Labor and Peace,* 29–31.

22. Franklin K. Lane, *Why We Are Fighting Germany,* in Franklin K. Lane and Newton D. Baker, *Nation in Arms,* War Information Series, No. 2 (Washington, D.C., 1917), 4.

23. See "Secretary Lane's Speech at Americanization Conference, Interior Department, Washington, D.C., April 3, 1918," p. 6, Daniels papers, Box 87, Folder: "Special Correspondence, Lane, Franklin K. Miscellany."

Democracy and Americanism were equated in this speech, and a portion of it is worth repeating for the insight it offers into Lane's thoughts about assimilating immigrants and America's meaning in world affairs. Democracy, Lane said, "must have a self-protecting sense as well as a creative spirit." Americanism was to have a new definition: "We want it to mean help; we want it to mean sympathy; we want it to mean understanding; we want it to mean largeness of view, and not smallness or narrowness. We want it to mean, not patronage, but the largest human fellowship. . . ." He continued:

> So we are here for the making of a more perfect nation, a nation in which there will be harmony between the capitalists and the workmen . . . harmony between the man who is born on this soil and the man who is not born on this soil. . . .
> Liberty enlightening the world! We are the bearers of that torch. It must be a human torch, lighting the path down which will come a finer civilization. It must be a torch for the curing of the nations. It must be a light that will be broad and not narrow, catholic and not insolent, sympathetic, human, essentially Divine.
> . . . We are fashioning a new people. We are doing the unprecedented thing in saying that Slav, Teuton, Celt, and the other races that make up the civilized world are capable of being blended here, and we say this upon the theory that blood alone does not control the destiny of man, that out of his environment, his education, the food that he eats, the neighbors that he has, the work that he does, there can be formed and realized a spirit, an ideal which will master his blood. In this sense we are all internationalists.

. . . Let us make America more worthy of our own dreams. . . . We shall make America better worth while to Americans and of higher service to the world. [Ibid., 1, 2, 7, 9, 10, 14]

24. Franklin K. Lane, "How to Make Americans," *Forum* 61 (Apr. 1919): 405. "Americanism is entirely an attitude of mind," Lane said. He wanted to impress on immigrants that America was an unfinished country with "limitless possibilities." A knowledge of American history and langauge was essential to the assimilation process, as was the desire to work. America was to be interpreted "in terms of fair play; in terms of the square deal." Ibid., 401–4, 406.

25. [Franklin K. Lane, with assitance of Frances Davenport and Elizabeth Donnan], *The Battle Line of Democracy: Prose and Poetry of the World War*, Red, White and Blue Series, No. 3 (Washington, D.C., 1917), 64, 75. Almost one hundred thousand copies of this volume were printed.

At least one other member of the CPI, Rudolph Altrocchi of the University of Chicago, who served in Italy, was fascinated with the poet's part in promoting patriotism. See Rudolph Altrocchi, "D'Annunzio as an Orator [letter to editor]," *Nation* 101 (Dec. 23, 1915), supplement, p. 4; and Rudolph Altrocchi, "'Mais Ici . . .' [letter to the editor]," ibid. (July 1, 1915): 13–14.

26. The best treatment of Stuart P. Sherman's thought is found in Hoeveler, *New Humanism*. Sherman is also discussed in Henry F. May, *End of American Innocence: A Study of the First Years of Our Own Time, 1912–1917* (Chicago, 1959, 1964), 74, 77, 354, 389–91.

27. Stuart P. Sherman, *Americans* (New York, 1922), ix.

28. Ibid., xi; Hoeveler, *New Humanism*, 145. For a discussion of Sherman's ideas on democracy, religion, and developing national unity, see ibid., especially 144–47, 157–58.

29. Stuart P. Sherman, "Why Mr. Roosevelt and the Rest of Us Are at War," *Nation* 105 (Nov. 15, 1917): 535; Guy Stanton Ford to Stuart P. Sherman, Dec. 8, 1917, CPI papers, CPI 3–A1, Box 66, L–1–616. Although Sherman did not mention Roosevelt by name, his criticism of the former chief executive continued in his pamphlet for the CPI: *American and Allied Ideals: An Appeal to Those Who Are Neither Hot nor Cold*, War Information Series, No. 12 (Washington, D.C., 1918). About a quarter of a million copies of Sherman's pamphlet were printed.

It must be said in Sherman's behalf that the idea of America controlling the world by force of arms was, if anything, even more abhorrent than that of Germany dominating the world. Sherman opposed appealing to race prejudice, to raising the flag in the name of Anglo-Saxonism, or to what he called old-fashioned nationalism, which glorified power but which had no principles to check its expansion. International and national ideals were not necessarily incompatible. The cause for which the United States fought was a sound basis for supernational principles, because America had been founded largely upon international principles by men of international outlook. America was fighting not for separatism or exclusion but for international law, international justice, international honor, international truth. Just as the ideas of a company and a regiment went together, so did those of internationalism and nationalism. Ibid., 11–13, 14, 21.

30. The address was given first to the National Council of Teachers of English on Dec. 1, 1917, and then again two weeks later to about two hundred people at the University of Michigan. Ford learned of the address from both J. M. Thomas and Laurence Larson and agreed to publish it, intending to send it to college graduates, ministers, lawyers, and any other influential persons. Stuart P. Sherman, *Journal* (Dec. 1, 13, 14, 1917), Stuart Pratt Sherman Papers, University of Illinois Archives, Urbana, Box 11. Also see Jacob Zeitlin and Homer Woodbridge, eds., *Life and Letters of Stuart P. Sherman* (2 vols., Freeport, N.Y., 1929, 1971), 1:356; J. M. Thomas to Guy Stanton Ford, Dec. 4, 1917, CPI papers, CPI 3–A1, Box 66, L–1–616; Ford to Thomas, Dec. 8, 1917, ibid.; Laurence M. Larson to E. B. Greene, Feb. 15, 1918, NBHS papers, Ac. 3699, Box 11, Folder: "Prof. L. M. Larson"; Guy Stanton Ford to Stuart Sherman, Jan. 23, 1918, CPI papers, CPI 3–A1, Box 66, L–1–642.

31. Sherman was aware of the potential dangers in asking teachers to become out-and-out propagandists for America—the temptation they would face to lie, to hate the opposition, to yield to "megalomania and national egotism." Sherman, *American and Allied Ideals*, 3–4.

Interestingly, some months earlier, perhaps in a more pessimistic mood, Sherman had confided to Paul E. More that "no ideal is worth fighting for. People who fight for ideals are deficient in imagination." Stuart P. Sherman to Paul E. More, May 11, 1917, Sherman papers, Box 4.

32. Sherman, *American and Allied Ideals*, 5–6.

33. In 1917, Sherman had written a book expressing strong reservations about trends in literature that encouraged men to "return to nature," to abandon internal restraint of instinct. He dealt with such writers as H. G. Wells and "the barbaric naturalism" of Theodore Dreiser. This work is essential background for understanding Sherman's CPI pamphlet. See Stuart P. Sherman, *On Contemporary Literature* (New York, 1917). Sherman later told More that "democracy is anti-naturalistic" and that "aristocracy is essentially naturalistic." Sherman to More, Jan. 20, [1918], Sherman papers, Box 4.

34. Sherman, *American and Allied Ideals*, 7.

35. Ibid., 17, 18–20.

36. Ibid., 9. Sherman expanded his ideas about Puritanism after the war, and some of his ideas on this subject—such as contending that Plato, Socrates, Confucius, and Buddha were within the Puritan tradition—gave ammunition to his critics. See Stuart P. Sherman, *Genius of America: Studies in Behalf of the Younger Generation* (New York, 1923), 35–75, especially 57.

37. Sherman, *American and Allied Ideals*, 6.

38. Ibid., 7.

39. Ibid., 9.

40. Ibid., 10. If Sherman made an effort to define that which was best in the American spirit, what would preserve democracy at home, there was a disturbing aspect to his thought: it has been suggested that his ideas hinted of fascism. See Robert E. Spiller et al., eds., *Literary History of the United States: History* (New York, 1946, 1963), 1152. Shortly after the war, Sherman was to write about the "national genius"—that although it was possible to persuade men to buy Liberty bonds, to invest in a nationalized railroad, or to enlist into the army, none of these things could make the citizen cry "O beautiful, my country!" This work was the task of the poet, the public man, the artist, who had an important part to play in national preparation by giving meaning and purpose to America, "so that our hosts of new unlearned citizens may come to understand her as they understand the divine compassion—by often kneeling before some shrine of the Virgin." When art acted in such a manner, it allowed citizens to transcend their lives and "live in the presence, as Burke declared, of our 'canonized' forefathers and in a kind of reverent apprehension of our posterity, happily conscious of a noble and distinguished national thought and feeling, 'above the vulgar practice of the hour.'" Because leaders like Lincoln communed with the national genius, obeying its urgings, America ceased "to be a body politic" and sometimes in the speeches and letters of such leaders became "a living soul." Sherman, *Genius of America*, 29, 30, 31. Sherman's ideas about "The National Genius" had been originally published in *Atlantic Monthly* (Jan. 1921).

41. Becker, comp., *America's War Aims and Peace Program*; Carl Becker, *United States: An Experiment in Democracy* (New York, 1920). This work was later published under the title *Our Great Experiment in Democracy: A History of the United States* (New York, 1927). See Guy Stanton Ford to Mrs. Charlotte Watkins Smith, July 11, 1952, Ford papers, Folder 50. See also "Reminiscences of Guy Stanton Ford," 3: 551. It is difficult to know if other books like Becker's were started for the CPI and finished after the war. The literature produced during the war and in the years immediately after it by members of the committee forms a fairly sizable volume of works seeking to explain American values. In addition to the books and articles mentioned elsewhere in this study, one might include Harvey O'Higgins, *Some Distinguished Americans: Imaginary Portraits* (Freeport, N.Y., 1922, 1971); George Creel, *Sons of the Eagle: Soaring Figures from America's Past* (Indianapolis, 1925); and Evert Boutell Greene, *Foundations of American Nationality* (New York, 1922).

42. "Reminiscences of Guy Stanton Ford," 3: 551.

43. Carl Becker to Samuel B. Harding, May 23, 1918, CPI papers, CPI 3–A1, Box 77, M–2E–53.

44. Becker, *Our Great Experiment in Democracy*, 1, 185.

45. Ibid., 332.

46. Ibid., 209, 223–24.

47. Ibid., 232–33, 246.

48. My conclusion that Americanism was used in some ways as a secular

religion in 1917–18 derives from several studies. Although there is considerable disagreement over the use of the term "civil religion," several works have been helpful, including Will Herberg, "America's Civil Religion: What It Is and Whence It Comes," *Modern Age* 17 (Summer 1973): 226–33; Herberg, *Protestant—Catholic—Jew: An Essay in American Religious Sociology* (Garden City, N.Y., 1955), 75–89; Sidney E. Mead, "American Protestantism since the Civil War: I. From Denominationalism to Americanism," *Journal of Religion* 36 (Jan. 1956): 1–16; Mead, "Amerian Protestantism since the Civil War: II. From Americanism to Christianity," ibid. (Apr. 1956): 67–89; Mead, "The 'Nation with the Soul of a Church,'" *Church History* 36 (Sept. 1967): 262–83; Robert N. Bellah, "Civil Religion in America," *Daedalus* 96 (Winter 1967): 1–21; Robert T. Handy, *Christian America: Protestant Hopes and Historical Realities* (New York, 1971): 139–43; Conrad Cherry, *God's New Israel: Religious Interpretations of American Destiny* (Englewood Cliffs, N.J., 1971), 271–77; J. L. G., "'Civil Religion': Clarifying the Semantic Problem," *Journal of Church and State* 16 (Spring 1974): 187–95; Alfred Balitzer, "Some Thoughts about Civil Religion," ibid. (Winter 1974): 31–50; John F. Wilson, "A Historian's Approach to Civil Religion," Russell E. Richey and Donald G. Jones, eds., *American Civil Religion* (New York, 1974), 115–38; Robert D. Linder, "Civil Religion in Historical Perspective: The Reality That Underlies the Concept," *Journal of Church and State* 17 (Autumn 1975): 399–421; and Philip Gleason, "Blurring the Line of Separation: Education, Civil Religion, and Teaching about Religion," ibid. 19 (Autumn 1977): 524–29, and especially the definition of civil religion on 525–26. Also helpful have been Carlton J. H. Hayes, *Nationalism, a Religion* (New York, 1960); and George Mosse's discussion of "The New Politics" in his *Nationalization of the Masses: Political Symbolism and Mass Movements in Germany from the Napoleonic Wars through the Third Reich* (New York, 1975), especially 1–20.

49. See *Creel Report*, 17.

50. United States Committee on Public Information, *American Loyalty by Citizens of German Descent*, War Information Series, No. 6 (Washington, D.C., 1917), 11–16. F. W. Lehmann was a former president of the American Bar Association and solicitor general of the United States under William Howard Taft. Franz Sigel's statement had first appeared in the New York *Times*.

51. Joseph Buffington, *Friendly Words to the Foreign Born*, Loyalty Leaflets, No. 1, (Washington, D.C., 1918?), p. 4.

52. Ibid., 6, 9.

53. The committee considered, but did not publish, Buffington's address "De-Prussianizing the Soul of Germany." At least one CPI pamphlet writer, Elihu Root, was enthusiastic about this essay. Root expressed the hope that American participation could produce a "spiritual revolution" in Germany, restoring that country to the political ideals of men like Francis Lieber. Samuel B. Harding to George Creel, May 29, 1918, CPI papers, CPI 3–A1, Box 72, L–1–1785; Elihu Root to Joseph Buffington, Sept. 7, 1918, Elihu

Root Papers, Library of Congress Annex, Washington, D.C., Box 136, Folder: "B–F 1918."

The *Battle Line of Democracy* also tried to reach hyphenated Americans with such essays as C. Kotzenabe's "German-American Loyalty" (79–80) and Otto H. Kahn's "A Message to the German Born" (81–82).

54. *Creel Report*, 78–79. In 1916, Creel argued that the melting pot had not worked and that unassimilated immigrants threatened "the permanence of American institutions as gravely as any menace of foreign foe." After the war he argued that the "overwhelming majority of aliens" had demonstrated "an almost passionate desire to serve America" but that they had been hindered "by the meannesses of chauvinism and the brutalities of prejudice, as well as the short-sightedness of ignorance." George Creel, "The Hopes of the Hyphenated," *Century* 91 (Jan. 1916): 350; and Creel, "Our 'Aliens'—Were they Loyal or Disloyal?" *Everybody's Magazine* 40 (Mar. 1919): 36.

55. Samuel B. Harding to Burrall Russell, June 1, 1918, CPI papers, CPI 3–A1, Box 71, L–1–1524. On Harding and Sperry see also Wallace Henry Moore, "The Conflict concerning the German Language and German Propaganda in the Public Secondary Schools of the United States, 1917–1919" (doctoral dissertation, Stanford University, 1937), 39–40, 100–104.

56. For Claxton's position see ibid., 30–32. For Wilson's position see George Creel to P. P. Claxton, Mar. 5, 1918, CPI papers, CPI 1–A1, Box 6, Folder 119.

57. George Creel to S. H. Clark, Dec. 1, 1917, CPI papers, CPI 1–A1, Box 6, Folder 117.

58. Guy Stanton Ford to Mr. Rosicky, Apr. 22, 1918, ibid., CPI 3–A1, Box 70, L–1–1313; Guy Stanton Ford to Frank W. Boynton, Aug. 31, 1918, ibid., Box 73, L–1–1988; Guy Stanton Ford to Stuart Sherman, Jan. 23, 1918, Sherman papers, Box 1.

For other discussions of the CPI's approach to immigrants, see Robert E. Park, *Immigrant Press and Its Control* (New York, 1922), 444–47. Hermann Hagedorn contends that the CPI was hostile to hyphenated Americans, but Edward Hartmann, Daniel E. Weinberg, and John Higham do not portray the committee in this fashion. Higham says the CPI exemplified a "liberal" approach to Americanizing the immigrant. Hermann Hagedorn, *Hyphenated Family: An American Saga* (New York, 1960), 233–35, 242, 244–49; Edward George Hartmann, *Movement to Americanize the Immigrant* (New York, 1947, 1967), 187–209; Weinberg, "The Ethnic Technician and the Foreign-Born," 218; John Higham, *Strangers in the Land: Patterns of American Nativism, 1860–1925* (New York, 1955, 1967), 216, 247, 277, and especially 252–53. Frederick Luebke notes that the CPI approached immigrants in a reasonable, humane manner but perhaps inadvertently encouraged intolerance. "Despite the sensible efforts of the Creel Committee to encourage and counsel rather than to command and threaten, it also contributed immeasurably to the climate of intolerance." Luebke, *Bonds of Loyalty*, 213.

59. In his autobiography, Creel said that he called for truth to counteract German lies, not propaganda as the enemy employed it but propaganda "in the true sense of the word, meaning the 'propagation of faith.' " Writing less than a week before Pearl Harbor, Ford observed that by 1941 the word "propaganda" had come to have a much different meaning than it had had when he worked for the CPI. See George Creel to Woodrow Wilson, July 23, 1918, Creel papers, Container 2; Creel, *Rebel at Large*, 158; and Guy Stanton Ford to L. D. Coffman, Dec. 2, 1941, Ford papers, Folder 43.

60. George Creel to Richard Ely (assistant director, Bureau of War Trade Intelligence), Sept. 4, 1918, CPI papers, CPI 3–A1, Box 67, L–1–825.

61. ". . . no program of materialism has ever received the approval of the American people," Creel argued. See George Creel, "Public Opinion as a War Measure," *National Marine* (June 1918), 31, 32.

62. Creel to Wilson, May 31, 1918, Creel papers, Container 2; Creel to Wilson, Sept. 25, 1918, ibid.; Creel to Daniels, Oct. 25, 1917, Daniels papers, Box 73, Folder: "Creel, George 1917." A statement prepared by Daniels to be delivered in New York is attached to Daniels to Creel, Oct. 30, 1917, ibid.

63. Creel to Wilson, Nov. 8, 1918, Creel papers, Container 2.

64. George Creel to Joseph Davies, undated, CPI papers, CPI 3–A1, Box 67, L–1–801. This letter may have been originally drafted by Ford. See statement dated Mar. 5, 1918, Ford papers, Folder 163. It should be noted that Ford very often drafted statements that were signed by President Wilson, Creel, or such other officials as Secretary of War Baker. A collection of such drafts is found in Ford papers, Folder 163. Creel saw the war as bound up with "the defeat of greed, the heartening of patriotism, the strengthening of character, the restoration of idealism, and an invigorated conception of the obligation of American citizenship," in short, that same "passionate devotion" to the "spirit of Concord" that had "carried Washington to victory." Creel, "The Sweat of War," 717.

65. Creel, "Public Opinion as a War Measure," 32.

66. Guy Stanton Ford to W. H. Stout, Dec. 2, 1918, CPI papers, CPI 3–A1, Box 74, L–1–2294.

67. Guy Stanton Ford to A. M. Simons, Oct. 9, 1917, ibid.

68. A. M. Simons to Guy Stanton Ford, ibid.

69. Frederic L. Paxson to A. M. Simons, Sept. 4, 1917, ibid.

There is also evidence that Simons prepared an article on the eight-hour day that was sent abroad by the CPI. See Ernest Poole to A. M. Simons, June 10, 1918, Algie M. Simons Papers, Wisconsin State Historical Society, Madison, Box 2, Folder: "Correspondence 1918, Jan.–July."

The CPI emphasized liberal or reform movements in other countries. Creel assured Paul Kellogg, of *Survey*, that he never spoke of the British Labour party except in terms of endorsement. Wallace Notestein, who prepared one of the strongest attacks against the German government, told Ford that not all of the passages he had used from German sources were discreditable to the Germans, especially when they explained German economic schemes. George Creel to Paul Kellogg, Apr. 5, 1918, CPI papers, CPI 1–A1, Box 14, Folder 362; Wallace Notestein to Guy Stanton Ford, Aug. 5, 1917, ibid., CPI 3–A1, Box 78, M–3–2. Notestein's pamphlet, compiled with Elmer E. Stoll, was *Conquest and Kultur: Aims of the Germans in Their Own Words*, Red, White and Blue Series, No. 5 (Washington, D.C., 1918).

70. Frederic L. Paxson, Edward S. Corwin, and Samuel B. Harding, eds., *War Cyclopedia: A Handbook for Ready Reference on the Great War*, Red, White and Blue Series, No. 7 (Washington, D.C., 1918), 224.

71. Ibid., 88.

72. Edward S. Corwin, "War, the Constitution Moulder," Richard Loss, ed., *Presidential Power and the Constitution: Essays by Edward S. Corwin* (Ithaca, N.Y., 1976), 27. This essay was originally published in *New Republic* 11 (June 9, 1917): 153–55.

73. Paxson, Corwin, Harding, eds., *War Cyclopedia*, 218.

74. Ibid.

75. Ibid., 260.

76. Ibid., 296.

77. Ibid.; Corwin, "War, the Constitution Moulder," 23–24.

78. For a list of these titles see *Creel Report*, 16–17.

79. When Congress cut the committee's appropriation, Creel informed Maisel that aid to the alliance from the CPI would be stopped Aug. 1, 1918. Creel wanted to turn control of the alliance over to Babson. Creel did influence President Wilson to give money to the alliance to set up, in late summer and autumn of 1918, a labor loyalty press in Laredo, Tex., to influence South American labor. In December 1918 the CPI appropriated ten thousand dollars to the alliance to promote Americanism among laborers in the fight against bolshevism. See George Creel to Robert Maisel, July 12, 1918, CPI papers, CPI 1–A1, Box 17, Folder 3; Maisel to Creel, July 15, 1918, ibid.; George Creel to Samuel Gompers, July 17, 1918, ibid.; and George Creel to Roger Babson, July 17, 1918, ibid. See also Grubbs, *Struggle for Labor Loyalty*, 120–21; and Lorwin, *American Federation of Labor*, 153. One pamphlet, *Labor's Red, White and Blue Book*, described the creation of the American Alliance for Labor and Democracy; see pp. 10–11.

80. Most of these pamphlets contained each theme in varying degrees. Those pamphlets especially emphasizing the danger of Prussian militarism were Frederic C. Walcott, *The Prussian System*, Loyalty Leaflets, No. 2 (Washington, D.C., 1918?); *Labor and War*; Elihu Root, *Plain Issues of the War*, Loyalty Leaflets, No. 5 (Washington, D.C., 1918?); John R. Commons, *German Socialists and the War* [American Alliance for Labor and Democracy], Loyalty Leaflets, No. 4 (Washington, D.C., 1918?).

Pamphlets stressing increased productivity and telling workingmen that they were better off in the United States than anywhere else included John R. Commons, *Who Is Paying for This War?* [American Alliance for Labor and

Democracy], Loyalty Leaflets, No. 3 (Washington, D.C., 1918?); Commons, *Why Workingmen Support the War* [American Alliance for Labor and Democracy], Loyalty Leaflets, No. 2 (Washington, D.C., 1918?); *Labor and the War*, 9; *Ways to Serve the Nation*; and United States Committee on Public Information, *What Really Matters: A Letter by an Unnamed Writer, Quoted by Rev. Joseph H. Odell in an Article in the* Atlantic Monthly *for February, 1918*, Loyalty Leaflets, No. 7 (Washington, D.C., 1918).

All of the CPI's Loyalty Leaflets circulated between 500,000 and 600,000 copies, except Root's *Plain Issues of the War*, whose printing was about 112,000 copies. Each publication for the American Alliance for Labor and Democracy circulated slightly over 300,000 copies, except *Labor's Red, White and Blue Book* (99,385) and *What Can Your Local Branch Do?* (Washington, D.C.?, 1918?) (15,000). See *Creel Report*, 16–17.

81. A. M. Simons to Guy Stanton Ford, Dec. 3, 1917, CPI papers, CPI 3–A1, Box 64, L–1–283; Simons to Ford, Dec. 18, 1917, ibid. Ford considered publishing *Why Workingmen Support the War* under the CPI heading but decided that "some phrasing in the first four pages would lead conservatives and some labor employers to cry 'Bolsheviki.'" Guy Stanton Ford to George Creel, Sept. 30, 1918, quoted in Gruber, *Mars and Minerva*, 151. Ford had fewer reservations about sending "radical" literature into Russia or Latin America. In fact, he apparently encouraged such material for those countries. Ibid., 150.

82. Commons, *Why Workingmen Support the War*, 3.

83. Ibid., 4.

84. Ibid., 6, 5.

85. Commons, *Who Is Paying for This War?* [5, 7].

86. *Labor's Red, White and Blue Book*, 7.

87. Ibid., 8–9.

88. *Labor and the War*, 10, 11. This speech was printed also in the committee's *War, Labor and Peace*, 7–14.

89. A. M. Simons to Guy Stanton Ford, Apr. 19, 1918, CPI papers, CPI 3–A1, Box 64, L–1–283; Simons to Ford, Apr. 26, 1918, ibid.; Ford to Simons, Apr. 19, 1918, ibid.

90. [Woodrow Wilson], *A War Message to the Farmer*, 4–7. This message was originally presented to a Farmers' Conference at Urbana, Ill., Jan. 31, 1918.

91. *National Service Handbook*, 1.   92. Ibid., 84.

93. Ibid., 6.   94. Ibid., 6–9.

95. These tasks would also be important to the period of postwar reconstruction. Ibid., 10.

96. United States Committee on Public Information, War Department, *Home Reading Course for Citizen-Soldiers*, War Information Series, No. 9 (Washington, D.C., 1917), 5.

97. Ibid., 3, 55.

98. Charles Merz, *First Session of the War Congress*, War Information Series, No. 10 (Washington, D.C., 1917).

99. *The Activities of the Committee on Public Information*, War Information Series, No. 17 (Washington, D.C., 1918).

100. "Reminiscences of Guy Stanton Ford," 551–52.

101. See Yehoshua Arieli, *Individualism and Nationalism in American Ideology* (Cambridge, Mass., 1964), 13, 20.

CHAPTER FOUR

1. George Creel, *War, the World, and Wilson* (New York, 1920), 120–21.

2. "Reminiscences of Guy Stanton Ford," 383.

3. Hans Kohn, *Idea of Nationalism: A Study in Its Origins and Background* (New York, 1944), 310; see also 289, 291–92, 324–25. See also Arieli, *Individualism and Nationalism in American Ideology*, 20–21; Louis L. Snyder, *Varieties of Nationalism: A Comparative Study* (Hinsdale, Ill., 1976), 203; and Ralph Henry Gabriel, *Course of American Democratic Thought: An Intellectual History since 1815* (New York, 1940), 19–23.

Daniel Smith argued that the American opposition to totalitarianism in Nazi Germany and Stalinist Russia in the 1930s and 1940s had its "immediate roots" in the Great War, "when American officials proclaimed the concept of an evil authoritarian or statist menace." Daniel M. Smith, "Authoritarianism and American Policy Makers in Two World Wars," *Pacific Historical Review* 43 (Aug. 1974): 303.

4. Harold Lasswell observed that "the psychological resistances to war in modern nations" are so great "that every war must appear to be a war of defence against a menacing, murderous aggressor." Lasswell noted common themes in the propaganda of belligerents during World War I, among them vilifying and attributing all guilt to the enemy. The themes chosen for emphasis, Lasswell contended, "depend upon the moral code of the nation whose animosity is to be aroused." Lasswell says little about the CPI, although some committee literature fits into his interpretation. Lasswell, *Propaganda Technique in World War I*, 47–101, especially 47, 77.

5. Ford maintained to the end of his career that he had never regretted anything he did during the war. The pamphlets, he felt, had not been the result of momentary passion but rather had sought to discuss fundamental issues. "Reminiscences of Guy Stanton Ford," 419. This quotation may have been originally drafted by Ford and used by Creel. See Ford Papers, Folder 163, and Creel, *How We Advertised America*.

6. For the image of Germany in best-selling novels, see Melvin Small, "Historians Look at Public Opinion," Melvin Small, ed., *Public Opinion and Historians* (Detroit, 1970), 26. For treatment of Germany in American school books, see Ruth Miller Elson, *Guardians of Tradition: American Schoolbooks of the*

Nineteenth Century (Lincoln, 1964), 143, 145. On the German-language press see Wittke, *German-Language Press in America*, 236.

7. See Luebke, *Bonds of Loyalty*.

8. Elihu Root, who wrote a pamphlet for the CPI, was concerned as early as April 1900 about a possible German challenge to the Monroe Doctrine. See Richard W. Leopold, *Elihu Root and the Conservative Tradition* (Boston, 1954), 59–60. See also Daniel M. Smith, "National Interest and American Intervention, 1917: An Historiographical Appraisal," *Journal of American History* 52 (June 1965): 9–10; George F. Kennan, *American Diplomacy, 1900–1950* (Chicago, 1951), 70–71; and Alfred Vagts, "Hopes and Fears of an American-German War, 1870–1915," *Political Science Quarterly* 54 (Dec. 1939): 514–35. By the 1890s there was also considerable anti-American sentiment in Germany. See Ernest R. May, *Imperial Democracy: The Emergence of America as a Great Power* (New York, 1961), 185–88.

9. Although it overemphasizes the importance of British propaganda on American opinion, the best study of this subject is Peterson, *Propaganda for War*. Also useful is Squires, *British Propaganda*. On the German-language press prior to April 1917, see Wittke, *German-Language Press in America*, 236–61.

For how Americans saw Germany before 1917 see also Luebke, *Bonds of Loyalty*, 69–81; Clara Eve Schieber, *Transformation of American Sentiment toward Germany, 1870–1914* (New York, 1923); Melvin Small, "The American Image of Germany, 1906–1914" (doctoral dissertation, University of Michigan, 1965); and Fred A. Sonderman, "The Wilson Administration's Image of Germany" (doctoral dissertation, Yale University, 1953).

10. Wilson's fondness for English institutions and his reservations about Germany stemming from what he believed to be the unrepresentative nature of German government can be traced to well before 1914. See Harley Notter, *Origins of the Foreign Policy of Woodrow Wilson* (New York, 1937, 1965), 42, 45–46, 77–78, 100.

11. For Brand Whitlock's experience in Belgium see David W. Southern, "The Ordeal of Brand Whitlock, Minister to Belgium, 1914–1922," *Northwest Ohio Quarterly* 41 (Summer 1969): 113–26.

12. See Gruber, *Mars and Minerva*, 117, 123–24. For another study dealing with historians as propagandists and the dilemma confronting them during the war, see Blakey, *Historians on the Homefront*.

13. See Small, "The American Image of Germany, 1906–1914," 115–18; Charles Franklin Thwing, *American and the German University: One Hundred Years of History* (New York, 1928), 69–77; and Charles Baskervill Robson, "The Influence of German Thought on Political Theory in the United States in the Nineteenth Century: An Introductory Study" (doctoral dissertation, University of North Carolina, 1930), 351.

14. Sylvia D. Fries, "*Staatstheorie* and the New American Science of Politics," *Journal of the History of Ideas* 34 (July–Sept. 1974): 391. For other works discussing German influence on American universities and German ideas

about government that had an audience in the United States in the late nineteenth and early twentieth centuries, see Thwing, *American and the German University*, 78–95; Robson, "The Influence of German Thought on Political Theory in the United States in the Nineteenth Century," 314–75; Thomas I. Cook and Arnaud B. Leavelle, "German Idealism and American Theories of the Democratic Community," *Journal of Politics* 5 (Aug. 1943): 213–36; Anna Haddow, *Political Science in American Colleges and Universities* (New York, 1939); Ralph G. Hoxie, *History of the Faculty of Political Science, Columbia University* (New York, 1955); Henry A. Pochmann, with the assistance of Arthur R. Schutz and others, *German Culture in America: Philosophical and Literary Influences, 1600–1900* (Madison, Wis., 1957), 307–23, 474–92.

15. Evarts B. Greene did attend Treitschke's lectures at the University of Berlin when he studied in Germany some years before Ford.

16. Ford, *Hanover and Prussia*.

17. Comments on militarism did not dominate Ford's diary but rather were sprinkled throughout a generally positive description of German society. Ford, "My Year Abroad" (Diary) (1899), Ford Papers, legal folder 5(1).

18. "Reminiscences of Guy Stanton Ford," 174–77, 179–80, especially 176.

19. Guy Stanton Ford, "Boyen's Military Law," *American Historical Review* 20 (Apr. 1915): 528–38.

20. Guy Stanton Ford, *Stein and the Era of Reform in Prussia, 1807–1815* (Gloucester, Mass., 1922, 1965). During the last half of the 1915–16 academic year, Ford had taken a sabbatical leave to finish his work on Stein. Ford considered publishing this book during the war for propaganda purposes but abandoned the idea.

21. Ford continued his opposition to authoritarian government after the war and in 1935 edited a work on the dangers of dictatorship, saying that "we do not yet know what kind of drug in the political materia medica propaganda is." Guy Stanton Ford, ed., *Dictatorship in the Modern World* (Minneapolis, 1935), v.

While at Columbia, both Ford and James T. Shotwell studied with John W. Burgess. Neither was impressed with Burgess's lectures, which often consisted of the professor reading page proofs from one of his books (Ford stopped attending the class). Burgess had been influenced by German doctrines of national sovereignty, and Shotwell believed that Burgess did not appreciate the parliamentary system and the safeguards it extended to freedom. "Reminiscences of Guy Stanton Ford," 190; James T. Shotwell, *Autobiography of James T. Shotwell* (Indianapolis, 1961), 44.

22. This list would also include Sydney B. Fay and Greene. Fay was asked to write on the following topics for the CPI's *War Cyclopedia*: hegemony, Berlin to Bagdad, Drang nach Osten, place in the sun, von Bernhardi, Machiavelli, Marx, William II, Charles I, and Franz Joseph. CPI papers, CPI 3–Al, Box 77, M–2E–19. Greene prepared pamphlets, one of which was *Lieber and*

Schurz: Two Loyal Americans of German Birth, War Information Series, No. 19 (Washington, D.C., 1918). He also helped justify American intervention (see Chapter 5 below).

23. In 1955, Walter Metzger pointed out the need for more information about the contact American students had with German universities during the nineteenth century. Recently, Carol Gruber examined the attitudes of a few scholars who wrote during World War I, persons not treated in this study. In discussing the complicated and sometimes anguished response to the war of Arthur T. Hadley, Henry Farnam, Albert Bushnell Hart, and James Henry Breasted, each of whom had spent considerable time studying in Germany, she observes that such people often had feelings of fondness for learning experiences, appreciation for intellectual stimulation received, and admiration for certain aspects of German culture. Close contacts had often been maintained with German scholars, and the war demanded a very difficult choice of loyalties. Gruber, *Mars and Minerva*, 70–80. See Walter P. Metzger, *Academic Freedom in the Age of the University* (New York, 1955), 93.

24. Charles Downer Hazen, "When France Failed—and Why: A Great Historian's Warning to Unawakened America," *American Magazine* 80 (Dec. 1915): 46–47, 94.

25. Charles D. Hazen, "Brief List of Books upon Recent European History," *History Teacher's Magazine* 8 (June 1917): 196–97.

26. Charles Downer Hazen, "Prussianism in Poland," *World's Work* 37 (Nov. 1918): 39–44; Hazen, "Why Alsace-Lorraine Must Be Returned to France," ibid. (Dec. 1918): 188–202.

Hazen also had interesting views on the relation between nationalism and democracy. Shortly after the war he commented on the peace treaty and the overwhelming power of nationalism. The nationalist spirit and the democratic spirit, he believed, were the two most powerful forces in modern history. Nationalism was "enormously superior as a vital force in determining the activities and shaping the destinies of men than its rival . . . internationalism." In Germany the nationalistic spirit had proved stronger than democracy, arresting its development. In other countries, such as Italy, Greece, Serbia, and Rumania, nationalism and democracy had gone hand in hand and were intimately involved in each other's destiny. Democracy in these countries would not have been possible had it not been for the nationalistic spirit. "Nationalism has, in many cases, been the very shield and buckler of democracy. . . . It is the lever that moves the world." Hazen believed that the peace treaty recognized nationalism, that the League of Nations was built on this foundation, and that peace required the willingness of Britain and the United States to aid France in event of an unprovoked attack by Germany. Hazen, "The Peace Treaty and World Politics," ibid. (World-Peace Supplement) (Apr. 1919): i–ii, vii.

27. Charles Downer Hazen, *Europe since 1815* (New York, 1910), 322, 324, 325, 328, 481, 728.

28. Charles D. Hazen, *The Government of Germany*, War Information Series, No. 3 (Washington, D.C., 1917).

29. Charles D. Hazen to James T. Shotwell, July 3, 1917, NBHS papers, Ac. 3699, Box 3.

30. See New York *Times*, July 1, 1917.

31. Waldo G. Leland to Guy Stanton Ford, July 5, 1917, NBHS papers, Ac. 3699, Box 2; Waldo G. Leland to Charles D. Hazen, July 5, 1917, ibid., Box 3.

32. Hazen, *The Government of Germany*, 5. See also Hazen, *Europe since 1815*, 325–27.

33. The Bundesrat was little more than an organization of princes, Hazen believed, each of whom claimed to rule by divine right. Hazen, *The Government of Germany*, 7–8.

34. Ibid., 8, 10, 15.

35. Ibid., 7.

36. Ibid., 15, 16. The almost absolute power of the Prussian crown was supported by German publicists, who taught "that the complete, uncontrolled power of the 'Government' (*Regierung*) is in the power of the prince; that the granting of constitutions did not mean the recognition of popular sovereignty in the slightest degree; that legislatures are not representations of the people but are mere organs of the State." Ibid., 13. By contrast, Hazen pointed out that the struggle for liberty throughout English history had brought Parliament's supremacy over the king and the military. Ibid., 16.

37. *Creel Report*, 16.

38. For example, Wallace Notestein, "The Interest of Seventeenth Century England for Students of American Institutions," *History Teacher's Magazine* 8 (Dec. 1917): 350–51. Notestein was asked to write on several topics for the *War Cyclopedia*, including the moral bankruptcy of German government, Kultur, and "Will to War." Samuel B. Harding to Wallace Notestein, May 17, 1918, CPI papers, CPI 3–A1, Box 77, M–2E–105.

39. Both Notestein and Stoll annotated *President's Flag Day Address*.

40. Wallace Notestein to Evarts B. Greene, May 11, 1918, NBHS papers, Ac. 3699, Box 12, Folder: "Public Information Committee"; Wallace Notestein to Waldo G. Leland, May 12, 1918, ibid.

41. Wallace Notestein to G. S. Ford, May 17, 1917, CPI papers, CPI 3–A1, Box 62, L–1–19.

42. Ford to Notestein, Feb. 28, 1918, ibid., Box 78, M–3cc–1. An essay, "War after War," containing excerpts from German publications concerning Germany's intentions after the war is in ibid., Box 63, L–1–202.

43. Notestein to Ford, Aug. 5, 1917, ibid., Box 78, M–3–2.

44. Ibid.

45. Notestein and Stoll, comp., *Conquest and Kultur*, 14. Samuel B. Harding prepared a pamphlet to be used in the classroom that outlined the history of the Great War, placing responsibility for the fighting largely on Germany's

desire for "a place in the sun." Germans saw the war as part of their world mission and often justified their actions in biological terms. Harding, *Study of the Great War*, 5–7.

46. Notestein and Stoll, comp., *Conquest and Kultur*, 18; Quotation from General Friedrich von Bernhardi, *Germany and the Next War*, translated by Allen H. Powles (London, 1912, 1914), 154.

47. Quoted in Notestein and Stoll, comp., *Conquest and Kultur*, 29.

48. Ibid., 29, 30; first quotation from Friedrich Nietzsche, *Beyond Good and Evil: Prelude to a Philosophy of the Future*, translated by Helen Zimmern (New York, 1907), 226; second quotation from Heinrich von Treitschke, *Politics*, translated by Blanche Dugdale and Torben de Bille (2 vols., London, 1916), 1: 95.

49. Notestein and Stoll, comp., *Conquest and Kultur*, 32, 38; First quotation, Treitschke, *Politics*, 1: 69, second quotation, ibid., 2: 599.

50. Notestein and Stoll, comp., *Conquest and Kultur*, 47–62.

51. Greene, *Lieber and Schurz*. Lasswell observed that "it is always difficult for many simple minds inside a nation to attach personal traits to so dispersed an entity as a whole nation." It is important that some single individual or small group of leaders be singled out and loaded down "with the whole decalogue of sins." Lasswell, *Propaganda Technique in World War I*, 89.

52. Charles Altschul, *German Militarism and Its German Critics: Fully Illustrated by Extracts from German Newspapers*, War Information Series, No. 13 (Mar. 1918). See also *Creel Report*, 16. About one-quarter of the pamphlet's distribution was in German, the remainder in English.

53. C. Altschul to Guy Stanton Ford, Jan. 12, 1918, CPI papers, CPI 3–A1, Box 67, L–1–752.

54. Altschul to Ford, Aug. 13, 1918, ibid., Box 70, L–1–1385.

55. J. T. Shotwell to Guy Stanton Ford, Dec. 12, 1917, ibid., Box 63, L–1–163. Despite Ford's reservations about the pamphlet's length, it was published without major reductions.

Shotwell wrote the introduction to a book written by Altschul in 1917. Charles Altschul, *American Revolution in Our School Text-Books: An Attempt to Trace the Influence of Early School Education on the Feeling towards England in the United States* (New York, 1917), v–vii.

56. Altschul, *German Militarism and Its German Critics*, 8–15.

57. Ibid., 20–36.   58. Ibid., 37.

59. Ibid., 20, 37.   60. Ibid., 5.

61. Ibid., 38.

62. Walcott, *The Prussian System*. Walcott, of the United States Food Administration, originally delivered this message on Sept. 12, 1917, to a conference of Food Administration agents.

63. Ibid., 6.

64. Ibid., 5–6.

65. Ibid., 3, 7, 8. At the time (Sept. 1917), Walcott hoped Germany's rebirth would be similar to the one he believed was then occurring in Russia.

66. Dana C. Munro, George C. Sellery, and August C. Krey, eds., *German*

War Practices: Part I: Treatment of Civilians, Red, White and Blue Series, No. 6 (Washington, D.C., 1918); and Dana C. Munro, George C. Sellery, and August C. Krey, eds., *German Treatment of Conquered Territory: Being Part II of "German War Practices,"* Red, White and Blue Series, No. 8 (Washington, D.C., 1918).

67. Quotation from the advertisement for this pamphlet at the end of most CPI publications printed in 1918.

68. Munro, Sellery, Krey, eds., *German War Practices, Part I*. For Hoover's statement see p. 79; for Walcott's see pp. 13, 53–54, 86–87; for Kellogg's, see pp. 88–91. For statements by Whitlock see pp. 32–33, 47–49, 53, 54–55, 73, 74–75, 78; for Gerard, see pp. 76–77; for Irwin, see p. 41.

69. Ibid., 23–25. Belgium was a theme emphasized by other committee writers: Carl L. Becker, "German Attempts to Divide Belgium," World Peace Foundation, *A League of Nations* 1 (Aug. 1918): 307–40. For S. S. McClure, see note 100 below.

The Bryce Report, which was so effective in convincing Americans and others of German atrocities, has subsequently been shown to be an exaggerated, untrustworthy account. See James Morgan Read, *Atrocity Propaganda, 1914–1919* (New Haven, 1941), 201–8. Read's work is still perhaps the best study on World War I atrocity propaganda.

70. Munro, Sellery, Krey, eds., *German War Practices, Part I*, 13–16.

71. Ibid., 5–6, 9.

72. Ibid., 7–9.

73. Ibid., 82, 84. Germans were accused of having raped women in China, also. Ibid., 8.

Read does argue that Belgian deportations were in violation of existing international law, although there was probably "less actual human suffering than the propaganda of the time asserted." Read does not deal with the CPI's discussion of this subject, however. See Read, *Atrocity Propaganda, 1914–1919*, 168–86, especially 186.

74. Munro, Sellery, Krey, eds., *German War Practices, Part I*, 32–33, 39–40. Evidence indicates that Germans did use Belgian civilians as shields, if for no other reason than for protection from snipers. See Read, *Atrocity Propaganda, 1914–1919*, pp. 87–88.

75. Munro, Sellery, Krey, eds., *German War Practices, Part I*, 12.

76. Munro, Sellery, Krey, eds., *German Treatment of Conquered Territory*, 5–6.

77. Ibid., 5.

78. Ibid., 33.

79. Ibid., 47. Ford says he forbade the use of the word "Hun" and that it slipped by him only once. "Reminiscences of Guy Stanton Ford," 383. This term was not commonly used in the literature of Ford's division, but "Hun" did appear in at least one other CPI pamphlet. See John S. P. Tatlock, *Why America Fights Germany*, War Information Series, No. 15 (Washington, D.C., 1918), 7.

80. Munro, Sellery, Krey, eds., *German Treatment of Conquered Territory*, 7.

81. Ibid., 8.

82. Ibid., 9.

83. The threat of German economic competition after the war also worried other committee writers. Herbert Houston called for a league of nations established along lines similar to those countries then fighting Germany. Its aim would have been to check German postwar economic expansion. Houston believed that Germany, whose industrial capacity had not been damaged, planned to gain a stranglehold on the world's economy after the war, and his league would preserve world peace by aggressively providing protection against the German "mailed fist." In addition to making the enemy pay for the reconstruction of the economies of Belgium, France, Italy, and even Russia, Houston wanted an international banking system (modeled on the American Federal Reserve System), an international food board, and an international chamber of commerce. Under certain conditions, Houston's league would have been able to deny offending countries freedom of the seas. Herbert S. Houston, "The Place of Business in a League of Nations: A Plan for a New World of Assured Fairness to All—A Complete Defense against Economic Penetration and Kaiserism in General," *Printer's Ink* 104 (July 11, 1918): 28, 31–32, 37–38. The substance of this article was delivered to the Associated Advertising Clubs of the World in San Francisco on July 9, 1918. See also Herbert S. Houston, *Blocking New Wars* (Garden City, N.Y., 1918); and Houston, "Doing the World's International Work," *World's Work* 37 (Feb. 1919): 438–40.

84. Munro, Sellery, Krey, eds., *German Treatment of Conquered Territory.* For requisitioned articles see pp. 13–22; for destruction of Louvain, pp. 40–46; for evacuation of northern France, pp. 47–56; for statements by Whitlock, pp. 36–39, 43–46, 56, 59–61; for Gibson, pp. 46, 57; for Kellogg, p. 36; for Hoover, p. 55; for Sharp, pp. 50–53; for Penfield, pp. 53–55; for diaries and a letter from German soldiers, pp. 33–35.

85. The government printed 1,592,801 copies of *German War Practices, Part I,* and 720,848 copies of *German Treatment of Conquered Territory. Creel Report,* 15, 16.

86. George Winfield Scott and James Wilford Garner, *The German War Code: Contrasted with the War Manuals of the United States, Great Britain, and France,* War Information Series, No. 11 (Washington, D.C., 1918).

87. He later became associate editor of the *Journal of International Law,* and he was president of the American Political Science Association in 1924.

Incidentally, Garner was also interested in defining and promoting "Americanism" and spoke on the subject, although not for the CPI, during this period. See James W. Garner Papers, University of Illinois Archives, Urbana, Box 2, Folder: "Americanism."

88. J. W. Garner to Guy Stanton Ford, June 11, 1917, CPI papers, CPI 3–A1, Box 62, L–1–34.

89. Guy Stanton Ford to Wallace Notestein, June 28, 1917, ibid., L–1–19.

90. Ford to Garner, June 11, 1917, ibid., L–1–34.

91. Scott and Garner, *The German War Code*, 2.

92. Ibid., 3, 5, 6.   93. Ibid., 7, 8.

94. Ibid., 9.   95. Ibid., 9–11.

96. Ibid., 13.   97. Ibid., 11, 15.

These publications tried to give the appearance of documentation, and it is evident that Ford did hold to standards of proof in the material he published. Both he and Creel worried about unsubstantiated accounts of atrocities, lest the committee destroy its credibility. Ford had opportunity to publish material that was largely imaginative. A few of the writings turned down by the committee included "The Meaning of the German Superman! Its Creation by Nietzsche, the Self-avowed Anti-Christ; How this Mental Image Hypnotized the German Race," "Damning Revelation of Germany's Turpitude: A Confession from a Partner in a Nation's Crime," "The Devil and Kaiser Bill" (poem), and "The Evil and Fate of Autocracy" (poem). For copies of these writings see CPI papers, CPI 3–A1, Box 68, L–1–885; ibid., Box 69, L–1–1283; ibid., Box 72, L–1–1816. One must bear in mind in considering the one-sided nature of CPI pamphlets that the strongest criticism of the committee came from those groups who believed it had not been militant enough in condemning the enemy. See Bean, "George Creel and His Critics" 197–265.

98. United States Committee on Public Information, *Germany's Confession: The Lichnowsky Memorandum* (Washington, D.C., 1918?); *Creel Report*, 16; George Creel to Robert L. Maddox, July 3, 1918, CPI papers, CPI 1–A1, Box 17, Folder 2.

The British and French also used Lichnowsky's work for propaganda purposes. For a fine treatment of Lichnowsky and the war, see Harry F. Young, *Prince Lichnowsky and the Great War* (Athens, Ga., 1977), especially 145–61.

99. *German-Bolshevik Conspiracy*. See also Edgar G. Sisson, *One Hundred Red Days: A Personal Chronicle of the Bolshevik Revolution* (New Haven, 1931). Recent scholarship treats these documents as almost surely forgeries. George Kennan, "The Sisson Documents," *Journal of Modern History* 28 (June 1956): 130–54; Blakey, *Historians on the Homefront*, 98–104; Gruber, *Mars and Minerva*, 151–57; William Appleman Williams, *American-Russian Relations, 1781–1947* (New York, 1952), 154–56; and Christopher Lasch, *American Liberals and the Russian Revolution* (New York, 1962), 112–18.

Although Lenin may not have taken money or orders from the German government, evidence does indicate that the German government gave substantial financial support to the Bolsheviks. See George Katkov, "German Foreign Office Documents on Financial Support to the Bolsheviks in 1917," *International Affairs* [London] 32 (Apr. 1956): 181–89. On German support for Lenin and his followers, see also Werner Hahlweg, "Lenins Reise durch Deutschland im April 1917," *Vierteljahrshefte fur Zeitgeschichte* 5 (Oct. 1957): 307–33.

100. S. S. McClure's association with the CPI is only slightly mentioned in Peter Lyon, *Success Story: The Life and Times of S. S. McClure* (Deland, Fla.,

1963), 385. See Guy Stanton Ford to S. S. McClure, Dec. 11, 1917, CPI papers, CPI 3–A1, Box 66, L–1–623; McClure to Ford, Dec. 13, 1917, ibid.; Samuel B. Harding to P. J. Lally, Jan. 5, 1918, ibid., Box 67, L–1–692; Guy Stanton Ford to Herbert Putnam (Library of Congress), Jan. 2, 1918, ibid., Box 64, L–1–338; Guy Stanton Ford to C. D. Lee, Mar. 1, 1918, ibid., Box 63, Folder 3.

McClure argued that Japan did not pose a threat to the United States in the Far East. For newspaper clippings on McClure's lectures about the Far East, see S. S. McClure Papers, Lilly Library, Indiana University, Bloomington, Boxes "McClure Mss. Printed—Writings 1908–1920" and "McClure Mss. Printed—Clippings 1917–1922."

German atrocities, especially in Belgium, were a favorite theme for McClure's lectures and writings. For example, McClure's talk before the Detroit Athletic Club was headlined "Audience Shudders as McClure Recounts Outrages by Germans." Detroit *Times*, Dec. 5, 1917 (see "McClure Mss. Printed—Clippings 1917–1922"). Earlier McClure had also written about the invasion of Belgium, though not for the CPI: S. S. McClure, *Obstacles to Peace* (Boston, 1917), 114–32, 171–231 (German atrocities in other countries were also condemned). In April 1919, McClure traveled to Belgium and wrote a pamphlet for the Belgian government on German abuses there. He also called for heavy German reparations. [S. S. McClure], "Mr. S. S. McClure's Trip, Easter, 1919: An American Opinion on the German Atrocities in Belgium" (Brussels, 1919).

101. This work was apparently never published as a book. S. S. McClure to Hattie (Harriet H. McClure), Jan. 12, 1918, McClure papers, "McClure Mss. 1917, Nov.–1918, May"; McClure to "My Beloved Wife," Mar. 27, 1918, ibid. McClure planned to call this book *The Road to Hell*; its purpose was to help "win this war" for the government. McClure to Hattie, Apr. 3, 1918, ibid. Also see S. S. McClure to Herbert S. Houston, Mar. 4, 1918, CPI papers, CPI 14–A3.

102. Harvey O'Higgins, *The German Whisper* (Washington, D.C., 1918?), 3. Shotwell suggested to Ford that O'Higgins write this pamphlet. J. T. Shotwell to Guy Stanton Ford, Nov. 28, 1917, CPI papers, CPI 3–A1, Box 63, L–1–163.

103. O'Higgins, *The German Whisper*, 7–16, 19–22.

104. Ibid., 29.

105. United States Committee on Public Information, *The Kaiserite in America: One Hundred and One German Lies Published Especially for the Commercial Travelers of America* (Washington, D.C., 1918?). See also *Creel Report*, 16.

106. *The Kaiserite in America*, 8–9.

107. Ibid., 15, 44.

108. Ibid., 3–4.

109. Earl E. Sperry and Willis M. West, *German Plots and Intrigues in the United States during the Period of Our Neutrality*, Red, White and Blue Series,

No. 10 (Washington, D.C., 1918). This pamphlet had a small circulation, only slightly more than 125,000.

110. E. E. Sperry to James T. Shotwell, May 26, 1917, NBHS papers, Ac. 3699, Box 6; Sperry to Shotwell, May 9, 1917, ibid.; Sperry to Shotwell, May 21, 1917, ibid.; Sperry to Shotwell, May 28, 1917, ibid.; E. E. Sperry to Charles H. Hull, June 3, 1917, ibid.; Sperry to Hull, June 4, 1917, ibid.

111. Sperry and West, *German Plots and Intrigues in the United States*, 8–9.

112. Leubke notes that the National German-American Alliance, following a meeting of national and state officials in February 1917, "promoted every effort to avert war—mass meetings, peace resolutions, popular referenda—while proclaiming total and explicit loyalty to the United States." After the United States entered the war, the alliance pursued "an explicitly patriotic course. It issued a call to all members to meet every responsibility imposed by citizenship. Although it was subsequently accused of dilatory patriotism, the alliance took much pride in its participation in the several Liberty bond drives. Absolute loyalty to the United States was a constant theme in its literature, as was the requirement of proper conduct. But the various alliances understandably hesitated to display sympathy for America's allies and they were less than eager to publicly condemn Germany's war aims or to blame the war on the Kaiser, as the superpatriots demanded." See Luebke, *Bonds of Loyalty*, 201, 231.

113. Before 1917, there were apparently German efforts to have the United States intervene in Mexico in order to divert American attention and supplies from the war in Europe. Though it is questionable that the Germans sponsored or participated in Pancho Villa's attack on the United States, the German Foreign Office, once having received news of the raid, probably tried to provide arms for Villa. For literature on this issue and the question whether Germany used Mexico as a base for sabotage in the United States, see Friedrich Katz, "Alemania y Francisco Villa," *Historia Mexicana* 12 (July–Sept. 1962): 88–102; Michael C. Meyer, "The Mexican-German Conspiracy of 1915," *The Americas* 23 (July 1966): 76–89; Friedrich Katz, "Pancho Villa and the Attack on Columbus, New Mexico," *American Historical Review* 83 (Feb. 1978): 126–28; James A. Sandos, "German Involvement in Northern Mexico, 1915–1916: A New Look at the Columbus Raid," *Hispanic American Historical Review* 50 (Feb. 1970): 70–88; and Charles H. Harris III and Louis R. Sadler, "The Plan of San Diego and the Mexican-United States War Crisis of 1916: A Reexamination," ibid. 58 (Aug. 1978): especially 402–3.

114. Sperry and West, *German Plots and Intrigues in the United States*, 9–38, 42–54.

115. Ibid., 56–58. The pamphlet also asserted that the American Correspondence Film Company had been a front for German propaganda films. Ibid., 58.

116. James Read writes that "the best evidence seems to indicate that the German actions in Belgium were not characterized by 'every refinement' of

'cruelty and bestiality,' although isolated acts of perversion may have taken place. The Belgian civil population almost certainly did not commit revolting atrocities on the invaders in any significant number of cases. However, at least 5,000 Belgian civilians were killed as a result of the German invasion. The Germans had little or no right to consider all resistance in Belgium illegal. This attitude led not only to the execution of many Belgians who were fighting the invaders according to the rules of international law, but also to the massacre of hundreds of hostages for which no satisfactory justification can be offered." Read, *Atrocity Propaganda, 1914–1919*, 102–3.

117. On the origins of the war and German war aims see Luigi Albertini, *Origins of the War of 1914*, translated and edited by Isabella M. Massey (London, 1953): Fritz Fischer, *Germany's Aims in the First World War* (London, 1961, 1967); and works by Fischer's students. On German militarism see Gordon Craig, *Politics of the Prussian Army, 1640–1945* (New York, 1955); Gerhard Ritter, *Sword and the Scepter: The Problem of Militarism in Germany*. Volume I: *The Prussian Tradition 1740–1890* (Coral Gables, Fla., 1964, 1969); and Gerhard Ritter, *Sword and the Scepter: The Problem of Militarism in Germany*. Volume II: *The European Powers and the Wilhelminian Empire, 1890–1914* (Coral Gables, Fla., 1965, 1970). For a comprehensive view see Volker R. Berghahn, *Germany and the Approach of War in 1914* (New York, 1973); and Gordon Craig, *Germany 1866–1945* (New York, 1978).

CHAPTER FIVE

1. United States Committee on Public Information, *America's Answer* (film), Reel 1, Subtitle 18.

2. For studies dealing with the American idea of mission see Gabriel, *Course of American Democratic Thought*, 339–70; Edward McNall Burns, *American Idea of Mission: Concepts of National Purpose and Destiny* (New Brunswick, 1957); Albert K. Weinberg, *Manifest Destiny: A Study of Nationalist Expansionism in American History* (Gloucester, Mass., 1958); Frederick Merk, in collaboration with Lois Bannister Merk, *Manifest Destiny and Mission in American History: A Reinterpretation* (New York, 1963); Ernest Lee Tuveson, *Redeemer Nation: The Idea of America's Millennial Role* (Chicago, 1968); Winthrop S. Hudson, ed., *Nationalism and Religion in America: Concepts of American Identity and Mission* (New York, 1970); Cherry, *God's New Israel*; David Wells, "New Perspective on Wilsonian Diplomacy: The Secular Evangelism of American Political Economy [review essay]," *Perspectives in American History* 6 (1972): 389–419; and Kurt Glaser, "Nineteenth-Century Messianism and Twentieth-Century Interventionism," *Modern Age* 17 (Winter 1973): 16–32. It has been suggested that one reason for the "missionary" character of American nationalism was interpretation of the national ideology in terms of political and social values that were thought to be universally valid. Arieli, *Individualism and Nationalism in American Ideology*, 26.

3. Wilson's appeal was significant. Hofstadter noted that "the traditional American idea had been not that the United States was to lead, rescue, or redeem Europe, but that it was to take its own people in a totally different direction which Europe was presumably incapable of following. The United States was to be a kind of non-Europe or anti-Europe." Hofstadter, *Age of Reform*, 279, 280. See also Daniel J. Boorstin, *America and the Image of Europe: Reflections on American Thought* (New York, 1960), 20–21.

4. Isolationist attitudes were strong when the war began in 1914 and no doubt persisted in 1917–18, even though the majority of Americans favored the war. The CPI tried to combat such beliefs. On isolation during this period see Selig Adler, *Isolationist Impulse: Its Twentieth-Century Reaction* (New York, 1957), 32; Osgood, *Ideals and Self-Interest in America's Foreign Relations*, 278; John Milton Cooper, Jr., *Vanity of Power: American Isolationism and the First World War, 1914–1917* (Westport, Conn., 1969); Kevin J. O'Keefe, *A Thousand Deadlines: The New York City Press and American Neutrality, 1914–1917* (The Hague, 1972), 30–31; and Ray A. Billington, "The Origins of Middle Western Isolationism," Carl N. Degler, ed., *Pivotal Interpretations of American History* (2 vols., New York, 1966), 2: 254–57.

5. [Bullard and Poole], *How the War Came to America*; Poole, *Bridge*, 264–65; Creel, *How We Advertised America*, 103.

6. Bullard, *Diplomacy of the Great War*, 285.

7. Ideally, Bullard hoped for a permanent world court. [Bullard and Poole], *How the War Came to America*, 5.

8. Ibid., 9.

9. Ibid., 7. Here Bullard was drawing on a May 27, 1916, speech by President Wilson before the League to Enforce Peace.

10. Ibid., 11, 15.

11. Ibid., 2, 16. Democracy, Bullard would write elsewhere, was not static. It was "a dynamic concept, an evolutionary development, a constant warfare —but a constant growth." Arthur Bullard, "Letters from an American Friend: II. The American Ideal of Democracy," 6, in CPI papers, CPI 3–A1, Box 76, L–3–113.

12. Waldo G. Leland to Charles H. Haskins, June 26, 1917, NBHS papers, Ac. 3699, Box 3; Haskins to Leland, June 27, 1917, ibid. See also *Creel Report*, 15.

13. Lane, *Why We Are Fighting Germany*, 3, 4, 6, 7; Robert Lansing, *America's Future at Stake*, in Robert Lansing and Louis F. Post, *A War of Self-Defense*, War Information Series, No. 5 (Washington, D.C., 1917), 6–7; Root, *Plain Issues of the War*, 3–4, 9, 10–11, 15; Louis F. Post, *The German Attack*, in Robert Lansing and Louis F. Post, *A War of Self-Defense*, War Information Series, No. 5 (Washington, D.C., 1917), 22. Post's essay first appeared in *Public*, July 27 and Aug. 3, 1917.

14. *Creel Report*, 16.

15. Guy Stanton Ford to C. D. Lee, Feb. 25, 1918, CPI papers, CPI 3–A1,

Box 63, Folder 3; Tatlock, *Why America Fights Germany*, 7, 9, 12–13. Tatlock did not believe that German blood had caused the war, and he felt that most German-Americans were loyal.

16. Tatlock, *Why America Fights Germany*, 9–10. This story, which undoubtedly made a profound impression on readers when it appeared in 1918, is one of the most frequently cited passages in CPI literature. See Mock and Larson, *Words That Won the War*, 166–67; and Peter Buitenhuis's more recent "The Selling of the Great War," *Canadian Review of American Studies* 7 (Fall 1976): 145.

17. Notestein and Stoll, comp., *Conquest and Kultur*, 95–105.

18. Ibid., 95–96, 97.

19. Ibid., 98–103.

20. Ibid., 104.

21. Although there has been one doctoral thesis written on Greene, there is no good full-scale biography of him. See Jack Randolph Kirby, "Evarts Boutell Greene: The Career of a Professional Historian" (doctoral dissertation, University of Illinois, 1969). Correspondence from Greene may be found in the NBHS papers; in the University of Illinois Historical Survey, Urbana; and in CPI papers, CPI 3–Al, Box 62, Folder 7, L–1–141.

22. Evarts B. Greene, *American Interest in Popular Government Abroad*, War Information Series, No. 8 (Washington, D.C., 1917), 4–5.

23. Ibid., 5.

24. Ibid., 6, 7–9. Earlier, Greene had used Daniel Webster to demonstrate American interest in political liberty abroad. Evarts B. Greene, "A Speech by Daniel Webster [letter to the editor]," *Nation* 105 (Aug. 9, 1917): 146–47.

25. Greene, *American Interest in Popular Government Abroad*, 10–12, 14, 15.

26. Ibid., 3, 16. Greene also had prepared a bibliography and topical outline on "The Contact of the Western Powers with the Far East." Evarts B. Greene to Waldo G. Leland, May 5, 1917, NBHS papers, Ac. 3699, Box 3, Folder: "Evarts B. Greene."

27. Frederick Jackson Turner to Charles H. Haskins, May 2, 1917, NBHS papers, Ac. 3699, Box 3, Folder: "Charles H. Haskins."

28. Dexter Perkins to [Waldo G. Leland], May 11, 1917, ibid., Box 6.

29. See Sherman, *American and Allied Ideals*, 6.

30. For Lowell's essay see [Lane], *Battle Line of Democracy*, 69–71. For Belgium, see 84–94; for France, 95–106; for Britain, 107–28; for Russia, 129–30; for Italy, 131–33. After the first revolution, Russia was often included in this community of ideals.

31. Guy Stanton Ford, "Foreword," in Notestein and Stoll, comp., *Conquest and Kultur*, 5.

How to deal with the American Revolution in Fourth of July oratory worried the committee's writers. Sherman recognized the opening it left for the anti-English orator and advised keeping "the flaming Irishman" off the stump. He suggested that speakers stress the reconciliation to a common cause. Moreover, England had really not been at war with America in 1776; the problem had been "only a little ring of musty old drones from the German heir." The Fourth of July should be an Independence Day for all democratic nations, celebrating a unity of spirit. Had not Burke supported the colonies, and Thomas Paine referred to America as the "cause of all mankind"? See Stuart P. Sherman to Samuel B. Harding, May 24, 1918, CPI papers, CPI 3–A1, Box 72, L–1–1736; Sherman to Harding, May 26, 1917, ibid., Box 66, L–1–642. For articles in *History Teacher's Magazine* dealing with the American Revolution, see Evarts B. Greene, "The American Revolution and the British Empire," *History Teacher's Magazine* 8 (Nov. 1917): 292–94; and James Sullivan, "Some Aspects of American Experience—1775–1783," ibid. (Dec. 1917): 351–52. Sullivan, who was a member of the State Department of Education in Albany, New York, was eager to show American teachers that the revolution was a conflict not so much between Englishmen and Americans as between two parties (Whig and Tory) in both countries, representing different ideals of government. Sullivan hoped to show "how ardent was the support of the colonists by the great Whig leaders in England." James Sullivan to Evarts B. Greene, Oct. 11, 1917, NBHS papers, Ac. 3699, Box 6, Folder: "James Sullivan."

32. Carl Russell Fish to Evarts B. Greene, May 17, 1917, NBHS papers, Ac. 3699, Box 3, Folder: "Evarts B. Greene"; Greene to Fish, May 21, 1917, ibid., Box 2; and E. B. Greene to S. P. R. Chadwick, Oct. 25, 1917, ibid.

Ironically, Greene in 1918 published "The Problems of Historical Scholarship and Teaching as Affected by the War," in which he warned that history was subject to abuse because the war brought a temptation to present facts to fit preconceived theories. This approach, he said, had been used by German historians like Treitschke to justify a monarchical government and encourage extreme national egoism. In reviewing Greene's work with *History Teacher's Magazine* it is hard not to conclude that he too fell victim to abusing history. E. B. Greene, "The Problems of Historical Scholarship and Teaching as Affected by the War," National Education Association of the United States, *Addresses and Proceedings of the Fifty-Sixth Annual Meeting, Pittsburgh, Pennsylvania, June 29–July 6* (1918), 56: 199.

33. Evarts B. Greene, "Suggestions on the Relation of American to European History," *History Teacher's Magazine* 8 (Sept. 1917): 218–19; Greene, "The American Revolution and the British Empire," 292–94; Greene, "The Interaction of European and American Politics, 1823–1861," ibid. 9 (Mar. 1918): 142–43.

34. Greene, "The American Revolution and the British Empire," 292; Greene, "Suggestions on the Relation of American to European History," 218, 219.

35. St. George L. Sioussat, "English Foundations of American Institutional Life," *History Teacher's Magazine* 8 (Oct. 1917): 260–61; Arthur Lyon

Cross, "Suggested Points for Emphasis in the Tudor Period, 1485–1603," ibid. (Nov. 1917): 290–92. An article similar to that by Sioussat was Notestein's "The Interest of Seventeenth Century England for Students of American Institutions," 350–51.

36. Evarts B. Greene to Arthur L. Cross, Sept. 27, 1917, NBHS papers, Ac. 3699, Box 2; Evarts B. Greene to James Sullivan, Oct. 15, 1917, ibid., Box 6, Folder: "James Sullivan"; Sullivan, "Some Aspects of American Experience—1775–1783," 351–52.

37. Evarts B. Greene, to T. C. Smith, July 17, 1917, NBHS papers, Ac. 3699, Box 6; Evarts B. Greene to Albert Bushnell Hart, July 21, 1917, ibid., Box 3 (Greene did not receive an answer from Hart and thus turned to Carl Becker for the article—Evarts B. Greene to A. E. McKinley, Dec. 4, 1917, ibid., Box 5); Evarts B. Greene to E. D. Adams, July 21, 1917, ibid., Box 1; Tenney Frank to Evarts B. Greene, Nov. 10, 1917, ibid., Box 2.

38. Arthur W. Dunn to Evarts B. Greene, June 30, 1917, ibid., Box 1; W. H. Gardiner (of *History Circle*) to James T. Shotwell, Oct. 18, 1917, ibid., Box 3; W. H. Gardiner to W. G. Leland, Oct. 30, 1917, ibid.

39. Speech before the United States Senate by Woodrow Wilson, Jan. 22, 1917.

40. Carl Becker to Frederick Jackson Turner, May 14, 1917, NBHS papers, Ac. 3699, Box 1. Becker thought that "history ought to be the most useful of studies for the solution of problems growing out of the war." He also felt history could aid the war effort in many ways. Precedents for executive usurpation could be gotten from the Civil War; a negative example of how to deal with a defeated Germany could be had from looking at American Reconstruction. Ibid.

41. Albert E. McKinley to Evarts B. Greene, July 28, 1917, ibid., Box 5; Evarts B. Greene to Albert Bushnell Hart, July 21, 1917, ibid., Box 3; Greene to McKinley, Dec. 4, 1917, ibid., Box 5; [Evarts B. Greene] to Carl Becker, Nov. 28, 1917, ibid., Box 1. For Becker's article see Carl Becker, "The Monroe Doctrine and the War," *History Teacher's Magazine* 9 (Feb. 1918): 87–90. Also see *Minnesota History Bulletin* 2 (May 1917): 61–68 (all citations from this latter source).

42. Becker, "The Monroe Doctrine and the War," 62–63.

43. Ibid., 66, 67.

44. Ibid., 62, 65, 67, 68.

45. Guy Stanton Ford to Carl Becker, June 19, 1918, CPI papers, CPI 3–A1, Box 76, L–3–104; Ford to Becker, June 28, 1918, ibid. A copy of an early draft of Becker's essay "The Monroe Doctrine" is in ibid., Box 62, L–1–134, Folder 5. Quotations are from this draft, p. [10].

46. Becker, *United States: An Experiment in Democracy*, 140. Interestingly, Becker did not believe that using American intervention in Russia to suppress Lenin's government was in the spirit of the Monroe Doctrine:

Whether we abandon or maintain the Monroe Doctrine is less important than whether we hold fast to or depart from our profoundest traditions. We shall certainly depart from them if, having for a hundred years in the name of democracy defended the right of American peoples to govern themselves in their own way, we now, in behalf of "law and order," deny that right to any European people because they choose to govern themselves according to democratic forms that are not agreeable to us. To raise an army in defense of Belgium and France against German aggressions may well have been no more than a wider application of the Monroe Doctrine but to send American soldiers into Russia for the suppression of the soviet government of Lenine is indeed to abandon the Monroe Doctrine for the ideals and the methods of the "Holy Alliance." [Ibid., 140–41]

47. Andrew C. McLaughlin, *The Great War: From Spectator to Participant*, War Information Series, No. 4 (Aug. 1917); *Creel Report*, 16.

McLaughlin was responsible also for having one of his colleagues at Chicago submit an essay to *History Teacher's Magazine* on the ending of America's "splendid isolation." A. C. McLaughlin to W. G. Leland, May 17, 1917, NBHS papers, Ac. 3699, Box 5, Folder: "A. C. McLaughlin." See Arthur P. Scott, "The Passing of Splendid Isolation," *History Teacher's Magazine* 8 (June 1917): 192–95.

48. McLaughlin, *Great War*, 6, 13, 14, 16. McLaughlin, realizing that British-American relations had not always been cordial, argued that the American Revolution was essentially "an English revolution, in which Englishmen of this side of the ocean were striving for the development and maintenance of liberty. . . ." Britain became a true friend of the United States when it became a democracy, with the passage of the second Reform Bill in 1867. France had become America's "real friend" with the fall of Napoleon III and the firm establishment of republican institutions. Ibid., 13–15.

49. McLaughlin's lectures were published in Andrew Cunningham McLaughlin, *America and Britain* (New York, 1919). McLaughlin's mission is discussed in Blakey, *Historians on the Homefront*, 70–77. Material on this lecture tour is also found in the Andrew C. McLaughlin Papers, University of Chicago Archives, Box 2.

Although not specifically mentioned in his CPI pamphlet, McLaughlin, during his speaking tour in England in 1918, emphasized the Anglo-Saxon heritage common to both Britain and the United States. See Andrew C. McLaughlin to George B. Adams, Oct. 3, 1918, ibid., Box 2, Folder 6. See also draft of lecture written in Hotel Arundel, London, in 1918, ibid., Folder 8.

50. McLaughlin, *America and Britain*, 128. For his lecture on the Monroe Doctrine see 97–173. McLaughlin had been influenced by Albert Bushnell Hart's views on the doctrine, and he acknowledged his indebtedness (ibid., vii). See also Albert Bushnell Hart, *Monroe Doctrine: An Interpretation* (Boston, 1916).

51. McLaughlin, *America and Britain*, 149–53.

52. Ibid., 166.

53. Ibid., 172–73. For McLaughlin's discussion of making the doctrine worldwide, see 164–73.

54. Guy Stanton Ford to I. J. Cox, Nov. 30, 1917, CPI papers, CPI 3–A1, Box 67, L–1–576, Folder 2.

55. Guy Stanton Ford, "Foreword," in *War Message and the Facts Behind It*, 3.

Bullard quoted President Wilson's speech of Jan. 22, 1917. [Bullard and Poole], *How the War Came to America*, 12. Creel made this argument shortly after the war in Creel, *War, the World, and Wilson*, 40, 122–23, 209, 315.

56. I. J. Cox to Guy Stanton Ford, Nov. 30, 1917, CPI papers, CPI 3–A1, Box 67, L–1–576, Folder 2; George G. Wilson to Guy Stanton Ford, Feb. 4, 1918, ibid., Box 62, L–1–144. See George Grafton Wilson, "The Monroe Doctrine after the War," World Peace Foundation, *A League of Nations* 1 (June 1918): 253–305. Wilson also prepared an address, "The Monroe Doctrine and the League to Enforce Peace." Ford to Wilson, Feb. 8, 1918, CPI papers, CPI 3–A1, Box 62, L–1–144; Wilson to Ford, July 28, 1917, ibid.

Shotwell considered Elbert J. Benton's essay "Fitting the Monroe Doctrine to Modern World Politics" for publication in *Century*, before rejecting it because of length. *Century* did publish other articles on the subject. James T. Shotwell to Elbert J. Benton (Western Reserve University), June 29, 1917, NBHS papers, Ac. 3699, Box 1; Shotwell to Benton, July 25, 1917, ibid. For example, see Herbert Adams Gibbons, "The Monroe Doctrine for the World," *Century* 94 (May 1917): 151–54.

57. James T. Shotwell to Earl Sperry, June 29, 1917, NBHS papers, Ac. 3699, Box 6.

58. Paxson, Corwin, and Harding, eds., *War Cyclopedia*, 176–77, 281–84. Greene wrote the entries on "United States, Champion of Free Government" and "United States, Isolation of." Evarts B. Greene to Samuel Harding, May 28, 1918, CPI papers, CPI 3–A1, Box 89, Folder 11.

59. How did these arguments square with Wilson's proposal for the United States to join a League of Nations? The CPI wound up most of its activities before debate over the issue. Some people felt that one of the committee's mistakes was failure to advertise the League. Although Ford assured other people that America was definitely committed to the League, only a few committee publications dealt with the question. The *National School Service*, as we shall see in the next chapter, promoted the League in public schools. One of the last CPI pamphlets, by Becker, entitled *America's War Aims and Peace Program*, dealt with the League. Noting the breakdown of national isolation, Becker supported the League of Nations. At the same time he believed that no organization for world peace was possible unless all member nations realized that a ruling idea of modern times was that government must be based on "consent of the governed." Unless member governments were subject to popular will a League of Nations would have little chance. Becker, *America's*

War Aims and Peace Program, 26, 48–51. For criticism of the CPI for failing to advertise the League, see [Edward L. Bernays], *Biography of an Idea: Memoirs of Public Relations Counsel Edward L. Bernays* (New York, 1965), 160–77; and "The Peace Treaty as the World's Greatest Advertising Failure," *Literary Digest* 63 (Dec. 20, 1919): 130–36. For Ford's views on the League see Guy Stanton Ford to George H. Shibley, Oct. 19, 1918, CPI papers, CPI 3–A1, Box 74, L–1–2136.

60. Quoted in Lewis Paul Todd, *Wartime Relations of the Federal Government and the Public Schools, 1917–1918* (New York, 1945), 57. Hereafter cited as *Wartime Relations*.

61. This observation about Wilsonian internationalism has been made by Nye, *This Almost Chosen People*, 88. Daniel Boorstin argues that Wilson's program "was a projection of the American image onto Europe." Boorstin, *America and the Image of Europe*, 22.

Chapter Six

1. Ford, "A New Educational Agency," 208.

2. Louis Snyder, *Meaning of Nationalism* (New Brunswick, 1954), 110. See also Boyd C. Shafer, *Nationalism: Myth and Reality* (New York, 1955), 121. Shafer notes that by the twentieth century in Europe and the United States, the one major purpose everywhere "of education, at all levels, came to be the making of 'good citizens,' and that meant, in popular thinking, the making of national patriots." Boyd C. Shafer, *Faces of Nationalism: New Realities and Old Myths* (New York, 1972), 195.

3. Shafer, *Nationalism: Myth and Reality*, 183–86; Edward H. Reiser, *Nationalism and Education since 1789: A Social and Political History of Modern Education* (New York, 1922), 7–319; Cecilia Hatrick Bason, *Study of the Homeland and Civilization in the Elementary Schools of Germany: With Special Reference to the Education of Teachers* (New York, 1937); Howard Marraro, *Nationalism in Italian Education* (New York, 1927); Gregor Ziemer, *Education for Death: The Making of a Nazi* (New York, 1941).

4. The *National School Service* has received only slight attention from scholars and usually has been described as solely an expression of wartime propaganda designed to stir up patriotic sentiment. Thus, Lewis Todd asserted that the *NSS* manifested "a parochial patriotism," that it gave instruction in patriotism rather than lessons in citizenship. Todd's analysis of the *NSS* was incomplete, however, as his study was based apparently on only a partial reading of the bulletin. Similar conclusions about the nature of the *NSS* are reached by George Blakey. Studies by Cedric Larson and James Mock, and by C. H. Hamlin, barely mention the *NSS* and contain misleading statements about the bulletin's circulation. This chapter will argue that the *National School Service* did try to promote patriotism but that it also must be put against a larger background than the war. It made a significant effort to

define the nature of citizenship in a democratic society and must be seen as an expression of reformist literature during these years. See Todd, *Wartime Relations*, 63–65, 86–90; Blakey, *Historians on the Homefront*, 122–24; Mock and Larson, *Words That Won the War*, 68; and C. H. Hamlin, "Educators Present Arms: The Use of the Schools and Colleges As Agents of War Propaganda, 1914–1918," in Charles Chatfield, ed., *Propaganda and Myth in Time of War* (New York, 1973), 31–32.

5. For the National Security League see Robert D. Ward, "The Origin and Activities of the National Security League, 1914–1919," *Mississippi Valley Historical Review* 47 (June 1960): 51–65; and Blakey, *Historians on the Homefront*. Blakey also discusses the National Board for Historical Service and the Committee on Public Information. The Student Army Training Corps (SATC), which replaced the Reserve Officers' Training Corps, is discussed in Gruber, *Mars and Minerva*, 213–52; and Evarts B. Greene, "Co-Operation between Colleges and Secondary Schools in Promoting Education for Citizenship," *Association of American Colleges Bulletin: Address at Fifth Annual Meeting* 5 (Apr. 1919): 103–11. For the SATC's operation in Iowa, see Louis P. Koch, "Drill on the Campus: The Student's Army Training Corps, 1918," *Palimpsest* 56 (Nov.–Dec. 1975): 184–91.

After the war, Evarts Greene, who was chairman of the Committee on Education for Citizenship of the American Council on Education, acknowledged that the SATC program had been a "bad dream" but argued that the experience had benefits. He had been responsible for the War Issues Course at the University of Illinois, a class that involved three thousand students. The course sought to offer instruction on the history of the war, the ideals of the nations involved as manifested in their governments, and how those ideals found expression in philosophy and literature. The course continued at Illinois through the 1918–19 school year, and Greene believed that it offered opportunity to instruct students in the responsibilities of citizenship —the duties of a citizen-soldier and "the even more complex conflicts of civil life." What bothered him was that university training had become too departmentalized, that students had lost a "sense of larger relationships." He believed that a war issues course, properly conducted, could create a "new type of citizen" able to deal with modern problems. Greene, "Co-Operation between Colleges and Secondary Schools in Promoting Education for Citizenship," 103, 105, 109, 110.

Of course, may CPI pamphlets were designed for classroom use. For instance, Harding's *Study of the Great War* traced the background of the conflict in slightly under one hundred pages. He found its causes in German and Austrian aggression and argued that the duty of all citizens was "to support the war whole-heartedly." Once the decision was made to enter the conflict, Harding said, "arguments against the war. . . [were] enemy arguments." Harding, *Study of the Great War*, 72; the second quotation was taken from a speech by Elihu Root in Chicago, Sept. 14, 1917, quoted in ibid.

6. Quoted in Todd, *Wartime Relations*, 87.

7. Guy Stanton Ford to Alva Groth, Jan. 24, 1918, CPI papers, CPI 3–A1, Box 67, L–1–810. The lack of direction in public education had worried Ford early in his career, even while he was teaching in Iowa. In 1898 he had written that "educationally speaking too many towns are simply drifting —ships without chart, compass or commander." Guy Stanton Ford, ed., "Educational Column," newspaper clipping in Ford papers, legal folder 3(1).

8. Such a plan was also favored by Dean Coffman of the University of Minnesota; William C. Bagley and G. D. Strayer, both of Columbia; and Harry Pratt Judson, president of the University of Chicago. Guy Stanton Ford to Frank Strong (Chancellor, University of Kansas), Mar. 12, 1918, CPI papers, CPI 3–A1, Box 69, L–1–1123.

9. Among those departments represented in the meeting with P. P. Claxton on Feb. 13, 1918, were the Food and Fuel Administrations, the Junior Red Cross, the War Savings Committee, the CPI, the Bureau of Education, the Liberty Loan Publicity Committee, the Internal Revenue Bureau, the Four Minute Men, the Boys' Working Reserve, the Council of National Defense, and the National Council of Patriotic Societies. Creel was enthusiastic about such a bulletin, but he was not eager to have his committee foot the entire cost of the publication. Philander P. Claxton to George Creel, Mar. 5, 1918, CPI papers, CPI 1–A1, Box 6, Folder 119; Creel to Claxton, Mar. 8, 1918, ibid.

10. See Statement, undated, ibid., CPI 3–A7, Box 89, C–101. The Emergency Council on Education was composed of twenty national associations on education. Its function was "the more complete mobilization of the educational forces of the country for the purposes of the war." P. L. Campbell (secretary-treasurer, Emergency Council on Education) to J. J. Pettijohn (associate director, Speaking Division, CPI), July 12, 1918, ibid., CPI 12–A1, Box 189, Z–1–18.

11. The following people composed the *NSS*'s advisory editorial board: Mary C. C. Bradford, state superintendent of public instruction, Denver, Colo.; J. A. C. Chandler, superintendent of public schools, Richmond, Va.; L. D. Coffman, dean, College of Education, University of Minnesota; R. J. Condon, superintendent of public schools, Cincinnati, Ohio; Dr. Thomas E. Finegan, deputy commissioner and assistant commissioner for elementary education, Albany, N.Y.; Alice Florer, assistant state superintendent, Lincoln, Nebr.; Rev. Augustine F. Hickey, diocesan supervisor of schools, Boston, Mass.; F. M. Hunter, superintendent of public schools, Oakland, Calif.; D. B. Waldo, president, State Normal School, Kalamazoo, Mich.; and H. G. Williams, president, National Educational Press Association, Columbus, Ohio.

In their correspondence with Ford and Searson, some of the board members revealed their hopes for the bulletin. Chandler wanted the first bulletin to emphasize preparing the teacher for Americanization and "spreading the gospel of American ideals of democracy." Subsequent issues should focus on methods by which these ideas could be communicated. Coffman also wanted the bulletin to stress the ideals of American democracy. Finegan was worried about the foreign born. He believed that the melting pot was not working, that it heated the nationalities in America but failed to "melt and merge" them. The school, he wrote, "should be democracy's nursery" and should encourage students to read books that would stimulate ideals. It was most important that students read and speak English. J. A. C. Chandler to Guy Stanton Ford, May 22, 1918, CPI papers, CPI 3–A7, Folder 2 (A–1); L. D. Coffman to J. W. Searson, May 10, 1918, ibid., (A–2); Thomas E. Finegan to Guy Stanton Ford, May 14, 1918, ibid., (A–6).

12. [J. W. Searson] to E. G. Gowans (state superintendent of public instruction, Salt Lake City, Utah), May 22, 1918, ibid., Folder 3, A–1–31. The cost of the *NSS* per issue ran from $4,500 to $5,800 and by the end of the war was representing a heavy drain on the limited finances of the CPI. Guy Stanton Ford to Augusta Drake, Oct. 11, 1918, ibid., CPI 3–A1, Box 74, L–1–2175; Guy Stanton Ford to C. D. Lee, Oct. 16, 1918, ibid., Box 63, Folder 3.

13. J. W. Searson sent out over three hundred letters to various educational leaders requesting suggestions for the proposed bulletin. Their replies are found in the CPI papers in the National Archives. See CPI 3–A7 (A–1 to A–25, A1–1–75, and B–1 to B–250). It is difficult to know how many persons, if any, opposed such a bulletin. Such opponents, if they existed, may have felt it best to remain silent, given the political climate of 1918.

14. William H. Kilpatrick to Guy Stanton Ford, May 16, 1918, ibid., CPI 3–A7, Folder 6, B–52; E. S. Evenden to J. W. Searson, May 14, 1918, ibid., Folder 5, B–4.

15. *National School Service* 1 (Sept. 1, 1918): 9.

16. For a brief biographical sketch of Bagley's early career, see Henry C. Johnson, Jr., and Erwin V. Johanningmeier, *Teachers for the Prairie: The University of Illinois and the Schools, 1868–1945* (Urbana, Ill., 1972), 160–64.

17. During his career, Bagley wrote or coauthored more than 20 books and 140 articles. His works included William Chandler Bagley, *Educative Process* (New York, 1905); Bagley, *Classroom Management* (New York, 1907); Bagley, *Craftsmanship in Teaching* (New York, 1911); Stephen Sheldon Colvin and Bagley, *Human Behavior: A First Book in Psychology for Teachers* (New York, 1913); Bagley, *School Discipline* (New York, 1914); Charles A. Beard and Bagley, *History of the American People* (New York, 1918). Bagley's postwar books included Bagley and W. S. Learned, *Preparation of Teachers* (New York, 1919); Bagley and J. A. H. Keith, *Nation and the Schools* (New York, 1920); Bagley and Charles A. Beard, *Our Old World Background* (New York, 1922); and Bagley, *Determinism in Education* (New York, 1925).

18. Bagley, *Educative Process*, 58–65. On the general theme of Bagley and the socially efficient individual, see also Erwin Virgil Johanningmeier, "A Study of William Chandler Bagley's Educational Doctrines and His Program

for Teacher Preparation, 1895–1918" (doctoral dissertation, University of Illinois, 1967), especially chapter 3, " 'Social Efficiency' as the Ultimate Aim of Education," pp. 37–78).

19. I. L. Kandel, *William Chandler Bagley: Stalwart Educator* (New York, 1961), 48.

20. Ibid., 49; W. C. Bagley, "Some Handicaps to Education in a Democracy," *School and Society* 3 (June 3, 1916): 813, 814.

21. Gene D. Phillips, "The Educational Thought of William C. Bagley" (doctoral dissertation, Indiana University, 1952), 164–65.

22. Beard and Bagley, *History of the American People*, v.

23. W. C. Bagley, "Education and Our Democracy," National Education Association of the United States, *Addresses and Proceedings of the Fifty-Sixth Annual Meeting Held at Pittsburgh, Pennsylvania June 29–July 6* 56 (1918): 55–58. See also Bagley, "Some Handicaps to Education in a Democracy," 808.

Bagley also saw early in his career the potential of schools for enhancing national prestige. He saw the part of education in increasing the national power of Japan and Germany. Germans had not entrusted education to "immature women and feeble men." Bagley, *Educative Process*, 34–35.

Although the *NSS* is not analyzed, a general treatment of "The Nation and the Schools" in Bagley's thought is found in Johanningmeier, "A Study of William Chandler Bagley's Educational Doctrines and His Program for Teacher Preparation, 1895–1918," 302–33.

24. See Charles A. Coulomb, Armand J. Gerson, and Albert E. McKinley, *Outline of an Emergency Course of Instruction on the War* (Teacher's Leaflet, No. 4, 1918). See also Albert E. McKinley, Charles A. Coulomb, and Armand J. Gerson, *World War: A School History of the Great War* (New York, 1918); Todd, *Wartime Relations*, 58–63, 237.

25. See J. W. Searson to Dr. Nathan G. Schaffer (Department of Public Instruction, Harrisburg, Pa.), Oct. 16, 1918, CPI papers, CPI 3–A7, Folder 1, a–1–18; and [J. W. Searson] to Edith K. O. Clark (Superintendent, Cheyenne, Wyo.), Oct. 16, 1918, ibid., a–1–16.

26. It has been suggested—incorrectly—that the *NSS* found its way into twenty million homes because it was distributed to schoolchildren. Mock and Larson, *Words That Won the War*, 68; Hamlin, "Educators Present Arms," 31–32.

27. See J. W. Searson to Blanche A. Cheney, Sept. 21, 1918, CPI papers, CPI 3–A7, Folder 5, C–214; and [J. W. Searson] to H. D. Ramsay (Superintendent, Fort Scott, Kans.), Oct. 21, 1918, ibid., Folder 4, a–1–57.

28. *National School Service* 1 (Oct. 15, 1918): 8; Guy Stanton Ford, "To Teachers in U.S . . . ," Ford papers, Folder 163.

29. [J. W. Searson] to Thomas E. Finegan (State Department of Education, Albany, N.Y.), June 5, 1918, CPI papers, CPI 3–A7, Folder 2, a–6; *National School Service*, 1 (Nov. 1, 1918): 8.

30. Ibid. (May 1, 1919): 11.

31. See ibid., 9. A rough estimate of the percentage of the *NSS* given over to each type of article is as follows: Americanization, citizenship, and the nature of the German government—18 percent; thrift, food, and fuel conservation—19 percent; public health and community sanitation—5 percent; study of the Great War—12 percent; the Red Cross and other practical activities—17 percent; support of the League of Nations—5 percent. Articles emphasizing German autocracy made up less than 2 percent of the *NSS*. Much of the remainder of the publication was composed of statements from government officials, poems, or material on postwar reconstruction.

32. *National School Service* 1 (Sept. 1, 1918): 15. See also ibid., 4. As part of their war work, students were expected to assist in making these ideals a reality in every nation.

33. Ibid. (May 1, 1919): 11; ibid. (Apr. 1, 1919): 11.

34. Ibid. (Apr. 1, 1919): 11.

35. Ibid., 6. The *NSS* reprinted these ideas from an article in the Washington *Herald*.

36. For these and other similar statistics, see *National School Service* 1 (Apr. 1, 1919): 1, 4.

37. Ibid. (Feb. 15, 1919): 16; ibid. (Feb. 1, 1919): 13.

38. Ibid. (Feb. 15, 1919): 6, 7, 8; ibid. (Mar. 15, 1919): 8.

39. Hofstadter, *Age of Reform*, 9. See also Maldyn Allen Jones, *American Immigration* (Chicago, 1960), 231–32.

40. *National School Service* 1 (Apr. 1, 1919): 8.

41. Ibid. (Feb. 15, 1919): 16. From the bulletin of the National Americanization Committee.

42. *National School Service* 1 (Apr. 1, 1919): 4, 13. This entire issue was devoted to Americanization and good citizenship. Page 4 lists seventeen ways in which a teacher could promote Americanization.

43. The National Security League was less sympathetic to immigrants than was the CPI. As mentioned, Higham noted that the CPI practiced "liberal Americanization" but that such an approach depended greatly on the high degree of national unity that existed during the war. The decline of national unity after the war weakened this school of Americanization. Higham, *Strangers in the Land*, 253.

44. *National School Service* 1 (Mar. 1, 1919): 12.

45. Ibid. (Nov. 15, 1918): 8; ibid. (Oct. 1, 1918): 16; ibid. (Sept. 1, 1918): 6.

46. Ibid. (Feb. 15, 1919): 8. See also ibid. (Feb. 1, 1919): 8.

47. Ibid. (Jan. 1, 1919): 11; ibid. (Sept. 1, 1918): 8. See also ibid., 13.

48. United States Committee on Public Information, *Division of Four Minute Men School Bulletin*, No. 4 (Nov. 15, 1918), 3. See also *National School Service* 1 (Apr. 1, 1919): 11.

49. *National School Service* 1 (Nov. 1, 1918): 1, 5. See also ibid. (May 1, 1919): 8.

50. Ibid. (Apr. 1, 1919), 8.

51. Bagley had prepared a study attempting to determine what geographical and historical facts should be taught in elementary schools by noting how often they appeared in current periodical and newspaper literature. W. C. Bagley, "The Determination of Minimum Essentials in Elementary Geography and History," *Fourteenth Yearbook of the National Society for the Study of Education. Part I: Minimum Essentials in Elementary-School Subjects—Standards and Current Practices* (Chicago, 1915), 131–46.

52. *National School Service* 1 (Sept. 1, 1918): 1–4; ibid. (Sept. 15, 1918): 1–3; ibid. (Oct. 1, 1918): 1–2, 7; ibid. (Oct. 15, 1918): 1–2.

53. Ibid. (May 1, 1919): 11.

54. Ibid. (Sept. 15, 1918): 12, 13.

55. As an example see ibid. (Oct. 1, 1918): 14–15.

56. Ibid. (Jan. 1, 1919): 14. See also ibid. (Jan. 15, 1919): 14–15; ibid. (Feb. 15, 1919): 14–15; ibid. (Mar. 15, 1919): 14; and ibid. (Apr. 15, 1919): 14–15.

57. Ibid. (Sept. 1, 1918): 6.

58. Ibid. (Mar. 1, 1919): 1.

59. Ibid. (Sept. 1, 1918): 13–14. See also "Sugar Geography," ibid. (Oct. 15, 1918): 13; ibid. (Oct. 1, 1918): 15; ibid. (Oct. 15, 1918): 7.

60. Ibid. (Oct. 15, 1918): 6; ibid. (Nov. 15, 1918): 15.

61. Ibid. (Dec. 1, 1918): 1, 6. See also ibid., 7, 14–15.

62. Ibid. (Sept. 1, 1918): 13.

63. For example, see ibid. (Oct. 1, 1918): 15; and ibid. (Nov. 15, 1918): 11. See also ibid., 9.

64. Ibid. (Oct. 15, 1918): 1, 2–3. See also ibid. (Nov. 1, 1918): 6; ibid. (Jan. 1, 1919): 6.

65. Bagley, *Educative Process*, 346. See also ibid., 347, 348.

66. For example, see *National School Service* 1 (Jan. 1, 1919): 10; ibid. (Jan. 15, 1919): 15; ibid. (Feb. 1, 1919); 1, 4, 12; ibid. (Mar. 15, 1919): 15; and ibid. (May 1, 1919): 7.

67. Ibid. (Dec. 1, 1918): 8. See also Bagley, "Education and Our Democracy," 57.

68. Alice Florer to J. W. Searson, Aug. 6, 1918, and Searson to Florer, Aug. 12, 1918, CPI papers, CPI 3–A7, Folder 2, A–8.

69. *National School Service* 1 (Sept. 15, 1918): 11.

70. See ibid. For a proposed program running through August 1919, see ibid. (Oct. 1, 1918): 11.

71. Woodrow Wilson to "Mr. Chairman," Mar. 13, 1918, CPI papers, CPI 12–A1, Box 180, B–3–3. A copy of this letter was sent to each state chairman associated with the Council of National Defense.

72. *National School Service* 1 (Dec. 15, 1918): 4–5; ibid. (Mar. 1, 1919): 8. See also ibid. (Feb. 15, 1919): 2.

73. Ibid. (Apr. 1, 1919): 15. The writer was Celia Erickson.

74. Ford, "America's Fight for Public Opinion," 25.

75. Carl Becker, *Our Great Experiment in Democracy*, 274–75.

76. Ideas that subordinated the citizen to the higher goals of the state were widespread during these years and by no means confined to the *NSS* or to educational thought in general. Robert D. Ward, in a recent study of the universal military training movement, argues that such thinking antedated the war and survived well into the postwar period. Ward examines the views of Leonard Wood, John J. Pershing, and others, including some educational leaders, emphasizing the antidemocratic nature of their ideas. See Robert D. Ward, "The Coercive Idea: Universal Training and American Military Policy, 1900–1952," unpublished manuscript.

77. This suggestion was made by Edwin M. Canine, superintendent of schools, East Chicago, Ind. Edwin M. Canine to J. W. Searson, May 31, 1918, CPI papers, CPI 3–A7, Folder 1, B–200.

78. For an interesting account of the intellectual developments challenging democratic theory, see Edward A. Purcell, Jr., *Crisis of Democratic Theory: Scientific Naturalism and the Problem of Value* (Lexington, Ky., 1973).

CHAPTER SEVEN

1. Letter from Woodrow Wilson to "The Fifteen Thousand Four-Minute Men of the United States," in "The War Work of the Four-Minute Men: With an Introductory Letter by President Wilson," *Touchstone* 3 (Sept. 1918): 504. This statement was undoubtedly prepared by Guy Stanton Ford, forwarded to the president by Creel, and signed by Wilson. See Ford papers, Folder 163; and memo attached to Creel to Wilson, Nov. 4, 1917, Wilson papers, Reel 355.

2. Quotation, Bertram G. Nelson, "The Four Minute Men," Montaville Flowers, ed., *What Every American Should Know about the War: A Series of Studies by the Greatest Authorities of Europe and America Covering Every Aspect of the Great Struggle, Delivered at the National Conference of American Lectures, Washington, D.C., April 8–13, 1918* (New York, 1918), 252.

3. Creel, *How We Advertised America*, 86; Wayne A. Nicholas, "Crossroads Oratory—A Study of the Four Minute Men of World War I" (doctoral dissertation, Columbia University, New York, 1954), 68–69. In later years, Creel claimed that there were 150,000 Four Minute Men. Creel, *Rebel at Large*, 162.

4. Marguerite Edith Jenison, *War-Time Organizations of Illinois* (Springfield, Ill., 1923), 46.

5. United States Committee on Public Information, *Four Minute Men News*, Edition F (Dec. 24, 1918): 5.

6. The figure of 400 million may be high. Creel provides confusing information, saying in one place that 134 million persons heard the speeches while in another contending that the audience was 400 million people. See Creel, *How We Advertised America*, 85, 94.

7. Scholars who have considered the Creel committee's use of speakers have focused on the Four Minute Men but have neglected the Speaking Division . For example, see Mock and Larson, *Words That Won the War*, 113– 30; Nicholas, "Crossroads Oratory"; Jeanne Graham, "The Four Minute Men: Volunteers for Propaganda," *Southern Speech Journal* 32 (Fall 1966): 49–57; and Carol Oukrop, "The Four Minute Men Became National Network during World War I," *Journalism Quarterly* 52 (Winter 1975): 632–37.

8. *Four Minute Men News*, Edition F, 1–2.

9. Ibid., 2; Creel, *How We Advertised America*, 84–85.

10. The division was organized on three levels: national, state, and local. The organizational plan for the division was outlined in United States Committee on Public Information, *Four Minute Men Bulletin*, No. 7 (June 25, 1917); and ibid., No. 7A (Nov. 25, 1917).

11. Nicholas, "Crossroads Oratory," 66–67.

12. Ibid., 67. William H. Ingersoll possessed a background in advertising and sales management and was a partner in the company that manufactured the famous dollar watch. He had been marketing manager for Robert H. Ingersoll and Brother of New York. A former president of the Advertising Men's League of New York and first chairman for the educational committee of the Association of National Advertisers, he had been chairman of the National Commission of the Associated Advertising Clubs of the World from 1914 to 1915. He had also been a lecturer at New York University and the Harvard Business School. See *Four Minute Men News*, Edition E (Oct. 1, 1918): 11, 17. Ryerson, Blair, and Ingersoll each served full time as division director and without salary (Blair and Ingersoll received nominal salaries of one dollar per month and one dollar per year respectively).

13. *Four Minute Men News*, Edition F, supplement (Dec. 24, 1918): vi. Nelson was a professor in the public speaking department at the University of Chicago.

14. Nelson, "The Four Minute Men," 256.

The business concerns of the Four Minute Men Division of the CPI were handled largely by Keith J. Evans, a member of the original organization, who was business manager from July 1917 to August 1918. He then entered the army. Gardner Corning of New York followed Evans. Stanley H. Renton of Brooklyn was assistant business manager until, in July 1918, he was succeeded by George A. Ross of Crawfordsville, Ind. *Four Minute Men News*, Edition F, 4.

15. Ibid., Edition D (June 29, 1918): 3; Nicholas, "Crossroads Oratory," 112–13.

16. Clark made these remarks before Four Minute Men in Pittsburgh. *Four Minute Men News*, Edition B [Jan. 1918]: 5.

Samuel Hopkins Adams joined the National Advisory Council in the spring of 1918. He wrote some of the division's bulletins and spoke frequently in the eastern United States. Other members of the council were Ingersoll (its first member), Mac Martin, and Samuel F. B. Morse. This body expanded under the leadership of Ingersoll. For material written by Adams see ibid., Edition C [April 1918]: 2.

17. Ibid., Edition F, 3; and *Four Minute Men Bulletin*, No. 7A, 3.

18. *Four Minute Men News*, Edition F, 3. Emphasis was on chairmen who were energetic as well as competent. Usually they were above average in their community in educational background and career success. Nicholas, "Crossroads Oratory," 73.

19. *Four Minute Men News*, Edition F, 5.

20. Nicholas, "Crossroads Oratory," 71.

21. Ibid., 71–72.

22. Rather late in the war—September 1918—a special bulletin was prepared for four-minute singing. "A singing Army can not be beaten," and singing was thought to give momentum to the army behind the lines, the workers who supplied the fighting men. This bulletin contained detailed instructions on how to organize four-minute singing (the four-minute time limit was emphasized), and it contained music and lyrics for "America," "The Star-Spangled Banner," "Dixie," "Columbia, the Gem of the Ocean," "Tramp, Tramp, Tramp," and several other well-known patriotic songs. See *Four Minute Men Bulletin*, No. 38 (for General Use) (Sept. 10, 1918).

23. Mock and Larson, *Words That Won the War*, 125.

24. Creel estimated that Four Minute Men cost the federal government only slightly more than $100,000. He said that voluntary contributions to the Four Minute Men were twenty-five times greater than the federal expenditure. In addition to this amount would have been the cost of paying speakers, had they not been voluntary, and the rent that normally would have been paid for theaters. In all, the Four Minute Men received over $9.3 million in services for its $100,000 investment. Creel, *How We Advertised America*, 94–98.

25. See *Four Minute Men Bulletin*, No. 33a (July 4, 1918).

26. *Four Minute Men News*, Edition D, 1.

27. *Four Minute Men Bulletin*, No. 7A, 6. In Cincinnati the captain of the city's Four Minute Men (he was also the vice-mayor) sat on a committee, made up of a Four Minute Man, a motion-picture theater manager, and a teacher of speech, which evaluated would-be speakers, offered advice for improvement, and classified them so that the best speakers would be sent to the most important theaters. B. C. Van Wye, "Speech Training for Patriotic Service," *Quarterly Journal of Speech Education* 4 (Oct. 1918): 269.

28. Nicholas, "Crossroads Oratory," 82.

29. George Creel to William H. Ingersoll, Oct. 28, 1918, CPI papers, CPI 1–A1, Box 14, Folder 331.

30. Although movie audiences were the major focus of the Four Minute Men, the division by no means confined its efforts to theaters. As the section expanded, a Women's Division was organized to cover women's clubs. Junior Four Minute Men were enrolled, and young people "rallied with a whoop."

Some two hundred thousand schools held contests to see who could present the best junior four-minute speech. College Four Minute Men were established in September 1918. At Vassar this program was coordinated with public speaking courses offered to women and worked so well that it continued after the national organization disbanded. In addition to supporting the Liberty Loans and the United War Work Campaign, the Vassar speakers were a force for promoting public health in Dutchess County and surrounding areas. By the end of the war the Four Minute Men covered nearly every type of meeting place, including labor unions, factories, social clubs, lodges, Sunday schools, churches, and synagogues. In Illinois nearly two thousand ministers enrolled as Four Minute Men. The division expanded to include the army, and three *Four Minute Men Army Bulletins* were published. Four issues of a special *School Bulletin* were published, which were devoted to the Third and Fourth Liberty Loans, war savings stamps, and the Red Cross Christmas Roll Call. See Creel, *How We Advertised America*, 91.

For the Four Minute Men program at Vassar, see Mary Yost, "Training Four Minute Men at Vassar," *Quarterly Journal of Speech Education* 5 (May 1919): 246–53. For their efforts on behalf of public health, see 251, 252. There were other instances where the Four Minute Men assisted in public health matters. When an influenza epidemic broke out in the autumn of 1918, New York health authorities asked for help. George W. Carpenter, the city's Four Minute Man chairman, instructed his speakers to discuss ways to prevent the flu and to treat its victims. George W. Carpenter to "All Four Minute Men," Oct. 31, 1918, CPI papers, CPI 14–A–2 (Sept.–Dec. 1918).

A special effort to reach factory workers was made by speaking during the noon hour. See George W. Carpenter to "All Speakers," Aug. 16, 1918, ibid. (July–Aug. 1918). For ministers who were Four Minute Men, see Jenison, *War-Time Organizations of Illinois*, 46. The army bulletins were entitled "Why We Are Fighting," "Insurance For Soldiers and Sailors," and "Back of the Trenches."

31. It is difficult to say how closely the CPI's instructions were followed by Four Minute Men at the state and local levels. Information for most states is incomplete, but in Connecticut there is evidence to suggest that the State Council of Defense had greater control over Four Minute Men than did the CPI and that often committee expectations were frustrated. See Bruce Fraser, "Yankees at War: Social Mobilization on the Connecticut Homefront, 1917–1918" (doctoral dissertation, Columbia University, 1976), 221, 225; see also 216–33.

32. Sometimes speakers who exceeded the four-minute limit were silenced by members of the audience; in Kentucky violence was used to stop a Four Minute Man who had gone on for nearly twenty minutes. In New York a few theater managers complained that Four Minute Men held down movie attendance. Bean, "George Creel and His Critics," 263–64.

33. *Four Minute Men Bulletin*, No. 7A, 5–6. The speaker was informed that he was "an accredited speaker for a Government office created by order of the President and [was] morally bound to conduct himself with the dignity proper for the service." *Four Minute Men News*, Edition F, 3.

34. Ibid., 2–3. The content of these bulletins had wider circulation than that given by Four Minute Men. Division headquarters prepared articles and released them through chairmen and publicity managers for use in local papers. One estimate indicated that the Four Minute Men secured at least nine hundred thousand lines of newspaper publicity. During the influenza epidemic in the autumn of 1918, when public meetings were banned, newspapers gave space daily to four-minute speeches prepared by members of the organization. Creel calculated that this publicity given to the government would have cost $750,000. *Creel Report*, 28–29.

35. *Four Minute Men Bulletin*, No. 24 (Feb. 18, 1918); ibid., No. 21 (May 27, 1918).

36. Ibid., No. 33 (June 29, 1918): 14.

37. Ibid., 11. The *Four Minute Men Bulletins* also supported internationalism and the League of Nations. See bulletins 44 and 46. Also see Elmer E. Cornwell, Jr., "Wilson, Creel, and the Presidency," *Public Opinion Quarterly* 23 (Summer 1959): 200–201.

38. *Four Minute Men Bulletin*, No. 33, 1.

39. Ibid., 2.   40. Ibid., 15.

41. Ibid., 4.   42. Ibid., 5, 6.

43. Ibid., 10.   44. Ibid., 6.

45. Ibid., No. 26 (Mar. 11, 1918): 1, 3.

46. Ibid., No. 41 (Oct. 15, 1918): 5. Statements on the importance of fire prevention included ones from President Wilson and from Secretaries McAdoo, Daniels, and Lane.

47. Ibid., No. 29 (Apr. 6, 1918): 11.

48. See ibid., No. 1 (May 12, 1917); ibid., No. 2 (May 16, 1917); ibid., No. 5 (June 14, 1917); ibid., No. 6 (June 16, 1917); ibid., No. 8 (June 25, 1917); ibid., No. 9 (June 26, 1917); ibid., No. 10 (July 8, 1917); ibid., No. 18 (Oct. 29, 1917); ibid., Supplement 18a (Oct. 29, 1917); ibid., No. 19 (Nov. 12, 1917); ibid., No. 20B (Dec. 17, 1917); ibid., No. 21 (Jan. 2, 1918); ibid., No. 23 (Feb. 11, 1918); ibid., No. 27 (Mar. 25, 1918); ibid., No. 30 (May 13, 1918); ibid., No. 32 (June 24, 1918); ibid., No. 35 (Aug 26, 1918); ibid., No. 37 (Aug. 21, 1918); ibid., No. 40 (Oct. 20, 1918); ibid., No. 43 (Dec. 7, 1918); ibid., No. 45 (Dec. 15, 1918).

49. For discussion of appeals to hate and fear and the necessity of basing such appeals on fact, see *Four Minute Men News*, Edition B, 1–2. Ingersoll believed that reason and emotion were both part of human nature. It was necessary first to convince people's reason and then to "prompt their feelings to induce action." He believed that four-minute speeches should be ads rather than addresses. See William H. Ingersoll, "The Body," in George William

Poole and Jonathan John Buzzell, eds., *Letters That Make Good: A Desk Book for Business Men* (Boston, 1913, 1915), 49–50; and Nicholas, "Crossroads Oratory," 283.

50. *Four Minute Men News*, Edition D, 14–15.

51. *Four Minute Men Bulletin*, No. 21 (Jan. 2, 1918): 10. For other atrocity stories approved by the Four Minute Men, see ibid., 8. Often these stories were taken from the CPI pamphlet "German War Practices."

52. Ibid., No. 39 (Sept. 12, 1918): 27–28.

53. Ibid., No. 20 (Nov. 26, 1917): 8. The Four Minute Men made a variety of appeals: to the willingness to do one's "bit," to national honor and local pride (especially in financial campaigns to see which area could do the most), to desire for punishment and retribution for Germany's wrongdoing, to desire to assist soldiers, to self-interest and financial gain, to humanitarian feeling. For an analysis of appeals made by these speakers, see Nicholas, "Crossroads Oratory," 164–72.

54. *Creel Report*, 32. Within just a few weeks after America entered the war, more than a dozen national speakers' bureaus had been established by government departments or by other organizations seeking to further the national interest. Many more speaking campaigns had been launched at the state level by councils of defense or other associations. Competition for speakers, duplication of effort, and a general failure to coordinate these attempts into an effective campaign had been the result. The Speaking Division sought to remedy this chaotic situation.

55. From May until September 1917, Bestor had been chairman of the committee of lecturers and entertainments in training camps for the YMCA War Council, and secretary of the Committee on Patriotism through Education for the National Security League. He was selected for the CPI post at a meeting in the Food Administration Building on Sept. 14, 1917. For the people present at this meeting, see Guy Stanton Ford to Arthur E. Bestor, Sept. 14, 1917, CPI papers, CPI 12–A2, Box 189, Folder: "Reports— Speaking Division." President Wilson thought Bestor an excellent choice. Woodrow Wilson to George Creel, undated, in *Creel Report*, 32.

56. Arthur E. Bestor, "Mobilizing the Mind of America," *Independent* 94 (Aug. 31, 1918): 290.

57. Memorandum, Arthur E. Bestor to Edgar Sisson, Oct. 5, 1917, CPI papers, CPI 12-A1, Box 176, A–1–12.

58. All of Bestor's activities with the National Security League were in connection with the Committee on Patriotism through Education. During the first week of the Chautauqua season in 1917, that institution and the NSL committee conducted at Chautauqua a training camp for speakers engaged in patriotic service. Upon his appointment as director of the Speaking Division, Bestor asked that his title as secretary of the committee be eliminated; eventually, at Creel's request, he resigned from membership in the committee. Arthur E. Bestor to Guy S. Ford, Oct. 22, 1917, CPI papers, CPI 12–A1,

Box 177, A–1–18; Arthur E. Bestor to George Creel, Oct. 22, 1917, ibid., Box 180, B–2–4 (Creel's reply written on this letter); Arthur E. Bestor to Robert M. McElroy, Oct. 24, 1917, ibid., Box 177, A–3–8.

59. Arthur E. Bestor, "Chautauqua's Chance To-Day," *Independent* 91 (July 7, 1917): 17, 18. Promoting a spirit of democratic idealism in the United States that would bring about national unity had been one of Bestor's concerns long before the war. See, for example, a Fourth of July oration given in 1910 entitled "The New Patriotism." Arthur Bestor Papers, University of Illinois Archives, Urbana, Box 116.

60. J. J. Pettijohn had been director of the extension division of Indiana University and had been in charge of the Indiana State Speakers' Bureau. W. Frank McClure, publicity director of the Redpath Bureau in Chicago, helped with publicity matters during Nov. 1917.

61. Government departments represented on the Advisory Committee included the Treasury Department, Department of Labor, Department of Agriculture, Department of the Interior, Council of National Defense, Woman's Committee on National Defense, Food Administration, Secretary of War's Commission on Training Camp Activities, American Red Cross, Four Minute Men, National War Savings Committee, and the CPI. Nongovernmental organizations represented included the American Alliance for Labor and Democracy, League for National Unity, National Community Center Association, Knights of Columbus, International Lyceum Association, National Committee of Patriotic and Defense Societies, National War Work Council, YMCA, National Security League, League to Enforce Peace, Chamber of Commerce of the United States, International Association of Rotary Clubs, Open Forum, American Civic Association, Associated Advertising Clubs, Association of Intercollegiate Alumnae, National Americanization Committee, Church Peace Union, General Federation of Women's Clubs, and American-Russian Chamber of Commerce. See United States Committee on Public Information, Speaking Division Bulletin, No. 1 (Jan. 1918): 3.

62. Because the Speaking Division was primarily a coordinating agency, there were relatively few orators under its direct control, but the division did keep a file of over ten thousand names of people who were considered good speakers and who were also thought to be community opinion makers. In addition, a catalog of three hundred of the most effective speakers was maintained, so that the division could make direct recommendations to organizations in need of speakers. Bestor also tried to enlist a corps of speakers, ten or twelve of whom would be at his disposal on short notice for strategic situations. Solomon Clark was among those asked to be in the latter group. Creel, *How We Advertised America*, 150–51; Arthur E. Bestor to S. H. Clark, Sept. 29, 1917, CPI papers, CPI 12–A1, Box 178, A–6–12. For a list of over five hundred speakers see ibid., Box 184, L–1–1.

63. Bestor, "Mobilizing the Mind of America," 300. This address was delivered at the Chautauqua Institution on Independence Day. For an address by Bestor before the state war conference of the New Jersey Council of

Defense, Trenton, on May 7, 1918, see Arthur E. Bestor, "The War and Making of Public Opinion," *New Jersey Municipalities* 2 (Oct. 1918): 231–32, 247–48.

64. See Arthur E. Bestor to Milton J. Davies (Institute of Arts and Sciences, Columbia University), Dec. 28, 1917, CPI papers, CPI 12–A1, Box 185, P–2–1. Bestor submitted "America and the War" to be considered for the CPI's War Information Series; it was submitted also to the NSL. Arthur E. Bestor to Guy S. Ford, Oct. 1, 1917, ibid., Box 177, A–1–18. Even after the war, Bestor continued to stress national unity, saying that "emphasis upon the rights of the nation over and above the rights of any individual or organization is the . . . thing that the public needs and wants." Arthur E. Bestor, "The Old World and the New Order," *Proceedings and Papers of the Indiana State Teachers' Association* (Oct. 30, 31, and Nov. 1, 1919): 230.

65. Even then, Bestor often had a disagreeable time. Arthur E. Bestor to Judge William L. Ransom (Public Service Commission, New York City), Dec. 7, 1917, CPI papers, CPI 12–A1, Box 185, R–3–2.

66. S. H. Clark to Guy S. Ford, Dec. 3, 1917, ibid., Box 178, A–6–12; S. H. Clark to George Creel, Mar. 2, 1918, ibid.

67. Arthur E. Bestor to S. H. Clark, Dec. 21, 1917, ibid.; Clark to Bestor, Mar. 15, 1918, ibid. Clark also believed that speakers, including himself, should be paid more for their efforts in behalf of the government. S. H. Clark (memorandum) to A. E. Bestor, W. M. Blair, and George Creel, Dec. 22, 1917, ibid.

68. When the Food Administration curtailed its speaking service in early Mar. 1918, Addams's speaking engagements were put under the auspices of the CPI. Although her fragile health hindered her travel, with Bestor's assistance a speaking engagement was also set up in early May for the General Federation of Women's Clubs in Hot Springs, Ark. Herbert Hoover to Jane Addams, Mar. 2, 1918, Jane Addams Correspondence, Swarthmore College Peace Collection, Swarthmore, Pa. Reel 1.5; Arthur E. Bestor to George Creel, Jan. 30, 1918, CPI papers, CPI 12–Al, Box 180, B–2–4; Jane Addams to Arthur Bestor, Jan. 24, 1918, ibid., Box 179, A–10–10; Bestor to Addams, Jan. 31, 1918, ibid.; Addams to Bestor, Feb. 9, 1918, ibid.; Bestor to Addams, Feb. 19, 1918, ibid.; Addams to Bestor, Mar. 1, 1918, ibid.

69. Jane Addams, *Second Twenty Years at Hull-House, September 1909 to September 1929: With a Record of a Growing World Consciousness* (New York, 1930), ix, 144. During her speaking tour, Addams tried to interest high school girls in the War Garden movement and encouraged women's organizations to support food conservation measures. She hoped such organizations would place themselves "at the disposal of the state" during the war crisis, but she also expressed the belief that a league of nations might come out of the allied countries' attempt to solve the food problem. See San Francisco *Examiner*, Mar. 29, 1918, p. 10; ibid., Mar. 28, 1918, p. 11. See also ibid., p. 15; ibid., Mar. 24, 1918, p. 10; and Los Angeles *Times*, Mar. 20, 1918, p. 5.

70. Charles Edward Russell to George Creel, CPI papers, CPI 1–A1, Box

24, Folder 15. Russell wrote extensively about Russia and bolshevism during this period. See Charles Edward Russell, *Unchained Russia* (New York, 1918); and Russell, *Bolshevism and the United States* (Indianapolis, 1919).

71. "Address of Charles Edward Russell," in *America's Message to the Russian People: Addresses by the Diplomatic Mission of the United States to Russia in the Year 1917* (Boston, 1918), 153, 154.

72. The Socialist party expelled Russell while he was in Russia as a member of the Root mission. Russell rejected the view that American entry into the war had been dictated by the capitalists, and he believed that an Allied defeat would mean the triumph of German imperialism and treaty breaking, making impossible any sort of just international order. Russell, *Bare Hands and Stone Walls*, 282–98.

73. Charles Edward Russell, "The New Socialist Alignment," *Harper's Magazine* 136 (Mar. 1918): 568–69, 570.

He would write in 1919 that "the crowning grandeur of this war, surpassing even the magnificence of the fall of autocracy, the death of militarism, the dawn of democracy in lands always strange to it . . . is the promise that the industrial system that has cursed mankind and blighted so many millions of lives is passing with the other anomalies of the dead old Night." Russell, *After the Whirlwind: A Book of Reconstruction and Profitable Thanksgiving* (New York, 1919), 313.

74. These remarks were made before Russell began speaking under the auspices of Bestor's division. See New York *Times*, Sept. 16, 1917, Section 1, p. 1. Russell believed that "for freedom and the emancipation of men the Russian revolution was the grandest event in human history." From an address by Charles Edward Russell before the Council of Workmen's, Soldiers' and Peasants' Delegates, June 12, 1917, in *America's Message to the Russian People*, 143.

75. Edgar Sisson to Arthur E. Bestor, Sept. 28, 1917, CPI papers, CPI 12–A1, Box 176, A–1–12.

76. "Address of Charles Edward Russell at a Reception by the Union League Club of New York City, August 15, 1917," in *America's Message to the Russian People*, 151.

Russell's speeches often warned of German agents working in the United States—see, for example, his speech before the Indiana Red Cross in Indianapolis. Indianapolis *News*, Oct. 30, 1917, pp. 1, 22. He also believed that his efforts were being sabotaged by German agents and complained to Creel of their efforts to discredit him in Spartanburg, S.C. See Charles Edward Russell to George Creel, Feb. 23, 1918, CPI papers, CPI 1–A1, Box 24, Folder 15. Russell was apparently one of the more temperamental speakers Bestor had to contend with. Though he often spoke on behalf of the American Alliance for Labor and Democracy, he was very dissatisfied with that organization. He was also unhappy with certain aspects of his speaking schedule. He asked Creel to see that whoever arranged his schedule would avoid putting him into churches, because, he said, "a church is a deadly place for the kind of meetings I want to hold." Undated memorandum on Charles Edward Russell, ibid., CPI 12–A1, Box 176, A–1–13; quotations from Russell to Creel, Jan. 4, 1918, ibid., CPI 1–A1, Box 24, Folder 15.

77. *Congressional Record*, 56, Part 8, 65th Congress, 2d Session, House of Representatives, June 17, 1918, pp. 7911–12. See also Louis J. Alber to Arthur E. Bestor, Oct. 18, 1917, CPI papers, CPI 12–A1, Box 178, A–9–12; *Creel Report*, 39; H. H. Cherry (Bowling Green, Ky.) to Arthur E. Bestor, Feb. 12, 1918, CPI papers, CPI 12–A1, Box 177, A–2–8; J. N. Darling (?) to Samuel Hopkins Adams, Nov. 12, 1917, Russell papers, Container 8; Byron Shimp to Arthur E. Bestor, Feb. 21, 1918, CPI papers, CPI 12–A1, Box 176, A–1–13; telegram, Byron W. Shimp to ?, Feb. 20, 1918, ibid., CPI 12–A5, Box 189, Folder: "Telegrams: A. E. Bestor B. W. Shimp."

Russell confided to Creel that he believed the attacks on him resulted from criticisms he made of capitalism and corporate power in America. But the corporations did not control public opinion, he said, as evidenced by the response to the work of the CPI. Creel apparently had some affection for Russell. Upon appointing Russell to CPI offices in England in April 1918, Creel expressed admiration for Russell's work, saying that his fondness for him had been increased "a thousandfold the past year" and that he had "been one of the greatest single powers in acquainting America with our war aims and in arousing the people to a realization of the national task." Russell to Creel, Apr. 17, 1918, ibid., CPI 1–A1, Box 24, Folder 15; Creel to Russell, Apr. 22, 1918, ibid.

Other Americans speaking under division auspices included Ford, Tatlock, Bertram Nelson, and James Scherer. Scherer was the chief field agent for the State Councils Section of the Council of National Defense for one year. He gives an account of his speaking tours in James A. B. Scherer, *Nation at War* (New York, 1918), in which he also discusses Ford and other speakers associated with the Speaking Division.

78. Quoted from Mock and Larson, *Words That Won the War*, 129.

79. Other foreign speakers sent out by the division included Lieutenant Hector MacQuarrie from the British War Mission, who delivered more than ninety speeches in four months; and Crawford Vaughan, former prime minister of South Australia and a noted labor leader, who gave twenty-two addresses. Captain Roald Amundsen, who had observed American troops at the front, was successful before Scandinavian-American audiences and spoke more than a dozen times in six states in Mar. and Apr. 1918. The division also cooperated in arranging for speakers through such groups as the Friends of German Democracy and the American Alliance for Labor and Democracy. For a more complete list of prominent individuals sponsored by the Speaking Division, see *Creel Report*, 37–39. For Bestor's interest in using uniformed

speakers on active duty, see Arthur E. Bestor to George Creel, Dec. 4, 1917, CPI papers, CPI 12–A1, Box 180, B–2–4; and Arthur E. Bestor to George F. Porter, Mar. 1, 1918, ibid., Box 177, A–1–19.

80. Creel, *How We Advertised America*, 152; George Creel to General John J. Pershing, Sept. 30, 1918, CPI papers, CPI 1–A1, Box 21, Folder 28.

81. Scherer, *Nation at War*, 190. Small once remarked that in all his years of university teaching, he considered his association with Périgord to have been the most notable. When Germany invaded Belgium in autumn 1914, Périgord immediately left for France to enlist as a soldier. He won a field commission but was severely wounded and forced from front-line duty. In America, he became known as the "warrior priest." After the war, Périgord became a professor of French civilization at UCLA.

82. *Creel Report*, 38; J. J. Pettijohn to A. E. Bestor, Jan. 5, 1918, CPI papers, CPI 12–A1, Box 181, C–1–2; Albion Small to Arthur E. Bestor, undated (late Oct. 1917), ibid., Box 180, B–4–6.

83. Scherer, *Nation at War*, 193–94.

84. Ibid., 201. There are other excerpts from Périgord's speeches in this work.

85. See Byron W. Shimp, "Report of the Speaking Division, Committee on Public Information," undated, CPI papers, CPI 12–A2, Box 189, Folder: "Reports Speaking Division," 3–4. The first three bulletins from the Speaking Division were entitled *Purpose and Scope of the Work of the Speaking Division*, *The Issues of the War at a Glance*, and *Ships, Ships, and Yet More Ships—the Nation's Greatest Need*. At least three subsequent bulletins were published, but they were one-page newsletters signed by Bestor.

86. Arthur E. Bestor to George Creel, Dec. 31, 1917, CPI papers, CPI 12–A1, Box 180, B–2–4. See also Bestor to Creel, Feb. 7, 1918, ibid., CPI 1–A1, Box 2, Folder 40; Arthur E. Bestor to Harold L. Ickes (State Council of Defense, Chicago), Nov. 6, 1917, ibid., CPI 12–A1, Box 179, B–1–25; Arthur E. Bestor to Norman Angell, Feb. 7, 1918, ibid., Folder A–10–4/A–10–6; and "Address by Mr. Arthur E. Bestor," undated and apparently delivered in Pennsylvania, ibid., Box 176, A–1–16, p. 3.

87. "Address by Mr. Arthur E. Bestor," 4–5. It was probably Frederick Allen of the Council of National Defense who first suggested to Bestor the use of state councils. Frederick L. Allen to Arthur E. Bestor, Sept. 12, 1917, CPI papers, CPI 12–A1, Box 177, A–1–19.

88. George F. Porter, "Memorandum with Regard to Speaking and Information Campaign" (Confidential), undated, ibid., pp. 1–2.

89. Byron W. Shimp to Glenn N. Merry, Oct. 27, 1917, ibid., A–5–8. Speakers' bureaus also tried to persuade newspapers to give speakers the greatest possible publicity. To cooperate with the speakers' bureaus a committee was to be set up, which would represent the State Council of Defense, the State Division of the Woman's Committee, the Extension Division of the Department of Agriculture, the State Department of Education, the Extension

Division of the State University, the State Department of Labor, the State Community Organizer, the Four Minute Men, the Federal Food and Fuel Administrators, and patriotic societies that had carried on effective speaking campaigns or that had ready-made audiences.

90. Arthur E. Bestor to David F. Houston, Mar. 28, 1918, CPI papers, CPI 12–A1, Box 178, A–9–3; Arthur E. Bestor to Frederic Walcott, Apr. 8, 1918, ibid., Box 177, A–1–17.

91. For the suggested plan of organization for the states see Byron W. Shimp, "Report of the Speaking Division, Committee on Public Information," ibid., CPI 12–A2, Box 189, Folder: "Reports Speaking Division." Also see Council of National Defense, "State Council Speakers' Bureaus," Bulletin No. 72 (Nov. 16, 1917), ibid., CPI 12–A1, Box 177, A–1–19.

92. Woodrow Wilson to "Mr. Chairman," Mar. 13, 1918, ibid., Box 180, B–3–3.

93. In Connecticut an old-line elite concerned with preserving traditional values strongly influenced the state council and the entire mobilization effort. The state council maintained a "gate-keeping influence" over CPI material that appeared in the state and often presented the public with a version of the war different from that coming from Washington. See Fraser, "Yankees at War." For the operation of the CPI's Speaking Division in Connecticut, see ibid., 214–16.

94. George B. Chandler to Richard M. Bissell, Dec. 8, 1917, CPI papers, CPI 12–A1, Box 181, C–1–1, p. 4.

95. Form letter from George B. Chandler, Nov. 17, 1917, ibid.

96. "The Workman's Stake in the World War," ibid., CPI 3–A1, Box 71, L–1–1594, p. 1. A bibliography was also included with this outline.

97. Chandler to Bissell, Dec. 8, 1917, 5; "Confidential Report on Speakers and Rallies," undated, CPI papers, CPI 12–A1, Box 181, C–1–1.

98. This service also provided useful information about the working of the county and town auxiliary committees and furnished information for speakers' use. The publicity committee sent out at least two bulletins containing material for speeches. "Memorandum on Publicity Work of State Councils of Defense," Oct. 26, 1917, ibid., CPI 3–A1, Box 63, L–1–328, pp. 2, 4, 7.

99. Chandler to Bissell, Dec. 8, 1917, 6.

100. Ibid., 7.

101. Frederick L. Allen to Arthur E. Bestor, Apr. 12, 1918, CPI papers, CPI 12–A1, Box 177, A–1–19. Also see interview with Arthur E. Bestor, given to the Committee on Public Safety for the Commonwealth of Pennsylvania, ibid., Box 186, S–2–4.

102. The Minnesota Public Safety Commission especially objected to the Nonpartisan League's sponsoring CPI speakers. See Carol Elizabeth Jenson, "Agrarian Pioneer in Civil Liberties: The Nonpartisan League in Minnesota during World War I" (doctoral dissertation, University of Minnesota, 1968), 160–68.

103. M. P. Goodner (executive secretary, State Council of Defense, Olympia, Wash.) to Arthur E. Bestor, Feb. 21, 1918, CPI papers, CPI 12–A1, Box 181, C–2–4.

104. Allen to Bestor, Mar. 29, 1918, ibid., Box 177, A–1–19.

105. *Creel Report*, 35.

106. The state's speakers' bureau paid for the band's travel expenses only. Byron W. Shimp to T. J. Preston, Dec. 21, 1917, CPI papers, CPI 12–A1, Box 178, A–7–1; J. J. Pettijohn to A. E. Bestor, Dec. 27, 1917, ibid., C–1–2.

107. Indianapolis *News*, Dec. 14, 1917, p. 24.

CHAPTER EIGHT

1. William C. D'Arcy, "The Achievements of Advertising in a Year," *Printers' Ink* 104 (July 11, 1918): 17. This statement was from an address given to the Associated Advertising Clubs of the World.

2. Carlton J. H. Hayes, *Essays on Nationalism* (New York, 1926, 1966), 1; David M. Potter, "Advertising: The Institution of Abundance," *Yale Review* 43 (Autumn 1953): 50.

3. Very little has been written about the development of the advertising profession during the First World War. Many accounts mention the CPI, noting that the war was good publicity for the advertising profession, but generally they do not go beyond this assertion. Some works seem to reach different conclusions about the importance of the CPI. Thus, one account says "neither the concepts nor the techniques of the CPI added significantly to the development of publicity," and another argues that the committee, through Edward L. Bernays, used the "most modern psychological ideas." See Alan R. Raucher, *Public Relations and Business, 1900–1929* (Baltimore, 1968), 74; and Thomas C. Cochran, *American Business System: A Historical Perspective, 1900–1955* (Cambridge, Mass., 1957), 77.

Although Eric Goldman notes that the "American entrance into World War I brought a brilliant publicity for publicity," he says little about the CPI and confines his discussion of the committee mainly to Creel and Bernays. Otis Pease concentrates on the post-1920 era and tells us only that the CPI's use of advertisers "doubtless contributed to their enhanced prestige." See Eric F. Goldman, *Two-Way Street: The Emergence of the Public Relations Counsel* (Boston, 1948), 11; and Otis Pease, *Responsibilities of American Advertising: Private Control and Public Influence, 1920–1940* (New Haven, 1958), 17. James P. Wood mentions the CPI only briefly in his discussion of advertising during the war, and Frank Presbrey does not discuss the committee. Mock and Larson's section on the Division of Advertising is one of their most disappointing, as it does not go much beyond Creel's account in *How We Advertised America*. See James Playsted Wood, *Story of Advertising* (New York, 1958), 354–55; Frank Presbrey, *History and Development of Advertising* (New York, 1929, 1968), 565–70; and Mock and Larson, *Words That Won the War*, 72, 96–101. With the exception of the work by Mock and Larson, these studies have relied on Creel and Bernays as their sources of primary information.

4. Creel, *How We Advertised America*, 4, 156.

5. Edward L. Bernays, *Public Relations* (Norman, Okla., 1952), 72.

6. D'Arcy, "The Achievements of Advertising in a Year," 17.

7. Houston described the creation of the advisory board in a speech before the Advertising Association of Chicago on Apr. 6, 1917. See Herbert S. Houston, "A.A.C. of W. on Firing Line," *Judicious Advertising* 15 (Apr. 1917): 39–42.

A member of the committee on resolutions of the League to Enforce Peace (he claimed to have been involved in suggesting the name for the organization), Houston was a member of the committee that drafted the platform of the league at Independence Hall in Philadelphia in June 1915. He also was treasurer of the league. Houston was a member of the Committee of the Chamber of Commerce of the United States on Economic Results of the War, and chairman of the committee on Foreign Trade of the Council of Foreign Relations. He also had edited the Spanish edition of *World's Work*.

8. See Houston, "The New Morals of Advertising," 384–88; Herbert S. Houston, "Working Out Business Ethics," *World's Work* 30 (Sept. 1915): 559–64; Houston, "The Spirit of the Convention," *Judicious Advertising* 15 (June 1917): 75–76, quoting Houston's address to the AACW convention. See also Houston, "Advertising and Victory," ibid. 34 (Aug. 1917): 457; Houston, "A.A.C. of W. on Firing Line," 42; Houston, *Blocking New Wars*, 126.

9. In New York the effort had been placed entirely on a voluntary basis. Creel, *How We Advertised America*, 157. The "Chicago Plan" had been used in the First Liberty Loan drive, and it was estimated that it helped bring in one million dollars. In Muncie, Ind., for instance, it had doubled the quota of bonds. Ibid. Though businesses were allowed to place their names on donated advertising in the First Liberty Loan, in the Second Liberty Loan campaign—at least in Chicago, where Rankin was in charge—names of contributors were omitted from war advertisements. See William H. Rankin to George Creel, Sept. 21, 1918, CPI papers, CPI 1–A1, Box 23, Folder: "Rankin, Wm. H."

10. *Editor and Publisher* 50 (June 16, 1917): 16.

11. *Editor and Publisher* strongly backed the campaign for paid advertising.

12. New York *Times*, Sept. 13, 1917, p. 12.

13. Ibid., Sept. 20, 1917, p. 12. In a speech in Indianapolis, Houston estimated that businessmen had spent more than five million dollars advertising the Second Liberty Loan and that the government could have done the same job for as little as two million dollars. *Editor and Publisher* 50 (Nov. 17, 1917): 5.

14. Ibid. (Aug. 18, 1917): 27.

15. Ibid. (Nov. 3, 1917): 16; ibid. (Dec. 8, 1917): 19.

16. Ibid. (June 16, 1917): 6; ibid. (Sept. 15, 1917): 6. See also ibid. (Nov. 24, 1917): 9.

17. Ibid. (Aug. 25, 1917): 3.

18. New York *Times*, Sept. 15, 1917, p. 10.

19. Creel, *How We Advertised America*, 156–57.

20. See John Sullivan to George Creel, Nov. 22, 1917, CPI papers, CPI 1–C6, Folder: "Misc. Advertising"; Frank E. Long (president, Agricultural Publishers Association) to George Creel, Nov. 30, 1917, ibid.; Herman C. Halsted (president, Six Point League) to Carl Byoir, Dec. 15, 1917, ibid.

21. *Editor and Publisher* 50 (Dec. 8, 1917): 7.

22. Sullivan to Creel, Nov. 22, 1917. See also John Sullivan to Carl Byers [sic], Nov. 28, 1917, CPI papers, CPI 1–C6, Folder: "Misc. Advertising."

23. *Editor and Publisher* 50 (Jan. 26, 1918): 7. Plans for the Division of Advertising were announced on Dec. 18, 1917, at a meeting in the Hotel McAlpin in New York City. Mock and Larson, *Words That Won the War*, 96. The directors of the division were announced the following day. John Sullivan, "The Truth about the Division of Advertising," *Advertising News* 27 (July 20, 1918): 14.

24. See "Credit to Whom Credit Is Due," ibid. (July 27, 1918): 4–5. For John Sullivan's account of the division's creation, see ibid. (July 20, 1918): 14. For evidence that division members retained their views about paid advertising, see *Editor and Publisher* 50 (Feb. 23, 1918): 16.

25. The purpose of the AAAA was to cooperate with publishers' associations across the country in an effort to raise advertising standards. William H. Johns had been a founder of the AAAA. For Johns's election as president of the association, and for its platform, see ibid. (June 16, 1917): 3–4.

26. Johns was public spirited and at one time was director of the Society for Prevention of Cruelty to Children. Shortly after the war he became president of the Chamber of Commerce of the Borough of Queens, New York.

27. *Editor and Publisher* 51 (Mar. 1, 1919): 9.

28. *Creel Report*, 43–44. Also see Committee on Public Information, "Purpose and Scope of the Work of the Division of Advertising," Bulletin No. 1 (June 1, 1918), CPI papers, CPI 14–A2, Folder: "July–Aug; 1918."

29. Carl Byoir to O. C. Harn, Mar. ? 1918, CPI papers, CPI 14–A3, Folder: "Dec. 1917–Feb. 1918."

30. *Editor and Publisher* 50 (Feb. 23, 1918): 16. Byoir's horizons were not limited by his advertising accounts. After the war he went to Europe and at the urging of Bernays visited the latter's uncle, Sigmund Freud, in Vienna. Byoir had a part in introducing Freud's *General Introductory Lectures to Psychoanalysis* in the United States. See [Bernays], *Biography of an Idea*, 197–98.

31. C. E. Walberg to Carl Byoir, Feb. 6, 1918, CPI papers, CPI 1–C6, Folder: "Misc. Advertising"; Walberg to Byoir, undated, ibid.

The advertising division was assisted by Rankin, Clarence A. Hope, and Harold A. Lebair, who was to be treasurer of Sherman and Bryan, Inc. For Lebair's account of the work of the Division of Advertising, see Harold A. Lebair, "How Advertising Division Worked to Tremendous Achievement," *Editor and Publisher* 51 (Jan. 25, 1919): 15.

32. For the complete text of the executive order see *Creel Report*, 43.

33. United States Committee on Public Information, "Report on conference with the *Division of Advertising*" (Jan. 7, 1918), CPI papers, CPI 1–C6, Folder: "Misc. Advertising."

34. George Creel to William B. Wilson, Jan. 12, 1918, ibid.

35. For Johns's statement concerning the scope of the Division of Advertising, see New York *Times*, Jan. 20, 1917, p. 6.

36. Ralph Hayes was delegated to represent Secretary of War Baker; Edward E. Britton stood in for Secretary of the Navy Daniels; the Agriculture Department was represented by Clarence Qusley, the U.S. Food Administration by P. B. Noyes, the chairman of the U.S. Shipping Board by Robert D. Beinl, and the chairman of the Red Cross War Council by Clarence D. Newell; and Charles S. Ward was to be the agent for the General Secretary of the YMCA. "Statement," CPI papers, CPI 1–A2.

37. "Statement," ibid., CPI 1–C6, Folder: "Misc. Advertising." These advertising clubs usually appointed their own committees to work with the Division of Advertising. For the committee appointed by the American Association of Advertisers, see *Editor and Publisher* 50 (Jan. 12, 1918): 27. For committees appointed by the Associated Business Papers and the Agricultural Publishers Association see ibid. (Jan. 19, 1918): 29.

38. William H. Johns to J. Cotner, Jr. (of *American Boy*), Feb. 20, 1918, CPI papers, CPI 14–A1, Box 203, Folder: "America A to E"; William H. Johns to George French (editor, *Advertising News*), Mar. 11, 1918, ibid., Folder: "Abe-Ain"; William H. Johns to Frank B. White (Agricultural Publishers Association), Mar. 5, 1918, ibid., Folder: "Agricultural Publishers Assoc."; Carl Byoir to Fleming Newbold (Washington *Star*), Mar. 14, 1918, ibid., CPI 1–C6, Folder: "Misc. Advertising"; H. A. Lebair to *Journal of Acetylene Welding*, May 24, 1918, ibid., CPI 14–A1, Box 203, Folder: "Abe-Ain"; George Creel to Edward Percy Howard (of American Press), Jan. 2, 1918, ibid., CPI 14–A3, Folder: "Dec. 1917–Feb. 1918."

39. Collin Armstrong to "Fellow Members," Feb. 6, 1918, ibid., CPI 1–C6, Folder: "Misc. Advertising." Organizations such as the Agricultural Publishers Association made equally direct appeals to members. There were many businessmen, of course, who gave space without having been subjected to any pressure. See letter signed by Frank B. White, chairman, Frank E. Long, James M. Pierce, Marco Morrow, and Wm. A. Whitney, Feb. 28, 1918, ibid., CPI 14–A1, Box 203, Folder: "Agricultural Publishers Assoc." A portion of this letter is quoted in Mock and Larson, *Words That Won the War*, 99.

40. William H. Johns (WHJ) to C. E. Walberg, Mar. 11, 1918, ibid., CPI 14–A3, Folder: "March–April 1918." Mock and Larson also note the joining of a patriotic message with a commercial appeal, citing the example of *Wear-Ever Magazine*, which was put out by the Aluminum Cooking Utensil Company of New Kinsington, Pa. Mock and Larson, *Words That Won the War*, 99.

Byoir also urged flexibility in the government's policy of accepting advertising, letting contributors associate merchandise with the government's cause. Houston supported a similar plan. Carl R. Byoir to William H. Johns, Jan. 2, 1918, CPI papers, CPI 14–A3, Folder: "Dec. 1917–Feb. 1918." See Herbert S. Houston to "Chairman Johns and My Associates in the Division of Advertising," Aug. 9, 1918, ibid., CPI 14–A1, Box 215, Folder: "Herbert S. Houston."

41. Quoted from a poem by Wallace Irwin, "Thoughts Inspired by a War-Time Billboard," in Fairfax Downey, *Portrait of an Era as Drawn by C. D. Gibson* (New York, 1936), 332.

42. Downey, *Portrait of an Era*, 328. See also Mock and Larson, *Words That Won the War*, 101.

43. William H. Johns to Carl Byoir, Jan. 28, 1918, CPI papers, CPI 14–A3, Folder: "Dec. 1917–Feb. 1918."

44. Unfortunately, most of the records of the Division of Pictorial Publicity were not included in the CPI collection in the National Archives. Division of Classification, National Archives, *Classification Scheme: Records of the Committee on Public Information, 1917–1919* (Washington, D.C., 1938), xv.

45. Downey, *Portrait of an Era*, 324; Mock and Larson, *Words That Won the War*, 102. The entire operation of the Division of Pictorial Publicity cost the government $13,170.97. Ibid.

46. Philadelphia *Record*, Magazine Section, Jan. 27, 1918, p. 11.

47. Ibid., 1, 7.

48. Ibid., 7; *New York Times Magazine*, Jan. 20, 1918, p. 11.

49. Philadelphia *Record*, Magazine Section, Jan. 27, 1918, p. 1.

50. Ibid.

51. The executive committee of the division consisted of William J. Beauley, F. G. Cooper, C. B. Falls, Louis Fancher, Malvina Hoffman, Wallace Morgan, Herbert Paus, W. A. Rogers, John E. Sheridan, Harry Townsend, Frank J. Sheridan, Jr., Adolph Triedler, H. Devitt Welch, and C. D. Williams. Ibid. Also, artists in other cities maintained offices that stayed in contact with Gibson's bureau: Dennett Grover was in Chicago, Edmond C. Tarbell was in Boston, and Arthur T. Matthews was in San Francisco serving in this capacity. Mock and Larson, *Words That Won the War*, 102.

For a summary of the activities of the Division of Pictorial Publicity, see *Creel Report*, 40–43.

52. Clarence A. Hope (CAH) to Leila Mechlin (*American Magazine of Art*), May 11, 1918, CPI papers, CPI 14–A1, Box 203, Folder: "American F–L."

53. *Creel Report*, 45. Campaigns were also conducted for the Council of National Defense, United War Work drives, and Training Camp Activities.

54. C. T. Adams, "Memorandum on Copy for Shipbuilding Advertisement," Feb. 9, 1918, CPI papers, CPI 1–C6, Folder: "advertising copies & layouts."

55. "Purpose and Scope of the Work of the Division of Advertising," [3].

56. Hubert L. Towle to Carl Byoir, Mar. 4, 1918, CPI papers, CPI 1–C6, Folder: "advertising copies & layouts."

57. For an account of this campaign see "'Uncle Sam's Employment Agency' Launches Big Advertising Drive," *Printers' Ink* 104 (Aug. 1, 1918): 83–85, with a list of firms cooperating on 84–85. See also Creel, *How We Advertised America*, 164.

58. For statistics on the various media employed in behalf of the Selective Service law, see *Creel Report*, 45–46.

59. To communicate with businessmen, the advertising division often used such periodicals as *Printers' Ink* and *Editor and Publisher*. These publications carried speeches and interviews with division members. Bruce Bliven was helpful in this regard: he was on the staff of *Printers' Ink* during the war and relayed the CPI's message to the business community.

60. Herbert S. Houston (hsh) to Carl Byoir, June 28, 1918, CPI papers, CPI 14–A3, Folder: "June–Dec. 1918."

61. See a letter drawn up apparently by Houston as a proposed greeting to the AACW convention from Bernard Baruch. Houston to Byoir, June 28, 1918.

62. See Herbert S. Houston, "Business and the Mailed Fist," *Judicious Advertising* 16 (Aug. 1918): 25–30.

63. As noted above, in note 83 to Chapter 4, Houston argued that a league of nations should use economic sanctions against erring nations to enforce peace. In 1915 he had said that, through a world court, nations could bring such economic pressure to bear on errant countries as to compel obedience to court decrees. Business, he stated in 1918, was the "protector of democracy." Representative democracy could serve "as a bond of union in a league of nations." Houston, *Blocking New Wars*, 125, 147; Houston, "Doing the World's International Work," 438–40; Herbert S. Houston, "Commerce to Enforce Peace," *Judicious Advertising* 13 (July 1915): 45–48.

64. L. B. Jones to Carl Byoir, Apr. 25, 1918, CPI papers, CPI 14–A3, Folder: "June–Nov. 1918." The *Spies and Lies* poster later gave way to other ads in the interest of maintaining army morale. A similar poster was entitled *Have You Met This Kaiserite?* Clarence A. Hope to Aluminum Company of America (Messena, N.Y.), Oct. 15, 1918, ibid., CPI 14–A1, Box 203, Folder: "Alb-Alu."

65. Clarence A. Hope to R. J. Kaylor(Youngstown Sheet and Tube Company), Sept. 24, 1918, ibid., Folder: "Yale-Zuk."

Actually, even though the first two loans had been floated before establishment of the advertising division, some of the section's personnel had been instrumental in developing the government's strategy for selling bonds. Early in May 1917, the Committee on Plan and Scope of the National Advertising Advisory Board had submitted to the Treasury Department a "Plan for Advertising and Selling." This report outlined a plan for the sale of government bonds, and several people signed it who were later to serve in the CPI's Division of Advertising: Harn, D'Arcy, Rankin, Johns, and Jones. The plan was submitted to Houston, and as chairman of the advisory board he presented it to Secretary McAdoo. Designed to reach the "masses," it was to finance the government and teach thrift to working people. Bonds were to be distributed through the twelve Federal Reserve Banks, charged by the government with managing the Liberty Loan. Other channels of distribution were to center on these banks. A variety of devices was suggested to encourage purchase of bonds. Banks might offer part payment plans, whereby money would be lent at 3.5 percent interest. Large employers were urged to advance money to their workers. In major cities, chain stores and other enterprises could be enlisted to sell the Liberty Loan. In rural areas, RFD carriers could solicit subscriptions for bonds delivered through local post offices.

The committee recommended a two-phase approach to selling Liberty bonds. The first would employ advertising copy that would educate the public. The second and shorter phase would emphasize "buy now" and try to stimulate the public to respond. As Houston would say, "Publicity gives information, but advertising spurs to action."

Advertising was to fit the audience. For the wealthy the committee suggested an appeal emphasizing patriotism and noting that bonds were tax exempt. For the middle class, patriotism and thrift would be the themes. For the poor the government would stress that the investment was safe and that it would bring added income. For the foreign born it would be emphasized that Liberty bonds were a perfect way to demonstrate loyalty.

This plan was altered for the Second and Third Liberty Loan drives, but the design remained. After establishment of the Division of Advertising, the section still worked with and through the publicity departments of the Liberty Loan committees of the Federal Reserve Districts. But by the middle of 1918, given the large number of campaigns in behalf of the government, there was a need to make copy more compelling. Between the Third and Fourth Liberty Loan campaigns, there was a feeling that some transition was needed to prepare the public for yet another round of investment. *Keep Your Liberty Bond* posters were printed, urging buyers to hold their investments and not allow "crooks" and "get-rich-quick artists" to profit. The feeling of sacrifice that went with purchasing a bond, it was believed, was valuable in creating national unity. See "The Liberty War Loan: The National Advertising Advisory Board's Advertising and Selling Plan," prepared by the Committee on Plan and Scope of the National Advertising Advisory Board, May 3, 1917; Houston, "Advertising and Victory," 457; " 'Keep Your Liberty Bond,' Advertises Uncle Sam," *Printers' Ink* 104 (Sept. 5, 1918): 98. See also Clarence A. Hope (cah) to S. Roland Hall (Alpha Cement, Faston, Pa.), Sept. 5, 1918, and Hope to Hall, Sept. 12, 1918, CPI papers, CPI 14–A1, Box 203, Folder: "Alb-Alu."

66. "Purpose and Scope of the Work of the Division of Advertising," [3].

67. Frank Leroy Blanchard, "Red Cross Advertising Campaign Based upon Heart Appeal," *Printers' Ink* 103 (May 23, 1918): 104.

68. There are a few works that exercise caution in relating the CPI to gory war posters. For example, an examination of government war posters in

Minnesota found the evidence inconclusive on whether the CPI used atrocity material in its billboards there. See Willis H. Raff, "Coercion and Freedom in a War Situation: A Critical Analysis of Minnesota Culture during World War One" (doctoral dissertation, University of Minnesota, 1957), 223.

69. Mock and Larson argued that the Division of Pictorial Publicity never involved itself with competitions because it was felt that the great mass of entries would be worthless. Mock and Larson, *Words That Won the War*, 102.

70. See "Striking Posters Will Aid Drive for W.S.S.," *Printers' Ink* 103 (May 30, 1918): 97–98.

71. Douglas Emery, "Tells of Germany's Crimes to Help Sell Liberty Bonds," ibid. 104 (Sept. 5, 1918): 73.

72. R. C. Leffingwell, assistant secretary of the Treasury, and George R. Cooksey, assistant to Secretary of the Treasury McAdoo, were among the committee's members. See "New Liberty-Loan Posters Reflect the War Spirit," ibid. (Sept. 26, 1918): 100.

73. Copies of the posters by Walter Whitehead and F. Strothman can be found in the Thomas J. White War Poster Collection, University of Chicago Library, Special Collection. A copy of Joseph Pennell's poster is in the CPI papers, CPI 14 series. For a description of these and other such posters see *Printers' Ink* 104 (Sept. 26, 1918): 100, 105.

74. A large volume of CPI Posters put out through the Division of Advertising is filed in CPI 14–B3 (oversize). Several posters that came out of the division for the WSS were more low-key than those illustrations mentioned above. Often they appealed to patriotism or self-interest, urging Americans to do more than their bit, assuring them that savings stamps would protect American boys, informing the purchaser that for as little as $4.12 he could, by waiting a few years, buy $5.00.

75. Creel, *Rebel at Large*, 196.

76. Clarence A. Hope (cah) to L. B. Jones, July 26, 1918, CPI papers, CPI 14–A1, Box 215, Folder: "Lewis B. Jones." See also Jones to Hope, July 27, 1918, ibid., Folder: "Clarence A. Hope."

77. One magazine told its readers that if this many posters were laid flat on the ground they would cover 180 square miles. See "New Liberty-Loan Posters Reflect the War Spirit," 105.

A few of the Fourth Liberty Loan posters, such as *Our Casualty Lists—Let's Not Get Used to Them—Let's Stop Them*, contained an appeal to self-interest rather than fear, pointing out the money earned by bonds. Another poster used in connection with the Fourth Liberty Loan, which appeared in such publications as *American Lawyers Quarterly*, was entitled *I Am Public Opinion*. Public opinion was symbolized by a rather robust woman (a figure similar to Eugène Delacroix's *Liberty Leading the People*), and citizens were warned that they would be judged not by their talk but by aid given to the war. For this latter illustration see Emery, "Tells of Germany's Crimes to Help Sell Liberty Bonds," 74.

78. Carl Byoir to William H. Johns, Mar. 27, 1918, CPI papers, CPI 14–A3, Folder: "March–April 1918."

79. See Blanchard, "Red Cross Advertising Campaign Based Upon Heart Appeal," 104–6, 109.

80. The advertising schedule for this poster called for 20 women's periodicals with a circulation of 12 million copies; 26 theater programs with circulation of 0.5 million copies; 62 other magazines and some 334 farm and trade papers with a readership of about 32.5 million. Altogether, this poster had an estimated circulation of 57 million, or about 2.5 copies per family. See "Give U.S. $1,500,000 in Advertising," *Editor and Publisher* 51 (July 20, 1918): 10.

81. For a discussion of the woman's image in poster propaganda in the United States and in other countries, see Michele J. Shover, "Roles and Images of Women in World War I Propaganda," *Politics and Society* 5 (No. 4, 1975): 469–86.

82. Magazine and farm papers reached about six million people through seventeen advertisements worth about $13,400. Carl Byoir to William H. Johns, Apr. 3, 1918, CPI papers, CPI 14–A3, Folder: "June-Nov. 1918"; L. B. Jones to "Publicity Manager, USSGA Dept. of Interior," Apr. 7, 1918, ibid. See also "Purpose and Scope of the Work of the Division of Advertising," [3].

83. Creel, *How We Advertised America*, 159; *Creel Report*, 44. Detailed monthly reports of the activities of the Division of Advertising are in CPI papers, CPI 14–B3. The following totals summarize the space with which the Division of Advertising dealt:

	Insertions	Circulation	Amount
General magazines	1,512	351,409,159	$895,108.29
Farm papers	1,443	134,279,895	361,221.84
Trade and misc. publications	4,353	41,377,554	238,102.47
House organs	831	14,386,475	52,727.50
Outdoor display	7	—	8,550.00
Newspapers	653	6,272,636	17,567.60
College papers	377	1,107,429	12,337.01
Book jackets	116	—	7,700.00[a]
Theater curtains	75	—	1,500.00
TOTAL	9,367	548,833,148	$1,594,814.71

[a]Estimated

These totals do not include the thousands of dollars of other outdoor advertising used or the sixty thousand window displays, many of which were prepared by the national war service committee of the International Association of Display Men. Mock and Larson, *Words That Won the War*, 100–101.

84. Creel, *How We Advertised America*, 164–65.

85. It is not suggested that the CPI's Division of Advertising and Division of Pictorial Publicity were the first to see public opinion as irrational. Nor does it appear that the committee, as Cochran argues, used the latest Freudian techniques. In 1918, however, probably the majority of the adver-

tising community was already coming to perceive man to be essentially irrational. See Merle Curti, "The Changing Concept of 'Human Nature' in the Literature of American Advertising," *Business History Review* 41 (No. 4, 1967): 345–53, especially 347.

86. Walter Lippmann, *Public Opinion* (New York, 1922); Lippmann, *Phantom Public: A Sequel to Public Opinion* (New York, 1925); Edward L. Bernays, *Crystallizing Public Opinion* (New York, 1923); Bernays, "Manipulating Public Opinion: The Why and the How," *American Journal of Sociology*, 23 (May 1928): 958–71; Bernays, *Propaganda* (New York, 1928).

87. *American Press: A Weekly Journal for Newspaper Men* (New York, Dec. 29, 1917), 6. A copy of this publication is in CPI papers, CPI 14–A3, Folder: "Dec. 1917–Feb. 1918."

88. Creel, *How We Advertised America*, 165.

89. Men like Rankin and D'Arcy were quick to see the implications. Shortly after the war, Rankin argued that the same techniques employed in selling Liberty Bonds and the Red Cross should apply to commercial advertising. Such an approach would increase newspaper advertising tenfold. The war had demonstrated the power of advertising, and he expected it to be an important aspect of postwar reconstruction. D'Arcy emphasized the value of advertising. Business without advertising would be a nightmare in which the whole world would be confused, out of focus: "Advertising is a thing, a force, a necessary part of civilization, just as the church, the kindergarten, the school, and the college are necessary parts of the world's requirements today." See *Editor and Publisher* 51 (July 13, 1918): 26; William H. Rankin, "Advertising Will Play Big Part in Reconstruction," ibid. (Dec. 21, 1918): 17; W. C. D'Arcy, "Imagine World without Its Daily Newspapers," San Francisco *Examiner,* July 7, 1918, "Section for Ad Men," p. 7; William C. D'Arcy, "1919 Holds Rewards for Real Service," *Editor and Publisher* 51 (Jan. 18, 1919): 32.

Chapter Nine

1. United States Committee on Public Information, "Preliminary Statement to the Press of the United States" (May 28, 1917), 4.

2. Alexis de Tocqueville, *Democracy in America* (2 vols., New York, 1835, 1954), 2: 119.

3. Will Irwin, "The American Newspaper: A Study of Journalism in Its Relation to the Public: I.—'The Power of the Press,'" *Collier's* 46 (Jan. 21, 1911): 18.

4. George Creel, "The Press: The Greatest Power in the Land," *Mentor* 9 (June 1, 1921): [4].

5. Creel, *How We Advertised America*, 109.

6. Quoted in Paxson, Corwin, Harding, eds., *War Cyclopedia*, title page.

7. *Official U.S. Bulletin. Hearing before the Joint Committee on Printing. Sixty-Sixth Congress. First Session. Under Section II of Public Act No. 314, 65th Congress*

(Aug. 12, 1919), 19. See also Frank Hardee Allen, "Government Influence on News in the United States during the World War" (doctoral dissertation, University of Illinois, 1934), 146–61.

8. George Creel to Woodrow Wilson, Dec. 26, 1917, Creel Papers, Container 1; Wilson to Creel, Dec. 31, 1917, ibid.

After the Armistice the chairman of the Joint Committee on Printing suggested that the great increase in volume of material put out by government publicity bureaus occurred in late 1916 or early 1917. The committee's paper bill increased at the end of fiscal year 1916 from $917,000 to almost $5 million. Though a rise in paper prices may account for part of this increase, the growth is probably more indicative of the enlarged role given to government publicity. *Official U.S. Bulletin. Hearing before the Joint Committee on Printing*, 21.

9. *Creel Report*, 12. The CPI never coordinated all the information put out by government departments, because many of them, such as the Food Administration, the War Trade Board, and the Council of National Defense, kept their own publicity departments. The State Department, perhaps because of Lansing's antipathy for Creel, made slight use of the CPI. Mock and Larson, *Words That Won the War*, 92; Allen, "Government Influence on News," 154.

10. Memorandum, Leigh Reilly to George Creel, June 29, 1918, CPI papers, CPI 1–A1, Box 23, Folder 15; Mock and Larson, *Words That Won the War*, 92.

11. See, for example, memorandum to Woodrow Wilson, June 25, 1917, Wilson papers, Reel 355, case file no. 3856. Of course, the advance texts of presidential addresses were often given to Creel for release to ensure the widest possible circulation. See, for example, Creel to Wilson, Apr. 3, 1918, Creel papers, Container 2.

12. Leo Rosten, *Washington Correspondents* (New York, 1937), 68. Rosten does not examine the CPI's part in this development.

13. *Creel Report*, 13–14.

14. Allen, "Government Influence on News," 78.

15. *Creel Report*, 14. As mentioned, many CPI pamphlets and Four Minute Men Bulletins were reprinted in newspapers, too. The division's total cost during the war was slightly more than $76,000. Mock and Larson, *Words That Won the War*, 92.

16. Ibid., 89. Newspapers were not allowed to break releases ahead of schedule; if they did, they were denied access to future releases.

17. Creel, *How We Advertised America*, 71, 74–75.

18. Ibid., 73.

19. Ibid., 80.

20. Leigh Reilly had been managing editor of the Chicago *Herald* and previously, from 1906 to 1913, editor-in-chief of the Chicago *Evening Post*. He remained in charge of the division until the end of the war.

21. Leigh Reilly was paid $5,200 per year, and Marlen E. Pew and Arthur W. Crawford each received $3,900. Creel, *How We Advertised America*, 90. Crawford was the Washington correspondent of the Chicago *Herald*.

22. Other writers and officials assisted the division. John Wilbur Jenkins, dean of Baltimore newspapermen, concentrated on the Navy Department. Secretary Daniels was of great assistance to the CPI there, as were Admirals William S. Benson, Ralph Earle, Montgomery Taylor, and Leigh Palmer. In the War Department, Heywood Broun of the New York *Tribune* assisted briefly and was followed by Wallace Irwin; Pew was the most effective assistant in the War Department, however. Crawford focused on the quartermaster's department. Edwin Newdick of the *Christian Science Monitor* worked with the surgeon-general. The Aircraft Board was the responsibility of Carl H. Butman. John Calvin Mellet of the International News Service and Livy Richard served with various other bureaus in the War Department. Archibald Mattingly, Charles P. Sweeney, Garrard Harris, and E. H. Hitchcock were other newspapermen serving the Division of News. Durant and Charles Willoughby manned the division's reference desk. Creel, *How We Advertised America*, 81–83.

23. Military Intelligence also thought that McClure had gained control of the *Evening Mail* with German money, no doubt as a result of his connection with Edward Rumely. See Military Intelligence Branch, "Report on the Committee on Public Information," 11–13. This report, often based on second- or even third-hand information, urged Creel to avoid letting McConaughy, or any CPI member, gain a reputation for bolshevism; for that, it asserted, would be "hardly less than a crime." Ibid., 13.

24. Ibid., and George Creel to Marlborough Churchill, July 8, 1918, CPI papers, CPI 1–A1 Folder: "Military Intelligence Report on Cx on Px Ix."

25. See J. W. McConaughy, "Aeroplanes in War," *Munsey's Magazine* 55 (Aug. 1915): 465–74; McConaughy, "Trench Warfare: How Modern Armies Burrow and Fight Underground," ibid., (Sept. 1915): 655–62; McConaughy, "Blockades and Blockade-Runners," ibid. 56 (Nov. 1915): 220–23; McConaughy, "Ancient Names Wiped Out by War: How the Great Conflict Is Decimating Britain's Oldest Families," ibid. (Dec. 1915): 409–12.

26. See J. W. McConaughy, "South America: A Land of the Future," ibid. (Jan. 1916): 495–527; McConaughy, "The Balkan States: A Long History of Intrigue and Slaughter," ibid. 57 (Feb. 1916): 1–32; McConaughy, "The Strong Man of China: Yuan Shih-kai, to Whom His Country's Waking Millions Look at the Present Crisis," ibid. (Mar. 1916): 277–89. McConaughy also wrote two other articles on the political and diplomatic problems in Europe: "Trials of the Neutral Kings: Dynastic and Political Troubles Are the Lot of the Seven Sovereigns on the Fringe of the Great War," ibid. (May 1916): 624–32; and "Our Ambassadors in the War Zone," ibid. 59 (Dec. 1916): 416–25.

27. See J. W. McConaughy, "The Red Cross of Mercy: What a Woman

Can Do When Her Country Goes to War," ibid. (Oct. 1916): 1–19. Mc-
Conaughy, "The Havoc of Invasion: A Broad Trail of Ruin through Five Fair
Provinces of France," ibid. 57 (Apr. 1916): 435–49.

After stepping down as director of the news division, McConaughy be-
came editor of the *War News Digest*. Later he was sent to South America by
Creel. Mock and Larson, *Words That Won the War*, 91; George Creel to J. W.
McConaughy, June 18, 1918, CPI papers, CPI 1–A1, Box 17, Folder 32.

28. For criticism of Durant see Military Intelligence Branch, "Report on
the Committee on Public Information," 11. Durant also helped John Hearley
distribute American news in Italy. *Creel Report*, 192.

29. United States Committee on Public Information, "Division of News
Directory: Prepared for the Information of Press Correspondents" (Washing-
ton, D.C., 1918), 4. See also Military Intelligence Branch, "Report on the
Committee on Public Information," 11; Creel, *How We Advertised America*, 82;
Marlen Pew, "Mobilizing Our Boys: How the United States Boys' Working
Reserve Plans to Enlist a Million Young Americans for Useful War-Time
Service," *Munsey's Magazine* 61 (July 1917): 226–29.

Creel defended Pew, denying any socialist affiliation. See Creel to Churchill, July 8, 1918. Pew had been editor of the Newspaper Enterprise Association (1907–10), had been employed with the Boston *Traveler* (1910–12), and
was news manager of United Press Association (of which he had been an
organizer in 1912). He edited the Philadelphia *News-Post* (1912–14) and had
organized the Press Illustrating Service, Inc., between 1915 and 1917. Subsequent to the war he became editor and manager of International News
Service and editor of *Editor and Publisher*.

30. Military Intelligence Branch, "Report on the Committee on Public
Information," 15.

31. Creel to Churchill, July 8, 1918. Actually, in his enthusiasm, Strunsky
prepared captions that gave inaccurate information on the number of American airplanes sent to France (see pp. 212–13 above). Creel said, "What we
wanted was plain, wooden titles, rather than propaganda titles."

32. Creel, *How We Advertised America*, 91.

33. Ibid., 76–77. Creel felt that Pershing's expedition was to be regarded
mainly as "a fife and drum corps" and that every person should be able to go
with it who could raise the money and present the proper credentials. But, as
Creel related to Mark Sullivan, Pershing and other army officers protested
against large numbers of reporters being present. (Of course, every journalist
who went to the war zone had to put up a sizable bond that was forfeited if
the censor's instructions were disobeyed). George Creel (?) to Mark Sullivan,
Aug. 10, 1917, CPI papers, CPI 1–A1, Box 27, Folder 11.

34. *Creel Report*, 108–40.

35. Woodrow Wilson, *Constitutional Government in the United States* (New
York, 1908), 126–27.

36. *Creel Report*, 66.

37. The bulletin was sent free to newspapers and magazines for more than a year, until a paper shortage caused suspension of this practice. Most major newspapers and magazines, however, took out paid subscriptions and thus continued to receive the bulletin. United States Committee on Public Information, *Report of the Director of the Official U.S. Bulletin to the Chairman of the Committee on Public Information* (Washington, D.C., 1918), 10–11.

38. Mock and Larson, *Words That Won the War*, 94. The amount received from subscriptions increased from $1,644.20 a month in May 1917 to $3,821.10 in January 1919. *Creel Report*, 67. Congress did not allow the CPI to keep its receipts from paid subscriptions to the *Official Bulletin* (or on the sale of pamphlets). Only the Division of Films was allowed to keep its receipts. See Guy Stanton Ford (?) to A. C. Krey, July 31, 1918, CPI papers, CPI 3–A1, Box 63, L–1–275.

39. *Report of the Director of the Official U.S. Bulletin to the Chairman of the Committee on Public Information*, 11–12.

40. "Facts concerning Official Bulletin, Its Field and Function; How and Why Publication Was Authorized by President," 1, CPI papers, CPI 5–A3, Box 152, Folder: "Facts concerning Official Bulletin." See also *Official U.S. Bulletin. Hearing before the Joint Committee on Printing*, 7. The shortage of newsprint paper did give the government another chance to influence the distribution of news. The cost of paper per hundred pounds rose from $2.15 in 1916 to $3.25 in 1917. Yet in June 1917 a joint congressional committee forced the International Paper Company to sell paper to the bulletin at a low price. President Wilson three months later, acting on authority given him by the National Defense Act, ordered this company to sell newsprint paper to the *Official Bulletin* at $0.025 per pound. Allen, "Government Influence on News," 171. It might also be mentioned that new papers were forbidden to start except in special cases. Ibid., 174.

Interestingly, a New York *Times* editorial criticized the bulletin's first issue for not offering anything new, for failing to deliver "scoops." See "Another Esteemed Contemporary," New York *Times*, May 12, 1917, p. 10.

41. *Report of the Director of the Official U.S. Bulletin to the Chairman of the Committee on Public Information*, 4.

42. *Creel Report*, 63–64. See also "Facts concerning Official Bulletin, Its Field and Function," 2.

43. *Creel Report*, 64–66.

44. *Official U.S. Bulletin. Hearing before the Joint Committee on Printing*, 19.

45. Ibid., 53. It is therefore not surprising that Rochester wanted the *Official Bulletin* to continue after the Armistice. He wrote to Creel explaining the advantage of such a publication: it was an excellent medium of communication between government departments and a source of communication on treaties to be ratified, trade conditions and economic readjustments, and political and social changes brought about by the war. It would help lessen the need for inquiry by businessmen who dealt with the government, decreasing

the daily flow of mail inquiries coming into Washington. Unless the bulletin were put on a permanent basis, the government would lack an official organ and be "powerless to present, in its own way, its own program for regeneration." He suggested that a commission perhaps composed of cabinet members and a director appointed by the president could be in charge of publication. He suggested that an appropriation of $500,000 to $600,000 would take care of necessary costs. The government did not make the *Official Bulletin* permanent, and it was sold to Roger Babson in early 1919. The paper was last published under CPI auspices on Mar. 31, 1919. However, the phrase "Official Government News" continued to appear on the publication's legend for some time, leading critics to charge that Creel had allowed Roger Babson, who purchased the publication, to take over a government asset. Rochester continued to edit the bulletin after it became a private concern. Under Babson's management the publication was known as the *United States Bulletin* and later as *United States Service*. Memorandum, E. S. Rochester to George Creel, undated, CPI papers, CPI 1–A1, Box 23, Folder 28. Rochester also submitted an alternate plan calling for the publication to be run by a committee made up of assistant secretaries of various executive departments and a director. *Report of the Director of the Official U.S. Bulletin to the Chairman of the Committee on Public Information*, 15. Also see [Babson], *Actions and Reactions*, 254; and Mock and Larson, *Words That Won the War*, 92–96. It has been suggested that two legacies of the *Official Bulletin* were the *United States Daily* (later *United States News*), published by David Lawrence, and the *Federal Register*, started in July, 1935. Mock and Larson, *Words That Won the War*, 96.

46. *Creel Report*, 63.

47. *Official U.S. Bulletin. Hearing before the Joint Committee on Printing*, 21–22.

48. Allen, "Government Influence on News," 162. See also *Official Bulletin*, June 9, 1917, pp. 10–12, 14.

49. Ibid., Nov. 23, 1918, p. 38.

50. News is seldom objective, and the very process of selecting and reporting it often betrays the bias of the editor or reporter. See Lippmann, *Public Opinion*, 358–65; and Leonard Doob, *Public Opinion and Propaganda* (New York, 1948), 430–31.

51. *Creel Report*, 95–96. For a list of government departments giving out releases, see ibid., 96. Five of the foreign-language bureaus did not begin issuing news releases until November 1918.

52. Allen, "Government Influence on News," 94.

53. Mock and Larson, *Words That Won the War*, 44–45.

54. Creel wanted to gain control over some of the German papers and wrote to Mitchell Palmer that he hoped reports of Palmer's representatives taking over German papers were true, for, Creel said, "if we can put your representatives in editorial control, we will have some powerful weapons for real fighting." George Creel to Mitchell Palmer (Alien Property Custodian),

Apr. 23, 1918, CPI papers, CPI 1–A1, Box 21, Folder 6. Creel also worried about the support of Jewish dailies and suggested to Samuel Gompers that an appeal be made to wealthy Jews to start a daily that would serve the CPI's (that is, the government's) purposes. George Creel (?) to Samuel Gompers, July 26, 1917, ibid., Box 11, Folder 256.

55. "Bureau" and "division" often are used synonymously in CPI correspondence.

56. United States Committee on Public Information, *Bulletin for Cartoonists*, No. 22 (Nov. 9, 1918), 1.

57. *Creel Report*, 76–78. For a list of departments supplied, see ibid., 77.

58. *Bulletin for Cartoonists*, No. 5 (July 6, 1918): 2. Copies of the bulletins are in CPI papers, CPI 14–A2.

59. Ibid., No. 3 (June 21, 1918): 2.

60. Ibid., No. 6 (July 13, 1918): 3.

61. Ibid., No. 10 (Aug. 10, 1918): 2.

62. Ibid., No. 11 (Aug. 24, 1918): 1.

63. Ibid., No. 5 (July 6, 1918): 2–3.

64. Ibid., No. 8 (July 28, 1918): 2. See also ibid., No. 6 (July 13, 1918): 3; and ibid., No. 7 (July 20, 1918): 3.

65. Ibid., No. 6 (July 13, 1918): 2.

66. Ibid., No. 11 (Aug. 24, 1918: 2–3.

67. Ibid., No. 7 (July 20, 1918): 3.

68. For examples of bulletins specially emphasizing the Fourth Liberty Loan, see ibid., No. 15 (Sept. 21, 1918): and ibid., No. 16 (Sept. 28, 1918).

69. The CPI's use of film is dealt with in Mock and Larson, *Words That Won the War*, 136–51, 153–57. This study serves as the basis for the treatment of the CPI in Timothy J. Lyons, "Hollywood and World War I, 1914–1918," *Journal of Popular Film* 1 (No. 1, 1972): 25–27. The CPI and film are briefly mentioned in Clyde Jeavons, *A Pictorial History of War Films* (Secaucus, N.J., 1974), 31. For a discussion of propaganda films produced during the war, other than those pictures put out by the Committee on Public Information, see ibid., 21–35; Mock and Larson, *Words That Won the War*, 131–35, 151–53; and Charles Reed Mitchell, "New Message to America: James W. Gerard's *Beware* and World War I Propaganda," *Journal of Popular Film* 4 (No. 4, 1975): 275–95.

70. Mock and Larson, *Words That Won the War*, 132. Some films had been prepared before Apr. 1917, stressing preparedness.

71. Movie stars such as Theda Bara, Douglas Fairbanks and Mary Pickford demonstrated their patriotism by helping to sell Liberty bonds. Ibid., 135.

72. Brady had earlier recommended using motion pictures to spread national propaganda. Memorandum about William A. Brady, June 22, 1917, Wilson papers, Reel 355, case file no. 3856.

Incidentally, before the war, Creel had apparently tried his hand at screenwriting in Denver. See Robert Sobel, *The Manipulators: America in the Media Age* (Garden City, N.Y., 1976), 91–92.

73. Other members of the committee included Thomas H. Ince, Jesse L. Lasky, Carl Laemmle, Marcus Loew, Joseph M. Schenck, Louis J. Selznick, and Adolph Zukor. Mock and Larson, *Words That Won the War*, 135.

74. Creel, *How We Advertised America*, 118–19; *Creel Report*, 47. For the titles of some of the early films produced, see ibid., 47–48.

75. The list of Signal Corps films produced during the war is surprisingly large and covers many phases of the war effort. For a catalog describing over four hundred of these films, see Bauer, comp., *List of World War I Signal Corps Films*.

76. In California, North Dakota, and Michigan the state councils of defense were in charge of distributing government films.

77. *Creel Report*, 53.

78. Howard Herrick (publicity manager, CPI Division of Films) to George Newland (dramatic editor, Cincinnati *Post*), Apr. 19, 1918, CPI papers, CPI 10A–A1, Box 155, first folder.

79. Charles S. Hart to Managing Editor (Cincinnati *Times-Star*), Apr. 23, 1918, ibid., sixth folder.

80. United States Committee on Public Information, *Pershing's Crusaders*, (film) Reel 1, Subtitle 1.

81. Ibid., Reel 1, Subtitle 86.

82. Charles F. Hart ("Director") to Dennis F. O'Brien, Apr. 27, 1918, CPI papers, CPI 10A–A1, Box 155, eighth folder.

83. Charles S. Hart to Pathé Exchange, May 3, 1918, ibid., Box 155.

84. See telegram dated Apr. 8, 1918, ibid., seventh folder.

85. United States Committee on Public Information, *Official War Review*, (film), No. 18.

86. Mrs. Jane Stannard Johnson (?) (secretary of the Division of Films) to H. C. Hoagland, Apr. 24, 1918, CPI papers, CPI 10A–A1, Box 155, eighth folder.

87. *Creel Report*, 53–55.   88. Ibid., 56–57.

89. Ibid., 57–58.   90. Ibid., 58–59.

91. In addition to *Hearts of the World*, Griffith turned out other films with the war as a theme, including *The Great Love* and *The Greatest Thing in Life*. In addition, he filmed the House of Representatives for a proposed government propaganda film, and with Stanner Taylor he wrote the synopsis of a war film entitled *The Hun Within*. For Griffith's wartime films, see Robert M. Henderson, *D. W. Griffith: His Life and Work* (New York, 1972), 182–200; and Edward Wagenknecht and Anthony Slide, *Films of D. W. Griffith* (New York, 1975), 90–114.

92. George Creel to William A. Brady, Aug. 20, 1918, CPI papers, CPI 1–A1, Box 3, Folder 66.

93. Jane Stannard Johnson (?) to Mrs. Genie H. Rosenfeld (Woman's

Press Club, New York City), Apr. 23, 1918, ibid., CPI 10A–A1, Box 155, first folder. Mrs. Johnson had been advertising and publicity manager for Paramount and also a film critic. Mock and Larson discuss a few of the hate films and other movies, such as *The Yanks Are Coming* and *Patria*, which involved the CPI in controversy. Mock and Larson, *Words That Won the War*, 143–53.

94. Ibid., 141–42.

95. William A. Brady to Vance McCormick (War Trade Board), July 19, 1918, CPI papers, CPI 1–A1, Box 3, Folder 66.

96. *Creel Report*, 61.

97. Ibid., 61–62.

98. Mock and Larson, *Words That Won the War*, 155.

99. For example, see United States *Catalogue of Photographs and Stereopticon Slides*. A copy of this publication is in CPI papers, CPI 14–A3, Folder: "Dec. 1917–Feb. 1918."

100. *Creel Report*, 62–63.

101. Creel, *How We Advertised America*, 83. See also Walton E. Bean, "The Accuracy of Creel Committee News, 1917–19: An Examination of Cases," *Journalism Quarterly* 18 (Sept. 1941): 263–72. Bean, a staunch defender of Creel, deals with two charges made against the CPI: that it falsified a story about a submarine attack on an American convoy headed to Europe on the Fourth of July 1917; and that it gave false information on the number of American airplanes sent to France. Although Bean does not give evidence of having examined the other fifty-nine hundred or more news releases of the CPI, he nevertheless concludes that "it may be doubted that the CPI's record for honesty will ever be equalled in the official war news of a major power." Mock and Larson, though less adamant than Bean, nevertheless leave a similar impression about the honesty of the CPI's news. Mock and Larson, *Words That Won the War*, 92.

102. This episode was apparently the reason behind Creel's dismissal of Strunsky. See Bean, "The Accuracy of the Creel Committee News," 271; and Creel, *How We Advertised America*, 47.

103. Ibid., 47–49.

104. Ben B. Lindsey to George Creel, Aug. 16, 1918, CPI papers, CPI 1–A1, Box 16, Folder 401; Creel to Lindsey, Aug. 17, 1918, Lindsey Papers, Corresp. (Carded Series) 1897–1931, Aug.–Nov. 1918, Container 59.

CHAPTER TEN

1. Creel, *How We Advertised America*, 25.

2. For Germany, see Gerald D. Feldman, *Army, Industry, and Labor in Germany, 1914–1918* (Princeton, N.J., 1966), 31–32, 137, 429. For Austria-Hungary, see Hans Hautmann, "Bemerkungen zu den Kriegs- und Ausnahmsgesetzen in Österreichungarn und Deren Anwendung 1914–1918," *Zeitgeschichte* [Austria] 3 (No. 2, 1975): 31–37. For France, see Marc Ferro,

Great War, 1914–1918, translated by Nicole Stone (London, 1969, 1973), 125–26; Jean-Noël Jeanneney, "Les Archives des Commissions de Controle Postal aux Armée (1916–1918)," *Revue d'Histoire Moderne et Contemporaine* 15 (Jan.–Mar. 1968): 209–33; Georges Liens, "La Commission de Censure et la Commission de Controle Postal a Marseille pendant la Première Guerre Mondiale," ibid. 18 (Oct.–Dec. 1971): 649–67; Guy Pedroncini, "Les Cours martiales pendant la Grande Guerre," *Revue Historique* 252 (Oct.–Dec. 1974): 393–408. For Great Britain, see Peterson, *Propaganda for War*, 13; Deian Hopkin, "Domestic Censorship in the First World War," *Journal of Contemporary History* 5 (No. 4, 1970): 151–69; Thomas C. Kennedy, "Public Opinion and the Conscientious Objector, 1915–1919," *Journal of British Studies* 12 (May 1973): 105, 114–15; and John Rae, *Conscience and Politics: The British Government and the Conscientious Objector to Military Service, 1916–1919* (London, 1970).

3. Sixty-five were convicted for making threats against the chief executive and ten for sabotage. Apparently no one was executed.

Harold Hyman contended that the Wilson administration bears some responsibility for the abuses of the Loyal Legion of Loggers and Lumbermen, a paramilitary labor union that operated extralegally in the timber states of the Northwest. He also criticized the administration for its association with the American Protective League. The APL cooperated with the Department of Justice in tracking down German spies in the United States, and its membership grew from about 90,000 in the summer of 1917 to approximately 350,000 by the end of the war. Hyman believed the spy threat had subsided by mid-1917 to the point where the Justice Department no longer needed the APL and thus should have discontinued its operation. The APL's reputation has been one of irresponsibility and extralegal activity, and undoubtedly many of its members did at times operate outside the law. However, Joan M. Jensen, who has written the most thorough study of the league, has shown that Attorney General Thomas Gregory tried to keep this agency under control. Neither he nor President Wilson condoned the illegal activities of its members, but both preferred working through the APL to putting the pursuit of German spies under control of the military. For example, Gregory and Wilson opposed the Chamberlain bill, which would have given to the military jurisdiction over all spies. See Harold M. Hyman, *To Try Men's Souls: Loyalty Tests in American History* (Berkeley, Calif., 1959), 271–315; and Joan M. Jensen, *Price of Vigilance* (Chicago, 1968), 120–28, 170–71, 230–31. See also Mock and Larson, *Words That Won the War*, 83.

For Albert Burleson see Donald Johnson, "Wilson, Burleson, and Censorship in the First World War," *Journal of Southern History* 28 (Feb. 1962): 46–58.

4. During the war many states were dissatisfied with the strength of federal legislation and passed measures of their own. The provisions of many state laws were similar to federal statutes, and thus, after the Armistice, about

thirty states continued what was essentially the substance of the national Espionage and Sedition Acts. Often these measures were supplemented in the immediate postwar period with regulations designed to protect property and prevent revolutionary activity. See Mock, *Censorship, 1917*, 215. For restrictive measures taken by various state governments and for the postwar period, see ibid., 24–38 and 213–31, respectively; Zechariah Chafee, Jr., *Freedom of Speech* (New York, 1920), 399–405; and Paul L. Murphy, *Meaning of Freedom of Speech: First Amendment Freedoms from Wilson to FDR* (Westport, Conn., 1972), 41–45. For other studies dealing with state and local repression, see Carl Wittke, *German-Americans and the World War: (With Special Emphasis on Ohio's German-Language Press)* (Columbus, Ohio, 1936), 147–60, 172–96; Robert L. Morlan, *Political Prairie Fire: The Nonpartisan League, 1915–1922* (Minneapolis, 1955), 152–59, 162–73, 179–82; Julian F. Jaffe, *Crusade against Radicalism: New York during the Red Scare, 1914–1924* (Port Washington, N.Y., 1972), 67–69; Luebke, *Bonds of Loyalty*, 3–26, 254–55, 273–77, 279–83; and Margaret Entz, "War Bond Drives and the Kansas Mennonite Response," *Mennonite Life* 30 (Sept. 1975): 4–9.

5. State councils of defense and their county and local auxiliaries were important in coercing reluctant citizens to support the war. Among the works that treat these organizations are William James Breen, "The Council of National Defense: Industrial and Social Mobilization in the United States, 1916–1920" (doctoral dissertation, Duke University, 1968); O. A. Hilton, "Public Opinion and Civil Liberties in Wartime, 1917–1919," *Southwestern Social Quarterly* 28 (Dec. 1947): 202–8; Austin L. Venable, "The Arkansas Council of Defense in the First World War," *Arkansas Historical Quarterly* 2 (Mar. 1943): 116–26; Gerald Senn, "Molders of Thought, Directors of Action: The Arkansas Council of Defense, 1917–1918," ibid. 36 (Autumn 1977): 280–90; Fraser, "Yankees at War"; Jenison, *War-Time Organization of Illinois*; O. A. Hilton, "The Minnesota Commission of Public Safety in World War I, 1917–1919," *Bulletin of the Oklahoma and Mechanical College* 68 (May 15, 1951): 2–41; Jenson, "Agrarian Pioneer in Civil Liberties"; Robert N. Manley, "Language, Loyalty and Liberty: The Nebraska State Council of Defense and the Lutheran Churches, 1917–1918," *Concordia Historical Institute Quarterly* 37 (Apr. 1964): 1–16; O. A. Hilton, "The Oklahoma Council of Defense and the First World War," *Chronicles of Oklahoma* 20 (Mar. 1942): 18–42; and Karen Falk, "Public Opinion in Wisconsin during World War I," *Wisconsin Magazine of History* 25 (June 1942): 389–407.

6. See Hyman, *To Try Men's Souls*, 284–86. Also, for the National Security League, see Ward, "The Origin and Activities of the National Security League"; and Blakey, *Historians on the Homefront*.

7. John M. Blum, "Nativism, Anti-Radicalism, and the Foreign Scare, 1917–1920," *Midwest Journal* 3 (Winter 1950–51): 46–53; Higham, *Strangers in the Land*, 194–233; William Preston, Jr., *Aliens and Dissenters: Federal Suppression of Radicals, 1903–1933* (Cambridge, Mass., 1963); and John Braeman,

"World War One and the Crisis of American Liberty [review essay]," *American Quarterly* 16 (Spring 1964): 104–12, especially 111–12.

8. Luebke, *Bonds of Loyalty*, 27–81.

9. See Chapter 1, note 15, above. Censorship and the CPI are discussed in Mock, *Censorship, 1917*; Mock and Larson, *Words That Won the War*, 19–47; Carl Brent Swisher, "Civil Liberties in War Time," *Political Science Quarterly* 55 (Sept. 1940): 327; Peterson and Fite, *Opponents of War*, 20, 94–95; Allen, "Government Influence on News," 146–91; and Paul L. Murphy, *World War I and the Origin of Civil Liberties in the United States* (New York, 1979), chapter 4.

10. Whereas Creel wrote little on censorship in late 1916 and early 1917, Bullard, as noted in Chapter 1, wrote extensively on the subject.

11. Mock, *Censorship, 1917*, 42–43. As mentioned, both Bullard and Poole spent most of their time with the CPI in the Foreign Section.

12. Creel, *Rebel at Large*, 157. This account was written thirty years after the creation of the CPI. "Publicity, *not* suppression" was the language used in Creel's communication with Secretary of the Navy Daniels in late Mar. 1917. See Chapter 1, note 75, above.

13. Creel, *Rebel at Large*, 157; Creel, *How We Advertised America*, 16, 27. Actually, Creel did seek control of cable censorship for himself. Secretary of the Navy Daniels had originally recommended that the executive control of cable censorship be given to the Committee on Public Information, but Creel had insisted that Commander David W. Todd, director of Naval Communications, be put in charge. By mid-Aug. 1917, however, Creel wrote to Daniels expressing irritation over delays encountered in operating through Naval Communications. "It has become absolutely necessary that I have official recognition in order to avoid delay, red tape, and the routine of the present system. The press censorship is one of the principal features of the work, and it calls for top speed at every moment. . . . On occasions when time is important, I want to be able to go to any Department of the Navy, War, or State without delay." He urged that cable censorship be taken away from Naval Communications, that official authority for it be given to him as chairman of the CPI, and that the office of the chief censor be created in New York City. George Creel to Josephus Daniels, Aug. 16, 1917, Daniels papers, Box 73, Folder: "Creel, George 1917."

14. A voluntary agreement on censorship had been reached between representatives of the press and the Departments of State, War, and the Navy before the CPI had been created. On Apr. 16, Wilson supplemented this agreement with a warning statement on "Treason and Misprison of Treason," which said that acts or publications of information giving aid or comfort in any way to the enemies of the United States were treason. Mock and Larson, *Words That Won the War*, 77–78.

15. Although the statement was unsigned, Creel, Bullard, and Sisson presented themselves to the press to answer questions about the regulations. Creel, *How We Advertised America*, 19.

16. Many publications requested their readers to report infractions. Some newspaper associations, such as the Pittsburgh Press Club, developed an intelligence bureau to watch publications for the Department of Justice in some twenty-seven Pennsylvania counties. Mock and Larson, *Words That Won the War*, 83.

17. See "Preliminary Statement to the Press of the United States." See also Mock and Larson, *Words That Won the War*, 80–83. These regulations were revised from time to time during the war. See *Editor and Publisher* 50 (Aug. 4, 1917): 6; and ibid. (Jan. 5, 1918): 24.

18. Memorandum, Breckinridge Long to Woodrow Wilson, Nov. 19, 1917, Creel Papers, Container 1.

19. Wilson to Long, Nov. 20, 1917, ibid.

20. George Creel to Woodrow Wilson, Nov. 28, 1917, ibid.

21. Creel told Senator William E. Borah that he never favored any censorship law and that voluntary agreements were sufficient to protect military secrets. He desired "to open every Department of Government to the inspection of the people." George Creel to William E. Borah, Dec. 19, 1917, CPI papers, CPI 1–A1, Box 2, Folder 62.

22. *Editor and Publisher* 50 (Dec. 15, 1917): 10.

23. Ibid. (Jan. 26, 1918): 23; ibid. 51 (Aug. 17, 1918): 5. Although most newspapers were sufficiently loyal to meet Creel's standards, a few publications were not, and Creel was never satisfied with the profession's attempts at self-regulation. The Hearst-owned San Francisco *Examiner*, the Washington *Post*, and the New York *Evening Post* were among the major culprits. Creel, *How We Advertised America*, 25; Mock and Larson, *Words That Won the War*, 85–88.

24. Members of the Censorship Board included Creel, Robert L. Maddox, Eugene Russell White, Brigadier General Frank McIntyre, Captain Frederic Bulkley Hyde, Captain David W. Todd, and Paul Fuller, Jr. See Mock, *Censorship, 1917*, 57–59.

25. See Mock and Larson, *Words That Won the War*, 20–21.

26. "Reminiscences of Guy Stanton Ford," 385.

27. George Creel to R. L. Maddox, Dec. 12, 1917, CPI papers, CPI 1–A1, Box 17, Folder 2.

28. Creel to Maddox, June 20, 1918, ibid.; Creel to Maddox, Oct. 10, 1918, ibid. There are indications that Creel was not eager to have mail censorship imposed. For instance, after cable censorship was established for messages going into Central and South America, Creel argued that postal censorship "would be inadequate and ineffective." George Creel to Woodrow Wilson, July 19, 1917, Creel papers, Container 1. The CPI did try to justify mail censorship, however. One committee poster was entitled *Live News or Live Sammies—Which do You Prefer?* Censorship of letters from the front was for the safety of American soldiers, the CPI argued. CPI papers, CPI 1–C6, Folder: "advertising copies & layouts."

29. Both the majority and minority reports, with Wilson's reply, are in "Minutes of the Meeting of the Censorship Board," May 29, 1918, ibid., CPI 1–A1, Box 4, Folder: "Censorship Board." Hereafter cited as Minutes. For further information on this controversy see Minutes, Apr. 17, Apr. 24, Apr. 25, 1917, ibid.

30. The Censorship Board continued to advise and assist the Post Office Department in censorship matters. Albert Burleson, as Arthur Link notes, used his censorship powers capriciously. For example, in censoring newspapers he granted that "legitimate criticism" (which was vaguely defined) of the president and armed forces would be permitted, but he imposed a limit on such criticism: "this limit is reached when a newspaper begins to say that this Government got into the war wrong, that it is there for a wrong purpose, or anything else that impugns the motives of the Government, thereby encouraging insubordination. Newspapers cannot say that this Government is the tool of Wall Street, or munition makers, or the tool of anybody. Nor can anything be published designed and calculated to incite the people to violate this law. There can be no campaign against conscription and the Draft law; nothing that will interfere with enlistments or the raising of an army, or the sale of authorized bonds or the collections of authorized revenues." In short, anything that obstructed the war effort, injured the government, or aided the enemy's cause would not be tolerated. See *Editor and Publisher* 50 (Oct. 6, 1917): 5. On Burleson's attitude toward newspaper disloyalty, see ibid. (Nov. 3, 1917): 17. Also see Arthur Link, *American Epoch: A History of the United States since the 1890's* (New York, 1955), 214–15; and Johnson, "Wilson, Burleson, and Censorship in the First World War."

31. Minutes, Apr. 3, 1918, CPI papers, CPI 1–A1, Box 4, Folder: "Censorship Board."

32. Mock and Larson, *Words That Won the War*, 84.

33. Minutes, June 19, Aug. 27, Aug. 29, Sept. 5, 1918, CPI papers, CPI 1–A1, Box 4, Folder: "Censorship Board."

34. Minutes, Oct. 24, 1918, ibid. On the subject of banning books during the war, see Mock, *Censorship, 1917*, 153–71; and Blakey, *Historians on the Homefront*, 82–97.

35. *Motor Age* was published in Chicago and *Air Service Journal* in New York.

36. Robert L. Maddox to George Creel, Mar. 26, 1918, CPI papers, 1–A1, Box 17, Folder 2; Maddox to Creel, Apr. 2, 1918, ibid. Colonel Marlborough Churchill was particularly concerned about textbooks. See Minutes, Aug. 2, 1918, ibid., Box 4, Folder: "Censorship Board."

37. Maddox complied with Creel's instructions regarding Bolshevik literature. See Creel to Maddox, Mar. 8, 1918, ibid., Box 17, Folder 2; Maddox to Creel, Mar. 9, 1918, ibid. See also Minutes, Aug. 22, 1918, ibid., Box 4, Folder: "Censorship Board."

38. Creel to Maddox, July 3, 1918, ibid., Box 17, Folder 2.

39. Minutes, Aug. 22, 1918, ibid., Box 4, Folder: "Censorship Board."

40. Creel to Maddox, Oct. 16, 1918, ibid., Box 17, Folder 2; Creel to Maddox, Nov. 1, 1918, ibid. Creel wished to prevent anything published by the Free Press Defense League from leaving the country.

41. Ernest J. Chambers to George Creel, Apr. 2, 1918, ibid., Folder 104; George Creel to Albert Shaw, Apr. 5, 1918, ibid.; George Creel to Ernest J. Chambers, Apr. 5, 1918, ibid.; Shaw to Creel, Apr. 8, 1918, ibid.; Creel to Chambers, Apr. 11, 1918, ibid.; Chambers to Creel, Apr. 16, 1918, ibid.; Creel to Chambers, Apr. 19, 1918, ibid.; Chambers to Creel, Apr. 22, 1918, ibid.

42. Chambers to Creel, Jan. 7, 1918, ibid.; William Randolph Hearst to George Creel, May 3, 1917, ibid., Box 4, Folder: "Censorship, Mail." See also Mock and Larson, *Words That Won the War*, 86.

43. Chambers to Creel, Jan. 29, 1918, CPI papers, CPI 1–A1, Folder 104; Creel to Chambers, Feb. 6, 1918, ibid.

44. Chambers to Creel, Nov. 7, 1917, ibid.; Creel (?) to Chambers, Nov. 10, 1917, ibid.

45. Chambers to Creel, Dec. 8, 1917, ibid.; Ernest J. Chambers to Secretary of State of Canada, Dec. 8, 1917, ibid.; George Creel to Herbert Putnam, Dec. 12, 1917, ibid. The second edition of Kirkpatrick's book especially upset Chambers.

There also is evidence that Creel had some effect on Canadian publications. Creel asked Chambers to write to the editor of the Sherbrooke, P.Q., *Daily Record* about an editorial entitled "America as an Ally." In addition, he supplied Chambers with information on foreign publications that were suspected of having been financed with German money. Creel to Chambers, Apr. 23, 1918, ibid.; Chambers to Creel, Jan. 17, 1918, ibid. The latter letter involved information about a German-financed Mexican paper. Chambers thought that German money was also backing "some dirty little sheets" in Canada.

46. *Editor and Publisher* 50 (May 18, 1918): 32.

47. H. O'H., "The Issue," *Century* 95 (Jan. 1918): 405. It will be remembered that O'Higgins wrote two pamphlets for the CPI encouraging citizens to report suspected spies to the Department of Justice.

48. Harvey O'Higgins, "Freedom of Speech," ibid. (Dec. 1917): 302–3.

49. This address had first been published in the *Santa Fe Magazine* (Dec. 1917). See Arthur D. Call, comp., *The War for Peace: The Present War as Viewed by Friends of Peace*, War Information Series, No. 14 (Washington, D.C., 1918), 24–27. This pamphlet contained statements supporting the war and opposing a premature peace from such groups as the American Peace Society, the Carnegie Endowment for International Peace, the League to Enforce Peace, the American School Peace League, the World Peace Foundation, Belgian relief workers, and various women peace workers. More than three hundred thousand copies of this pamphlet were printed.

50. Ibid., 24. Apparently, Darrow engaged in rhetorical flights on other occasions. In an earlier speech at Madison Square Garden the New York *Times* quoted him as saying, "If President Wilson had not defied Germany he would have been a taitor (sic), and any man who refuses to back the President in this crisis is worse than a traitor." New York *Times*, Sept. 16, 1917, p. 3.

51. Call, comp., *The War for Peace: The Present War as Viewed by Friends of Peace*, 35.

52. Ibid., 37.

53. Edward S. Corwin to Samuel Harding, June 16, 1918, CPI papers, CPI 3–A1, Box 77, M–2E–15.

54. Edward S. Corwin, *National Supremacy: Treaty Power vs. State Power* (New York, 1913); Corwin, *President's Control of Foreign Relations* (Princeton, N.J., 1917). Perhaps the most comprehensive treatment of Corwin's thought is Gerald Joseph Garvey, "Corwin on the Constitution: The Content and Context of Modern American Constitutional Theory" (doctoral dissertation, Princeton University, 1962).

55. Edward S. Corwin, *Constitution and What It Means To-Day* (2d ed., Princeton, N.J., 1921), iv, vii.

Of course, during 1918 and through much of 1919 there were substantial differences between Holmes and Chafee over the meaning of the First Amendment. For the development of Holmes's thinking on this question, see Fred D. Ragan, "Justice Oliver Wendell Holmes, Jr., Zechariah Chafee, Jr., and the Clear and Present Danger Test for Free Speech: The First Year, 1919," *Journal of American History* 58 (June 1971): 24–45.

56. Edward S. Corwin to Zechariah Chafee, Dec. 3, 1920, Zechariah Chafee, Jr., Papers, Harvard Law School Library, Cambridge, Mass., Container 14, Folder 7: "Freedom of Discussion—Corr. Colt-Durant." This letter was part of a brief exchange on the First Amendment between Corwin and Chafee in late 1920 and early 1921. Two letters from Chafee to Corwin dated Nov. 16, 1920, and Jan. 3, 1921, are found in ibid. and also in the Edward S. Corwin Papers, Mudd Library, Princeton University, Princeton, N.J.

57. Edward S. Corwin, "Freedom of Speech and Press under the First Amendment: A Résumé," *Yale Law Journal* 30 (Nov. 1920): 48.

58. Ibid., 51, 55. For further information on Corwin's thoughts about Holmes and "clear and present danger," see Edward S. Corwin, "Bowing Out 'Clear and Present Danger,'" *Notre Dame Lawyer* 27 (Spring 1952): especially 325–43; and Samuel J. Konefsky, *Legacy of Holmes and Brandeis: A Study in the Influence of Ideas* (New York, 1956), 189, 191, 193, 194, 202, 205, 210.

Although Holmes stated the "clear and present danger" test for speech in *Schenck v. United States* (Mar. 3, 1919), he used it at that time "as a negative or restraining device rather than as a positive, libertarian or permissive rule. . . . For all practical purposes, [he] applied a bad-tendency test to free speech." It was probably not until the *Abrams* case (Nov. 10, 1919) that Holmes "began constructing the 'clear and present danger' formula to protect civil liberties."

Ragan, "Justice Oliver Wendell Holmes, Jr., Zechariah Chafee, Jr., and the Clear and Present Danger Test of Free Speech: The First Year, 1919," 36, 44.

59. Corwin, *Constitution and What It Means To-Day*, 88.

60. Paxson, Corwin, Harding, eds., *War Cyclopedia*, 101. After the war, Corwin continued to assert that "in time of war or public danger when even the privilege of the writ of habeas may be suspended . . . , measures of restraint may go to lengths not allowable in quieter times. Yet at all times, it is generally conceded, Congress may ban utterances calculated to incite to violence or a forcible breach of the law; and this means in practice that it may ban utterances which to a jury of twelve Americans may seem calculated to do this." He argued that "the cause of freedom of speech and press is largely in the custody of legislative majorities and juries, which so far as there is evidence to show, is just where the framers of the Constitution intended it to be." Corwin, *Constitution and What It Means To-Day*, 88–89; Corwin, "Freedom of Speech and Press under the First Amendment: A Résumé," 55. See also Edward S. Corwin, "Constitutional Law in 1919–1920. I: The Constitutional Decisions of the Supreme Court of the United States in the October Term, 1919," *American Political Science Review* 14 (Nov. 1920): 658.

61. See Article I, Section 8, Paragraph 18 of the U.S. Constitution.

62. Paxson, Corwin, Harding, eds., *War Cyclopedia*, 101.

63. Ibid.

64. Ibid., 103.

65. Corwin, "Freedom of Speech and Press under the First Amendment: A Résumé," 55.

CONCLUSION

1. *Bulletin for Cartoonists*, No. 11 (Aug. 24, 1918), 1.

2. Shafer, *Faces of Nationalism*, 345.

3. Kohn, *Idea of Nationalism*, 289, 323, 324; and Arieli, *Individualism and Nationalism in American Ideology*, 20–21. Here, Arieli was drawing on Alexis de Tocqueville.

4. Paxson, Corwin, Harding, eds., *War Cyclopedia*, 15.

5. *Labor and the War*, 15. Creel said to Wilson, "I find it hard always to think of you as a person, for you stand for America so absolutely in my mind and heart and are so inseparably connected with the tremendous events of the time." George Creel to Woodrow Wilson, Dec. 28, 1917, Creel papers, Container 1. For a good discussion of the CPI and the publicizing of the presidency, see Cornwell, Jr., "Wilson, Creel, and the Presidency," 189–202; and Elmer E. Cornwell, Jr., *Presidential Leadership of Public Opinion* (Bloomington, Ind., 1965), 48–57.

6. Creel, *War, the World, and Wilson*, 16.

7. Although this view is oversimplified, some scholars have argued that the First World War brought an important change in the way problems in

public opinion were seen. Stow Persons argues that before the war, on matters concerning the formation of opinion, interest focused "upon desirable social goals." After the war the emphasis shifted away from concern with worthy goals and began to center on how opinions were formed and how they could best be manipulated. Stow Persons, *American Minds: A History of Ideas* (New York, 1958), 374. Persons argues that in CPI propaganda "there was nothing essentially false or artificial," but that it did have the unfortunate effect of causing the public to think in stereotypes. Ibid., 375. Eric Goldman, in his study of the public relations counselor, places the Creel committee in the tradition of publicity that sought to "inform" the public rather than deceive or manipulate it. Goldman, *Two-Way Street*, 3, 11–12.

8. It is not especially surprising that Creel's efforts to mobilize opinion should manifest inconsistency. Much of the muckraking discussion of democracy was paradoxical and contradictory. See Stanley K. Schultz, "The Morality of Politics: The Muckrakers' Vision of Democracy," *Journal of American History* 52 (Dec. 1965): 527–47.

9. Two of the most vigorous critics of mass democracy after the war, Bernays and Lippmann, were associated with the CPI. Bernays, as mentioned, worked for the committee in Latin America. Lippmann, who was often critical of the CPI's efforts, served as an officer in a military intelligence unit in Europe that sent propaganda behind enemy lines. This unit, though separate from the CPI, often coordinated its effort with the committee's. Lippmann drew on this experience in writing *Public Opinion*. For works by Bernays and Lippmann see Chapter 8, note 86, above. See also "Reminiscences of Walter Lippmann" (1950), 87–88, Columbia Oral History Collection, Columbia University, New York.

It is also possible that the committee's endeavors had another long-range effect. Writers such as Stuart Sherman contended that democracy required inner restraints on natural appetites. Yet the CPI offered publicity to the advertising profession and undoubtedly acted as a stimulant to its growth. Modern advertising, particularly since the end of World War I, has probably encouraged unrestrained appetite. See Daniel Bell, *Cultural Contradictions of Capitalism* (New York, 1976), xi, 68–69.

10. Hitler, *Mein Kampf*, 181.

11. Lippmann made a partial list of organizations that were putting out propaganda during the war, in addition to the CPI. They included the Red Cross, Salvation Army, and YMCA (all of which the CPI's Division of Advertising assisted); the Jewish Welfare Board; and the several independent patriotic societies, such as the League to Enforce Peace, the League of Free Nations Association, the National Security League, and the publicity bureaus of the Allies. Lippmann, *Public Opinion*, 47. See also Allen, "Government Influence on the News."

12. See the chapter entitled "The Charges of Treasonable Moderation" in Bean, "George Creel and His Critics," 197–265.

13. For philosophical, literary, and social developments during this period, see Purcell, *Crisis of Democratic Theory*; May, *End of American Innocence*; and Nathan G. Hale, Jr., *Freud and the Americans: The Beginnings of Psychoanalysis in the United States, 1876–1917* (New York, 1971), especially 21, 29, 46, 267–73.

14. Cushing Strout, *New Heavens and New Earth: Political Religion in America* (New York, 1974), 252. Strout has correctly observed that the call for national unity "served as a defense also against the anxiety generated by a fearful awareness of economic, social, and cultural differences arising in an increasingly industrial and ethnically pluralistic country." Ibid. Henry May noted that "America went into the war in a period of apparent complacency and underlying, sharply increasing tension." May, *End of American Innocence*, 388.

15. "Danger comes in a democracy," Ingersoll said, "when its citizens busy themselves exclusively in their private affairs and give no time or thought to their public interests, thus making opportunity for political bosses, public waste and corruption. . . ." He proposed that local Four Minute Men organizations establish forums that would affiliate with state forums, which in turn would associate with some national organization. The local forums would meet once a month. Ingersoll suggested that money raised in local communities to commemorate those men killed in action could be put to no better use than the building of public halls for the local forums, helping to revive the old-time town meetings. Such memorials, and the instruction that would be heard in them, would assure that the men who fell in France had died for the cause of liberty. William H. Ingersoll, "What Shall the Four Minute Men Do in the Future?" *Four Minute Men News*, Edition F, supplement (Dec. 24, 1918), i–iii, vii.

16. Such an ideological renaissance is discussed in John Higham, "Hanging Together: Divergent Unities in American History," *Journal of American History* 61 (June 1974): 23–26, especially 25.

Essay On Sources

MORE than fifty manuscript collections were used in preparing this study. By far the largest and most valuable source was the Records of the Committee on Public Information, Record Group 63, in the National Archives. There are about 180 cubic feet of CPI records, perhaps half of which relate to the Domestic Section. Included are incoming and outgoing correspondence, statistical reports, confidential memoranda, mailing lists, card records, posters, and photographs. Of special value were George Creel's correspondence (CPI 1 series) and material relating to the divisions headed by Guy Stanton Ford and Arthur Bestor (CPI 3 and CPI 12 series). There is a large body of material pertaining to the Division of Advertising, although one wishes for more correspondence from this section's members revealing advertising strategy. Also disappointing was the lack of material relating to the Divisions of Work with the Foreign Born, Women's War Work, and Syndicated Features. The CPI collection is supplemented by an excellent seventy-eight-page finding aid prepared by Roscoe R. Hill and Frank Hardee Allen of the National Archives' Division of Classification, *Classification Scheme: Records of the Committee on Public Information, 1917–1919* (Washington, D.C., 1938). Although this collection is sizable, it represents only about a quarter of the original total of material relating to the CPI. The remainder was either lost or destroyed.

The Manuscript Division of the Library of Congress houses several important collections. The George Creel Papers were useful, although much of Creel's correspondence during the war, especially with President Woodrow Wilson, was of little value. Creel met regularly with Wilson to discuss the work of the CPI, but the substance of these conversations is only occasionally revealed in letters. The Woodrow Wilson Papers were of some value in attempting to determine the origins of the committee and Wilson's connection with its work. Creel's part in the CPI's creation, however, is best revealed in the Josephus Daniels Papers. The Daniels collection was also helpful in regard to matters involving censorship and the use of film, and it has interesting material on Franklin K. Lane's ideas on Americanization. Of less value were the Newton Diehl Baker Papers. The Robert Lansing Papers tend to confirm Lansing's slight role in both the creation of the Committee on Public Information and the CPI's subsequent work. The Benjamin B. Lindsey collection contains interesting correspondence between Lindsey and Creel relating to the former's wartime service. The Charles Edward Russell Papers include material on Russell's wartime speaking tours, with copies of speeches. Most valuable were the Papers of the National Board for Historical Service, in particular a great deal of correspondence to and from Evarts B. Greene regarding his work for the NBHS and *History Teacher's Magazine*. Correspondence from Carl Becker, Laurence Larson, Dana Munro, and other writers for the CPI is in this collection. The Brand Whitlock Papers, although not used extensively for this study, do contain a good deal of information about Whitlock's work in Belgium, including his interest in German atrocities. The Elihu Root collection reflects the former secretary of state's concern about German Kultur but has little about his association with the CPI. Letters from Herbert S. Houston written during 1917 and 1918 are found in the William Howard Taft Papers (both Houston and Taft were members of the League to Enforce Peace). Other collections examined in the Manuscript Division of the Library of Congress, but which were of little value for this work, were the papers of Charles Dana Gibson, Booth Tarkington, and Robert M. McElroy.

Material relating to the CPI is found in the Seeley G. Mudd Manuscript Library at Princeton University. Most helpful were the Arthur Bullard Papers. Although much of this collection pertains to Bullard's work in Russia, it includes information relating to his journalistic career before 1917. The Edward S. Corwin Papers were also worthwhile (Corwin is worthy of a good biography). Unfortunately, much of his outgoing correspondence is not found in this collection. Of particular interest was an exchange of letters in late 1920 and early 1921 between Corwin and Zechariah Chafee, Jr., regarding the First Amendment. Corwin's communication is found in the Chafee papers at the Harvard Law School Library. The Ray Stannard Baker Collection and the Robert Lansing Selected Papers (1915–1921) at the Mudd Library were examined but were not helpful in matters relating to the Committee on Public Information.

At Yale University the Edward M. House Collection was found important, especially in determining Bullard's influence in the weeks before the creation of the CPI. The House *Diary* also has some references to Bullard in the weeks prior to establishment of the committee. The Wallace Notestein Papers were of limited value, as were the Walter Lippmann Papers.

Collections at the New York Public Library Annex contain wartime correspondence to and from Creel. The Albert Shaw Papers, the Schwimmer-Lloyd Collection, and the National Civic Federation Papers all have interesting letters to and from the CPI's chairman. Ralph Easley's exchanges with Creel in the National Civic Federation Papers are particularly good in showing outside pressure on Creel while he was directing the CPI.

At Columbia University, Butler Library contains the James G. Phelps Stokes Papers, which shed light on Stokes's prowar activities. Several interviews in the Columbia Oral History Collection were also used, including those with Guy Stanton Ford, James T. Shotwell, Walter Lippmann, Bruce Bliven, Malcolm Davis, Heber Blankenhorn, Henry Seidel Canby, and DeWitt Clinton Poole. Reminiscences of Ford, Lippmann, and Blankenhorn were especially helpful. The Shotwell, Canby, and Poole interviews offer little on the CPI.

The S. S. McClure Papers in the Lilly Library at Indiana University give insight into McClure's participation in the war, especially in late 1917 and early 1918. The Upton Sinclair Papers in the Lilly Library were of small value.

The papers of several CPI writers are in the University of Illinois Archives. Perhaps most interesting are those of Stuart P. Sherman, whose correspondence, especially with Paul Elmer More, provides background for understanding Sherman's CPI pamphlet. There is correspondence from Sherman in the Harold N. Hillebrand Papers, although it was less helpful. The Laurence M. Larson Papers have correspondence with Guy Stanton Ford and Frederic Paxson regarding Larson's reports on immigrant newspapers in Illinois and regarding his work for the *War Cyclopedia*. The Arthur Bestor, Sr., Papers, still restricted, do not contain much correspondence relating to Bestor's work for the CPI (there is a considerable volume of Bestor's letters in the committee's papers), but the collection does contain copies of several wartime speeches. The Ernest J. Bogart, James G. Randall, and James W. Garner Papers have some material relating to work with the CPI. The Eugene V. Davenport Papers contain copies of wartime pamphlets by writers from the University of Illinois, including CPI publications. Correspondence from Greene and Larson is in the Papers of the Committee on the History of the Participation of the University in World War I, and in the Papers of the Dean's Office, College of Liberal Arts and Sciences, University Archives. There is considerable correspondence to and from Greene in the University of Illinois Historical Survey, "Illinois in World War I." Generally speaking, Greene's letters in these collections were disappointing, as few pertain to his work for the CPI. Most deal with his activities at the university as either dean or professor. There is much material relating to his efforts to promote the war at the University of Illinois, especially through the War Issues Course.

A substantial portion of Guy Stanton Ford's wartime correspondence is found in the CPI papers in Washington, but there is also a sizable collection of Ford's papers in the University of Minnesota Archives. Ford's correspondence with his wife during these years was useful in tracing his movement on a speaking tour in the western United States in 1918, made in cooperation with Bestor's division. This collection also contains copies of statements prepared by Ford but signed by other officials, including President Wilson, Creel, and Secretary of War Baker. In addition, Ford's diary kept during his stay in Germany as a student in 1899 gives a fascinating picture of Marburg and Berlin and demonstrates Ford's early concern with German militarism. The William Stearns Davis Papers and the August Krey Papers, also in the University of Minnesota Archives, were helpful. Davis's letters in early 1917 show him to have been a vehement critic of anyone who opposed war with Germany. Krey's papers have relatively little information on his writings for the CPI but do reveal that he also helped the committee by reading foreign-language newspapers. The William Anderson Papers in the University Archives are still uncataloged, and they, along with the Anderson collection in the Minnesota Historical Society, were of little use in preparing this study.

The Department of Special Collections in the Joseph Regenstein Library at the University of Chicago contains worthwhile material. The Andrew C. McLaughlin Papers reveal little new concerning McLaughlin's CPI pamphlet but do have drafts of speeches and lectures showing his ideas on the Monroe Doctrine and the League of Nations. In addition, there is information on McLaughlin's lecture tour in England for the National Board for Historical Service. The Charles E. Merriam Papers have some correspondence with such people as Lindsey and John Spargo, but virtually all of the material pertaining to the CPI deals with Merriam's work in Italy. A check of "An Inventory of Jane Addams Papers in the University of Chicago Library" turned up nothing about Addams's speaking tour in early 1918. The Addams papers at Hull House in the University of Chicago Circle contain many reproductions of her papers located at Swarthmore College.

Other records were examined. The Carl Becker Papers at Cornell University have some exchanges between Becker and Ford but very little on the former's activities for the CPI. The Algie M. Simons Papers at the State Historical Society of Wisconsin in Madison hold a good deal of material on Simons's work abroad during 1918. However, the John R. Commons Papers, located in the same place, reveal little about Commons's wartime pamphlets.

There are several collections of war posters, in addition to those found in the CPI papers. The Thomas J. White War Poster Collection in the Department of Special Collections at the University of Chicago's Joseph Regenstein Library is excellent. The George C. Marshall Research Foundation in Lexington, Va., also has a collection of war posters, to be published under the editorship of O. W. Riegel.

Memoirs, diaries, and autobiographies contain material on the CPI and its members. George Creel's *Rebel at Large* (New York, 1947) gives relatively little new information on his work with the committee and sometimes exaggerates his role in events, but is suggestive in regard to his early religious and educational training and his relation to Woodrow Wilson, before and during the war. Robert Lansing's *Memoirs* (Indianapolis, 1935) indicate that he had little influence on the CPI and that he had a low opinion of Creel. Josephus Daniels's *Wilson Era* (Chapel Hill, N.C., 1946) is much friendlier to Creel. Daniels is at pains to show that the CPI did not mean censorship but rather "public information" to mobilize "the *mind* of America." *The Cabinet Diaries of Josephus Daniels, 1913–1921* (E. David Cronon, ed., Lincoln, Nebr., 1963), have information on the CPI and were of use in reconstructing the committee's origins. There is little information on the committee in Newton D. Baker's *Why We Went to War* (New York, 1936).

Guy Stanton Ford's *On and Off the Campus* (Minneapolis, 1938) is disappointing, primarily because most of the book is made up of essays published before 1938. Unlike Ford's oral interview, this work reveals little about his years as a student in Germany and later at Columbia University and about what effects those experiences may have had on his subsequent views about Germany. James T. Shotwell's *Autobiography* (Indianapolis, 1961) has information about the CPI and its connection with the National Board for Historical Service. Will Irwin's *Propaganda and the News* (New York, 1936) is disorganized, but there are several chapters on German propaganda before 1917 and U.S. propaganda after that date. (Irwin's *Making of a Reporter* [New York, 1942] devotes a chapter to work with the CPI's Foreign Section). Ernest Poole's *Bridge* (New York, 1940) provides information about war service and makes interesting observations about some committee members, including his close friend Arthur Bullard. Charles Edward Russell's *Bare Hands and Stone Walls* (New York, 1933) does not treat speaking appearances for Arthur Bestor's division but is useful for understanding Russell's enthusiastic support of the war. Although expelled from the Socialist party, Russell believed that there was nothing in socialist dogma to prevent supporting the conflict.

Edward Bernays's *Public Relations* (Norman, Okla., 1952) and *Biography of an Idea* (New York, 1965) discuss the CPI's effect on public relations, specifically the committee's effect on Bernays's thinking about the subject. Roger W. Babson's *Actions and Reactions* (New York, 1935) treats work for the CPI and the attempt to promote better wartime relations between labor and management. Jane Addams's *Second Twenty Years at Hull-House* (New York, 1930) discusses her experience while working for the Food Administration but neglects her association with the CPI. Addams's *Peace and Bread in Time of War* (New York, 1922) does provide useful material on her wartime ideas. Edith Bolling Wilson's *My Memoir* (Indianapolis, 1938) contains only a few references to Creel. G. C. Sellery's *Some Ferments at Wisconsin, 1901–1947* (Madison, Wis., 1960) deals with faculty opposition to Robert M. La Follette's stand on the war but makes no mention of Sellery's writing for the Committee on Public Information. Ida M. Tarbell's *All in the Day's Work* (New York, 1939) discusses her desire to see reforms maintained during the war, although she does not deal with the CPI. Henry Canby, who in at least one account is credited with helping create the CPI, does not mention the committee in *American Memoir* (Boston, 1934, 1947). S. S. McClure's *My Autobiography* (New York, 1914, 1963), written before entry into the war, contains interesting material on McClure's earlier career.

Several members of the committee wrote accounts of the CPI—accounts that view the CPI in a favorable light. Creel's

How We Advertised America (New York, 1920) is easily the most detailed history of the propaganda agency by a committee member. Though much of the substance of this work is in the official *Creel Report* (New York, 1920)—an excellent source of information—the author's story was for almost twenty years the standard picture of the committee, and, indeed, much subsequent scholarship followed his organizational scheme. Creel denies that the CPI imposed anything other than a limited, voluntary censorship. For Creel the work of the committee was a crusade, an idealistic "fight for the mind of mankind." One comes away from Creel's work feeling that ideas, or ideals, played an important part in winning the war. Guy Stanton Ford's "America's Fight for Public Opinion," *Minnesota History Bulletin* 3 (Feb. 1919): 3–26, contends that the committee waged a "battle for men's opinions and for the conquest of their convictions," a struggle of equal importance to that taking place on the battlefield in Europe. The goal of the CPI was "mobilization and inspiration of public opinion . . . to arouse a patriotism that could be translated into action." Charles E. Merriam's "American Publicity in Italy," *American Political Science Review* 13 (Nov. 1919): 541–55, and Vira Whitehouse's *A Year as a Government Agent* (New York, 1920) describe the committee's work in Italy and Switzerland, respectively. Frederic L. Paxson argued that Creel was not a censor "in any exact sense" and that he used every means of displaying the American argument for participation in the war, which "as an hypothesis . . . was close-knit" and "largely true" (*American Diplomacy and the World War*, Boston, 1936). In an earlier work, Paxson contended that Creel "devoted his time to lifting the lid of secrecy" surrounding the war (*Recent History of the United States, 1865–1929*, Boston, 1929).

For articles by committee members one may refer either to notes in the present study or to the subsequent bibliographical listing. Pamphlets in the CPI's Red, White and Blue, War Information, and Loyalty Leaflet series were used, as were publications by the Committee for the Friends of German Democracy and the American Alliance for Labor and Democracy. *History Teacher's Magazine*, published under the auspices of the National Board for Historical Service, contains several articles by CPI writers. A check of periodicals turned up articles by people who wrote for the committee—articles that do not always appear in *Reader's Guide to Periodical Literature*. Among magazines searched were *American Magazine, Atlantic Monthly, Century, Cosmopolitan, Editor and Publisher, Harper's Weekly, Independent, Judicious Advertising, McClure's Magazine, Munsey's Magazine, Nation, North American Review, Outlook, Printers' Ink, Scribner's Magazine,* and *World's Work. Editor and Publisher* and *Printers' Ink* are excellent sources for material on the Division of Advertising. *Editor and Publisher* contains material relating to the press's reaction to wartime censorship. *Judicious Advertising* is a source of articles by Herbert Houston, William D'Arcy, Roger Babson, and William H. Ingersoll, among others.

Newspapers were useful in obtaining speeches by persons associated with the CPI. The New York *Times*, well indexed, was helpful. The Philadelphia *Record*, Indianapolis *News*, Los Angeles *Times*, Detroit *Times*, and San Francisco *Examiner* were used. The *Official Bulletin* remains one of the best sources on government activities during the war, although it has been relatively untapped by scholars.

Scores of secondary accounts of the war or the postwar period mention the CPI. Many of these works, rather than basing their conclusions about the committee on empirical evidence, reflect the climate of opinion in which they were written. Very few draw on the committee's papers. A theme of these secondary treatments of the CPI—beginning with revisionist writing in the early 1920s and carrying through into the 1970s —is that the committee perverted scholarship and truth during the war, overplayed the German threat, and was responsible for stirring hatreds that brought wartime and postwar hysteria. One result was to doom Wilson's efforts at Paris. Many writers accept either part or all of this view. Early attacks on the CPI are in works by Upton Sinclair (*Goose Step*, Pasadena, Calif., 1922), Harry Elmer Barnes ("The Drool Method in History," *American Mercury* 1 [Jan. 1924]: 31–38), and C. Hartley Grattan ("The Historians Cut Loose," ibid. 11 [Aug. 1927]: 414–30). Other authors in the 1920s accused the CPI of "exaggerations and misrepresentations" (Kirby Page, *War: Its Causes, Conse-*

quences and Cure, New York, 1923), of making "no effort . . . to present the truth," of perpetrating "the greatest fraud ever sold to the public in the name of patriotism and religion" (C. H. Hamlin, *War Myth in United States History*, New York, 1927). Peter Odegard perhaps summed up the disillusionment with propaganda techniques used in 1917 and 1918 when he wrote in 1930 that "truth was crucified during the war" (*American Public Mind*, New York, 1930). Similar views of the committee were presented by Arthur Ponsonby, *Falsehood in War-Time* (London, 1928); George Sylvester Viereck, *Spreading Germs of Hate* (New York, 1930); and O. W. Riegal, *Mobilizing for Chaos: The Story of the New Propaganda* (New Haven, Conn., 1934).

The CPI has been blamed for creating war and postwar hysteria by a variety of writers, including Viereck and Lucy M. Salmon (*Newspaper and Authority*, New York, 1923). Charles and Mary Beard accused the committee of "subduing . . . the minds of tender children" (*Rise of American Civilization: The Industrial Era*, New York, 1940). I. F. Stone referred to the committee's impact as "organized mass idiocy" ("Creel's Crusade," *Nation* 149 [Dec. 9, 1939]: 647–49). Although this view is less apparent in writings about the committee during the 1940s, it reemerged in the 1950s, 1960s, and 1970s. Robert K. Murray has argued that the CPI set a pattern that resulted in "indoctrination of hate, prejudice, and 100 percent Americanism on a colossal scale" (*Red Scare*, Minneapolis, 1955). Similar views of the committee are found in John Morton Blum's *Woodrow Wilson and the Politics of Morality* (Boston, 1956), William E. Leuchtenburg's *Perils of Prosperity, 1914–32* (Chicago, 1958), and Christopher Lasch's *New Radicalism in America [1889–1963]* (New York, 1965). Murray Levin's *Political Hysteria in America* (New York, 1971), a work seemingly influenced by the climate of the late 1960s and early 1970s, says that the CPI "nourished superpatriotic instincts. . . . One hundred percent Americanism was the committee's credo." More recently, Peter Buitenhuis ("The Selling of the Great War," *Canadian Review of American Studies* 7 [Fall 1976]: 139–50) has argued that, although the members of the CPI were idealistic and sincere, the committee's operations were nevertheless responsible for hysteria and postwar disillusionment. Buitenhuis also contends that, by creating stereotypes, the CPI played some part in the anticommunist hysteria of the 1920s and in the related "attacks on organized labor and the general waves of anti-radicalism" that were part of the two decades following the war. Even John Higham, who treats the CPI judiciously, says that anti-German and antiradical excitements were so "interlocked" that "no date marks the end of one or the beginning of the other," and that the CPI did help provide a logical connection between the two by publishing the Sisson documents in Nov. 1918 (*Strangers in the Land*, New York, 1955, 1967).

This picture of the Committee on Public Information has been popularized in many textbooks, including those by Thomas A. Bailey (*American Spirit*, Lexington, Mass., 1973) and Samuel Eliot Morison (*Oxford History of the American People*, New York, 1965). Morison and David Noble ("The New Republic and the Idea of Progress, 1914–1920," *Mississippi Valley Historical Review* 38 [Dec. 1951]: 387–402) argue that the committee whipped up emotions to the point where Wilson really had no chance at selling the results of the Paris Peace Conference to the American public. Failure of the United States to enter the League of Nations was largely the fault of the CPI, because it did not educate the American people on the issues of the war. Creel's explanation of why the CPI did not publicize the results of the peace conference more widely is in "Why the Peace Treaty Was Not Advertised," *Advertising and Selling* (Dec. 24, 1919): 32–36.

A few accounts draw a more favorable picture of the Committee on Public Information. Mark Sullivan, who did not have access to the CPI files, speaks of the committee in glowing terms. He calls Creel "an artist" who had "the floreating quality that dreams huge projects" (*Our Times: The United States, 1900–1933: Over Here, 1914–1918*, New York, 1933). My study does not agree with Sullivan's assertion that the CPI "was the shadow of a man," a reflection of Creel. Though not as enthusiastic as Sullivan, Robert E. Osgood says that while the committee helped raise "America's missionary fervor... to the peak of 1898," the United States was dedicating "its wealth, its military power, and its prestige to the service of the rest of the world" (*Ideals and Self-Interest in America's Foreign Relations*, Chicago, 1953). Arthur Walworth is perhaps more neutral when he blandly describes the committee's purpose as awakening "in American minds an appreciation of the causes and stakes of the war" (*Woodrow Wilson: World Prophet*, Boston, 1958, 1965).

By the 1930s the CPI had become the object of serious scholarship. Frank Hardee Allen's doctoral dissertation, "Government Influence on News in the United States during the World War" (University of Illinois, 1934), was completed before the committee's records opened. Drawing on such sources as *How We Advertised America*, the *Creel Report*, the *Congressional Record*, the New York *Times*, and Ray Stannard Baker's account of the Paris Peace Conference, Allen treats the government's effort to control news. Although the whole range of government activity in this realm is dealt with, the thesis discusses the CPI and particularly the committee's Division of News.

In 1938 the records of the CPI were made available to scholars, and the following year there appeared the first and only full-scale study of the committee based on those records. James R. Mock and Cedric Larson's *Words That Won the War* (Princeton, N.J., 1939) follows the organization of Creel's *How We Advertised America* and is a catalog of the CPI and its personnel. It is not footnoted, and the authors admit that they were able only to skim the CPI files, that there was such "an embarrassing wealth of material" that only a "small library" would do justice to the committee. The study perhaps adds most to Creel's account by showing that, contrary to Creel's assertion that he had no censorship powers as head of the CPI, he was a member of the Censorship Board, had close contacts with both the postmaster general and the Justice Department, and in fact did exercise influence in determining what material was to be censored. Still, this work presents a generally favorable view of Creel and the committee. It argues that Creel and the CPI did not create the hysterical atmosphere of 1917 and 1918 but had to cope with it (although the authors admit that some of the committee's work may have added fuel to the flames). Mock and Larson, perhaps attempting to draw lessons from the First

World War on the eve of the Second World War, saw the CPI as "a buffer between military dictatorship and civil life." Rather than emphasizing censorship, Creel sought to flood the channels of communication "with official, approved news and opinion." Though Creel may have been "too eager," other groups, such as the National Security League, wanted public opinion raised to higher intensity. To Mock and Larson, Creel and his committee tried to preserve liberalism through the ordeal of modern war. Mock followed this book with *Censorship, 1917* (Princeton, N.J., 1941), which deals not only with the CPI but also with the government's entire censorship effort. Like the previous study, this work is not footnoted.

Walton Bean's "George Creel and His Critics" (University of California, Berkeley, 1941), was the first doctoral thesis written from the CPI files. The work, which was directed by Frederic Paxson, focuses on criticisms of Creel and the committee— that the CPI distorted and censored news, that it was a partisan mouthpiece for Wilsonian ideas—and is a ringing defense of the CPI's chairman and his committee. One is sometimes left with the impression that this study is an extension of Creel's *How We Advertised America*. Perhaps Bean's last chapter is the most interesting. In it he argues that the strongest criticism of Creel and the CPI during the war came from the Right rather than from the Left. Like Mock and Larson, he contends that the CPI faced charges of not being patriotic enough and that Creel had to defend himself against such charges. The CPI acted as a lightning rod, drawing off criticism of Wilson.

Two more recent doctoral theses touching on the CPI have been published. Neither George Blakey's *Historians on the Homefront* (Lexington, Ky., 1970) nor Carol Gruber's *Mars and Minerva* (Baton Rouge, La., 1975) focuses exclusively on the Committee on Public Information. Blakey treats the National Security League and the National Board for Historical Service in addition to the CPI. Gruber's study deals with the years 1914–18 and with a somewhat different group of academicians who supported the war. Both authors discuss Ford's Division of Civic and Educational Publications, pointing out how historians and other scholars allowed government service to distort scholarship. The studies may reflect lessons from the 1960s and 1970s, but they do treat an important feature of the CPI's work. Both studies are well written. Gruber's account, published some years after Blakey's work, offers a perhaps more detailed explanation of why academicians took the positions they did during the war.

Other works do not make the CPI their focus but have drawn on the CPI papers. H. C. Peterson and Gilbert C. Fite, in *Opponents of War, 1917–1918* (Seattle, 1957), discuss the CPI's role in government censorship and repression of civil liberties. Creel is portrayed as concerned with possible disloyalty but also as worried about the "chauvinistic, reactionary state organizations" of the Council of National Defense. James Weinstein in *Corporate Ideal and the Liberal State* (Boston, 1968) was interested in the CPI's relation to labor. He argued that Creel secretly controlled the American Alliance for Labor and Democracy. Frank L. Grubbs, Jr.'s *Struggle for Labor Loyalty* (Durham, N.C., 1968) uses the committee's papers to explain the CPI's connection with the alliance.

There are areas relating to the Committee on Public Information that need more research, and one such area is biography. There are no published biographies of Creel, Bullard, Charles Edward Russell, Bestor, or, as mentioned, Edward S. Corwin, although manuscript collections exist for each man. Joseph Garvey's doctoral thesis, mentioned in Chapter 10, is the most lengthy treatment of Corwin's thought. There is no biography of Ford, who was certainly one of the most influential persons determining the content of government propaganda during the war. Although there are perhaps fewer records, studies could be done of Ernest Poole, Will Irwin, Harvey O'Higgins, Edgar Sisson, and Herbert S. Houston. Often, too, where biographies exist for people associated with the CPI, they deal inadequately with the war years. Peter Lyon's *Success Story* (Deland, Fla., 1963) does not do justice to McClure's role in the war, especially in late 1917 and early 1918. Mary E. Tomkins's *Ida M. Tarbell* (New York, 1974) is disappointing on activities during the war. William C. Bagley has been the subject of a biography (I. L. Kandel, *William Chandler Bagley: Stalwart*

Educator, New York, 1961) and of several doctoral dissertations, including Gene D. Phillips's "The Educational Thought of William C. Bagley" (Indiana University, 1952) and Erwin Virgil Johanningmeier's "A Study of William Chandler Bagley's Educational Doctrines and His Program for Teacher Preparation, 1895–1918" (University of Illinois, 1967). Nonetheless, one is left with the impression that the definitive study of Bagley has yet to be written. Greene is another person worthy of study. Jack Randolph Kirby's doctoral thesis, "Evarts Boutell Greene: The Career of a Professional Historian" (University of Illinois, 1969), provides only a superficial treatment of Greene's writings and career. Kent Kreuter and Gretchen Kreuter's *An American Dissenter* (Lexington, Ky., 1969) offers an account of Simons during 1917–18, and Barry Karl's *Charles E. Merriam and the Study of Politics* (Chicago, 1974) is a fine biography. John C. Farrell's *Beloved Lady: A History of Jane Addams' Ideas on Reform and Peace* (Baltimore, 1967) gives perhaps the best published account of Addams's wartime speeches. But there may be more to learn about these people's participation in the war.

Nationalism is one of the larger issues associated with the CPI. There is a need for more studies about American nationalism in the twentieth century, as there is no good comprehensive treatment of this subject. A step in the right direction is Arthur Harrison Ogle, Jr.'s doctoral thesis ("Nationalism and American Foreign Policy, 1898–1920: A Series of Case Studies on the Influence of an Idea," University of Virginia, 1971), which examines the nationalistic views of several Americans, including Woodrow Wilson. Among the material that has been written on nationalism, several works were helpful in preparing the present study. Carlton J. H. Hayes's *Essays on Nationalism* (New York, 1926), *Historical Evolution of Modern Nationalism* (New York, 1931, 1968), and *Nationalism: A Religion* (New York, 1960) are essential. Boyd Shafer's *Nationalism: Myth and Reality* (New York, 1955) and *Faces of Nationalism* (New York, 1972) are similarly important, as are Louis Snyder's *Meaning of Nationalism* (New Brunswick, N.J., 1954) and his more recent *Varieties of Nationalism* (Hinsdale, Ill., 1976). Leonard Doob's *Patriotism and Nationalism* (New Haven, Conn., 1964) is still good. Karl Deutsch's *Nationalism and Social Communication* (Cambridge, Mass., 1953) was suggestive as were Anthony D. Smith's *Theories of Nationalism* (London, 1971), and his "The Formation of Nationalist Movements," Anthony D. Smith, ed., *Nationalist Movements* (London, 1976), 1–30. David M. Potter's "The Historian's Use of Nationalism and Vice Versa," Don E. Fehrenbacher, ed., *History and American Society* (New York, 1973), 61–108, and Gale Stokes's "Cognition and the Function of Nationalism," *Journal of Interdisciplinary History* 4 (Spring 1974): 525–42, are important essays. For background on American nationalism and the idea of mission, I have used several works, including Merle Curti, *Roots of American Loyalty* (New York, 1946); Hans Kohn, *American Nationalism* (New York, 1957) (and the chapter on the same subject in Kohn's *Idea of Nationalism*, New York, 1943); Charles A. Beard, "Nationalism in American History," Waldo G. Leland, ed., *Nationalism* (Bloomington, Ind., 1934), 39–51; Paul C. Nagel, *This Sacred Trust: American Nationality, 1798–1898* (New York, 1971); Russel B. Nye, *This Almost Chosen People* (East Lansing, Mich., 1966); Yehoshua Arieli, *Individualism and Nationalism in American Ideology* (Cambridge, Mass., 1964); Edward McNall Burns, *American Idea of Mission* (New Brunswick, N.J., 1957); Ernest Tuveson, *Redeemer Nation* (Chicago, 1968); and Conrad Cherry, *God's New Israel* (Englewood Cliffs, N.J., 1971). Works cited in Chapter 3 of this study on civil or secular religion were also helpful.

There is considerable literature on progressivism and the war. Richard Hofstadter's *Age of Reform* (New York, 1955) has been challenged by more than two decades of scholarship but still is one of the most stimulating works on the progressive years. Charles Hirschfeld's "Nationalist Progressivism and World War I," *Mid-America* 45 (July 1963): 139–56; Allen F. Davis's "Welfare, Reform, and World War I," *American Quarterly* 19 (Fall 1967): 516–33; J. A. Thompson's "American Progressive Publicists and the First World War, 1914–1917," *Journal of American History* 58 (Sept. 1971): 364–83; and Louis Filler's *Appointment at Armageddon* (Westport, Conn., 1976) are all worthwhile studies.

Several accounts were useful in explaining anti-German

sentiment in 1917–18, including those works cited in Chapter 4 by Melvin Small, Ruth Miller Elson, Daniel M. Smith, Alfred Vagts, Carl Wittke, Clara Eve Schieber, George Blakey, and Carol Gruber. In addition, Frederick C. Luebke's *Bonds of Loyalty: German-Americans and World War I* (De Kalb, Ill., 1974) is both interesting and intelligently written. There is no question that emotions ran high during the Great War and that many persons were swept up in the hysteria of the period. However, there has been a tendency to ignore the differences between German and American political and military institutions. There were people who were worried about those differences and who offered a more thoughtful indictment of the enemy than did others, who were caught up in the emotions of the era. The concerns of the more thoughtful writers about German militarism can sometimes be traced to before the war. Certainly, if we are to believe a substantial portion of post-World War II scholarship on German history, their fears were well founded. More studies would be welcome on the experiences of Americans with German society before 1914, especially those of scholars who spent time studying in German universities. Such work could build on the findings of Gruber, Charles Franklin Thwing, Anna Haddow, Thomas I. Cook and Arnaud B. Leavelle, Ralph G. Hoxie, Henry A. Pochmann, Charles Baskervill Robson, and Sylvia D. Fries (also cited in Chapter 4). Not only could it perhaps better explain wartime attitudes toward Germany, but it would also illuminate an important period in American educational history.

Public speakers during the war have not received extensive treatment. Jeanne Graham's "The Four Minute Men: Volunteers for Propaganda," *Southern Speech Journal* 32 (Fall 1966): 49–57, and Carol Oukrop's "The Four Minute Men Became National Network during World War I," *Journalism Quarterly* 52 (Winter 1975): 632–37, do not add much to the account of Mock and Larson. Wayne A. Nicholas's doctoral thesis, "Crossroads' Oratory: A Study of the Four Minute Men of World War I" (Columbia University, 1953), is the most detailed study of the Four Minute Men. Based on the published *Four Minute Men Bulletins* and *Four Minute Men News*, this study is heavy with quotations and repetitious; it could have been condensed. It does present perhaps the best analysis of appeals used by the Four Minute Men. The Speaking Division has received virtually no historical analysis. James A. B. Scherer's *Nation at War* (New York, 1918) contains excerpts from speeches by such speakers as Paul Périgord, who was sent out by Bestor's division. Our knowledge of both the Four Minute Men and the Speaking division could profit from further state and local studies of their activities. Two doctoral dissertations have provided information in this area. Carol Elizabeth Jenson's "Agrarian Pioneer in Civil Liberties: The Nonpartisan League in Minnesota during World War I" (University of Minnesota, 1968) sheds light on the Speaking Division and the difficulties it encountered with the state's Commission on Public Safety. Bruce Fraser's "Yankees at War: Social Mobilization on the Connecticut Homefront, 1917–1918" (Columbia University, 1976) argues that orators for both the Speaking Division and Four Minute Men in Connecticut were more closely controlled by the state council of defense than by the CPI.

There is no good history of advertising during the years before and during the war. Otis Pease's *Responsibilities of American Advertising* (New Haven, Conn., 1958) has some introductory material on the CPI and the war but concentrates on the years 1920 to 1940. Advertising has unquestionably had a large inpact on modern society. David M. Potter's "Advertising: The Institution of Abundance," *Yale Review* 43 (Autumn 1953): 49–70 (later published in *People of Plenty: Economic Abundance and the American Character*, Chicago, 1954), provides a good introductory survey of advertising's development in the late nineteenth and twentieth centuries, and his conclusion that we need more studies on advertising in this century is still correct. In particular, advertising's relation to national power deserves more investigation. Stanley Kelley, Jr.'s *Professional Public Relations and Political Power* (Baltimore, 1956) is a fine study in this direction.

On public opinion theory, Stow Persons's *American Minds* (New York, 1958) was stimulating, as were Walter Lippmann's *Public Opinion* (New York, 1922) and Edward Bernays's *Crystal-*

lizing Public Opinion (New York, 1923), *Propaganda* (New York, 1928), and "Manipulating Public Opinion: The Why and the How," *American Journal of Sociology* 23 (May 1928): 958–71. These works should be read in contrast to Creel's "Public Opinion in War Time," *Annals of the American Academy of Political and Social Science* 78 (July 1918): 185–94, and "Propaganda and Morale," *American Journal of Sociology* 47 (Nov. 1941): 340–51. For propaganda techniques employed during the war one must begin with Harold D. Lasswell's *Propaganda Technique in World War I* (London, 1927). Although containing factual errors, this work was a pioneering study of comparative war propaganda. Part of Sydney Weinberg's doctoral dissertation, "Wartime Propaganda in a Democracy: America's Twentieth-Century Information Agencies" (Columbia University, 1969), deals with the CPI, although the major focus is on the post–1918 years, and the work is probably strongest on the Office of War Information during World War II. Jackson A. Giddens's doctoral thesis, "American Foreign Propaganda in World War I" (Fletcher School, Tufts University, 1967), treats the CPI's propaganda sent abroad. Leonard Doob's *Public Opinion and Propaganda* (New York, 1948) is a fine study of general propaganda techniques during the twentieth century.

Although the definitive study of censorship and civil liberties during the Great War remains to be written, several works dealing with this subject are useful. Zechariah Chafee, Jr.'s *Free Speech in the United States* (New York, 1920) is classic. Mock's *Censorship, 1917*, and portions of Mock and Larson's *Words That Won the War* provide good introductions to censorship measures taken in 1917–18. Though appropriately critical of actions taken by the Wilson administration and the CPI, Mock and Larson are nevertheless sensitive to the dilemmas facing democratic government in wartime. Another introduction to the period, somewhat briefer, is Harry Scheiber's *Wilson Administration and Civil Liberties, 1917–1921* (Ithaca, N.Y., 1960). There are a number of other studies (cited in Chapter 10) that are worthwhile, including the books by H. C. Peterson and Gilbert C. Fite and by William Preston. Also good are the articles by Donald Johnson, John M. Blum, John Braeman, Brent Swisher, and

Fred D. Ragan. Frank Hardee Allen's dissertation contains useful information, too. Other studies provide valuable background for this period. Donald Johnson's *Challenge to American Freedoms* (Lexington, Ky., 1963) treats the growth of the American Civil Liberties Union. Harold M. Hyman's *To Try Men's Souls: Loyalty Tests in American History* (Berkeley, Calif., 1959) criticizes the Wilson administration for the extralegal activities of the Loyal Legion of Loggers and Lumbermen and the American Protective League. Hyman's comments about the administration and the APL, however, must be placed against Joan M. Jensen's subsequent study, *Price of Vigilance* (Chicago, 1968). It is the most thoroughly researched treatment of that organization. Paul L. Murphy's *Meaning of Freedom of Speech: First Amendment Freedoms from Wilson to FDR* (Westport, Conn., 1972) is thought-provoking even though it concentrates mainly on the post-1918 period. Murphy also has an introductory work on First Amendment rights in *World War I and the Origin of Civil Liberties in the United States* (New York, 1979). For a fine discussion of the suppression of minority views by public opinion during World War I, see O. A. Hilton, "Public Opinion and Civil Liberties in Wartime, 1917–1919," *Southwestern Social Science Quarterly* 28 (Dec. 1947): 201–24.

There are areas related to civil liberties and World War I where important work remains to be done. Some of the most severe repression occurred at the state and local level and was very often the work of the state councils of defense and their county and local auxiliaries. A listing of some of the works dealing with these organizations is found in Chapter 10, but a thorough study of these agencies is still needed. Also cited in Chapter 10 are works by Gerald D. Feldman, Hans Hautmann, Marc Ferro, Jean-Noël Jeanneney, Georges Liens, and Deian Hopkin that touch on censorship in Europe, although, even when taken together, they still present only a fragmentary view of this subject. More information on censorship in Europe during the war would perhaps broaden our own perspective on how civil liberties fared in America. Finally, though many of the above authors touch on various aspects of First Amendment freedoms during the First World War, a good, detailed account of the Wilson administration and civil liberties is needed.

Doctoral dissertations and essays other than those mentioned above have been helpful. Wallace Henry Moore's "The Conflict Concerning the German Language and German Propaganda in the Public Secondary Schools of the United States, 1917–1919" (Stanford University, 1937) provided information about Samuel B. Harding and E. E. Sperry and their attitudes about teaching German in public schools. Charles Baskervill Robson's "The Influence of German Thought on Political Theory in the United States in the Nineteenth Century: An Introductory Study" (University of North Carolina, 1930), was helpful. American perceptions of Germany before and during the war are treated in Melvin Small's "The American Image of Germany, 1906–1914" (University of Michigan, 1965). Small's essay "Historians Look at Public Opinion," Melvin Small, ed., *Public Opinion and Historians* (Detroit, 1970), 13–32, points up difficulties of attempting to measure public opinion in the early twentieth century. I also profited from Alvar Ellegård's "Public Opinion and the Press: Reactions to Darwinism," *Journal of the History of Ideas* 19 (June 1958): 379–87, a fine account of difficulties and dangers in gauging public opinion through the press. Russell Buchanan's "American Editors Examine American War Aims and Plans in April, 1917," *Pacific Historical Review* 9 (Sept. 1940): 253–65, is a good summary of the editorial opinion of sixty-eight American newspapers. Fred A. Sondermann's thesis, "The Wilson Administration's Image of Germany" (Yale University, 1953), was not particularly helpful in preparing this study.

Other doctoral theses either touch the work of the CPI or individuals and issues connected with the committee. Ora Hilton's "The Control of Public Opinion in the United States during the World War" (University of Wisconsin, 1929) was followed by several articles listed in Chapter 10. Willis H. Ruff's "Coercion and Freedom in a War Situation: A Critical Analysis of Minnesota Culture during World War One" (University of Minnesota, 1957) has some information on CPI posters in Minnesota (pp. 223–24). Sally M. Miller's "Victor L. Berger and the Promise of Constructive Socialism, 1910–1920" (University of Toronto, 1966), and her subsequent book by the same title (Westport, Conn., 1973) contain information on Algie Simons. John David Hoeveler, Jr.'s "The New Humanism: An Aspect of Twentieth Century American Thought" (University of Illinois, 1971) and his later *New Humanism: A Critique of Modern America, 1900–1940* (Charlottesville, Va., 1977), use the Stuart Pratt Sherman correspondence in the University of Illinois Archives. Hoeveler's work is a stimulating study with a fine discussion of Sherman's thought, as well as of the ideas of Irving Babbitt, Paul E. More, Henry S. Canby, and others. Lance T. Ventry's "The Impact of the United States Committee on Public Information on Italian Participation in the First World War" (Catholic University of America, 1968) does not deal with the Domestic Section and is marred by factual inaccuracies.

Bibliography

MANUSCRIPT SOURCES

Bloomington, Ind.
  Lilly Library, Indiana University
    S. S. McClure Papers
    Upton Sinclair Papers
Cambridge, Mass.
  Harvard Law School Library
    Zechariah Chafee, Jr., Papers
Chicago, Ill.
  Joseph Regenstein Library, University of Chicago
    Jane Addams Papers
    Andrew C. McLaughlin Papers
    Charles E. Merriam Papers
    Thomas J. White War Poster Collection
Ithaca, N.Y.
  John M. Olin Library, Cornell University Libraries
    Carl Becker Papers
Lexington, Va.
  George C. Marshall Research Foundation
    Posters of World War I and World War II
Madison, Wis.
  State Historical Society of Wisconsin
    John R. Commons Papers
    Algie M. Simons Papers

Minneapolis, Minn.
  Minnesota Historical Society
    William Anderson Papers
  University of Minnesota Archives
    William Anderson Papers
    William Stearns Davis Papers
    Guy Stanton Ford Papers
    August Krey Papers
New Haven, Conn.
  Yale University Library
    Papers of Colonel E. M. House
    Walter Lippmann Papers
    Wallace Notestein Papers
New York, N.Y.
  Butler Library, Columbia University
    James G. Phelps Stokes Papers
  New York Public Library Annex
    National Civic Federation Papers
    Schwimmer-Lloyd Collection
    Albert Shaw Papers
Princeton, N.J.
  Seeley G. Mudd Manuscript Library, Princeton University
    Ray Stannard Baker Papers
    Arthur Bullard Papers
    Edward S. Corwin Papers
    Robert Lansing Selected Papers

Swarthmore, Pa.
  Swarthmore College Peace Collection
    Jane Addams Correspondence
Urbana, Ill.
  University of Illinois Archives
    Arthur Bestor, Sr., Papers
    Ernest J. Bogart Papers
    Committee on the History of
      the Participation of the
      University in World War I,
      1915–1923 (Evarts Greene
      and Laurence Larson
      correspondence)
    Eugene V. Davenport Papers
    James W. Garner Papers
    Harold N. Hillebrand Papers
    Laurence M. Larson Papers
    Liberal Arts and Sciences,
      Dean's Office, Departmental and Subject File
      (History Department,
      University of Illinois
      correspondence)
    James G. Randall Papers
    Stuart Pratt Sherman Papers

University of Illinois Historical
  Survey
    Illinois in World War I (Evarts
      Greene correspondence)
Washington, D.C.
  Library of Congress Annex
    Newton Diehl Baker Papers
    George Creel Papers
    Josephus Daniels Papers
    Charles Dana Gibson Papers
    Robert Lansing Papers
    Benjamin B. Lindsey Papers
    Robert M. McElroy Papers
    National Board for Historical
      Service Papers
    Elihu Root Papers
    Charles Edward Russell Papers
    William Howard Taft Papers
    Booth Tarkington Papers
    Brand Whitlock Papers
    Woodrow Wilson Papers
  National Archives
    Records of the Committee
      on Public Information,
      Record Group 63

Interviews, Columbia Oral History Collection, Columbia University

Heber Blankenhorn
Bruce Bliven
Henry Seidel Canby
Malcolm Davis

Guy Stanton Ford
Walter Lippmann
DeWitt Clinton Poole
James T. Shotwell

Memoirs, Diaries, Autobiographies, and Published Collections

Addams, Jane. *Second Twenty Years at Hull-House: September 1909 to September 1929: With a Record of a Growing World Consciousness.* New York, 1930.

[Babson, Roger W.] *Actions and Reactions: An Autobiography of Roger W. Babson.* New York, 1935.

Baker, Newton D. *Why We Went to War.* New York, 1936.

Baker, Ray Stannard. *American Chronicle: The Autobiography of Ray Stannard Baker.* New York, 1945.

[Bernays, Edward L.] *Biography of an Idea: Memoirs of Public Relations Counsel Edward L. Bernays.* New York, 1965.

[Bok, Edward]. *Americanization of Edward Bok: The Autobiography of a Dutch Boy Fifty Years After.* New York, 1921.

Canby, Henry Seidel. *American Memoir.* Boston, 1934, 1947.

Creel, George. *Rebel at Large: Recollections of Fifty Crowded Years.* New York, 1947.

Cronon, E. David, ed. *Cabinet Diaries of Josephus Daniels, 1913–1921.* Lincoln, Nebr., 1963.

Daniels, Josephus. *Wilson Era: Years of War and After, 1917–1923.* Chapel Hill, N.C., 1946.

Ford, Guy Stanton. *My Year Abroad* (Diary) (1899), Guy Stanton Ford Papers, University of Minnesota Archives, legal folder 4(l) and 5(l).

———. *On and Off the Campus.* Minneapolis, 1938.

House, Edward M. *Diary.* Yale University Library.

Irwin, Will. *Making of a Reporter.* New York, 1942.

Lane, Anne Wintermute, and Louise Herrick Wall, eds. *Letters of Franklin K. Lane: Personal and Political.* Boston, 1922.

[Lansing, Robert]. *War Memoirs of Robert Lansing, Secretary of State.* Indianapolis, 1935.

[MacArthur, Douglas]. *Reminiscences: General of the Army Douglas MacArthur.* New York, 1964.

———. *A Soldier Speaks: Public Papers and Speeches of General of the Army Douglas MacArthur.* New York, 1965.

McClure, S. S. *My Autobiography.* New York, 1914, 1963.

Poole, Ernest. *Bridge: My Own Story.* New York, 1940.

Russell, Charles Edward. *Bare Hands and Stone Walls: Some Recollections of a Side-Line Reformer.* New York, 1933.

Sellery, G. C. *Some Ferments at Wisconsin, 1901–1947: Memories and Reflections.* Madison, Wis., 1960.

Seymour, Charles, ed. *Intimate Papers of Colonel House.* 4 vols., Boston, 1928.

Sherman, Stuart P. *Journals* (1917–18), Stuart Pratt Sherman Papers, Box 11, University of Illinois Archives.

Shotwell, James T. *Autobiography of James T. Shotwell.* Indianapolis, 1961.

Sisson, Edgar G. *One Hundred Red Days: A Personal Chronicle of the Bolshevik Revolution.* New Haven, Conn., 1931.

Tarbell, Ida M. *All in the Day's Work.* New York, 1939.

Wilson, Edith Bolling. *My Memoir.* Indianapolis, 1938.

NEWSPAPERS

Detroit *Times*

Indianapolis *News*

Los Angeles *Times*

New York *Times*

Official Bulletin

Philadelphia *Record*

San Francisco *Examiner*

PERIODICALS

Advertising News
American Magazine
Atlantic Monthly
Century
Cosmopolitan
Editor and Publisher
Everybody's Magazine
Harper's Weekly
History Teacher's Magazine
   (Historical Outlook)

Independent
Judicious Advertising
McClure's Magazine
Munsey's Magazine
Nation
North American Review
Outlook
Printers' Ink
Scribner's Magazine
World's Work

MATERIAL BY PEOPLE ASSOCIATED WITH THE CPI AND
OTHER CONTEMPORARY PUBLISHED SOURCES

Adams, George B. "The English Background of American Institutions."
   Historical Outlook 60 (Nov. 1918): 423–25.

Adams, Samuel Hopkins. *Common Cause: A Novel of the War in America*. Boston,
   1918.

————. "The I. I. I.: A Story of the New Washington." *Everybody's Magazine*
   40 (Mar. 1919): 22–26, 90–95.

————. "Invaded America: I. Poisoning the Press." *Everybody's Magazine* 37
   (Dec. 1917): 9–16, 86.

————. "Invaded America: Wisconsin Joins the War." *Everybody's Magazine*
   38 (Jan. 1918): 28–33, 82, 84.

————. "Invaded America: The Winning Battle in the Middle West." *Everybody's Magazine* 38 (Feb. 1918): 30–32, 74–76, 78–83.

————. "Invaded America: Making Over the Alien." *Everybody's Magazine*
   38 (Mar. 1918): 55–56, 58, 60, 62, 64.

————. "Private Smith Is Cordially Invited." *World's Work* 36 (Sept. 1918):
   528–37.

Addams, Jane. "Americanization." *Papers and Proceedings: Fourteenth Annual
   Meeting, American Sociological Society, Held at Chicago, Ill., December 29–31,
   1919* 14 (1920): 206–15.

————. *Peace and Bread in Time of War*. New York, 1922.

————. "The World's Food Supply and Woman's Obligation." National Education Association of the United States, *Addresses and Proceedings of the
   Fifty-Sixth Annual Meeting Held at Pittsburgh, Pennsylvania, June 29–July 6,
   1918* 56: 108–13.

"Advertises in War Emergency; Uncovers Rich New Market." *Printers' Ink*
   104 (Sept. 12, 1918): 37–38, 40.

"Advertising Wins Many Recruits for Y.M.C.A. War Service." *Printers' Ink*
   104 (July 25, 1918): 59–60.

Altrocchi, Rudolph. "D'Annunzio as an Orator." *Nation* 101 (Dec. 23, 1915):
   4 (of supplement).

_____. " 'Mais Ici . . .' [letter to editor]," *Nation* 101 (July 1, 1915): 13–14.

_____. "A Prophetic Sonnet." *Nation* 104 (Apr. 29, 1917): 457.

_____. "Summons to Youth: Poem." *Poetry* 10 (July 1917): 191.

Altschul, Charles. *American Revolution in Our School Text-Books: An Attempt to Trace the Influence of Early School Education on the Feeling toward England in the United States.* New York, 1917.

_____. *German Militarism and Its German Critics: Fully Illustrated by Extracts from German Newspapers,* War Information Series, No. 13, Washington, D.C., 1918.

American Alliance for Labor and Democracy. *Labor's Red, White and Blue Book: The Official Record of the Organized Labor Movement of America in Relation to the World War.* New York, 1918?

Babson, Roger W. "Eliminating the Economic Causes of War." Geroge H. Blakeslee, ed., *Problems and Lessons of the War: Clark University Addresses, December 16, 17, and 18, 1915.* New York, 1916, 155–62.

_____. *Future of South America.* Boston, 1916.

_____. "The South American Plan." *Sagamore Sociological Conference (Eighth Year)* (Sagamore Beach, Mass., June 30–July 2, 1914), 35–36.

Bagley, W. C. "The Determination of Minimum Essentials in Elementary Geography and History." *Fourteenth Yearbook of the National Society for the Study of Education.* Part I: *Minimum Essentials in Elementary-School Subjects— Standards and Current Practices.* Chicago, 1915, 131–46.

_____. "Education and Our Democracy." National Education Association of the United States, *Addresses and Proceedings of the Fifty-Sixth Annual Meeting Held at Pittsburgh, Pennsylvania, June 29–July 6, 1918* 56: 55–58.

_____. *Educative Process.* New York, 1905, 1912.

_____. "Present-Day Minimal Essentials in United States History as Taught in the Seventh and Eighth Grades." *Sixteenth Yearbook of the National Society for the Study of Education:* Part I: *Second Report of the Committee on Minimal Essentials in Elementary-School Subjects.* Bloomington, Ind., 1917, 143–55.

_____. *School Discipline.* New York, 1914.

_____. "Some Handicaps to Education in a Democracy." *School and Society* 3 (June 3, 1916): 807–16.

Baker, Newton D. *War Measures and Purposes.* In Franklin K. Lane and Newton D. Baker, *Nation in Arms,* War Information Series, No. 2, Washington, D.C., 1917, 8–13.

Beard, Charles A. "A Call upon Every Citizen." *Harper's Magazine* 137 (Oct. 1918): 655–56.

Beard, Charles A., and Mary Ritter Beard. *American Citizenship.* New York, 1914.

Beard, Charles A., and William C. Bagley. *History of the American People.* New York, 1918.

Becker, Carl L. *America's War Aims and Peace Program,* War Information Series, No. 21, Washington, D.C., 1918.

_____. "Detachment and the Writing of History." *Atlantic Monthly* 106 (Oct. 1910): 524–36.

_____. "German Attempts to Divide Belgium." World Peace Foundation, *A League of Nations* 1 (Aug. 1918): 307–40.

_____. "German Historians and the Great War." *Dial* 60 (Feb. 17, 1916): 160–64.

_____. Letter to Editor. *Nation* 106 (Feb. 7, 1918): 142–43.

_____. "The Monroe Doctrine and the War." *Minnesota History Bulletin* 2 (May 1917): 61–68 (reprinted in *History Teacher's Magazine* 9 [Feb. 1918]: 87–90).

_____. *United States, an Experiment in Democracy.* New York, [1920].

Bernays, Edward L. *Crystallizing Public Opinion.* New York, 1923.

_____. "Manipulating Public Opinion: The Why and the How." *American Journal of Sociology* 33 (May 1928): 958–71.

_____. "The Press Agent Has His Day [letter]." *Printers' Ink* 110 (Feb. 26, 1920): 107–8.

_____. *Propaganda.* New York, 1928.

_____. *Public Relations.* Norman, Okla., 1952.

_____. *Public Relations, Edward L. Bernays, and the American Scene: Annotated Bibliography of and Reference Guide to Writings by Edward L. Bernays from 1917 to 1951.* Concord, N.H., 1951.

_____. "Public Relations." Edward L. Bernays, ed., *Careers for Men: A Practical Guide to Opportunity in Business: Written by Thirty-Eight Successful Americans.* New York, 1927, 1939.

_____. "Putting Politics on the Market." *Independent* 120 (May 19, 1928): 470–72.

Bestor, Arthur E. "Chautauqua's Chance To-Day." *Independent* 91 (July 7, 1917): 17–18.

_____. "Mobilizing the Mind of America." *Independent* 95 (Aug. 31, 1918): 290, 300.

_____. "The Old World and the New Order." *Proceedings and Papers of the Indiana State Teachers' Association* (Oct. 30, 31, and Nov. 1, 1919): 214–32.

_____. "The Speaking Division, Committee on Public Information." Montaville Flowers, ed., *What Every American Should Know About the War.* New York, 1918, 260–61.

_____. "The War and the Making of Public Opinion." *New Jersey Municipalities* 2 (Oct. 1918): 231–32, 247–48.

Blanchard, Frank Leroy. "Patriotic Posters Speed Up Production in Government Shipyards." *Printers' Ink* 104 (Sept. 5, 1918): 89–90, 92.

_____. "Red Cross Advertising Campaign Based upon Heart Appeal: Through Newspapers, Magazines, Trade Papers, Posters, Car Cards and Moving Pictures Is Carried in a Dramatic and Appealing Way the Cry for Help That Comes from Across the Sea." *Printers' Ink* 103 (May 23, 1918): 104–6, 109.

Blankenhorn, Heber. *Adventures in Propaganda: Letters from an Intelligence Officer in France.* New York, 1919.

_____. "The War of Morale: How America 'Shelled' the German Lines with Paper." *Harper's Magazine* 139 (Sept. 1919): 510–24.

Bliven, Bruce. "Fighting the German Spy with Advertising: Three New Official Campaigns, Prepared by the Division of Advertising, Committee on Public Information, Will Help to Counteract Enemy Propaganda and Maintain Our National Morale." *Printers' Ink* 103 (May 23, 1918): 17–20, 25–26.

———. "How Advertising Will Help 'Put Over' the Next Draft." *Printers' Ink* 104 (Aug. 22, 1918): 61–62, 64, 69.

———. "Keeping the Country Sold on the War: The National Committee of Patriotic Societies Is Doing Yeoman Service in Teaching Our Citizens What We Are Fighting For." *Printers' Ink* 103 (May 9, 1918): 41–44.

———. " 'Waking Up America': The Big Job of Making 110,000,000 People Realize What the War Means—What Is Being Done and By Whom." *Printers' Ink* 103 (May 2, 1918): 65–68.

———. "What British Advertisers Have Learned in War Time." *Printers' Ink* 104 (Aug. 8, 1918): 3–4, 6, 110, 112, 117.

Bogart, E. L. "Historical Novels in American History." *History Teacher's Magazine* 8 (Sept. 1917): 226–31.

Brady, William A. "Have the Movies Ideals?" *Forum* 59 (Mar. 1918): 307–15.

Brown, L. Ames. "Economics of Prohibition." *North American Review* 203 (Feb. 1916): 256–64.

———. "The Election and Prohibition." *North American Review* 204 (Dec. 1916): 850–56.

———. "The General Staff." *North American Review* 206 (Aug. 1917): 239.

———. "Is Prohibition America?" *North American Review* 203 (Mar. 1916): 413–19.

———. "Nation-Wide Prohibition." *Atlantic Monthly* 115 (June 1915): 735–47.

———. "A New Era of Good Feeling." *Atlantic Monthly* 115 (June 1915): 99–110.

———. "Preparedness for Peace: An Authorized Statement of President Wilson's Plans." *Collier's* 58 (Sept. 16, 1916): 12–13.

———. "The President and the Independent Voter." *World's Work* 32 (Sept. 1916): 494–98.

———. "President Wilson and Publicity." *Harper's Weekly* 58 (Nov. 1, 1913): 19–21.

———. "President Wilson's Mexican Policy." *Atlantic Monthly* 117 (June 1916): 732–44.

———. "Prohibition." *North American Review* 202 (Nov. 1915): 702–29.

———. "Prohibition or Temperance?" *North American Review* 203 (Apr. 1916): 564–71.

———. "Prohibition's Legislative Efforts." *North American Review* 204 (Oct. 1916): 589–93.

———. "Suffrage and Prohibition." *North American Review* 203 (Jan. 1916): 93–100.

———. "Wilson the Candidate." *American Review of Reviews* 54 (July 1916): 41–45.

Bullard, Arthur. *ABC's of Disarmament and the Pacific Problem.* New York, 1921.

————. *American Diplomacy in the Modern World*. Philadelphia, 1928.

————. "Are We a World Power?" *Century* 91 (Nov. 1915): 114–19.

————. "The British War Machine." *Outlook* 109 (Mar. 24, 1915): 683–86.

————. "Business and the War." *Outlook* 109 (Apr. 7, 1915): 832–35.

————. "Clausewitz and This War." *Outlook* 109 (Feb. 24, 1915): 433–36.

————. [Albert Edwards]. *Comrade Yetta*. New York, 1913.

————. "Democracy and Diplomacy." *Atlantic Monthly* 119 (Apr. 1917): 491–99.

————. *Diplomacy and the Great War*. New York, 1916.

————. "England and the Future of Democracy." *Outlook* 114 (Oct. 25, 1916): 416–19.

————. "English View-Points on the War." *Outlook* 110 (June 9, 1915): 327–34.

————. "How Strong Are the Germans?" *Outlook* 114 (Oct. 18, 1916): 380–84.

————. *Mobilising America*. New York, 1917.

————. "National Defense." *Century* 89 (Feb. 1915): 489–91.

————. "Our Relations with France." *Atlantic Monthly* 118 (Nov. 1916): 634–40.

————. "Our Relations with Great Britain." *Atlantic Monthly* 118 (Oct. 1916): 451–61.

————. *Russian Pendulum: Autocracy—Democracy—Bolshivism*. New York, 1919.

————. [Albert Edwards]. "Vox Populi." *Outlook* 91 (Apr. 3, 1909): 789–91.

————. "The War and Workingmen." *Outlook* 109 (Mar. 31, 1915): 770, 779–82.

————. "The Wrong Side of the Looking-Glass: Impressions of Topsy-Turvy Russia." *Harper's Magazine* 139 (Aug. 1919): 408–13.

[Bullard, Arthur, and Ernest Poole]. *How the War Came to America*, Red, White and Blue Series, No. 1, Washington, D.C., 1917.

Byoir, Carl. "The Presentation of Montessori Material." National Education Association of the United States, *Journal of Proceedings and Addresses of the Fiftieth Annual Meeting Held at Chicago, Illinois* (July 6–12, 1912), 613–18.

Call, Arthur D., comp. *War for Peace: The Present War as Viewed by Friends of Peace*, War Information Series, No. 14, Washington, D.C., 1918.

"Campaign to Aid New Draft Registration Uses Striking Copy." *Printers' Ink* 104 (Aug. 29, 1918): 28.

Canby, Henry Seidel. *Classic Americans: A Study of Eminent American Writers from Irving to Whitman, with an Introductory Survey of the Colonial Background of Our National Literature*. New York, 1931.

Carpenter, D. P. "Wanted—A New Vision in Factory Posters: Why Negative, Though Well-Intentioned, Posters Do More Harm Than Good to Employees." *Printers' Ink* 103 (May 9, 1918): 8, 10, 12.

"A Censor Censured." *Living Age* 320 (Feb. 23, 1924): 342–43.

"Censorship Muddle." *Nation* 104 (May 31, 1917): 648–49.

Chafee, Zechariah, Jr. *Freedom of Speech in the United States*. New York, 1920.

Citizens of German Descent. *American Loyalty*, War Information Series, No. 6, Washington, D.C., 1917.

Claxton, Philander P. "How Shall We Educate for the Democracy of the Future?" Montaville Flowers, ed., *What Every American Should Know About the War*. New York, 1918, 297–309.

Colvin, Stephen Sheldon, and William Chandler Bagley. *Human Behavior: A First Book in Psychology for Teachers*. New York, 1913.

Commons, John R. *German Socialists and the War* [American Alliance for Labor and Democracy], Loyalty Leaflets, No. 4, Washington, D.C., 1918.

_____. *Who Is Paying for this War?* Loyalty Leaflets, No. 3, Washington, D.C., 1918.

_____. *Why Workingmen Support the War*, Loyalty Leaflets, No. 2, Washington, D.C., 1918.

Corwin, Edward S. "Bowing Out 'Clear and Present Danger,' " *Notre Dame Lawyer* 27 (Spring 1952): 325–59.

_____. *Constitution and What It Means To-Day*. Princeton, N.J., 1920, 1921.

_____. "Constitutional Law in 1919–1920. I: The Constitutional Decisions of the Supreme Court of the United States in the October Term, 1919." *American Political Science Review* 14 (Nov. 1920): 635–58.

_____. "Freedom of Speech and Press under the First Amendment: A Résumé." *Yale Law Journal* 30 (Nov. 1920): 48–55.

"Creel: An Announcement." *Everybody's Magazine* 40 (Jan. 1919): 25.

"Creel Committee Lops Off Press Agent Stories: Sharp Reduction in Money Allowance by Congress Causes a Revision of Activities—Advertising Activities Not Affected." *Printers' Ink* 104 (July 18, 1918): 82, 85.

Creel Report: Complete Report of the Chairman of the Committee on Public Information, 1917: 1918: 1919. New York, 1920.

Creel, George. "Aid and Comfort to the Enemy." *Independent* 93 (Mar. 16, 1918): 446–47.

_____. "The American Newspaper: What It Is and What It Isn't." *Everybody's Magazine* 40 (Apr. 1919): 40–44, 92.

_____. "America's Fight for World Opinion." *Everybody's Magazine* 40 (Feb. 1919): 9–16.

_____. "America's First Year of War." *Independent* 93 (Mar. 30, 1918): 516–17.

_____. "America's Foremost City." *Harper's Weekly* 59 (Nov. 21, 1914): 495–97.

_____. "Beware the Super-patriots." *American Mercury* 51 (Sept. 1940): 33–41.

_____. "Can a Democractic Government Control Prices? An Interview with Joseph E. Davies of the Federal Trade Commission, Formerly U.S. Commissioner of Corporations." *Century* 93 (Feb. 1917): 605–11.

_____. "The Case for Mr. Garfield." *Independent* 93 (Mar. 9, 1918): 408–9.

_____. *Chivalry versus Justice: Why the Women of the Nation Demand the Right to Vote*. New York, 1915.

————. "Close the Gates!" *Collier's* 69 (May 6, 1922): 9–10.

————. "The Field of Publicity." Montaville Flowers, ed., *What Every American Should Know about the War*. New York, 1918, 4–12.

————. "The Fight for Public Opinion." *Scientific American* 118 (Apr. 6, 1918): 298.

————. "Flashing Democracy around the World." *World Outlook* 4 (Nov. 1918): 8.

————. "Four Million Citizen Defenders: What Universal Training Means in Dollars, Duty, and Defense." *Everybody's Magazine* 36 (May 1917): 545–54.

————. "German 'Efficiency.'" *Independent* 93 (Mar. 2, 1918): 344–45.

————. "German Lies about Versailles." *American Mercury* 56 (Jan. 1943): 54–62.

————. "The Ghastly Swindle." *Harper's Weekly* 59 (Aug. 29, 1914): 196–97.

————. "High Cost of Hate." *Everybody's Magazine* 30 (June 1914): 755–70.

————. "Hopes of the Hyphenated." *Century* 91 (Jan. 1916): 350–63.

————. *How We Advertised America: The First Telling of the Amazing Story of the Committee on Public Information That Carried the Gospel of Americanism to Every Corner of the Globe*. New York, 1920.

————. "The 'Lash' of Public Opinion." *Collier's* 74 (Nov. 22, 1924): 8–9, 46.

————. "The Lost Provinces." *Independent* 93 (Feb. 23, 1918): 310.

————. "Makers of Opinion: Personal Impressions of Mark Sullivan and Other Widely Read Reporters for the American Press." *Collier's* 65 (May 15, 1920): 20, 39, 42.

————. "Making Good on Guns." *Independent* 94 (Apr. 20, 1918): 120–39.

————. *Measuring Up Equal Suffrage: An Authoritative Estimate of Results in Colorado*. New York, [1912].

————. "Melting Pot or Dumping Ground?" *Collier's* 68 (Sept. 3, 1921): 9–10.

————. "A Message from the United States Government to the American People." *Independent* 93 (Feb. 9, 1918): 234–35.

————. "Military Training for Our Youth." *Century* 92 (May 1916): 20–26.

[Creel, George]. "Mr. George Creel Tells How Our Publicity Offensive Ended the War." *Literary Digest* 60 (Feb. 8, 1919): 58, 60.

————. "The Next Four Years: An Interview with the President." *Everybody's Magazine* 36 (Feb. 1917): 129–39.

————. "The Obvious Answer." *Independent* 94 (Apr. 27, 1918): 168, 173.

————. "Our 'Aliens'—Were They Loyal or Disloyal?" *Everybody's Magazine* (Mar. 1919): 36–38, 70–73.

————. "Our 'Visionary' President: An Interpretation of Woodrow Wilson." *Century* 89 (Dec. 1914): 192–200.

————. "Poisoners of Public Opinion." *Harper's Weekly* 59 (Nov. 7 and 14, 1914): 436–38 and 465–66.

————. "The Press: The Greatest Power in the Land." *Mentor* 9 (June 1, 1921): 3–12.

_____. "Propaganda and Morale." *American Journal of Sociology* 47 (Nov. 1941): 340–51.

_____. "Public Opinion as a War Measure." *National Marine* (June 1918), 30–38.

_____. "Public Opinion in War Time." *Annals of the American Academy of Political and Social Science* 78 (July 1918): 185–94.

_____. "Raemaekers—Man and Artist." *Century* 94 (June 1917): 256–59.

_____. "Rotting at the Core: The Amazing Facts of Germany's Internal Breakdown." *Independent* 94 (Apr. 13, 1918): 73, 103.

_____. *Sons of the Eagle: Soaring Figures from America's Past.* Indianapolis, 1917.

_____. "The Sweat of War: What It Means to Put One Million Men in the Field." *Everybody's Magazine* 36 (June 1917): 708–17.

_____. "Unite and Win." *Independent* 94 (Apr. 6, 1918): 5–6.

_____. "A War of Peoples." *Independent* 93 (Feb. 16, 1918): 268–69.

_____. *War, the World and Wilson.* New York, 1920.

_____. *What Have Women Done with the Vote?* New York, [1915].

_____. "Why the Peace Treaty Was Not Advertised." *Advertising and Selling* (Dec. 24, 1919), 32–36.

_____. *Wilson and the Issues.* New York, 1916.

Creel, George, Benjamin B. Lindsey, and Edwin Markham. *Children in Bondage: A Complete and Careful Presentation of the Problem of Child Labor—Its Crimes, and Its Cure.* New York, 1914.

D'Arcy, William C. "The Achievements of Advertising in a Year: Chief of These Is Its Service in the Fight for a Free World." *Printers' Ink* 104 (July 11, 1918): 17–18.

"Drive Now On to Sell Hundred Million of Farm Loan Bonds." *Printers' Ink* 103 (May 16, 1918): 73–74.

"Elaborating War News." *Nation* 105 (July 12, 1917): 30.

Emery, Douglas. "Tell of Germany's Crimes to Help Sell Liberty Bonds." *Printers' Ink* 104 (Sept. 5, 1918): 73–74, 79–80.

Farrar, Gilbert P. "Absorbing, Typographically, Liberty Loan Copy." *Printers' Ink* 104 (Sept. 12, 1918): 28, 31–32.

Finegan, Thomas E. "Training for National Service." National Education Association of the United States, *Addresses and Proceedings of the Fifty-Sixth Annual Meeting Held at Pittsburgh, Pennsylvania, June 29–July 6, 1918* 56: 49–50.

Fish, Carl Russell. "American Democracy." *Minnesota History Bulletin* 3 (Feb. 1920): 251–72.

Ford, Guy Stanton. "America's Fight for Public Opinion." *Minnesota History Bulletin* 3 (Feb. 1919): 3–26.

_____. "Boyen's Military Law." *American Historical Review* 20 (Apr. 1915): 528–38.

———. "The Committee on Public Information." *Historical Outlook* 11 (Mar. 1920): 97–100.

———. "The Department of Education, Committee on Public Information." Montaville Flowers, ed., *What Every American Should Know About the War*. New York, 1918, 262–64.

———. *Hanover and Prussia, 1795–1803: A Study in Neutrality*. New York, 1903.

———. "The Lost Year in Stein's Life." Guy Stanton Ford, *On and Off Campus*. Minneapolis, 1938, 161–203.

———. "A New Educational Agency." National Education Association of the United States, *Addresses and Proceedings of the Fifty-Sixth Annual Meeting Held at Pittsburgh, Pennsylvania, June 29–July 6, 1918* 56: 207–8.

———. "A New Evangel." Guy Stanton Ford, *On and Off Campus*. Minneapolis, 1938, 472–74.

———. "Two Eighteenth-Century German Publicists on the American Revolution." Guy Stanton Ford, *On and Off Campus*. Minneapolis, 1938, 264–97.

———. "Wöllner and the Prussian Religious Edict of 1788." Guy Stanton Ford, *On and Off Campus*. Minneapolis, 1938, 219–63.

———, ed. *Dictatorship in the Modern World*. Minneapolis, 1936.

Gardner, Edward Hall. "College Professors Give an Airing of Their Views on Advertising: Not a Waste, but a Producer of Wealth, Say They—Memorialize Congress on Zone Postage Increase." *Printers' Ink* 103 (May 16, 1918): 31–32.

Gibbons, Herbert Adams. "The Monroe Doctrine for the World." *Century* 94 (May 1917): 151–54.

Gompers, Samuel. "America Is an Ideal [Address of Samuel Gompers, President, American Federation of Labor, Delivered at the Lexington Avenue Theatre, New York City, Feb. 22, 1918]." United States Committee on Public Information Special Service for Employers, *Bulletin No. 3*, Washington, D.C.? 1918.

———. *American Labor and the War*. New York, 1919.

"Good Assistance Given Division of Advertising." *Printers' Ink* 103 (May 2, 1918): 25.

Greene, Evarts B. *American Interest in Popular Government Abroad*, War Information Series, No. 8, Washington, D.C., 1917.

———. "The American Revolution and the British Empire." *History Teacher's Magazine* 8 (Nov. 1917): 292–94.

———. "Co-operation between Colleges and Secondary Schools in Promoting Education for Citizenship." *Association of American Colleges Bulletin: Addresses at Fifth Annual Meeting* 5 (Apr. 1919): 103–11.

———. *Foundations of American Nationality*. New York, 1922.

———. "The Interaction of European and American Politics, 1823–1861." *History Teacher's Magazine* 9 (Mar. 1918): 142–43.

_____. "The Problems of Historical Scholarship and Teaching as Affected by the War." National Education Association of the United States, *Addresses and Proceedings of the Fifty-Sixth Annual Meeting Held at Pittsburgh, Pennsylvania, June 29–July 6, 1918* 56: 199–200.

_____. "A Speech by Daniel Webster." *Nation* 105 (Aug. 9, 1917): 146–47.

_____. "Suggestions on the Relation of American to European History." *History Teacher's Magazine* 8 (Sept. 1917): 218–19.

Hardie, Martin, and Arthur K. Sabin, eds. *War Posters Issued by Belligerent and Neutral Nations, 1914–1919*. London, 1920.

Harding, Samuel B. "Some Geographical Aspects of the War." *History Teacher's Magazine (War Supplement)* 9 (Apr. 1918): 217.

_____. *Study of the Great War: A Topical Outline, with Extensive Quotations and Reading References*, War Information Series, No. 16, Washington, D.C., 1918.

_____. "Topical Outline of the War." *History Teacher's Magazine (War Supplement)* 9 (Jan. 1918): 30–62.

_____. "What the War Should Do for Our History Methods." *History Teacher's Magazine* 10 (Apr. 1919): 189–90.

Hart, Albert Bushnell. *Monroe Doctrine: An Interpretation*. Boston, 1916.

_____. "The New United States." *Yale Review* 8 (Oct. 1918): 1–17.

Hazen, Charles D. "Brief List of Books upon Recent European History." *History Teacher's Magazine* 8 (June 1917): 196–97.

_____. *Europe since 1815*. New York, 1910.

_____. *Government of Germany*, War Information Series, No. 3, Washington, D.C., 1917.

_____. "The Peace Treaty and World Politics." *World's Work* (World-Peace Supplement) 38 (May 1919): i–vii.

_____. "Prussianism in Poland." *World's Work* 37 (Nov. 1918): 39–44.

_____. "When France Failed—and Why." *American Magazine* 80 (Dec. 1915): 46–47, 94.

_____. "Why Alsace-Lorraine Must be Returned to France." *World's Work* 37 (Dec. 1918): 188–202.

Houston, Herbert S. "A. A. C. of W. on Firing Line." *Judicious Advertising* 15 (Apr. 1917): 39–43.

_____. "Advertising and Victory." *World's Work* 34 (Aug. 1917): 457–60.

_____. "Again 'The Miracle of the Marne.'" *World's Work* 40 (Sept. 1920): 465–77.

_____. *Blocking New Wars*. Garden City, N.Y., 1918.

_____. "Commerce to Enforce Peace." *Judicious Advertising* 13 (July 1915): 45–48.

_____. "Doing the World's International Work." *World's Work* 37 (Feb. 1919): 438–40.

_____. *Los Estados Unidos ante el conflicto, el espíritu national en defense de sus ideals, historia de un peregrinaje patriotico*. New York, 1918.

———. "The New Morals of Advertising." *World's Work* 28 (Aug. 1914): 384–88.

———. "The Place of Business in a League of Nations: A Plan for a New World of Assured Fairness to All—A Complete Defense against Economic Penetration and Kaiserism in General." *Printers' Ink* 104 (July 11, 1918): 28, 31–32, 37–38.

———. "The Spirit of the Convention." *Judicious Advertising* 15 (June 1917): 75–77.

———. "Working Out Business Ethics: How Advertising Is Making and Enforcing a Code of Morality and Efficiency from Within—and How, Without, the Associated Advertising Clubs of the World Are Undertaking to Show the Public How It Is Served by Advertising." *World's Work* 30 (Sept. 1915): 559–64.

"How the Division of Advertising 'Sells Itself.'" *Printers' Ink* 104 (Aug. 15, 1918): 80.

"How the Fourth Liberty Loan Will Be Advertised." *Printers' Ink* 104 (Aug. 22, 1918): 106, 109–11.

"The Illustrious Mr. Creel and the Facts [editorial]." *Bellman* 25 (Mar. 15, 1919): 285–86.

Ingersoll, William H. "The Future of the Four Minute Men." *Quarterly Journal of Speech Education* 5 (Mar. 1919): 175–78.

Irwin, Will. "Age of Lies: How the Propagandist Attacks the Foundation of Public Opinion." *Sunset* 43 (Dec. 1919): 23–25.

———. "All the News That's Fit to Print." *Collier's* 47 (May 6, 1911): 17–19, 30.

———. (with comments by Clifford F. Weigle and David G. Clark). *American Newspaper*. Ames, Iowa, 1969.

———. *Babes of Belgium*. New York, [1915].

———. *Christ or Mars?* New York, 1923.

———. "England: The Puzzle: Are Her People Cool—or Asleep? Brave or Blind?" *American Magazine* 79 (Feb. 1915): 40–41, 78–83.

———. "The German Prisoners in France." Special feature service, United States Committee on Public Information, for release in morning newspapers, Sunday, Feb. 24, 1918.

———. "The 'Glory' of War." *American Magazine* 79 (Dec. 1914): 53–54, 72–75.

———. "Hats Off to France!" *American Magazine* 79 (Jan. 1915): 62–65.

———. *Latin at War*. New York, 1917.

———. *Men, Women and War*. New York, 1915.

———. "My Religion." In *They Believe*, as told by Will Irwin et al. New York, 1928, 81–86.

———. "Newspapers and Canned Thought." *Collier's* 73 (June 21, 1924): 13–14, 29.

———. *"The Next War": An Appeal to Common Sense*. New York, 1921.

_____. "Patriotism That Pays." *Nation* 119 (Nov. 12, 1924): 513–16.

_____. *Propaganda and the News, or What Makes You Think So?* New York, 1936.

_____. *A Reporter at Armageddon: Letters from the Front and behind the Lines of the Great War.* New York, 1918.

_____. *Splendid Story of the Battle of Ypres.* London, 1915.

_____. "What Is News?" *Collier's* 46 (Mar. 18, 1911): 17–18.

_____. "Why the Next War Won't Pay." *Collier's* 71 (June 16, 1923): 7–8.

_____. "Wreckage of War: Flashlight Pictures Taken on the Trail of the German Army." *American Magazine* 78 (Nov. 1914): 49, 70–73, 76–78.

Irwin, Will, and Emanuel Victor Voska. *Spy and Counter Spy.* London, [1941].

Irwin, Will, and Thomas M. Johnson. *What You Should Know about Spies and Saboteurs.* New York, 1943.

J. T. M. "German Attempts to Control Press through Advertising: Revelations concerning the German Science of Poisoning Public Opinion." *Printers' Ink* 103 (May 9, 1918): 3–4, 6, 130–32, 134.

_____. "How Germany Has Concealed Her Economic Strength: Even If Beaten in the Field She Is Calculating on a Peace of Economic Victory." *Printers' Ink* 103 (May 16, 1918): 17–20.

"'Keep Your Liberty Bond,' Advertises Uncle Sam." *Printers' Ink* 104 (Sept. 5, 1918): 98, 101.

Kerney, James. *Political Education of Woodrow Wilson.* New York, 1921.

Lamar, W. H. "Government's Attitude toward the Press." *Forum* 59 (Feb. 1918): 129–40.

Lane, Franklin K. "How to Make Americans: Take the Foreigner by the Hand—Show Him the Spirit of the Nation." *Forum* 61 (Apr. 1919): 399–406.

_____. "The Need of a Definite Program of Americanization of Our Foreign-Born Peoples." Edwin Wildman, ed., *Reconstructing America: Our Next Big Job.* Boston, 1919, 386–92.

_____. "What America Means [Address]." In Woodrow Wilson, Franklin K. Lane, and Theodore Roosevelt, *Americanism.* Washington, D.C.? 1920? 5–11.

_____. *Why We Are Fighting Germany.* In Franklin K. Lane and Newton D. Baker, *Nation in Arms,* War Information Series, No. 2, Washington, D.C., 1917, 3–7.

[Lane, Franklin K., with the assistance of Frances Davenport and Elizabeth Donnan]. *Battle Line of Democracy: Prose and Poetry of the World War,* Red, White and Blue Series, No. 3, Washington, D.C., 1917.

Lansing, Robert. *America's Future at Stake.* In Robert Lansing and Louis F. Post, *A War of Self-Defense,* War Information Series, No. 5, Washington, D.C., 1917, 3–10.

_____. "A New Era." *Everybody's Magazine* 40 (Jan. 1919): 52.

Larson, Laurence M. "Nationalism and the Coming Peace Conference." *Historical Outlook* 9 (Dec. 1918): 475–77.

———. "The Responsibility for the Great War." *University of Illinois Bulletin* 15 (Aug. 19. 1918).

———. "Territorial Problems of the Baltic Basin." *University of Illinois Bulletin* 16 (Dec. 30, 1918).

Latané, John H. "The League of Nations and the Monroe Doctrine." *World's Work* 37 (Feb. 1919): 441–44.

———. "The Monroe Doctrine and the American Policy of Isolation in Relation to a Just and Durable Peace." *Annals of the American Academy of Political and Social Science* 72 (July 1917): 100–109.

Lee, Ivy. "How Red Cross Money is Handled and Spent." *Review of Reviews* 56 (Dec. 1917): 615–16.

Lippmann, Walter. *Early Writings.* Introduction and annotations by Arthur Schlesinger, Jr. New York, 1970.

———. "Freud and the Layman." *New Republic* 2 (Apr. 17, 1915): 9–10.

———. *Liberty and the News.* New York, 1919.

———. *Phantom Public: A Sequel to "Public Opinion."* New York, 1925.

———. *Public Opinion.* New York, 1922.

———. *Stakes of Diplomacy.* New York, 1915.

———. "The World Conflict in Its Relation to American Democracy." *Annals of the American Academy of Political and Social Science* 72 (July 1917): 1–10.

Lippmann, Walter, and Charles Merz. "A Test of the News." *New Republic* Supplement 23 (Aug. 4, 1920): Part II.

Loss, Richard, ed. *Presidential Power and the Constitution: Essays by Edward S. Corwin.* Ithaca, N.Y., 1976.

McClure, S. S. *Mr. S. S. McClure's Trip. Easter, 1919: An American Opinion on the German Atrocities in Belgium.* Brussels, 1919.

———. *Obstacles to Peace.* Boston, 1917.

———. "Patriotism [editorial]." *McClure's Magazine* 21 (July 1903): 335–36.

McConaughy, J. W. "Aeroplanes in War." *Munsey's Magazine* 55 (Aug. 1915): 465–74.

———. "Ancient Names Wiped Out by War: How the Great Conflict Is Decimating Britain's Oldest Families." *Munsey's Magazine* 56 (Dec. 1915): 409–12.

———. "The Balkan States: A Long History of Intrigue and Slaughter." *Munsey's Magazine* 57 (Feb. 1916): 1–32.

———. "Blockade and Blockade-Runners." *Munsey's Magazine* 56 (Nov. 1915): 220–23.

———. "The Havoc of Invasion: A Broad Trail of Ruin through Five Fair Provinces of France." *Munsey's Magazine* 57 (Apr. 1916): 435–49.

———. "Our Ambassadors in the War Zone." *Munsey's Magazine* 59 (Dec. 1916): 416–25.

———. "The Red Cross of Mercy: What a Woman Can Do When Her Country Goes to War." *Munsey's Magazine* 59 (Oct. 1916): 1–19.

———. "South America: A Land of the Future." *Munsey's Magazine* 56 (Jan. 1916): 495–527.

_____. "The Strong Man of China: Yuan Shih-kai, to Whom His Country's Waking Millions Look at the Present Crisis." *Munsey's Magazine* 57 (Mar. 1916): 277–89.

_____. "Trench Warfare: How Modern Armies Burrow and Fight Underground." *Munsey's Magazine* 55 (Sept. 1915): 655–62.

_____. "Trials of the Neutral Kings: Dynastic and Political Troubles Are the Lot of the Seven Sovereigns on the Fringe of the Great War." *Munsey's Magazine* 57 (May 1916): 624–32.

Macfarlane, Peter Clark. "The Fortunes of Citizen Creel (An Everyday American Who Has Been Able to Keep Faith with His Belief That Life Need Never Be Dull)." *Collier's* 51 (July 19, 1913): 5–6, 24–28.

McLaughlin, Andrew Cunningham. *America and Britain.* New York, 1919.

_____. "American History and American Democracy." *American Historical Review* 20 (Jan. 1915): 255–76.

_____. "Chauvinism Repudiated." *Nation* 107 (Aug. 17, 1918): 171–72.

_____. "Democracy and the Constitution." *Proceedings of the American Antiquarian Society*, New Series, Part II, 22 (Oct. 1912): 293–320.

_____. *Great War: From Spectator to Participant*, War Information Series, No. 4, Washington, D.C., 1917.

_____. "Historians and the War." *Dial* 62 (May 17, 1917): 427–28.

_____. "Impressions of Britain in War-Time." *Historical Outlook* 9 (Dec. 1918): 473–75.

_____. "Sixteen Causes of War." *University of Chicago War Papers*, No. 4, Chicago, 1918.

_____. *Steps in the Development of American Democracy.* New York, 1920.

McLaughlin, Andrew C., and Albert Bushnell Hart. *Cyclopedia of American Government.* 3 vols., New York, 1914.

McLaughlin, Andrew C., William E. Dodd, Marcus W. Jernegan, and Arthur P. Scott. *Source Problems in United States History.* New York, 1918.

Merriam, Charles. *American Political Ideas: Studies in the Development of American Political Thought.* New York, 1920.

_____. "American Publicity in Italy." *American Political Science Review* 13 (Nov. 1919): 541–55.

_____. "Citizenship." *University of Chicago Magazine* 3 (July 1911): 276–82.

_____. *History of the Theory of Sovereignty since Rousseau.* New York, 1900, 1972.

_____. *Making of Citizens.* New York, 1931, 1966.

_____. *New Aspects of Politics.* Chicago, 1925.

[Merriam, Charles E., Bernard Fay, and Edward A. Ross]. "Discussion." Waldo G. Leland, ed., *Nationalism: Papers Presented at the Fourth Chicago Meeting of the American Association for the Advancement of Science.* Bloomington, Ind., 1934, 67–69.

Merry, Glenn N. "National Defense and Public Speaking." *Quarterly Journal of Speech Education* 4 (Jan. 1918): 53–60.

Merz, Charles. "American Moving Pictures as Foreign Ambassadors."

W. Brooke Graves, ed., *Readings in Public Opinion: Its Formation and Control*. New York, 1928, 370–80.

———. *First Session of the War Congress*, War Information Series, No. 10, Washington, D.C., 1917.

———. *Great American Band Wagon: A Study of Exaggerations*. New York, 1928.

"More Advertising Prescribed for Slack Sales of War Savings Stamps." *Printers' Ink* 103 (June 6, 1918): 107–8.

Moses, Bert. "What the War is Doing for Advertising." *Printers' Ink* 104 (Sept. 12, 1918): 30.

Munro, Dana C., George C. Sellery, and August C. Krey, eds. *German War Practices: Part I: Treatment of Civilians*, Red, White and Blue Series, No. 6, Washington, D.C., 1918.

———. *German Treatment of Conquered Territory: Being Part II of "German War Practices,"* Red, White and Blue Series, No. 8, Washington, D.C., 1918.

Myers, Gustavus. "Germany's Biggest Fraud—Social Reform." Montaville Flowers, ed., *What Every American Should Know about the War*. New York, 1918, 150–64.

Nelson, Bertram G. "The Four Minute Men." Montaville Flowers, ed., *What Every American Should Know about the War*. New York, 1918, 252–56.

"New Liberty-Loan Posters Reflect the War Spirit." *Printers' Ink* 104 (Sept. 26, 1918): 100, 105–6.

Notestein, Wallace. "The Interest of Seventeenth-Century England for Students of American Institutions." *History Teacher's Magazine* 8 (Dec. 1917): 350–51.

———. "Sentiment on the War in the Northwest." *Nation* 101 (Nov. 18, 1915): 595.

Notestein, Wallace, and Elmer E. Stoll, comps. *Conquest and Kultur: Aims of the Germans in Their Own Words*, Red, White and Blue Series, No. 5, Washington, D.C., 1918.

Official U.S. Bulletin. Hearing before the Joint Committee on Printing. Sixty-Sixth Congress. First Session. Under Section 11 of Public Act No. 314, 65th Congress. August 12, 1919. Washington, D.C., 1920.

O'Higgins, Harvey. "Freedom of Speech." *Century* 95 (Dec. 1917): 302–3.

———. *German Whisper*. Washington, D.C., 1918?

———. "The Issue." *Century* 95 (Jan. 1918): 405.

———. "Judge Ben Lindsey: Advance Agent of the New Freedom." *Cosmopolitan* 66 (Jan. 1919): 70–71, 103.

O'Higgins, Harvey (with Ben B. Lindsey). "The Doughboy's Religion." *Cosmopolitan* 66 (Mar. 1919): 64–67, 126–27.

———. "Horses' Rights for Women." *Cosmopolitan* 66 (May 1919): 71–75, 166, 168.

———. "Our National Faith-Cure." *Cosmopolitan* 66 (Apr. 1919): 30–33, 123–26.

O'Higgins, Harvey O., and Edward H. Reede. *American Mind in Action*. New York, 1920.

Parker, Sir Gilbert. "The United States and the War." *Harper's Magazine* 136 (Mar. 1918): 521–31.

Paxson, Frederic L. "The Spirit of Present History." *History Teacher's Magazine* 9 (June 1918): 318–19.

Paxson, Frederic L., and Carl Russell Fish. "Wisconsin and La Follette [letter to the editor]." *Nation* 106 (Mar. 21, 1918): 319.

Paxson, Frederic L., Edward S. Corwin, and Samuel B. Harding, eds. *War Cyclopedia: A Handbook for Ready Reference on the Great War*, Red, White and Blue Series, No. 7, Washington, D.C., 1918.

"The Peace Treaty as the World's Greatest Advertising Failure." *Literary Digest* 63 (Dec. 20, 1919): 130–36.

Pew, Marlen. "Mobilizing Our Boys." *Munsey's Magazine* 61 (July 1917): 226–29.

"Plans for Winning the War Discussed." *Survey* 40 (May 11, 1918): 162–63.

Poole, Ernest. *Blind: A Story of These Times*. New York, 1920.

———. *"The Dark People," Russia's Crisis*. New York, 1918.

———. "Face of My Enemy." *Everybody's Magazine* 32 (May 1915): 529–42.

———. "The Fighters and the Haters." *McClure's Magazine* 49 (Sept. 1917): 19.

———. *Harbor*. New York, 1915.

———. "Hoover." *Everybody's Magazine* 36 (June 1917): 654–56.

———. "The Theater of War." *American Magzine* 79 (June 1915): 29–30, 62, 64, 66, 68–71.

———. *Village: Russian Impressions*. New York, 1918.

———. "Why I Am No Longer a Pacifist." *McClure's Magazine* 49 (Aug. 1917): 19, 67.

Post, Louis F. *German Attack*. In Robert Lansing and Louis F. Post, *A War of Self-Defense*, War Information Series, No. 5, Washington, D.C., 1917, 11–22.

Report of the Director of the Official U.S. Bulletin to the Chairman of the Committee on Public Information. Washington, D.C., 1919.

Root, Elihu. *Plain Issues of the War*, Loyalty Leaflets, No. 5, Washington, D.C., 1918?

Russell, Charles Edward. "Address of Charles Edward Russell at a Reception by the Union League Club of New York City, August 15, 1917." In *America's Message to the Russian People: Addresses by the Members of the Special Diplomatic Mission of the United States to Russia in the Year 1917*. Boston, 1918, 150–54.

———. "Address of Charles Edward Russell at the Demonstration in Behalf of the Soldiers at Pavlosk-Voksal, June 20, 1917." In *America's Message to the Russian People: Addresses by the Members of the Special Diplomatic Mission of the United States to Russia in the Year 1917*. Boston, 1918, 148–49.

———. "Address of Charles Edward Russell before the Council of Workmen's, Soldiers', and Peasants' Delegates, June 12, 1917." In *America's Message to the Russian People: Addresses by the Members of the Special Diplomatic Mission of the United States to Russia in the Year 1917*. Boston, 1918, 143–47.

————. *After the Whirlwind: A Book of Reconstruction and Profitable Thanksgiving*. New York, 1919.

————. "Bolshevism: 'Autocracy's Twin Brother.'" Edwin Wildman, ed., *Reconstructing America: Our Next Big Job*. Boston, 1919, 278–79.

————. "The New Americanism." *Proceedings and Papers of the Indiana State Teachers' Association* (Oct. 30, 31, and Nov. 1, 1919), 270–94.

————. "The New Socialist Alignment." *Harper's Magazine* 136 (Mar. 1918): 563–70.

————. *These Shifting Scenes*. New York, 1914.

Scherer, James A. B. *Nation at War*. New York, 1918.

Scott, Arthur P. "The Passing of Splendid Isolation." *History Teacher's Magazine* 8 (June 1917): 192–95.

Scott, George Winfield, and James Wilford Garner. *German War Code: Contrasted with the War Manuals of the United States, Great Britain, and France*, War Information Series, No. 11, Washington, D.C., 1918.

Sherman, Stuart P. *American and Allied Ideals: An Appeal to Those Who Are Neither Hot nor Cold*, War Information Series, No. 12, Washington, D.C., 1918.

————. *Americans*. New York, 1923.

————. "Carlyle and Spy Mania." *Nation* 107 (Oct. 19, 1918): 449.

————. *Emotional Discovery of America and Other Essays*. Murray Hill, N.Y., 1932.

————. *Genius of America: Studies in Behalf of the Younger Generation*. New York, 1931.

————. *On Contemporary Literature*. New York, 1917.

————. *Points of View*. New York, 1923.

————. "Why Mr. Roosevelt and the Rest of Us Are at War." *Nation* 105 (Nov. 15, 1917): 532–37.

Shotwell, James T. "The National Board for Historical Service." *History Teacher's Magazine* 8 (June 1917): 199.

Simons, Algie M. "The Future of the Socialist Party." *New Republic* 9 (Dec. 2, 1916): 118–20.

————. "Pacificism vs. Revolution." *New Republic* 10 (Mar. 24, 1917): 220–21.

————. *Vision for Which We Fought: A Study in Reconstruction*. New York, 1919.

Sioussat, St. George L. "English Foundations of American Institutional Life." *History Teacher's Magazine* 8 (Oct. 1917): 260–61.

[Sisson, Edgar]. *German-Bolshevik Conspiracy*, War Information Series, No. 20, Washington, D.C., 1918.

Sperry, Earl E., and Willis M. West. *German Plots and Intrigues in the United*

States during the Period of Our Neutrality, Red, White and Blue Series, No. 10, Washington, D.C., 1918.

"Striking Posters Will Aid Drive for W. S. S. [war savings stamps]: Prize Winners in Three Competitions Announced—Adolph Triedler's Poster Takes $1,000 Prize." *Printers' Ink* 103 (May 30, 1918): 97–98.

Sullivan, John. "The Truth about the Division of Advertising." *Advertising News* 27 (July 20, 1918): 14.

Tarbell, Ida M. "'My Religion.'" In *They Believe*. New York, 1928, 29–38.

_____. *Rising of the Tide: The Story of Sabinsport*. New York, 1919.

Tarkington, Booth. "'Middle Western Apathy.'" *American Magazine* 83 (June 1917): 31–32, 118–22.

_____. "Using the Kaiser." *American Magazine* 86 (Aug. 1918): 44–45, 83–84, 87.

Tatlock, John S. P. *Why America Fights Germany*, War Information Series, No. 15, Washington, D.C., 1918.

Tattler. "National Miniatures: George Creel." *Nation* 105 (Nov. 22, 1917): 573–74.

Tumulty, Joseph P. *Woodrow Wilson as I Know Him*. Garden City, N.Y., 1921.

"Two Big Campaigns Coming to Raise War Funds." *Printers' Ink* 104 (Aug. 29, 1918): 25–27.

"Uncle Sam's Advertising Agency Reports Progress: The Division of Advertising, at a Luncheon in Washington, Recites Great Work Done since January." *Printers' Ink* 103 (May 16, 1918): 89–92, 96, 140–41.

"'Uncle Sam's Employment Agency' Launches Big Advertising Drive." *Printers' Ink* 104 (Aug. 1, 1918): 83–85.

"Uncle Sam's Money Pays for Marine Corps Advertising." *Printers' Ink* 104 (Aug. 1, 1918): 100–101.

"The United States Censorship Board at Washington." *American Review of Reviews* 57 (June 1918): 583.

United States Committee on Public Information. *Activities of the Committee on Public Information*, War Information Series, No. 17, Washington, D.C., 1918.

_____. *American Loyalty by Citizens of German Descent*, War Information Series, No. 6, Washington, D.C., 1917.

_____. *Bulletin for Cartoonists*, Nos. 1–25. Washington, D.C., 1917, 1918.

_____. *Four Minute Men Bulletin*, Nos. 1–46. Washington, D.C., 1917, 1918.

_____. *Four Minute Men News*, Nos. A–F. Washington, D.C., 1917, 1918.

_____. *Germany's Confession: The Lichnowsky Memorandum*. Washington, D.C., 1918.

_____. *Information concerning the Making and Distribution of Pictures That Show the Activities of the Army and Navy*. Washington, D.C., 1917.

_____. *Kaiserite in America: One Hundred and One German Lies, Published Especially for the Commercial Travelers of America*. Washington, D.C., 1918?

———. *Labor and the War: President Wilson's Address to the American Federation of Labor, Delivered at Buffalo, N.Y., November 12, 1917*, Loyalty Leaflets, No. 3, Washington, D.C., 1917?

———. *National Service Handbook*, Red, White and Blue Series, No. 2, Washington, D.C., 1917.

———. *President's Flag Day Address with Evidence of Germany's Plans*, Red, White and Blue Series, No. 4, Washington, D.C., 1917.

———. *School Bulletin*, Nos. 1–4. Washington, D.C., 1918.

———. *Selective Service Register. Issued for Provost Marshal General's Office, War Department, U.S.A., Washington, D.C.* New York, 1918.

———. *Semiofficial Summary of the Treaty of Peace between the Twenty-Seven Allied and Associated Powers and Germany as Handed to the German Plenipotentiaries at the Peace Conference on May 7, 1919.* Washington, D.C., 1919.

———. *War, Labor and Peace: Some Recent Addresses and Writings of President Wilson*, Red, White and Blue Series, No. 9. Washington, D.C., 1918.

———. *War Message and Facts behind It: Annotated Text of President Wilson's Message, April 2, 1917*, War Information Series, No. 1, Washington, D.C., 1917.

———. *A War Message to the Farmer* [from Woodrow Wilson], Loyalty Leaflets, No. 4, Washington, D.C., 1918.

———. *War Work of Women in Colleges.* Washington, D.C., 1918.

———. *Ways to Serve the Nation*, Loyalty Leaflets, No. 6, Washington, D.C., 1917?

———. *What Really Matters: A Letter by an Unnamed Writer, Quoted by Rev. Joseph H. Odell in an Article in the Atlantic Monthly for February, 1918*, Loyalty Leaflets, No. 7, Washington, D.C., 1918.

———, Division of Four Minute Men, *Army Bulletin*, Nos. 1–3. Washington, D.C., 1918.

———, Division of Industrial Relations, *Special Service Bulletin for Employers.* Washington, D.C., 1918.

———, Division of News, *Division of News Directory, Prepared for the Information of Press Correspondents.* Washington, D.C., 1918.

———, Division of Pictures, *Catalogue of Photographs and Stereopticon Slides Issued by the Division of Pictures, Committee on Public Information.* Washington, D.C., 1918.

———, Information Department, *Woman's Committee of the Council of National Defense—Organization Charts, May, 1917–1918.* Washington, D.C., 1918.

———, Speaking Division, *Bulletin*, Nos. 1–3. Washington, D.C., 1918.

———, War Department, *Home Reading Course for Citizen-Soldiers*, War Information Series, No. 9, Washington, D.C., 1917.

United States *Congressional Record*, House of Representatives, Volume 56, Part 8.

Van Loon, Hendrik W. "The Neutrals and the Allied Cause." *Century* 94 (Aug. 1917): 610–20.

———. "A New Historical Division." *Nation* 106 (May 25, 1918): 616–17.

————. "The Soul of Flanders." *Nation* 107 (Dec. 21, 1918): 776–77.

Van Wye, B. C. "Speech Training for Patriotic Service." *Quarterly Journal of Speech Education* 4 (Oct. 1918): 366–71.

Wagstaffe, William de. "The Creel Press Cabinet: An Insight into the Censorship." *Forum* 58 (Oct. 1917): 447–60.

Walcott, Frederic C. *Prussian System*, Loyalty Leaflets, No. 2, Washington, D.C., 1918.

"War Exhibit at San Francisco Convention: Allied War Exposition Opens in San Francisco July 7—First Shown in Its Entirety during Convention Week." *Printers' Ink* 103 (June 27, 1918): 72.

"War Programme for San Francisco Convention: L. E. Pratt, Chairman of the Committee, Outlines Principal Features of the Annual A. A. C. of W. Event—Publisher Kellogg, of San Francisco, Defends Chairman Creel." *Printers' Ink* 103 (May 9, 1918): 96.

"War Topics at Front in Convention of A.N.A. and A.B.C.: Speakers' Chief Aim Was to Point the Way to War's Successful Conclusion." *Printers' Ink* 103 (June 13, 1918): 45–48, 51.

"The War Work of the Four-Minute Men: With an Introductory Letter by President Wilson." *Touchstone* 3 (Sept. 1918): 304–7.

Well, Hulet M. *Wilson and the Issues of Today: A Socialist Revision of George Creel's Famous Book*. Seattle, Wash., 1918.

Whitehouse, Vira B. *A Year as a Government Agent*. New York, 1920.

Whitlock, Brand. "Belgium: The Closing Curtain." *Everybody's Magazine* 40 (Jan. 1919): 9–16, 64–68.

————. Randolph C. Downes, ed. "Letters to George Creel." *Northwest Ohio Quarterly* 28 (Autumn 1956): 170–80.

Wilhelm, Donald. "The Government's Own Publicity Work." *American Review of Reviews* 56 (Nov. 1917): 507–11.

————. "Our Uncensorious Censor." *Independent* 93 (Jan. 5, 1918): 20–21, 43.

Wilson, George Grafton. "The Monroe Doctrine After the War." World Peace Foundation, *A League of Nations* 1 (June 1918): 253–305.

Wilson, Woodrow. "Ad Men Using Their Professions to Exalt American Business." *Judicious Advertising* 14 (July 1916): 37–39.

————. "Americanism [address]." In Woodrow Wilson, Franklin K. Lane, and Theodore Roosevelt, *Americanism*. Washington, D. C.? 1920?, 1–4.

————. *Constitutional Government in the United States*. New York, 1908.

Yost, Mary. "Training Four Minute Men at Vassar." *Quarterly Journal of Speech Education* 5 (May 1919): 246–53.

Zook, George Frederick. *America at War: A Series of Illustrated Lectures on American War Activities*. Washington, D. C., 1918.

————. "The British Empire and What It Stands For." *Historical Outlook* 10 (Feb. 1919): 127–31.

————. "Use of Pictures and Lantern Slides in Study of the Great War." *Historical Outlook* 10 (Jan. 1919): 23–24.

Index

Publication of Supplementary Volumes to *The Papers of Woodrow Wilson* is assisted from time to time by the Woodrow Wilson Foundation in order to encourage scholarly work about Woodrow Wilson and his time. All volumes have passed the review procedures of the publishers and the Editor and the Editorial Advisory Committee of *The Papers of Woodrow Wilson*. Inquiries about the Series should be addressed to The Editor, Papers of Woodrow Wilson, Firestone Library, Princeton University, Princeton, N.J. 08540.

Raymond B. Fosdick, *Letters on the League of Nations: From the Files of Raymond B. Fosdick* (Princeton University Press, 1966).

Wilton B. Fowler, *British-American Relations, 1917–1918: The Role of Sir William Wiseman* (Princeton University Press, 1969).

John M. Mulder, *Woodrow Wilson: The Years of Preparation* (Princeton University Press, 1978).

George Egerton, *Great Britain and the Creation of the League of Nations: Strategy, Politics, and International Organization, 1914–1919* (The University of North Carolina Press, 1978).

Stephen Vaughn, *Holding Fast the Inner Lines: Democracy, Nationalism, and the Committee on Public Information* (The University of North Carolina Press, 1979).